EVERYONE
IS
ITALIAN
ON
SUNDAY

EVERYONE
IS
ITALIAN
ON
SUNDAY

Rachael Ray

ATRIA BOOKS

New York • London • Toronto • Sydney • New Delhi

ATRIA BOOKS

An Imprint of Simon & Schuster, Inc.
1230 Avenue of the Americas
New York, NY 10020

First Atria Books hardcover edition October 2015

ATRIA BOOKS and colophon are trademarks of Simon & Schuster, Inc.

For information about special discounts for bulk purchases, please contact Simon & Schuster Special Sales
at 1-866-506-1949 or business@simonandschuster.com.

The Simon & Schuster Speakers Bureau can bring authors to your live event.
For more information or to book an event, contact the Simon & Schuster Speakers Bureau
at 1-866-248-3049 or visit our website at www.simonspeakers.com.

Interior design by Jill Armus
Photography by Frances Janisch
Food styling by Mariana Velasquez
Prop styling by Karin Olsen

Photo of Rachael Ray on page ii © John Kernick 2011
Cocktail chapter by John Cusimano
Dessert chapter by Maria Betar

Manufactured in the United States of America

10 9 8 7 6 5 4 3 2 1

Library of Congress Cataloging-in-Publication Data is available.

ISBN 978-1-4767-6607-2
ISBN 978-1-4767-6608-9 (ebook)

To my family, thank you for making me an Italian
from my heart to my stomach.

CONTENTS

Aglio e Olio (page 139)

INTRODUCTION

For me, this book is the single most important work of my life. It represents decades of enjoying and working with food and the people I love most in this world. Inside, you'll find meals like the dandelion greens and fried eggs my husband and I were obsessed with for months, assorted primi piatti like baked ricotta with pistachios, instructions for how to bake pizza and calzones with or without a wood-burning oven, a recipe for the ultimate game day pulled pork sandwiches, and many more Italian goodies. The book even includes my sister Maria's favorite Italian desserts and my husband John's Italian ingredient–inspired cocktails. This book was written with one very important message in mind: Everyone is Italian on Sunday.

My grandfather was Sicilian, one of fourteen children, and one of the four that came to America. He settled in upstate New York and eventually became a wonderful stonemason who worked on the rebuilding of a historical site, Fort Ticonderoga. He was a strong man with lots of energy and a great sense of humor. He was a wonderful gardener and cook as well, played the concertina, and told great stories.

My mom was the eldest of my grandfather's ten children. She grew up in a modest home on a tiny peninsula on Lake George, but to hear her talk about her childhood, you might think she was born a princess who lived in a castle with all the riches and benefits of privilege. You never would have guessed she was the daughter of an immigrant stonemason who had to work eighty or more hours a week while growing and harvesting enough food for so many mouths. My mother's recollection of her childhood has always been my favorite bedtime story. Even now, all grown up, I conjure her memories like a treasured fairy tale.

Once upon a time, everyone would gather at my grandfather's house at the edge of the majestic Lake George on Sundays. From fellow Italian stoneworkers to neighbors from all around, all were welcome and none were turned away. The kitchen table was often moved outside to the lawn, because more people came to eat than any room in the house could hold.

Grandpa would cook all sorts of meats and sausages in a big pot of tomato sauce. Then he would serve them on a large platter and toss lots of spaghetti into the sauce. He would serve a huge salad of vegetables from his own garden, and down at the end of the table he would put out two big, five-gallon tubs of ice cream beside a wheelbarrow filled with ripe melons. With the garden machete—which hung from a string tied to his belt and was like an extension of his arm—Grandpa would slice through the melons, scoop out the seeds with his hand, and fill the sweet melon centers with vanilla ice cream. No matter how many came, there was always enough food for everyone. After the meal, the men would play their instruments and sing, and Zia (Aunt) Patrina would swirl her *moppina* (slang for dish towel) up in the air over her head and lead the kids in a dance around the fire.

Anyone can be an Italian on Sundays, and any day can be made to feel like a Sunday. The magic of an Italian Sunday is in human connections. Food is the great communicator, connecting generations and helping build memories and friendships. It gathers us together and teaches us the importance of sharing not just food, but the best of ourselves.

Italian food makes us smile. Think of the first time you successfully twirled spaghetti around the tines of your fork or saw lasagna piled high just waiting for that first bite. How many times have you taken a cheesy, gooey, or crispy bite of any Italian treat and it made you close your eyes in utter delight that anything could be so good? Even something as simple as a big, buttery bite of nutty Parmigiano-Reggiano followed by a large sip of red wine—wow!

The meaning of being Italian on Sunday is to prepare food with love, to savor it, and to share it with others, sometimes loudly, always with gusto. Being Italian on Sunday is about bringing out your lust for life and passion for all things: food, storytelling, wine, music, and each other. Being Italian on Sunday is about emotion and finding beauty in every delicious moment of our lives.

Clockwise from upper left:
Rum French Toast (page 14);
Bloody Johnnys (page 2),
Golden Beets with Lemon-
Dijon Dressing and Radishes
(page 29); Frittata Soufflé
with Tomatoes, Pancetta,
and Leeks (page 5).

CHAPTER 1

BRUNCH

The Italians may not have a meal they call "brunch," but every day, around midday, they have a heavy meal, followed by a nap or rest, and then their "second day" begins around 3 p.m. or so. (The day ends with a light supper sometime between 9 p.m. and midnight.) So in a sense, Italians have brunch every single day, and every single recipe in this book could be part of an endless brunch buffet.

For me, on the other hand, brunch is a luxury specific to weekends, especially those I can spend up in the country, in the mountains where I grew up. I love to cook special late-morning and midday meals for visiting friends (who refer to our house as "The Inn"). But even if I don't have a crowd to feed, I wake up early, take a run to menu-plan and burn off a few calories, and then I hit the kitchen. While I'm cooking, John mixes up his Bloody Johnnys (page 2) or some new concoction, or pops some champagne (I'll have bitters and a twist, please), and the day just gets better from there.

BLOODY JOHNNYS

Prep a pitcher of Bloody Johnny mix, put out a bottle of vodka, glasses, a bucket of ice, and a bar spoon, and your guests can mix their drinks to taste. Garnish the bloodies with any or all of the following: a celery stalk, olives, lemon and lime wedges, pickled veggies, fresh cilantro sprigs, etc. Go crazy . . .

1 (48-ounce) bottle Spicy Hot V8 vegetable juice
Grated zest and juice of 1 lemon
Grated zest and juice of 1 lime
2 tablespoons horseradish, or to taste
13 dashes of Tabasco sauce, or to taste
2 ounces Worcestershire sauce
1 teaspoon celery salt
1 teaspoon pepper

Combine all the ingredients in a sealable pitcher or container. Shake well and refrigerate until cold.

To make one cocktail, pour 1½ ounces vodka into an ice-filled Collins glass and add the Bloody Johnny mix. Stir and garnish as you like.

PROSCIUTTO AND EGG ROLLS

It's more the New Yorker in me than the Italian in me that loves an egg sandwich. This baked egg roll (just a stuffed kaiser roll) is a favorite among our houseguests running out to sled or ski in the winter. It always gets a big reaction, so the next time you work hard entertaining overnight, go easy on yourself the next morning with this recipe.

3 tablespoons butter
1 clove garlic, smashed
1 small sprig fresh rosemary
4 to 6 sesame-topped white rolls
4 to 6 slices prosciutto or prosciutto cotto (cooked ham)
1½ cups shredded Fontina, young pecorino, or young provolone cheese (easy melting cheeses)
4 to 6 large free-range organic eggs
Salt and pepper
Minced fresh chives and thyme

Position a rack in the center of the oven and preheat the oven to 350°F.

In a small saucepan, melt the butter over medium heat. Add the garlic and rosemary to infuse. When the foam subsides, remove from the heat and stir well with a pastry brush.

Use a knife to cut a circle 2½ to 3 inches in diameter into each roll top, cutting about ¾ inch into the roll (not all the way through). Pull the round piece of bread off the roll (it will be the "cap") and hollow out the inside of the roll. You want to make the roll into a nest for the ham and egg. Brush the insides of the "nest" and the underside (noncrust side) of the "cap" with the garlic-rosemary butter. Line the nest with ham, allowing the ham to come up over the edges of the nest a bit like flower petals. Fill each nest with cheese, then crack an egg on top and season with salt and pepper.

Place the rolls and caps (crust side down) on a baking sheet and bake until the eggs have set to soft-medium centers, the ham is crisp at the edges, and the bread is toasted, 10 to 12 minutes. Garnish with chives and thyme and serve with the caps set alongside. When the cap is set into place, it will burst the yolk—yum!

DANDELION GREENS AND FRIED EGGS

==== SERVES 4 ====

John and I love this meal so much that we made it every Sunday for a couple of months straight when the dandelion greens were growing, well, like the weeds they are. Like a great song that gets overplayed on the radio, this had to come off the brunch menu for a while but it's back on and we're trying not to wear it out. You could also make this with Basted Eggs (page 9) instead of fried eggs.

¼ cup plus 2 tablespoons good olive oil
6 to 8 flat anchovy fillets, or to taste
4 large cloves garlic, thinly sliced
1 teaspoon crushed red pepper flakes, or 2 small fresh red chiles, halved
1 large bunch dandelion greens, stemmed and coarsely chopped (6 to 8 cups)
Freshly grated nutmeg
Juice of ½ lemon, or a splash of dry vermouth
4 large free-range organic eggs
Salt and black pepper
Minced fresh chives
Crusty bread (see Tip)

In a large skillet, heat ¼ cup of the oil (4 turns of the pan) over medium heat. Add the anchovies, cover the pan with a splatter screen or lid, and shake until the anchovies begin to break up. Reduce the heat a bit, uncover, and stir until the anchovies melt into the oil. Add the garlic and red pepper flakes and stir for 2 to 3 minutes. Add the greens and cook until tender-crisp, tossing for a couple of minutes in the garlicky oil. Season with nutmeg and douse with the lemon juice.

In a large nonstick skillet, heat the remaining 2 tablespoons oil (2 turns of the pan) over medium heat. Add the eggs and cook for 2 minutes, then flip and cook for 1 minute more; season with salt and black pepper.

Top the greens with the eggs. Sprinkle with chives. Serve with crusty bread.

SOMETIMES I serve this brunch with charred bread rubbed with garlic, dressed with oil and sea salt, or with thinly sliced browned baby potatoes. A hunk of crusty bread works just fine as well. The point is, serve it with something you can use to mop up the yolks.

GRILLED CAESAR SALAD WITH POACHED EGGS

==== SERVES 4 ====

Who doesn't love a good Caesar salad? This version makes a fun summer lunch or brunch with chilled *rosato* (rosé).

1 rounded teaspoon anchovy paste, or 4 flat anchovy fillets, pasted
1½ teaspoons Worcestershire sauce
1 rounded teaspoon Dijon mustard
Juice of 1 lemon
3 large cloves garlic: 1 pasted or grated, 2 halved
Salt and pepper
⅓ cup EVOO, plus more for drizzling
A handful of freshly grated pecorino cheese, plus more for serving
4 slices ciabatta bread
2 large romaine lettuce hearts, halved lengthwise, cleaned, and dried
Olive oil cooking spray
4 Poached Eggs (see box)

Heat a grill or grill pan to medium-high heat.

In a large bowl, whisk the anchovy paste, Worcestershire sauce, mustard, lemon juice, garlic paste, and pepper. While whisking, stream in the ⅓ cup EVOO to emulsify. Stir in the pecorino.

Char the bread on the grill. Rub with the cut garlic, drizzle with some EVOO, and season with salt. Set the garlic croutons aside.

Coat the lettuce lightly with olive oil spray and season with salt and pepper. Grill on both sides to mark and char.

Make the Poached Eggs.

Serve the charred romaine on plates topped with dressing, a garlic crouton, a poached egg, and a little extra grated cheese.

BASICS

POACHED EGGS

=== SERVES 4 TO 6 ===

A splash of white vinegar
4 to 6 large free-range organic eggs

In a deep skillet, heat a couple inches of water with the vinegar to a low rolling boil. Crack the eggs into individual ramekins or custard cups. Whisk the water in circles to create swirls, slide the eggs into the simmering water one at a time, and poach for 3 to 4 minutes for soft to medium eggs.

SCAFATA AND POACHED EGGS WITH BRUSCHETTA

SERVES 4

Scafata is fava beans cooked with escarole. I like to serve it in late spring and early summer to celebrate a bounty of great produce. All you really need are the favas, escarole, and garlic, but I use a half dozen more ingredients when they're available. Use as many of the green ingredients as you can find.

¼ cup olive oil

½ pound purple or green asparagus, thinly sliced on an angle

1 small fresh or dried red chile, halved lengthwise

1 small bunch ramps (wild leeks), whites finely chopped and green tops cut into 1-inch pieces (see Tip)

5 or 6 garlic scapes, chopped (see Tip)

1 cup fresh or thawed frozen peeled fava beans or edamame

1 cup shelled fresh peas

Salt and black pepper

1 head escarole, washed and coarsely chopped

½ cup chicken or vegetable stock

4 Poached Eggs (page 3)

4 slices ciabatta or white peasant bread

1 clove garlic, halved

EVOO, for drizzling

Flaky sea salt

1 cup loosely packed chopped mixed fresh herbs: flat-leaf parsley, basil or tarragon, and mint

Juice of 1 lemon

In a large skillet, heat the olive oil (4 turns of the pan) over medium-high heat. Add the asparagus and toss for 2 minutes. Add the chile, ramp whites, and garlic scapes and toss to combine. Add the fava beans and peas, season with salt and black pepper, and cook, stirring constantly, for 3 to 4 minutes. Wilt the escarole in the pan, add the stock, and reduce the heat to low.

Make the Poached Eggs.

Toast the bread or char on both sides under the broiler, then rub the bruschetta with the cut garlic, drizzle with EVOO, and season with flaky sea salt.

Stir the ramp greens and herbs into the scafata and douse the mixture with the lemon juice. Serve in shallow bowls topped with poached eggs, with the bruschetta alongside.

TIP

Instead of the ramps, you can use small spring onions or scallions, whites finely chopped and light green parts sliced on an angle. If you don't have garlic scapes, substitute 4 cloves garlic, thinly sliced.

FRITTATA SOUFFLÉ WITH TOMATOES, PANCETTA, AND LEEKS

SERVES 4 TO 6

This is my equivalent of a BLT in a frittata. The technique can be used with any filling ingredients but be careful not to make the fillings or toppings too heavy. For example, you can stir some potato into your frittata, but it should be very finely chopped and browned or shredded. And heavier ingredients, by weight, should be used sparingly. By folding in the egg whites, the frittata reaches new heights—literally.

8 large free-range organic eggs
1 teaspoon dry mustard
3 tablespoons freshly grated
    Parmigiano-Reggiano cheese
⅓ cup grated Fontina Val d'Aosta
    or Gruyère cheese
Salt and pepper
1 tablespoon good olive oil
¼ pound sliced pancetta,
    chopped
2 leeks, halved lengthwise,
    cut crosswise into 1-inch
    half-moons, washed well
    and dried
2 cloves garlic, finely chopped
2 tablespoons finely chopped
    fresh thyme
2 tablespoons butter
12 cherry or grape tomatoes,
    quartered

Preheat the oven to 375°F.
    Separate the eggs, placing the whites in one bowl and the yolks in another. Whisk the whites until medium-firm peaks form. Whisk the yolks with the mustard, cheeses, salt, and pepper.
    In an 8- or 9-inch ovenproof skillet, heat the oil (1 turn of the pan) over medium to medium-high heat. Add the pancetta and brown lightly, about 2 minutes. Add the leeks, garlic, and thyme and cook until lightly browned, 4 to 5 minutes. Transfer the leek mixture to a plate.
    Add the butter to the skillet and melt over medium to medium-high heat. When the foam subsides, fold the egg whites into the yolk mixture and pour the mixture into the skillet. Scatter the leek mixture over the eggs as they begin to set and the edges firm up. Dot the frittata with the tomatoes and transfer the pan to the oven. Bake until golden and puffed, 15 to 18 minutes. Let cool for 10 minutes.

RATATOUILLE FRITTATA

SERVES 4

Yes, ratatouille is French, not Italian, but who cares? The combination of zucchini, eggplant, and tomatoes is meant to be, and this frittata is spectacular.

1 tablespoon butter
¼ pound thinly sliced speck
    (smoky ham) or prosciutto
3 to 4 cups Ratatouille (page 345)
8 large free-range organic eggs
⅓ cup milk
1½ cups freshly grated
    Parmigiano-Reggiano cheese
Pepper

Position a rack in the center of the oven and preheat the oven to 400°F.
    Rub an 8- to 9-inch ovenproof skillet with the butter. Line the pan with overlapping slices of speck, letting it hang slightly over the edges.
    Spread half the ratatouille in the bottom of the pan. In a bowl, whisk the eggs, milk, and Parm. Season with pepper. Stir the remaining ratatouille into the eggs and pour the mixture into the skillet. Fold the edges of the ham in. Bake until set, 20 to 25 minutes. Let cool on a cooling rack for 10 minutes, then invert onto a serving plate.

VARIATION

Caponata Frittata

Swap in the same amount of Caponata (page 31) for the ratatouille.

TRUFFLE EGGS AND GRILLED BRIOCHE WITH WARM TALEGGIO AND HONEY

SERVES 4

The Best Breakfast EVER: This meal should be illegal, it is so sinful and rich, but thankfully they will not lock you up if you decide to give it a try.

8 large Araucana (pale green shelled eggs) or other free-range organic eggs
1 white or black truffle
4 slices (about ¾ inch thick) brioche bread
⅓ pound ripe Taleggio cheese
Acacia or truffle honey
3 tablespoons good-quality butter, cut into small pieces
Sea salt and pepper
3 tablespoons minced fresh chives

Store the eggs and the truffle in the same plastic food storage bag overnight. The truffle will perfume the eggs through their porous shells.

Heat a griddle or nonstick skillet over medium heat and grill the bread until deep golden on both sides. In a small saucepan, melt the Taleggio over medium-low heat, or put the cheese in a bowl and microwave until melted. Slather the bread with the cheese and drizzle with honey. Cut the bread from corner to corner on an angle.

In a bowl, beat the eggs. Beat in the bits of butter and season with salt and a few grinds of pepper. Shave or grate in some truffle (I usually put in 1 to 2 tablespoons).

Heat a nonstick skillet over medium heat. Pour in the eggs and scramble them, constantly moving the spoon or spatula in small circles to develop lots of curds. Add the chives and adjust the seasonings.

Top the buttery eggs with more shaved truffle and serve with the Taleggio toast alongside.

FLATBREAD PIZZAS WITH GREENS, RICOTTA, AND EGGS

SERVES 4

The idea of having pizza for breakfast is fun. I must admit that there has been more than a morning or two in my life when cold pizza was not only breakfast, but somehow seemed like the most delicious breakfast choice, period. This is an easy, but elegant, means to that end.

2 tablespoons olive oil
2 or 3 flat anchovy fillets (to taste)
1 leek, halved lengthwise, cut crosswise into half-moons, washed well and dried
2 or 3 large cloves garlic (to taste), sliced
1 large bunch dandelion greens or flat kale, stemmed and sliced
Freshly grated nutmeg
Salt and pepper
1 cup fresh ricotta cheese, homemade (see box, page 40) or store-bought, drained and crumbled
2 tablespoons fresh thyme leaves
1 teaspoon grated lemon zest (from an organic lemon)
4 large flatbreads or pocketless pitas

Olive oil cooking spray
1 ball (about 8 ounces) fior di latte cheese (fresh mozzarella), excess moisture pressed out, diced or shredded
1 cup freshly grated Parmigiano-Reggiano cheese
1 tablespoon butter
4 large free-range organic eggs

Heat a grill to medium-high heat.

In a large skillet, heat the oil (2 turns of the pan) over medium heat. Add the anchovies, cover the pan with a splatter screen or lid, and shake until the anchovies begin to break up. Reduce the heat a bit, uncover, and stir until the anchovies melt into the oil. Add the leek and garlic and stir for 2 minutes. Wilt in the greens and season with a little nutmeg, salt, and pepper.

In a bowl, mix the ricotta, thyme, and lemon zest.

Spray the bread lightly with olive oil. Working in batches if necessary, grill the bread until crisp on one side, flip, then top with dollops of the ricotta and some of the greens, mozzarella, and Parm. Cover the grill and cook for 5 minutes to melt the cheeses.

In a large skillet, melt the butter over medium heat. Crack in the eggs and cook over-easy. Season with salt and pepper.

Top each pizza with an egg.

CROQUE MADAME, ITALIAN-STYLE

What's not to love? Bread layered with *besciamella* sauce, ham, and cheese, then baked and topped with a basted egg? *Si.* Yes. Please.

2½ cups milk
4 tablespoons (½ stick) butter
3 tablespoons flour
Salt and pepper
Freshly grated nutmeg
1 rounded tablespoon Dijon mustard
¼ cup freshly grated Parmigiano-Reggiano cheese
4 large slices (½ inch thick) rustic peasant-style bread (long oval slices)
8 thin slices prosciutto cotto (cooked ham)
About 2 cups loosely packed shredded Fontina Val d'Aosta or Gruyère cheese (shred on the large holes of a box grater)
4 Basted Eggs (see Basics box)
Minced fresh chives, for garnish

Preheat the oven to 375°F.

In a small saucepan, warm the milk over low heat.

Heat a deep medium skillet over medium heat and melt the butter. When it foams, add the flour and whisk for 1 minute. Add the warm milk and cook until just thick enough to coat the back of a spoon. Season with salt, pepper, and nutmeg. Stir in the mustard and Parm and remove from the heat.

Arrange the bread slices on a nonstick or parchment paper–lined baking sheet. Cover the bread with the white sauce and arrange the ham in a thin layer lightly piled on top. Top with cheese and bake until golden, 15 to 18 minutes.

Meanwhile, make the Basted Eggs.

Serve the eggs on the baked toasts. Garnish with chives.

VARIATIONS

Variations abound with this meal. Sometimes I layer a half dozen thin spears of blanched asparagus between the ham and cheese. Or sometimes a bed of sherry-sautéed mushrooms, or garlicky wilted spinach or wilted greens on top of the croque and under the egg. For something entirely special, I add shaved truffle to the white sauce and a couple extra shaves atop the egg.

DEVILED HAM AND ASPARAGUS MELTS WITH BASTED EGGS

Deviled Cotto Ham (page 39)
4 large slices (½ inch thick) rustic peasant-style bread (long oval slices)
32 to 40 pencil-thin asparagus spears
¾ pound Fontina Val d'Aosta cheese, shredded on the large holes of a box grater
4 Basted Eggs (see Basics box)
Salt and pepper

Position a rack in the center of the oven and preheat the oven to 375°F.

Make the Deviled Cotto Ham. Evenly spread each slice of bread with a ¼-inch-thick layer of deviled ham and place the bread on a baking sheet.

Fill a bowl with ice and water. In a skillet, bring 2 inches of water to a boil. Add the asparagus and cook for 3 minutes. Cold-shock in the ice bath, then remove and dry the spears on a kitchen towel or paper towels.

Arrange 8 to 10 spears on each slice of ham-topped bread and top the body of the asparagus and most of the ham with shredded Fontina, leaving the tips and ends of the asparagus exposed. Bake until the bread is toasted on the bottom and the cheese is melted and lightly browned, 15 to 18 minutes.

Meanwhile, make the Basted Eggs.

Serve a basted egg on each toast and season with salt and pepper.

BASICS

BASTED EGGS

SERVES 4

3 tablespoons butter
4 large free-range organic eggs
Salt and pepper

In a large nonstick skillet, melt the butter over medium-low heat. When it foams, add the eggs, leaving a little room around each. When each egg white has set, baste with butter by tipping the pan and spooning the butter over the top of the yolks. Season with salt and pepper, cover the pan, and cook for 2 minutes.

QUICK POLENTA WITH ASPARAGUS, LEEKS, AND POACHED EGGS

A friend of mine was visiting for the weekend and she had fairly recently gone gluten-free due to a health issue. This was one of our brunch creations, and given how much she used to enjoy a big bowl of pasta, I loved seeing how pleased she was with this creamy, cheesy bowl of polenta topped with asparagus and perfectly poached eggs. This is a bowl of comfort that is so pretty you almost don't want to eat it . . . almost.

3 tablespoons olive oil

¾ pound mixed mushrooms, coarsely chopped (tiny mushrooms can just be stemmed)

1 bunch asparagus, thinly sliced on an angle

1 large or 2 medium leeks (white and light green parts), halved lengthwise, thinly sliced crosswise into half-moons, washed well and dried

3 cloves garlic, sliced

2 tablespoons fresh thyme leaves, chopped

Salt and pepper

⅓ cup dry sherry

3 cups chicken stock

1½ cups stone-ground cornmeal (I like Indian Head brand)

3 tablespoons butter

½ cup freshly grated Parmigiano-Reggiano cheese

⅛ to ¼ teaspoon freshly grated nutmeg (to taste)

4 Poached Eggs (page 3)

In a large skillet, heat the oil (3 turns of the pan) over medium-high heat. Add the mushrooms and brown well, 12 to 15 minutes. Add the asparagus, leeks, garlic, and thyme and season with salt and pepper. Stir for 5 minutes more, then add the sherry and cook until it has evaporated.

In a small saucepan, bring the stock and 1½ cups water to a boil. Reduce the heat to a simmer, whisk in the cornmeal, and cook until thickened, 3 to 5 minutes. Add the butter, Parm, nutmeg, salt, and pepper. Remove from the heat. If the polenta gets too thick, add more hot water.

Make the Poached Eggs.

Spoon the polenta into shallow bowls, make a well in the center, and fill the well with the mushroom and asparagus mixture. Top with a poached egg.

POLENTA WITH TIPSY MUSHROOMS, POACHED EGGS, AND GREEN SALAD

Serve this all on the same plate to encourage the diners to eat the meal in unison: The creamy yolks running into the soft polenta mixed with the earthy mushrooms and the bright bite of lemon-dressed greens. Please do not confine this menu to brunches as it makes a delicious warm, comforting dinner as well. I really love having breakfast-style foods and/or eggs for dinner.

Rachael's Polenta (page 179)

3 tablespoons butter

2 tablespoons olive oil

1½ pounds mixed mushrooms: a combination of cremini plus hen-of-the-woods (maitake) or shiitake, sliced

2 tablespoons fresh thyme leaves, chopped

1 shallot, chopped

2 cloves garlic, chopped

Salt and pepper

About ¾ cup sherry or Marsala

6 Poached Eggs (page 3)

Mixed Greens Salad (page 25)

Make Rachael's Polenta and keep warm.

In a large skillet, melt the butter into the oil over medium-high heat. Add the mushrooms and brown. Add the thyme, shallot, and garlic and season with salt and pepper. Stir for 2 to 3 minutes more. Add the sherry and reduce until almost evaporated.

Make the Poached Eggs and Mixed Greens Salad.

To serve, pour puddles of the creamy, thick polenta into shallow bowls. Nest the poached eggs in the polenta, scatter the mushrooms around the edges, and pile the greens along one side to leave the other elements of the dish partially exposed.

PARMIGIANO-REGGIANO FRENCH TOAST WITH SAUSAGE PATTIES AND WARM HONEY

I love dishes that are salty and sweet at the same time. This meal is unexpected for diners who think they know what French toast tastes like. Not so fast. This French toast has an Italian twist: Parmigiano-Reggiano cheese.

1½ pounds ground pork
¼ cup dry white or red wine
1 teaspoon fennel seeds
1 teaspoon granulated garlic
1 teaspoon granulated onion
1 teaspoon ground sage
2 teaspoons coarsely ground pepper
1½ teaspoons kosher salt
2 tablespoons EVOO
5 large free-range organic eggs
1 cup milk
Freshly grated nutmeg
2 cups freshly grated Parmigiano-Reggiano cheese
8 slices (¾ inch thick) good-quality Italian or white bread
3 to 4 tablespoons butter, melted
Warm honey, for drizzling
Fresh berries of any type, for garnish

Preheat the oven on its lowest setting. Heat a griddle pan over medium-high heat.

In a large bowl, mix the pork, wine, fennel seeds, garlic, onion, sage, 1 teaspoon of the pepper, 1 teaspoon of the salt, and the EVOO. Form the pork mixture into 8 small, thin patties. Place the patties on the griddle pan and cook for 3 to 4 minutes on each side. Transfer to a baking sheet to keep warm in the oven.

Reduce the heat under the griddle to medium for the French toast.

In a bowl, whisk the eggs, milk, a little nutmeg, the Parm, and the remaining 1 teaspoon pepper and ½ teaspoon salt. Coat the bread slices in the egg batter.

Coat the griddle pan with some melted butter and add the soaked bread. Cook until golden and cooked through. Add more butter to the pan as needed.

Serve the Parmesan French toast with the sausage patties. Drizzle with warm honey and garnish with a few fresh berries.

PANETTONE FRENCH TOAST

Panettone (brioche-style golden bread spiked with citrus and dried fruit) is delicious as is, but it's even better when toasted or griddled. To make it even richer than that, soak the bread in custard and slow-cook it in melted butter to a deep golden brown. This is what we have for brunch every Christmas Day. I always buy two or three panettone so we can keep making this dish well into January. The custard makes a nice coating for French toast made with brioche, cinnamon bread, or cinnamon-raisin bread the rest of the year.

3 large free-range organic eggs
1 cup half-and-half
1 teaspoon almond extract
Freshly grated nutmeg
6 slices (about 1½ inches thick) panettone (from a loaf about 5 inches wide)
5 tablespoons butter, melted

TOPPING SUGGESTIONS:
Warm honey
Warm maple syrup
Warm fruit syrup
Ricotta or mascarpone cheese sweetened with powdered sugar
Mixed berries doused with Grand Marnier or amaretto

Preheat the oven to its lowest setting.

In a shallow bowl, whisk the eggs, half-and-half, and almond extract. Add a little nutmeg.

Heat a large nonstick griddle over medium heat. Coat the panettone 2 slices at a time in the custard. Liberally grease the griddle with melted butter. Add the bread and cook until deeply golden, puffed, and cooked through. Transfer the cooked toast slices to a baking sheet and keep warm in the oven. Brush the griddle with more butter and repeat.

Serve with the toppings of your choice.

VARIATIONS

Brioche French Toast

Substitute 6 thick slices of brioche for the panettone. Stale bread is fine and, in fact, preferred.

Almond French Toast

Dip one side of the custard-soaked bread in sliced almonds for added crunch.

Rum French Toast

Use rum extract instead of almond extract in the custard recipe, or use both extracts together.

MEATBALLS AND OATMEAL FOR BRUNCH

WOW. This meal may sound odd—meatballs for breakfast—and unusual, yes, but once you've had this combo, you'll be hooked. You will long for it to be cold enough outside to make it again. Here's how you serve this brunch: Make a bed of the oatmeal in shallow bowls and top with the meatballs. You will be surprised how the presentation will lift this from odd to almost elegant.

Breakfast Sausage Meatballs
SERVES 4

¼ teaspoon baking soda
1 tablespoon very hot water
1½ teaspoons kosher salt
1 to 1½ cups homemade coarse dry bread crumbs
Milk, for moistening the bread
1¼ to 1½ pounds ground pork, chicken, or turkey
2 tablespoons dry white wine
1 large free-range organic egg, lightly beaten
2 tablespoons EVOO
2 cloves garlic, grated or minced
1½ teaspoons granulated onion
1½ teaspoons ground sage (if using pork) or poultry seasoning (if using chicken or turkey)
1 teaspoon ground coriander
½ teaspoon crushed red pepper flakes
⅛ teaspoon freshly grated nutmeg
Black pepper
⅓ to ½ cup freshly grated Parmigiano-Reggiano cheese

Preheat the oven to 400°F. Line a baking sheet with parchment paper.

In a small bowl, combine the baking soda, hot water, and salt and stir to dissolve.

In another bowl, moisten the bread crumbs with milk, then squeeze out the excess liquid.

In a large bowl, combine the meat, wine, and baking soda mixture. Add the bread crumbs, egg, EVOO, garlic, onion, sage, coriander, red pepper flakes, nutmeg, black pepper, and Parm and stir to combine with a spatula.

Roll meatballs about the size of large walnuts (I use a small scoop to roll faster) and arrange them on the baking sheet. Bake until cooked through and light golden, 18 to 20 minutes.

TIP

To make bread crumbs, pulse crustless stale white or peasant bread in a food processor into large flakes.

Savory Fennel, Rosemary, and Honey Oatmeal
SERVES 4

¼ cup pignoli (pine nuts)
1 tablespoon fennel seeds
2 cups milk
3 tablespoons butter
1 teaspoon sea salt
1⅔ cups rolled oats
½ cup golden raisins
Leaves from 3 or 4 small sprigs fresh rosemary, coarsely chopped
3 tablespoons acacia honey, or more to taste

In a medium pot, toast the pine nuts and fennel seeds over medium heat. Add 4 cups water, the milk, butter, salt, oats, raisins, and rosemary. Bring to a simmer, but do not boil. Cook until tender, about 20 minutes. Stir in honey to taste.

BUTTERNUT SQUASH GALETTE

SERVES 6

I serve this often as a brunch item, but with a simple salad it's a terrific light supper perfect for early fall. Sometimes I add pepper to the crust dough for an extra spicy twist. If I prepare the dish for a guest with egg allergies, I brush the dough with buttermilk instead of egg wash to brown the crust.

DOUGH:

6 ounces (1½ sticks) very cold butter, cut into cubes
3 cups flour
1½ teaspoons salt
9 tablespoons ice water (see Tip)

FILLING:

3 tablespoons butter
2 Honeycrisp or Gala apples, peeled and thinly sliced
1 onion, thinly sliced
1 small butternut squash, peeled, seeded, and thinly sliced
2 tablespoons fresh thyme leaves, chopped
8 fresh sage leaves, very thinly sliced
Salt and pepper
Freshly grated nutmeg

1 large free-range organic egg, beaten with a splash of water
Gorgonzola cheese, blue cheese, or smoked blue cheese
Acacia honey, for drizzling

Make the dough: In a food processor, combine the butter, flour, and salt and pulse until small pieces form. Continue to pulse, pouring the cold water through the feed tube, pulsing until the dough just comes together. Turn it out onto a lightly floured surface and press it into a round, flat disk. Wrap the dough in plastic and refrigerate for at least 1 hour or up to 24 hours. (Or freeze it for later use; it will be good for up to 3 months. Thaw until pliable but still chilled.)

Make the filling: In a large skillet, melt the butter over medium heat. Add the apples, onion, squash, thyme, and sage; season with salt, pepper, and nutmeg. Cook until just tender, about 15 minutes. Let cool a bit until easy to handle.

Position a rack in the center of the oven and preheat the oven to 375°F. Line a baking sheet with parchment paper.

On a lightly floured surface, roll the chilled dough out into a large round, ⅛ inch thick and 13 to 15 inches in diameter. Place the dough on the lined baking sheet and arrange the apple-squash mixture over the dough, slightly mounded in the center and with a 2-inch border around the edges. Fold the edges of the dough in, overlapping and pleating the dough every few inches as you go around the galette.

Bake the galette for 30 minutes. Brush the edges with the beaten egg and return to the oven to bake until the crust is deep golden, about 15 minutes.

Serve topped with blue cheese and drizzled with honey.

TIP

Here's how I get really ice-cold water when making doughs: I use a cocktail shaker to shake the water with ice and then I strain it right into the processor.

GALETTE WITH RICOTTA AND GREENS

As with any savory galette, this is not only an elegant brunch item but makes a tasty light supper, too. For the greens, you can use all chard or mix it with tender, stemmed Tuscan kale. If there's anyone who will be eating this who has an egg allergy, use buttermilk instead of the egg wash to brush the crust.

DOUGH:

6 ounces (1½ sticks) very cold butter, cut into cubes
1½ cups flour
1 cup whole wheat flour
1½ teaspoons kosher salt
½ cup ice-cold water (see Tip, page 16)

FILLING:

3½ tablespoons olive oil
12 green or purple asparagus spears, thinly sliced on an angle
Salt and black pepper
2 tablespoons butter
½ pound cremini mushrooms, thinly sliced
¼ pound hen-of-the-woods mushrooms (maitake), root cut away and mushrooms separated
2 shallots, finely chopped
2 tablespoons fresh thyme leaves, chopped
¼ cup sherry or Marsala
3 cloves garlic, chopped
¾ pound Swiss or rainbow chard or a mixture of chard and Tuscan kale, stemmed and chopped (about 8 cups)

Freshly grated nutmeg
1 cup fresh ricotta cheese, homemade (see box, page 40) or store-bought, drained
½ cup walnuts, toasted
2 teaspoons grated lemon zest (from an organic lemon)
1 cup freshly grated Parmigiano-Reggiano cheese

1 large free-range organic egg, beaten
¾ cup loosely packed chopped mixed fresh herbs: tarragon, flat-leaf parsley, mint, and/or chives
½ teaspoon crushed red pepper flakes
Juice of ½ lemon
Flaky sea salt

Make the dough: In a food processor, combine the butter, flours, and salt and pulse until small pieces form. Continue to pulse, pouring the cold water through the feed tube, pulsing until the dough just comes together. Turn it out onto a lightly floured surface and press it into a round, flat disk. Wrap the dough in plastic and chill in the refrigerator for at least 1 hour or up to 24 hours (or freeze it for up to 3 months; thaw until pliable but still chilled).

Make the filling: In a large skillet, heat 1 tablespoon of the oil (1 turn of the pan) over medium-high heat. Add the asparagus and cook until tender-crisp, about 2 minutes. Season with salt and black pepper and transfer to a plate.

Return the skillet to the heat and add ½ tablespoon of the oil (½ turn of the pan). Add the butter and when the foam subsides, add the mushrooms and brown well, 7 to 8 minutes. Add the shallots and thyme, stir for 1 to 2 minutes, then add the sherry and cook until it has evaporated. Transfer the mushroom mixture to a plate and set aside.

Return the skillet to the heat and add the remaining 2 tablespoons oil (2 turns of the pan). Add the garlic and stir for 1 minute. Add the greens to wilt, then season with a few grates of nutmeg, salt, and black pepper.

Position a rack in the center of the oven and preheat the oven to 375°F. Line a baking sheet with parchment paper.

In a food processor, combine the ricotta, walnuts, lemon zest, and ½ cup of the Parm; season with salt and black pepper. Pulse to combine.

On a lightly floured surface, roll the chilled dough out into a large round ⅛ inch thick and 13 to 15 inches in diameter. Place the dough on the prepared baking sheet and spread the ricotta mixture over the top, leaving a 2-inch border. Top with the mushrooms, asparagus, and greens. Scatter the remaining ½ cup Parm over the top. Fold the edges of the dough in, overlapping and pleating the dough every few inches as you go around the galette.

Bake the galette for 30 minutes, then brush the edges liberally with beaten egg and bake until the crust is deep golden at the edges, about 15 minutes.

Top the galette with the herbs, red pepper flakes, lemon juice, and flaky sea salt. Cut into wedges and serve.

SPAGHETTI PIE

SERVES 6

My grandpa used to make a breakfast of garlic, oil, chopped cold spaghetti, and eggs. I always toss leftover pasta with the sauce. You want all of the pasta to taste good. I never end up with just "naked" cold spaghetti. This dish is a great way to use up leftover spaghetti, either carbonara or spaghetti Bolognese. Of course, if you don't have any of those, you can just cook up about ¼ pound spaghetti to al dente and cold-shock it before proceeding with the recipe method.

3 to 4 tablespoons good olive oil

¼ pound pancetta, finely chopped

2 or 3 cloves garlic (to taste), chopped

½ teaspoon crushed red pepper flakes

2 to 3 cups cold leftover spaghetti carbonara, Bolognese, or plain spaghetti, coarsely chopped

7 large free-range organic eggs

¼ cup finely chopped fresh flat-leaf parsley

1 cup freshly grated Parmigiano-Reggiano or Grana Padano cheese

Salt and black pepper

Position a rack in the center of the oven and preheat the oven to 375°F.

In an 8- or 9-inch ovenproof skillet, heat the oil (3 to 4 turns of the pan) over medium heat. Add the pancetta and render, stirring, for 2 to 3 minutes. Add the garlic and red pepper flakes and stir for 1 minute. Add the cold pasta and toss for 2 minutes just to heat through.

In a bowl, beat the eggs, parsley, cheese, a little salt, and black pepper. Pour the mixture over the spaghetti and stir to combine. Cook for 1 minute to set, then transfer to the oven and bake the frittata until set and golden, about 15 minutes. Let cool for 10 minutes, then invert onto a plate and serve.

HAM AND HAY PIE

SERVES 6

This is a frittata baked in a pan that is lined with ham. Of all the brunch items included here, this is probably the most popular among my friends and family. "Hay" refers to the shredded cabbage, and we have a lot of cabbage in our garden during the summer and early fall.

2 tablespoons butter, plus more for the pan

⅓ pound sliced speck (smoky ham) or prosciutto di Parma

1 tablespoon olive oil

1 small onion, halved and thinly sliced

3 or 4 cloves garlic (to taste), chopped or thinly sliced

1 small potato, peeled and cut into ¼-inch cubes

½ small head green cabbage, shredded (3 to 4 cups)

A few leaves fresh sage, thinly sliced

Salt and pepper

Freshly grated nutmeg

7 large free-range organic eggs

About ½ cup milk

2 cups freshly grated Parmigiano-Reggiano or Grana Padano cheese

Position a rack in the center of the oven and preheat the oven to 400°F.

Grease an 8- or 9-inch oven-proof skillet with a little butter.

Using 4 or 5 slices of ham, line the pan with an even, overlapping layer, letting the ends hang over the sides of the pan. Coarsely chop the remaining ham.

In a second skillet, heat the oil (1 turn of the pan) over medium heat. Add the 2 tablespoons butter to melt. When it foams, add the onion, garlic, potato, cabbage, and sage. Season with salt, pepper, and nutmeg. Cook, stirring, until the vegetables are softened, 12 to 15 minutes. Add the chopped ham and toss for 2 to 3 minutes more. Remove from the heat.

Add one-third of the "hay" (the cabbage mixture) to the ham-lined skillet. In a bowl, beat the eggs, milk, and cheese and season with salt and pepper. Stir the remaining hay into the eggs, add to the skillet, and fold the ham ends in. Bake the pie until just firm and golden, 16 to 18 minutes. Let cool for 10 minutes on a cooling rack, then invert onto a plate to serve.

On plate in center: Butternut-Sage Crostini (page 39); Veal and Sage Meatballs with Gorgonzola (page 53); Plums with Speck (page 29); Shaved Raw Artichoke Salad (page 24). Cocktails: Grapefruit Martini (page 369); and Brooklyn Township (page 368).

CHAPTER 2

STARTERS, SALADS, AND SMALL BITES

What Americans call first courses, the Italians call *primi piatti* (literally, "first dishes"). This chapter is filled with ideas for starting a meal, but you really need to check out a number of other chapters, too, to get a full picture of the possibilities. For example, a classic "first dish" for an Italian meal is pasta (though in this country we think of pasta as an entrée). So the pasta chapter, which is the largest in this book, could be considered a chapter completely dedicated to primi piatti. You also need to check out the risotto and soup chapters, both classic ways to kick off a dinner. So my advice is, mark your favorites in this chapter, but if you are building a buffet or looking for the perfect first course and have a few extra minutes, thumb through the whole book before settling on your choice.

FAMILY-SIZE CAESAR

Use all romaine for this salad, or try my favorite, a mixture of flat Tuscan kale (or baby kale) and romaine. The kale gives the salad a stronger chew and flavor, and also keeps the greens from looking too wilted if anyone goes back for seconds. The croutons take longer than the salad to prepare but man, are they good. Beware of snacking on too many before the salad is served.

CROUTONS:

¼ cup olive oil

2 large cloves garlic, smashed

4 tablespoons (½ stick) good-quality butter

1½ teaspoons coarsely ground pepper

4 to 5 cups stale peasant or good-quality Italian white bread cubes

A handful of freshly grated Parmigiano-Reggiano cheese

A handful of freshly grated Pecorino Romano cheese

DRESSING AND SALAD:

3 large cloves garlic: 1 smashed and 2 pasted or grated

2 teaspoons anchovy paste, or 7 or 8 flat anchovy fillets, pasted

1 large organic egg yolk (see Tip)

2 teaspoons Worcestershire sauce

2 teaspoons Dijon mustard

¼ cup fresh lemon juice

Pepper

¾ to 1 cup EVOO

¾ to 1 cup freshly grated pecorino cheese

2 heads romaine lettuce, coarsely chopped, or 1 head romaine and 1 bunch Tuscan kale (also called black, lacinato, or dinosaur kale), stemmed and cut into 1-inch pieces

Preheat the oven to 350°F.

Make the croutons: In a large skillet, heat the oil (4 turns of the pan) and garlic over medium heat. Melt the butter into the oil and add the pepper. Swirl for 2 minutes after the butter melts. Toss the bread cubes with the garlic oil on a baking sheet, spread in a single layer, and top with the cheeses. Bake until deeply golden and fragrant, 10 to 15 minutes.

Make the dressing and salad: Rub the inside of a large wooden salad bowl with the smashed garlic clove. Add the garlic paste, anchovy paste, egg yolk,

Worcestershire sauce, mustard, lemon juice, and pepper and whisk. While whisking, stream in the EVOO to emulsify. Stir in the pecorino. Taste and adjust the seasonings.

Add the chopped greens and croutons to the bowl and toss to combine. Adjust the pepper and pecorino to taste.

THE DRESSING contains a raw egg yolk, which may be omitted if you have concerns about eating uncooked egg. I buy organic Araucana eggs because I feel that eggs farmed in a smaller, humane, controlled environment probably have less of a chance of carrying salmonella. (Then again, I'm a cook, not a doctor, so I think Caesar salad with carbonara and poached eggs on polenta are worth the risk.)

SESAME-ANCHOVY CAESAR SALAD

Tahini is not a traditional ingredient in Italian cooking, but it makes a delicious eggless Caesar-style dressing. The salad can be easily made dairy-free as well by simply omitting the Romano cheese from the dressing and making garlic-rubbed croutons (instead of the traditional croutons made with butter and cheese).

2 large cloves garlic: 1 finely grated or pasted, 1 halved
Juice of 1 lemon
¼ cup tahini
2 teaspoons anchovy paste
Coarsely ground pepper
⅓ cup EVOO, plus more for the croutons
A generous handful of grated Romano cheese (optional)
3 or 4 slices rustic white bread
Flaky sea salt
6 to 8 cups chopped romaine lettuce, kale leaves, or a combination

In a large salad bowl, whisk the grated garlic, lemon juice, tahini, anchovy paste, pepper, and about 3 tablespoons water to thin the tahini a bit. While whisking, slowly stream in the EVOO to emulsify. Taste, adjust the seasonings, and stir in the Romano (if using).

Under the broiler or in a toaster, toast the bread. Rub the toast with the cut garlic and dress with a little EVOO and flaky sea salt. Cut into cubes.

Add the greens and croutons to the bowl with the dressing and toss well.

CELERY, PORTOBELLO, AND PARSLEY SALAD

Use this salad with menus featuring veal or beef as the main course. A sliced small strip steak topped with this salad is a very simple and delicious quick meal; it is something I make for myself when cooking for one because of its simplicity and flavor, but John loves it, too.

4 or 5 ribs celery with leafy tops, very thinly sliced on an angle
4 portobello mushroom caps, gills scraped, very thinly sliced
1 cup fresh flat-leaf parsley tops, coarsely chopped
2 cups baby kale or arugula
Juice of 1½ lemons
¼ cup EVOO
Salt and pepper
Pecorino or Parmigiano-Reggiano cheese, shaved into curls with a vegetable peeler (optional)

In a bowl, combine the celery, mushrooms, parsley, kale, lemon juice, EVOO, salt, and pepper and let the salad stand for a few minutes for the mushrooms to soften and mellow and for the flavors to combine. If you want, add shaved pecorino just before serving.

SHAVED RAW ARTICHOKE SALAD

SERVES 8 TO 10

3 lemons, halved
16 baby artichokes (about 1½ pounds)
2 or 3 ribs celery with leafy tops, very thinly sliced on an angle
1 cup fresh flat-leaf parsley tops, chopped
A couple of handfuls of baby or wild arugula
¼ cup EVOO
Salt and pepper
1 cup shaved Parmigiano-Reggiano cheese
¼ cup fresh tarragon leaves (optional)

Fill a bowl with water and a little ice. Squeeze in the juice of one lemon and the juiced rinds.

Trim the artichokes down to the pale yellow and pale purple leaves. Keep as much of the baby stems intact as possible and trim a scant ½ inch from the tops. Using a mandoline or the slicer blade on a box grater, shave the raw artichokes almost as thin as potato chips, dropping them into the ice water as you go. Leave the artichokes in the water until ready to assemble your salad.

Drain the artichokes and dry on a kitchen towel. Transfer to a shallow serving bowl and combine with the celery, parsley, and arugula. Squeeze the juice of the remaining 2 lemons over everything, dress with the EVOO, and season with salt and pepper. Just before serving, add the shaved Parm and tarragon (if using).

CHERRY TOMATO AND RED ONION SALAD

SERVES 6

2 pints cherry tomatoes, halved
1 cup fresh flat-leaf parsley tops, chopped
1 small red onion, chopped
¼ cup olive oil
Salt and pepper

In a bowl, combine the tomatoes, parsley, onion, and oil. Season with salt and pepper. Let stand for 10 to 15 minutes before serving.

GRAPEFRUIT WITH GIN AND MINT

Well, the title is the recipe, pretty much. Section red grapefruit or a combination of red and yellow. Or else you can peel the grapefruit, cut them into large disks, and remove the seeds. Arrange the grapefruit on a platter and douse it with good, herbaceous gin—a liberal sprinkle around the platter. Top with chopped fresh mint. My mother invented this dish and it is delicious and refreshing.

ARUGULA SALAD WITH SAGE AND WHITE BALSAMIC VINAIGRETTE

SERVES 4

This is my absolute favorite topping for Veal Milanese (page 277).

1 small clove garlic, pasted
2 or 3 leaves fresh sage, very thinly sliced or mashed together with the garlic using a mortar and pestle
1 small shallot, grated (about 1½ tablespoons)
1 tablespoon fresh lemon juice
2 tablespoons white balsamic vinegar
2 teaspoons light honey (such as acacia)
⅓ cup EVOO
Salt and pepper
5 ounces arugula, baby kale, or a combination (6 cups)
1 pint cherry or grape tomatoes, halved

In a small bowl, whisk the garlic, sage, shallot, lemon juice, vinegar, and honey. Still whisking, stream in the EVOO to emulsify. Season with salt and pepper. Put the greens and tomatoes in a large serving bowl, add the dressing, and toss to coat.

MIXED GREENS SALAD

SERVES 6

Juice of 1 lemon
1 tablespoon white wine vinegar
1 tablespoon honey
2 teaspoons Dijon mustard
2 tablespoons grated shallot or onion
¼ cup EVOO
Salt and pepper
1 head frisée, separated into leaves
4 cups baby arugula
3 cups baby spinach

In a small bowl, whisk the lemon juice, vinegar, honey, mustard, and grated shallot. Still whisking, stream in the EVOO to emulsify. Season with salt and pepper. Put the greens in a large serving bowl, add the dressing, and toss to coat.

MIXED CITRUS SALAD

SERVES 6 TO 8

Tarragon is a favorite flavor of mine. It tastes like a marriage of basil and fresh fennel, two more of my loves.

4 blood oranges or navel oranges
2 red or yellow grapefruit, or 1 of each color
1 bunch spring onions or scallions, thinly sliced on an angle
½ cup fresh tarragon leaves, coarsely chopped
EVOO, for drizzling
Salt and pepper

Trim the tops and bottoms of the oranges and grapefruit. Stand them upright and use a sharp knife to cut away the peel and membranes, following the curve of the fruit. Cut the citrus crosswise into disks. Shingle the slices on a large platter and top with the spring onions and tarragon. Drizzle liberally with EVOO (about 3 tablespoons) and season with salt and pepper.

ORANGE AND ARUGULA SALAD

SERVES 4

½ small red onion, very thinly sliced
Juice of 1 lemon
Salt and pepper
1 blood orange or navel orange
6 cups packed wild arugula, baby kale, or a combination
2 tablespoons EVOO

In a salad bowl, combine the onion, lemon juice, and a little salt and let sit to "bleed out" (this tames the boldness of the onion and lets the flavors meld a little) while you prep the remaining ingredients.

Trim the top and bottom of the orange. Stand it upright and use a sharp knife to cut away the peel and the membranes, following the curve of the fruit. Working over a bowl, use the knife to release the orange segments from between the membranes, letting them fall into the bowl as you do so. Chop the segments and add them (and any juices) to the bowl with the onion.

Add the arugula and EVOO and season with salt and pepper. Toss to combine.

ORANGE, OREGANO, AND RED ONION SALAD

SERVES 6 TO 8

This is a Sicilian classic. I add briny, salty capote capers (which are larger than nonpareil capers) to mine to balance the sweetness of the oranges.

6 navel oranges or blood oranges, or a mixture of both
1 small red onion, very thinly sliced
Leaves from 2 sprigs fresh oregano, finely chopped
EVOO, for drizzling
A fat handful of flat-leaf parsley tops, coarsely chopped
3 tablespoons capote capers
Salt and pepper

Trim the tops and bottoms of the oranges. Stand them upright and use a sharp knife to cut away the peel and membranes, following the curve of the fruit. Cut the oranges crosswise into disks.

Shingle the oranges and onion slices on a large platter. Top with the oregano and drizzle liberally with EVOO (about 3 tablespoons). Scatter the parsley and capers around the platter and season with salt and pepper.

THE 3 B'S: BERRIES, BALSAMIC, AND BASIL

This combination is a fabulous salad on its own, but I often use it to top grilled, sliced pork tenderloin as well. It is a magical combination. I like to mix in blackcaps or blackberries as well.

2 pints strawberries, hulled and quartered

1 pint blackberries or blackcaps (black raspberries)

Pinch of salt

3 tablespoons balsamic reduction (see box) or aged syrupy balsamic vinegar

½ cup fresh basil leaves, torn or thinly sliced

In a bowl, combine the berries, salt, balsamic reduction, and basil. Let stand for 30 minutes, toss, and serve.

BASICS

BALSAMIC REDUCTION

Thick, syrupy balsamic reduction—aka balsamic drizzle or glaze—can be purchased (including my own brand of it) or you can make your own: In a small pot, combine ¾ cup balsamic vinegar (eyeball the amount) and heat to a low rolling simmer. Add 3 tablespoons light brown sugar and cook until the vinegar has reduced to about ¼ cup syrup.

BEET CARPACCIO WITH CHILES AND MINT

I love beets and they grow so well in the Adirondacks. I use them in pasta and rice dishes, but salads are my favorite recipes for beets.

BEETS:

4 to 6 medium beets, any color

Olive oil, for drizzling

Salt and black pepper

DRESSING:

3 tablespoons white wine vinegar or white balsamic vinegar

2 teaspoons sugar

2 small fresh red chiles, finely chopped

¼ cup minced fresh chives

⅓ cup good olive oil

Salt and black pepper

SALAD:

1 small red onion, very thinly sliced

1 cup chopped celery tops or beet greens

About 4 cups baby or wild arugula

½ cup packed fresh mint leaves, chopped

1 cup crumbled ricotta salata cheese

½ cup pistachios, toasted

Preheat the oven to 400°F.

Make the beets: Trim the beets, then drizzle them with a little oil and rub it all over. Season with salt and black pepper. Enclose the beets and a splash of water in a foil pouch (if using golden beets as well as red, wrap the golden beets in a separate packet). Roast until tender, about 40 minutes. Let the beets cool, then peel by wiping away the skin with paper towels. Chill until ready to serve.

Make the dressing: In a small bowl, whisk all the dressing ingredients.

Make the salad: When ready to serve, very thinly slice the beets with a mandoline or the slicer blade on a large box grater. Shingle the beets and onion on a serving platter. Top with the celery tops, arugula, and mint. Pour the dressing over the top. Top each serving individually with ricotta salata and pistachios.

BEET CARPACCIO WITH CAMPARI VINAIGRETTE

SERVES 4 TO 6

Sweet and bitter are the components of this simple citrusy salad. This one is just so pretty to look at.

BEETS:
4 to 6 medium red beets
EVOO, for drizzling
Salt and pepper

DRESSING:
1 shot (1½ ounces) Campari
2 tablespoons white wine vinegar or white balsamic vinegar
1 teaspoon sugar
1 shallot, grated
2 teaspoons Dijon mustard
2 tablespoons fresh thyme leaves, finely chopped
⅓ cup good olive oil
Salt and pepper

SALAD:
1 small red grapefruit
1 orange
About 3 cups baby or wild arugula
1 small red onion, very thinly sliced
½ cup fresh tarragon leaves, coarsely chopped

Preheat the oven to 400°F.

Make the beets: Trim the beets, then drizzle them with a little EVOO and rub it all over. Season with salt and pepper. Enclose the beets and a splash of water in a foil pouch. Roast until tender, about 40 minutes. Let the beets cool, then peel them by wiping away the skin with paper towels. Chill until ready to serve.

Make the dressing: In a small bowl, whisk all the dressing ingredients.

Make the salad: When ready to serve, very thinly slice the beets with a mandoline or the slicer blade on a large box grater. Trim the tops and bottoms of the grapefruit and orange. Stand them upright and use a sharp knife to cut away the peel and membranes, following the curve of the fruit. Cut the citrus crosswise into disks.

On a platter, make a bed of arugula. Arrange the beets, onion, grapefruit, and orange over the greens and scatter with the tarragon. Pour the dressing over the salad and serve.

GOLDEN BEETS WITH LEMON-DIJON DRESSING AND RADISHES

SERVES 6

This is a sweet and spicy mix of baby golden beets and radishes—it's a colorful summer dish.

BEETS:
12 to 16 baby golden beets
Olive oil, for drizzling
Salt and pepper

DRESSING:
2 to 3 tablespoons acacia honey
1 small shallot, grated
1 rounded tablespoon Dijon mustard
Grated zest and juice of 1 organic lemon
2 tablespoons white wine vinegar
⅓ cup olive oil

SALAD:
1 bunch radishes, trimmed and quartered
½ cup chopped celery
1 bunch scallions, chopped
½ cup fresh flat-leaf parsley leaves, coarsely chopped
Salt and pepper

Preheat the oven to 400°F.

Make the beets: Trim the beets, then drizzle them with a little oil and rub it all over. Season with salt and pepper. Enclose the beets and a splash of water in a foil pouch. Roast until tender, 35 to 40 minutes. Let the beets cool, then peel by wiping away the skin with paper towels. Chill until ready to serve.

Make the dressing: In a small bowl, whisk all the dressing ingredients.

Make the salad: Quarter the beets. In a bowl, combine the beets, radishes, celery, scallions, and parsley. Add the dressing and toss to combine. Adjust the seasonings.

PLUMS WITH SPECK

That's the recipe—so simple and simply delicious. Slice small ripe plums on either side of the pit, creating 2 portions. Season liberally with black pepper. Wrap the lower half of the plum with a thin slice of speck. It will wrap around twice. Tuck in the edges and shingle on a serving plate.

PEARS AND YOUNG PECORINO

SERVES 4

If you have an Italian market or very large cheese shop in your neighborhood, look for cacio e pere, young pecorino cheese made with bits of pear running through the cheese itself. Any young pecorino will be delicious with this dish. I often serve this as a dessert rather than a starter, but it works beautifully as a first course as well. Serve it nice and hot.

2 Anjou pears
Fresh lemon juice
24 to 28 thin slices young
    pecorino cheese
Acacia honey or truffle honey,
    for drizzling

Preheat the oven to 400°F.

Halve and slice the pears (6 or 7 slices per half) and drizzle with lemon juice.

Shingle the pear and cheese in a baking dish. Bake for 7 to 8 minutes to melt the cheese and warm the pears. Drizzle with honey and serve immediately while warm and "melty."

MELON AND PROSCIUTTO WITH LIME AND PEPPER

Arrange wedges of ripe orange, green, or yellow melon on a platter with prosciutto di Parma piled alongside. Or wrap the melon slices individually with prosciutto. In my family, we like to douse the melon with lime juice and season it with pepper, so we add lime wedges to the serving platter and place the pepper mill alongside it.

ROASTED BUTTERNUT SQUASH AND PROSCIUTTO

SERVES 6 TO 8

This is our family's winter version of prosciutto and melon. We cut the squash to look like wedges of cantaloupe or hand melon (an heirloom melon), then serve them with prosciutto alongside or wrapped around the squash. It's a visual pun and a very tasty one at that.

1 large butternut squash
Olive oil, for drizzling
Salt and pepper
Freshly grated nutmeg
1 pound thinly sliced prosciutto
    di Parma

Preheat the oven to 400°F.

Cut the round bottom of the butternut squash away from the narrow top half. Trim the end and top of the squash, then sit each half upright and trim away the skin following the curve of the vegetable. Halve the round end of the squash and scoop out the seeds with a large spoon. Cut the squash into 1½- to 2-inch-wide wedges similar in shape and size to melon wedges.

Arrange the squash on a large rimmed baking sheet and drizzle with oil, tossing to coat the squash lightly but evenly. Season with salt, pepper, and a few grates of nutmeg. Roast until tender and lightly browned at the edges, 25 to 30 minutes.

Arrange the squash stacked or layered on two-thirds of a large platter. Loosely pile the prosciutto in pretty ribbons in the empty one-third of the platter, alongside the pile of roasted squash wedges. Serve at room temperature. To eat, wrap the prosciutto around the squash.

GIARDINIERA

Serve as an appetizer or pulse in a food processor to create a relish for sandwiches (see the Ultimate Pulled Pork Sandwiches, page 230).

1 large head cauliflower

⅓ cup kosher salt

1 red bell pepper, quartered and cut into ½-inch slices

2 red finger peppers or banana peppers, cut into thin rings

2 carrots, cut into ¼-inch-thick slices

3 or 4 ribs celery with leafy tops, cut into 1-inch-thick pieces

½ pound green beans

6 large cloves garlic, smashed

1 to 1½ cups large pitted or pimiento-stuffed Sicilian or Spanish olives

2 or 3 sprigs fresh oregano or marjoram

4 or 5 sprigs fresh thyme

2 cups white balsamic vinegar or white wine vinegar

¼ cup sugar

2 tablespoons sea salt

3 or 4 fresh bay leaves

1 tablespoon black peppercorns

1 tablespoon fennel seeds

Trim the cauliflower leaves, then cut a deep cross into the cauliflower stem. In a wide pot, bring 4 to 5 inches of water to a boil. Add the kosher salt and the cauliflower. Keep at a rolling simmer and cook, partially covered, until the cauliflower is tender but still firm (not mushy), 7 to 8 minutes. Drain very well and let cool. Cut into generous florets.

Divide the cauliflower, bell pepper, finger peppers, carrots, celery, green beans, garlic, olives, oregano sprigs, and thyme sprigs among several jars (or put them in one large nonreactive container).

In a saucepan, combine the vinegar, 3 cups water, the sugar, sea salt, bay leaves, peppercorns, and fennel seeds and cook over medium heat, stirring to dissolve the sugar and salt in the brine, for 2 to 3 minutes. Pour the hot brine over the vegetables, cover, and let come to room temperature. Then refrigerate and brine for at least 3 days and up to 7 days before serving.

CAPONATA

We eat caponata (an eggplant and vegetable appetizer) often. It's great as a snack at brunch, lunch, or on buffets, cold out of the fridge at midnight, or stacked on a sandwich. Sometimes we enjoy it as a hot entrée served on a bed of creamy polenta, or on bread topped with cheese as a makeshift pizza, or even tossed with pasta and cheese. Most recipes for this sweet-and-sour dish include sugar and vinegar, but we use neither; instead, we add golden raisins for sweetness. I also leave some of the skin attached to the chopped eggplant for a nicer look and a bitter balance.

Salt

1 large eggplant, half the skin peeled (in stripes) and cut into ¾-inch cubes

¼ cup olive oil

1 large yellow or red onion, chopped

2 or 3 ribs celery with leafy tops, chopped

1 red bell pepper, diced

1 cubanelle or other mild green pepper, diced

1 fresh chile or cherry pepper, chopped

4 cloves garlic, thinly sliced

1 cup Sicilian olives, pitted and chopped

A small handful of golden raisins

1 (28- to 32-ounce) can San Marzano tomatoes (look for DOP on the label)

A few leaves of torn fresh basil

¼ cup fresh flat-leaf parsley tops, chopped

¼ cup pignoli (pine nuts), toasted

Salt the eggplant and let drain on paper towels for 20 to 30 minutes.

In a large Dutch oven, heat the oil (4 turns of the pan) over medium-high heat. Add the eggplant, onion, celery, bell pepper, cubanelle, chile, garlic, olives, and raisins. Add the tomatoes, breaking them up with your hands, and add the juices from the can. Cook, partially covered but stirring occasionally, until the caponata comes together and the vegetables are tender, about 20 minutes.

Stir in the basil and the parsley. Garnish with the toasted pine nuts.

MARINATED EGGPLANT

Many traditional recipes for pickled eggplant or eggplant under oil call for them to cure or marinate for 2 weeks to 2 months before eating. I have tried this eggplant recipe, which takes just 2 days to prepare, versus eggplant I let marinate for 6 weeks. I prefer the fresher version. The eggplant had more bite, a better chew, and a bigger flavor that wasn't just about salt and vinegar on the tongue. Serve this with crusty bread or small toasts.

3 tablespoons kosher salt

2 pounds eggplant, peeled and cut into sticks ¼ inch thick and 2 to 3 inches long

1½ cups white wine vinegar or white balsamic vinegar

5 or 6 cloves garlic, very thinly sliced

Leaves from 2 sprigs fresh oregano or marjoram, coarsely chopped

1 teaspoon crushed red pepper flakes

1 teaspoon fennel seeds

A handful of fresh flat-leaf parsley leaves

A small handful of fresh mint leaves

1 cup olive oil

Salt the eggplant and drain in a strainer set over a bowl or in the sink for 3 to 4 hours.

In a deep wide skillet, bring the vinegar and 3 cups water to a low rolling boil. Add the eggplant and cook for 4 to 5 minutes. Drain in the strainer, then set the strainer over a large bowl. Place plastic over the eggplant and weight it down with a sack of beans or a heavy can. Refrigerate overnight.

The next day, layer the eggplant into a jar, scattering in the garlic, oregano, red pepper flakes, fennel seeds, parsley, and mint. Cover with the oil and refrigerate overnight. Serve at room temperature.

PREPPING AND COOKING ARTICHOKES

- **TO PREP:** Fill a bowl with water and a little ice and the juice and juiced shell of 1 lemon. Trim the stems but leave intact. Pull off the dark outer leaves until you reach the pale leaves. With scissors, trim the spiny tops. As you finish trimming each artichoke, transfer it to the cold lemon water to keep it from browning.
- **TO STEAM:** Set up a steamer. Rub the cut surfaces of the artichokes with a cut lemon half. Steam the artichokes until they're nice and tender, and the leaves can be pulled off easily, about 30 minutes. Then cool them upside down so they can drain while they're cooling. Carefully pull out the center leaves and scrape out the choke (all the little fibers at the center), leaving the artichoke intact.
- **TO BOIL:** Cook the artichokes in a large pot of boiling salted water with lemon juice, 15 to 20 minutes. I also put a kitchen towel on top to keep the artichokes from bobbing around and to keep them submerged in the water. Cool them upside down so they can drain while they're cooling, then carefully pull out the center leaves and scrape out the choke.

ARTICHOKE DIPPERS AND DIPPING SAUCES

Prep and steam artichokes (see box, page 32) and serve them with a sauce for dipping the leaves into (don't forget a discard bowl). For a hot dip, try Bagna Cauda (page 37). For a room-temp dip, try Garlic Butter with Parsley and Mint (page 311). Or, for cold dips, here are four favorites among our houseguests:

Sweet Basil Aioli

MAKES 1½ CUPS

1 free-range organic egg yolk
1 clove garlic, pasted
Grated zest and juice of 1 organic
   lemon or Meyer lemon
Fine sea salt
⅔ to ¾ cup olive oil
3 tablespoons heavy cream
2 teaspoons acacia honey
½ cup fresh basil leaves,
   shredded or torn

In a small bowl, whisk the egg yolk, garlic, and lemon zest and juice. Season with salt. While whisking, slowly stream in the oil, pouring it down the side of the bowl, to emulsify. Stir in the cream, honey, and basil. Adjust the salt.

Savory Anchovy-Basil Aioli

MAKES 1½ CUPS

1 free-range organic egg yolk
1 clove garlic, pasted
Grated zest and juice of
   1 organic lemon
Fine sea salt
⅔ to ¾ cup olive oil
3 tablespoons heavy cream
2 or 3 flat anchovy fillets,
   minced, or 1 teaspoon
   anchovy paste
½ cup fresh basil leaves,
   shredded or torn
Pepper

Toasted fresh bread crumbs
   or panko bread crumbs,
   for garnish (optional)

In a small bowl, whisk the egg yolk, garlic, and lemon zest and juice. Season with salt. While whisking, slowly stream in the oil, pouring it down the side of the bowl, to emulsify. Stir in the cream, anchovies, basil, and pepper. Adjust the seasonings. If desired, garnish with bread crumbs.

Garlicky Mixed Herb Aioli

MAKES 1¼ CUPS

1 free-range organic egg yolk
2 small cloves garlic, pasted
Juice of 1 lemon
1 tablespoon Dijon mustard
Fine sea salt
⅔ to ¾ cup grapeseed oil or
   olive oil
Pepper
⅓ to ½ cup finely chopped
   mixed fresh herbs: chives,
   flat-leaf parsley, tarragon,
   and thyme

In a small bowl, whisk the egg yolk, garlic, lemon juice, and mustard. Season with salt. While whisking, slowly stream in the oil, pouring it down the side of the bowl, to emulsify. Stir in pepper and the herbs. Adjust the seasonings.

Dijon and Shallot Vinaigrette

MAKES 1¼ CUPS

1 large shallot, peeled
Salt and pepper
Grated zest and juice of
   1 organic lemon
2 tablespoons white balsamic
   vinegar or white wine
   vinegar
2 tablespoons fresh thyme
   leaves, finely chopped
1 teaspoon fennel pollen or
   ground fennel
2 tablespoons Dijon mustard
3 tablespoons acacia honey
¾ cup EVOO

Grate the shallot into a bowl. Season with salt and pepper and let stand for 5 minutes. Whisk in the lemon zest and juice, vinegar, thyme, fennel pollen, mustard, and honey. While whisking, slowly stream in the EVOO to emulsify. Adjust the seasonings.

SPICY ITALIAN-STYLE DEVILED EGGS

MAKES 24 PIECES

'Nduja—a spicy pork and hot pepper paste (see box, page 123)—is rendered a bit and combined with hard-boiled egg yolks to make the most insanely delicious and seriously devilish stuffed eggs ever. My mother goes crazy for these. Any leftovers I turn into egg salad just by chopping them up; it's delicious on toast with lettuce, tomato, and minced giardiniera relish.

12 free-range organic eggs
2 tablespoons EVOO
1 teaspoon fennel seeds
2 large cloves garlic, chopped
3 to 4 tablespoons 'nduja
¼ cup grated or minced onion
1 plum tomato, seeded and finely chopped
A small handful of fresh flat-leaf parsley tops, very finely chopped
1 fresh red chile, minced, for garnish

Place the eggs in a medium saucepan with water to cover. Bring to a rapid rolling boil. Cover the pan, remove from the heat, and let stand for 10 minutes. Crack the shells and let stand for 10 minutes in very cold water. Peel the eggs. Halve them lengthwise and remove the yolks. Set the whites and yolks aside separately.

In a small skillet, heat the EVOO (2 turns of the pan) over medium heat. Add the fennel seeds, garlic, and 'nduja. Once the 'nduja melts, add the onion and stir for a minute or two. Add the tomato, stir, and remove from the heat. Transfer to a bowl and let cool completely.

Mash the egg yolks into the cooled 'nduja mixture. Transfer the egg yolk mixture into a small plastic food storage bag. Snip off one corner of the bag to make a small opening and pipe the spicy egg yolk filling into the egg white halves. Sprinkle the eggs with bits of parsley and chile.

CAESAR-STUFFED EGGS

MAKES 32 PIECES

These stuffed eggs taste like Caesar salad. They're always a hit. Chopped leftovers are delicious as a salad on charred Italian bread.

16 large free-range organic eggs
2 tablespoons lemon juice
2 teaspoons Dijon mustard
Fine sea salt
⅔ cup olive oil
2 cloves garlic, grated or pasted
1 tablespoon anchovy paste
1 tablespoon Worcestershire sauce
1½ to 2 teaspoons coarsely ground pepper
½ cup freshly grated Pecorino Romano cheese, or ¼ cup pecorino and ¼ cup Parmigiano-Reggiano cheese
1 cup packed finely chopped romaine lettuce hearts, plus more for garnish

Place the eggs in a medium saucepan with water to cover. Bring to a rapid rolling boil. Cover the pan, remove from the heat, and let stand for 10 minutes.

Crack the shells and let stand for 10 minutes in very cold water. Peel the eggs. Halve them lengthwise and remove the yolks. Set the whites and yolks aside separately.

In a medium bowl, whisk the lemon juice and mustard. Season with salt. While whisking, stream in the oil slowly, pouring it down the side of the bowl, to emulsify. Stir in the garlic, anchovy paste, Worcestershire sauce, pepper, and cheese. Taste and adjust the flavors—it should taste like a thick Caesar dressing.

Mash the egg yolks into the dressing. Stir in the chopped lettuce. Spoon the mixture into a small plastic food storage bag. Snip off one corner of the bag to make a small opening and pipe the Caesar filling into the egg white halves. Garnish with a bit more finely chopped lettuce.

GRILLED EGGPLANT INVOLTINI

This is a special-looking, foolproof party snack. It works well as a simple supper, too.

1 large eggplant
Salt
2 tablespoons olive oil,
    for brushing
Pepper
1½ cups fresh cow or sheep's milk
    ricotta cheese
½ cup freshly grated Parmigiano-
    Reggiano or Pecorino Romano
    cheese
¼ cup walnuts, toasted and finely
    chopped or processed
1 teaspoon grated lemon zest
    (from an organic lemon)
2 tablespoons fresh thyme leaves,
    chopped
8 slices speck (smoky ham) or
    prosciutto di Parma
3 to 4 cups wild arugula or baby
    kale
1 cup cherry or grape tomatoes,
    quartered
½ small red onion, finely chopped
EVOO, for drizzling

Heat a grill or grill pan to medium-high heat.

Trim two opposite rounded sides of the eggplant to square it off a bit, then cut the eggplant lengthwise into eight ⅛-inch-thick slices. Salt the thin eggplant "steaks" liberally and drain for 10 minutes, then pat dry. Brush the eggplant with oil on both sides and season with pepper. Grill the eggplant for 2 minutes on each side until marked and tender. Transfer to a work surface.

In a bowl, combine the ricotta, Parm, walnuts, lemon zest, and thyme. Season with salt and pepper.

Layer each piece of eggplant with speck, spread with the cheese mixture, top with a layer of arugula, and scatter some tomato and onion over the top. Roll up the layered eggplant, drizzle with EVOO, and serve.

BAGNA CAUDA

Bagna cauda is a wonderful dip for vegetables. With a little adaptation it also makes a great pasta sauce (see Straw and Hay Pasta with Vegetables in Bagna Cauda Sauce, page 151). Serve the dip with crusty warm or charred bread and an assortment of vegetables (see Tip).

1 large head garlic (10 to 12 cloves),
    cloves separated, unpeeled
Sea salt
2 tablespoons olive oil
2 tablespoons butter
12 good-quality flat anchovy fillets
2 cups heavy cream
Pepper
¼ cup fresh flat-leaf parsley
    leaves, finely chopped

Bring a small pot of water to a low boil. Add the garlic and simmer for 20 minutes. Let cool, then drain, peel, and mash into a paste. Season with a little sea salt.

In a small pot, heat the oil (2 turns of the pan) over medium heat. Melt the butter into the oil. Add the anchovies, cover the pan with a splatter screen or lid, and shake until the anchovies begin to break up. Reduce the heat a bit, uncover, and stir until the anchovies melt. Add the cream and whisk in the garlic paste. Cook until the cream has reduced by half. Season with pepper.

Serve the bagna cauda in a warm shallow dish or fondue pot, garnished with the parsley.

TIP

BLANCH assorted farm-fresh vegetables—such as asparagus, baby golden beets, baby carrots, baby zucchini, cauliflower or purple cauliflower, haricots verts, pattypan squash, and/or sugar snap peas—for dipping. Bring a few inches of water to a boil in a large pot and season with salt. Fill a large bowl with ice and water. Cut the vegetables into similar shapes and sizes but keep them separate. Blanch the vegetables one type at a time until tender-crisp: 1 to 2 minutes for delicate vegetables like asparagus and thin beans, 3 minutes for firmer vegetables. After each batch, transfer them to the prepared ice bath with a spider or small strainer. Drain well.

DEVILED LENTILS

If you have trouble finding Norcia lentils, you can substitute French Puy lentils, which will cook a bit quicker. This is a wonderful dish to add to any buffet, but we love it as brunch topped with 3-minute poached eggs as well.

About 1 pound Norcia lentils (see box)
2 onions: 1 quartered, 1 finely chopped
2 fresh bay leaves
Salt
2 tablespoons olive oil
¼ pound 'nduja (see box, page 123)
1 carrot, chopped
2 or 3 ribs celery with leafy tops, chopped
3 or 4 cloves garlic, chopped
2 tablespoons fresh thyme leaves
2 tablespoons fresh rosemary leaves, chopped
1 tablespoon grated orange zest (from an organic orange)
1 cup chicken stock
A handful of chopped fresh flat-leaf parsley

In a large saucepan, combine the lentils with water to cover (a couple of quarts). Add the quartered onion and the bay leaves and bring the water to a boil. Salt the water and cook the lentils at a low rolling boil until tender, 35 to 40 minutes. Drain. Fish out and discard the bay leaves and onion quarters.

Heat a skillet or pan over medium to medium-high heat, then add the oil (2 turns of the pan). Add the 'nduja and melt it down. Add the chopped onion, carrot, celery, garlic, thyme, rosemary, and orange zest and stir until the vegetables have softened, 3 to 5 minutes. Add the lentils and stock and simmer for a few minutes to allow the flavors to combine and the liquid to almost evaporate. Stir in the parsley and serve the lentils warm, at room temp, or as a cold salad.

NORCIA LENTILS

Lenticchie di Castelluccio di Norcia are small, firm, round lentils grown in the mountains of Umbria. They're our favorite lentil, and we love and eat them so often that I order four or five 500-gram bags of Norcia lentils at a time online.

POOR MAN'S CAVIAR

When you process the flesh of a roasted eggplant, the seeds make the pureed flesh vaguely resemble a bowl of nutty fresh caviar. Eggplant is much cheaper than osetra eggs, and my family probably prefers the flavor of the roasted eggplant. (I'm still down with both.)

⅓ cup olive oil
2 or 3 cloves garlic, smashed
½ teaspoon crushed red pepper flakes
1 sprig fresh rosemary
1 large eggplant
Salt and black pepper
A small handful of fresh flat-leaf parsley leaves
Small toasts, for serving
Garnishes: crème fraîche or mascarpone, minced red onion, minced hard-boiled egg, minced giardiniera relish

In a small saucepan, warm the oil, garlic, red pepper flakes, and rosemary. Let the garlic oil gently bubble away for a couple of minutes, then set aside to infuse and cool. Discard the rosemary stem but reserve the garlic.

Preheat the oven to 425°F.

Halve the eggplant lengthwise and score the flesh with a sharp knife in a 1-inch crosshatch pattern, running your knife between the flesh and skin as well. Brush the flesh with the infused oil and season with salt and black pepper. Set the eggplant halves cut side down on a baking sheet and roast until very tender, about 30 minutes. Let cool.

When cool enough to handle, scoop the flesh of the eggplant into a food processor. Add the reserved garlic from the oil and a few leaves of parsley. Pulse into a spread. Taste and adjust the seasonings.

Serve with toasts and garnishes of your choice.

DEVILED COTTO HAM

MAKES 2½ CUPS

This is a delicious snack for a buffet served with toast points or charred bread. Also see the brunch chapter for Deviled Ham and Asparagus Melts with Basted Eggs (page 9).

1 pound deli-sliced prosciutto cotto (cooked ham), torn or coarsely chopped

2 ribs celery with leafy tops, coarsely chopped

½ red onion, coarsely chopped

2 cloves garlic, chopped

2 tablespoons fresh thyme leaves, chopped

1 teaspoon crushed red pepper flakes

2 teaspoons to 1 tablespoon Tabasco sauce (to taste)

2 tablespoons Worcestershire sauce

3 tablespoons Dijon mustard

3 tablespoons good-quality pickle relish

Put everything in a food processor and pulse into a very finely chopped spread.

BUTTERNUT-SAGE CROSTINI

SERVES 6

1 large butternut squash, halved lengthwise and seeded

Olive oil, for brushing and drizzling

Salt and pepper

Freshly grated nutmeg

1 baguette, cut on an angle into ¼-inch slices

2 cloves garlic, halved

Flaky sea salt (optional)

4 tablespoons (½ stick) butter

12 fresh sage leaves

½ cup freshly grated Parmigiano-Reggiano cheese

Preheat the oven to 400°F.

Brush the cut sides of the squash with oil and season with salt, pepper, and nutmeg. Place on a baking sheet and roast until tender, 35 to 40 minutes. Let cool. When cool enough to handle, scrape the roasted squash flesh into a food processor and puree.

At the same time, scatter the baguette slices on a large baking sheet and toast or char on both sides. Rub the toasted bread with cut garlic, drizzle or brush the bread with oil, and season with flaky sea salt, if desired.

In a small skillet, melt the butter over medium heat. When the foam subsides, add the sage leaves and cook until crisp. Remove the sage leaves and add the browned butter to the squash puree. Stir in the Parm and half the sage. Taste and adjust the seasonings.

Transfer to a bowl and garnish with the remaining sage. Serve with the toasts for topping.

FRESH RICOTTA CHEESE

MAKES ABOUT 1 POUND (2 CUPS)

Homemade ricotta is wonderful in recipes, but is best savored when served as a crostini, spread on toasted rounds of bread, drizzled with EVOO or honey, and sprinkled with a pinch of flaky sea salt. I serve fresh ricotta as an appetizer the way chef Andrew Carmellini prepares it at his restaurant Locanda Verde in New York's TriBeCa: chopped fresh thyme, EVOO, and pepper. We also love to add orange blossom or truffle honey in generous, fat drizzles over the top of the cheese, especially if we are serving the cheese at brunch. Other nice complements to the ricotta are Fava Bean Spread (page 43) and Classic Salsa Verde (page 262). Serve ricotta with charred peasant-style white bread.

2 quarts whole milk
1 cup heavy cream
¼ cup fresh lemon juice
1 teaspoon sea salt

In a nonreactive pot, heat the milk and cream until it reaches 200°F (use a candy thermometer). Remove from the heat and add the lemon juice and salt. Stir a few turns to combine and let stand for 10 minutes to curdle the milk.

Meanwhile, line a large strainer with two layers of cheesecloth and place over a large glass bowl.

Ladle the milk mixture into the lined strainer and leave to drain for 1 hour at room temperature. Transfer to a container and chill. The fresh ricotta will keep for 3 to 4 days.

RICOTTA-MASCARPONE CHEESE SPREAD

MAKES ABOUT 2 CUPS

This spread goes fast at any gathering. I love it with charred bread, but it's also delicious when spread on halved small ripe tomatoes.

1 cup fresh ricotta cheese, homemade (see box) or store-bought
½ cup mascarpone cheese
¼ cup heavy cream
1 tablespoon grated lemon zest (from an organic lemon)
1 large clove garlic, pasted
2 tablespoons finely chopped fresh thyme leaves
3 tablespoons finely chopped fresh flat-leaf parsley
3 tablespoons finely chopped fresh chives
1 teaspoon fine sea salt
12 to 15 grinds of pepper

In a bowl, stir all the ingredients until smooth. Line a strainer with two layers of cheesecloth and place it over a bowl. Spoon the mixture into the strainer and refrigerate several hours or overnight.

BAKED RICOTTA WITH PISTACHIOS

SERVES 6 TO 8

Baked cheese is delicious all on its own, served with flatbreads or crackers or charred toast. Ripe fresh fruits are also delicious with baked ricotta. At holidays, top this stunner of a snack with roasted grapes, roasted cherry tomatoes, or roasted pitted cherries. I roast all three of these fruits as toppers with thinly sliced shallots and a fat drizzle of good-quality balsamic vinegar.

Butter, for greasing the baking dish
1 pound fresh ricotta cheese, homemade (see box, page 40) or store-bought, drained
½ cup freshly grated Parmigiano-Reggiano cheese
½ cup Italian pistachios, toasted and finely chopped
1 large free-range organic egg, beaten
2 tablespoons fresh thyme leaves
1 tablespoon grated lemon zest (from an organic lemon)
Salt and pepper
Freshly grated nutmeg

Preheat the oven to 350°F. Butter a large ramekin or small soufflé dish. Line the sides with doubled parchment paper to give the dish a 2- to 3-inch collar.

In a bowl, stir the ricotta, Parm, pistachios, egg, thyme, lemon zest, salt, pepper, and a few grates of nutmeg. Scrape into the ramekin, set it on a baking sheet, and bake until just set, about 45 minutes. Let cool for 30 minutes or so.

Remove the parchment paper collar and turn out the baked ricotta onto a serving dish.

TRUFFLE AND MASCARPONE PROFITEROLES

MAKES 20 TO 24

PROFITEROLES:
8 tablespoons (¾ stick) butter, cut into pieces
½ teaspoon salt
1 cup flour
⅛ teaspoon baking powder
4 large free-range organic eggs

FILLING:
2 cups mascarpone cheese
¼ cup heavy cream
1 teaspoon natural truffle oil
3 to 4 tablespoons minced fresh chives
Shaved white truffle
Sea salt

Preheat the oven to 400°F. Line a baking sheet with parchment paper.

Make the profiteroles: In a saucepan, combine 1 cup water, the butter, and salt and bring to a low boil. Stir in the flour and baking powder and stir until the dough pulls away from the sides of the pan. Transfer the hot dough to the bowl of a stand mixer fitted with the paddle attachment. With the mixer running on medium-low speed, add the eggs, one at a time, and beat until incorporated. Once the sides of the mixer bowl cool to room temp, spoon the dough into a plastic food storage bag. Snip off one corner of the bag to make a pastry bag.

Anchor the parchment paper to the baking sheet by piping a dab of dough under each corner. Pipe 20 to 24 rounds (at least 1 inch in diameter) of dough onto the baking sheet, then pat the top of each mound of dough down with wet fingertips to smooth them a bit. Bake until golden and small beads of moisture have stopped forming on the puffs, about 25 minutes. Cool to room temp and set aside until ready to fill and serve.

Make the filling: In a bowl, stir the mascarpone, cream, truffle oil, and chives. Add shaved truffle and sea salt to taste. Spoon the mixture into a small plastic food storage bag. Snip off one corner of the bag to make a small opening for piping.

Poke a hole in the bottom of each profiterole with a chopstick or wooden dowel, fill with truffle-mascarpone cream, and serve.

FAVA BEAN SPREAD

Serve this spread on small charred toasts.

1½ to 2 cups shelled fresh fava beans
½ to ¾ cup freshly grated pecorino cheese
2 cloves garlic, peeled
1 cup combined fresh flat-leaf parsley and mint leaves
Juice of 1 lemon
Salt and pepper
3 to 4 tablespoons EVOO

Bring a saucepan of water to a boil. Add the fava beans and blanch for 3 to 4 minutes. Drain and let cool. Peel the skins off the favas; the beans will split into 2 bright green pieces as you pop them out of their skins.

In a food processor, combine the peeled favas, pecorino, garlic, parsley/mint mixture, lemon juice, salt, pepper, and EVOO. Pulse into a thick spread. Taste and adjust the seasonings.

TUSCAN CHICKEN LIVER SPREAD

My friend Torello, the owner and operator of Il Latini in Florence, Italy, serves a warm coarsely ground liver spread on hot fried bread rounds as a warm crostini. I simply cannot stop eating this addictive, rich snack. My mom, Elsa, makes the most delicious chicken liver pâté I have ever eaten. Here is Mom's recipe. Traditionally, we serve the spread chilled, then brought back to room temp just before placing it out with sprouted wheat toast planks, fine mustards, sliced cornichons, and very thinly sliced shallots for topping. (My guests often fight over the leftovers, if there are any.) When I am longing for Il Latini, I serve my mom's recipe warm on crispy toasts pan-fried in EVOO.

4 ounces (1 stick) butter, cut into small pieces
2 large onions, thinly sliced
1 fresh or dried bay leaf
1 pound chicken livers, cleaned, trimmed, and patted dry
½ teaspoon ground thyme
Salt and pepper
3 ounces (6 tablespoons) dry sherry or cognac

In a large skillet, melt the butter over medium heat. Add the onions and bay leaf and cook, stirring occasionally, until the onions are tender and browned, 20 to 25 minutes.

Push the onions to the side of the pan and increase the heat to high. Add the chicken livers to the center of the pan and cook until browned, then stir in the onions and season with the thyme, salt, and pepper. Deglaze the pan with the sherry. Fish out and discard the bay leaf.

In a food processor, puree the liver and onions until smooth. Pack the spread into a crock and serve warm or cool (press a piece of plastic wrap directly onto the surface of the spread if not serving immediately).

BAKED STUFFED ARTICHOKES

SERVES 6 TO 8

We often serve these artichokes as a nibble before dinner, as they are a family favorite on my mom's side. My grandfather Emmanuel created the recipe, and what makes it delicious are the anchovies melted into the EVOO to give a natural salty flavor to the deeply toasted bread crumbs. We make these every Christmas because once baked, they resemble Christmas stars. We also make them on or around my brother's birthday in late summer, as he is my grandfather's namesake.

1 lemon

2 large artichokes

About ½ cup EVOO, plus more for drizzling

10 to 12 good-quality flat anchovy fillets

Cloves from 1 head garlic, finely chopped

2½ cups bread crumbs

Coarsely ground pepper

Tops from 1 bunch fresh flat-leaf parsley, finely chopped

1 cup freshly grated Parmigiano-Reggiano cheese

Set up a bowl of cold lemon water and trim the artichokes as directed on page 32, but instead of snipping off the pointy ends, leave them on for the "star" effect. Cook, drain, and remove the chokes from the artichokes as directed.

Preheat the oven to 400°F.

In a skillet, heat the EVOO over medium heat. Add the anchovies, cover the pan with a splatter screen or lid, and shake until the anchovies begin to break up. Reduce the heat a bit, uncover, and stir until the anchovies melt into the oil. Add the garlic and stir for a minute more to combine, then add the bread crumbs. Work the oil and garlic into the bread crumbs and toast to deep golden brown. Add lots of pepper and remove the pan from the heat. Let cool, then stir in the parsley and Parm.

Arrange the artichokes in a baking dish. Add enough water to barely coat the bottom of the dish. Spoon the bread crumb stuffing into the spaces between the artichoke leaves. When the artichoke is fully stuffed, it will look like a giant star. Loosely cover the dish with foil and put into the oven until the artichokes are heated through. Uncover and drizzle them with EVOO. Bake, uncovered, to re-crisp the crumbs. Serve from the baking dish, with bowls alongside for the discarded leaves.

SPINACH AND ARTICHOKE–STUFFED MUSHROOMS

MAKES 24 TO 30

This is a bite or two of everyone's favorite dip stuffed in a cremini mushroom cap. It is a nice alternative to the fatty traditional dip that is mostly cheese and mayo and very little spinach and artichokes.

24 to 30 cremini mushrooms, stems removed and reserved
3 tablespoons olive oil
Salt and pepper
1 small onion, coarsely chopped
2 cloves garlic, grated or pasted
1 (10-ounce) box frozen chopped spinach, thawed and wrung dry in a kitchen towel
1 cup water-packed canned or thawed frozen artichoke hearts
Freshly grated nutmeg
1 cup freshly grated Parmigiano-Reggiano cheese
2 free-range organic egg yolks
¼ cup pignoli (pine nuts), toasted
½ cup heavy cream

Preheat the oven to 425°F.

Place the mushroom caps on a rimmed baking sheet, stemmed side down (so that the liquids drain away from the mushrooms as they start to shrink). Drizzle with 1 tablespoon of the oil and season with salt and pepper. Roast until tender, 10 to 12 minutes. Remove from the oven. Leave the oven on.

Meanwhile, chop the reserved mushroom stems. In a small skillet, heat 1 tablespoon of the oil (1 turn of the pan). Add the mushroom stems and brown. Add the onion and garlic, season with salt and pepper, and cook to soften. Let cool, then transfer to a food processor. Add the spinach and artichoke hearts. Season with salt, pepper, and nutmeg and pulse-chop. Pulse in the remaining 1 tablespoon oil, the Parm, egg yolks, pine nuts, and cream. Transfer to a bowl.

Flip the mushroom caps over and fill them with the spinach-artichoke mixture, mounding it up a bit. Bake until the filling is cooked through, 12 to 15 minutes.

SALAD-STUFFED ARTICHOKES

To stuff a cooked artichoke and turn it into a cold salad lunch, prep and cook the artichoke as directed on page 32. Dress the inside and heart with EVOO, salt, and pepper. Fill the center with lots of Cherry Tomato and Red Onion Salad (page 24). You can mix line-caught, sustainable tuna and/or wild arugula leaves into this dish as well. Serve with a ramekin of your favorite dipper (see box, page 33) alongside for extra flavor and fun.

FONTINA VAL D'AOSTA AND HERB GOUGÈRES

MAKES 20 TO 24

Everyone loves a warm cheese puff. These disappear so fast, you may want to make a double batch. Cheese puffs do freeze really well and reheat in a moderate oven, but there are rarely enough left to freeze.

6 tablespoons (¾ stick) butter, cut into pieces

½ teaspoon salt

1 cup flour

⅛ teaspoon baking powder

4 large free-range organic eggs

1 cup grated Fontina Val d'Aosta or Gruyère cheese

3 to 4 tablespoons minced mixed fresh herbs: thyme, chives, and rosemary

Preheat the oven to 400°F. Line a baking sheet with parchment paper.

In a saucepan, combine 1 cup water, the butter, and salt and bring to a low boil. Stir in the flour and baking powder and stir until the dough pulls away from the sides of the pan. Transfer the hot dough to the bowl of a stand mixer fitted with the paddle attachment. With the mixer running on medium-low speed, add the eggs, one at a time, and beat until incorporated. Once the sides of the mixer bowl cool to room temp, beat in the Fontina and herbs. Spoon the dough into a plastic food storage bag. Snip off one corner of the bag to make a pastry bag.

Anchor the parchment paper to the baking sheet by piping a dab of dough under each corner. Pipe 20 to 24 rounds (at least 1 inch in diameter) of dough onto the baking sheet, then pat the top of each mound of dough down with wet fingertips to smooth them a bit. Bake until golden and small beads of moisture have stopped forming on the puffs, about 25 minutes. Serve hot.

SAUSAGE AND RICOTTA-STUFFED MUSHROOMS

MAKES 24 TO 30

24 to 30 medium-large cremini mushrooms, stems removed and reserved

1 tablespoon olive oil, plus more for drizzling

Salt and pepper

½ pound Sweet Italian Sausage with Fennel (page 237)

1½ cups fresh ricotta cheese, homemade (see box, page 40) or store-bought, well drained

1 large free-range organic egg, lightly beaten

½ cup freshly grated Parmigiano-Reggiano cheese

½ cup fresh flat-leaf parsley tops, or 5 ounces frozen chopped spinach, thawed and wrung dry in a kitchen towel

⅛ teaspoon freshly grated nutmeg

Preheat the oven to 425°F.

Place the mushroom caps on a rimmed baking sheet, stemmed side down (so that the liquids drain away from the mushrooms as they start to shrink). Drizzle with oil and season with salt and pepper. Roast until tender, 10 to 12 minutes. Remove from the oven. Leave the oven on.

Meanwhile, finely chop the reserved mushroom stems. In a skillet, heat the oil (1 turn of the pan). Add the sausage, breaking it up into crumbles as it browns. Add the mushroom stems and brown. Remove from the heat and set aside until cool enough to handle.

In a bowl, combine the sausage-mushroom mixture, ricotta, egg, Parm, parsley, and nutmeg. Season with salt and pepper.

Flip the mushroom caps over and fill with the ricotta stuffing, mounding it up a bit. Bake until the filling is cooked through, 12 to 15 minutes. Serve hot.

MUSHROOM-STUFFED MUSHROOMS

These are my favorite stuffed mushrooms because that's what you taste: mushrooms.

MUSHROOMS:

32 to 36 large cremini
    mushrooms, stems removed
    and reserved
2 tablespoons olive oil, plus more
    for drizzling
Pepper
Porcini salt or sea salt
4 tablespoons (½ stick) butter
3 tablespoons fresh thyme leaves
4 cloves garlic, grated or pasted
½ cup dry sherry or Marsala
1 bunch spinach (see Tip),
    stemmed and chopped, or
    2 cups packed baby kale,
    chopped
1 cup panko bread crumbs or
    lightly toasted homemade
    bread crumbs
1 free-range organic egg, beaten
1 cup loosely packed freshly
    grated Parmigiano-Reggiano
    cheese

BESCIAMELLA:

2 tablespoons butter
2 tablespoons flour
1 cup milk
Salt and pepper
Freshly grated nutmeg
1 free-range organic egg yolk

Preheat the oven to 425°F.

Make the mushrooms: Place the mushroom caps on a baking sheet, stemmed side down (so that the liquids drain away from the mushrooms as they start to shrink). Drizzle with oil and season with pepper and porcini salt. Roast until tender, 10 to 12 minutes. Remove from the oven. Leave the oven on.

Meanwhile, finely chop the reserved mushroom stems. In a skillet, melt the butter in the oil (2 turns of the pan) over medium-high heat. Add the mushroom stems and cook until tender, about 12 minutes. Add the thyme and garlic. Add the sherry and stir to deglaze the pan.

Wilt in the spinach. Transfer the mixture to a bowl and let cool, then stir in the panko so the bread crumbs can absorb the liquids from the spinach and mushrooms. Stir in the egg and Parm.

Flip the mushroom caps over and stuff them using a small scoop or spoon (I overfill them). Arrange them tightly in a small baking dish.

Before the stuffed mushrooms go in the oven, make the bescia-mella: In a small saucepan, melt the butter over medium heat. Whisk in the flour and cook for 1 minute. Whisk in the milk and season with salt, pepper, and a few grates of nutmeg. Beat the egg yolk in a small bowl. Whisk a little of the sauce into the egg yolk to temper it, then stir the warmed egg yolk back into the sauce.

Spoon the besciamella over the top of each mushroom cap, then bake until the besciamella is bubbling and browned on top, 10 to 12 minutes.

TIP

This is fresh farm spinach with flat-looking leaves, not the stuff in the bag that's like dark, dark, dark green.

ITALIAN WINGS

Yeah, I know, there is nothing super "Italian" about hot wings, but I use 'nduja (a paste of hot pepper sausage—see page 123 for more info) to make these delicious, addictive wings. In the summer, my husband slow-smokes the wings (1 hour in the smoker at 325°F). But the rest of the year, we parboil and roast the wings, a method that gives us crispy wings without frying.

36 chicken drumettes
Salt and pepper
4 ounces (1 stick) butter
⅓ pound 'nduja
4 large cloves garlic, finely chopped
3 tablespoons fresh rosemary leaves, coarsely chopped
3 tablespoons white balsamic vinegar or white wine vinegar
1 large bulb fennel, quartered, cored, and cut into sticks
6 ribs celery with leafy tops, cut into sticks

Position a rack in the center of the oven and preheat the oven to 475°F.

Bring a pot of water to a boil. Add the wings and cook for 5 minutes. Drain well. Arrange the wings on a baking sheet, season with salt and pepper, and roast until crispy, 15 to 20 minutes.

Meanwhile, in a saucepan, melt the butter over medium heat. Add the 'nduja and melt it into the butter. Stir in the garlic and rosemary and cook for 2 minutes to infuse. Add the vinegar and remove from the heat.

When the wings are done, transfer them to a bowl and toss with the 'nduja sauce. Serve with fennel and celery sticks.

SWORDFISH POLPETTE

These fish balls are roasted in the oven and are a bite-size, rolled-up version of my Swordfish Cutlets (page 204). If you like these flavors, try the cutlets some night.

1¼ to 1½ pounds swordfish (trimmed weight), all skin and bloodlines removed, coarsely chopped
Salt and pepper
1 cup loosely packed fresh flat-leaf parsley tops
Grated zest of 2 organic lemons
3 or 4 cloves garlic (to taste), finely chopped
1 large free-range organic egg, beaten
3 tablespoons grated onion
1 plum tomato, seeded and finely chopped
3 tablespoons EVOO
½ cup fresh bread crumbs

Preheat the oven to 375°F. Line a baking sheet with parchment paper.

In a food processor, pulse-chop the fish into very fine pieces, then transfer to a bowl. Season with salt and pepper.

On a cutting board, chop the parsley, then add the lemon zest and garlic and continue chopping these together to form a gremolata. Add the gremolata to the fish, along with the egg, onion, tomato, EVOO, and bread crumbs. Mix to combine.

Use a 2-ounce scoop or spoon out about 2 rounded tablespoons of the swordfish mixture and roll one test ball (about the size of an oversize walnut). Roast for 10 to 12 minutes to taste for seasoning. Adjust the seasonings, if necessary, then roll the remaining balls and roast until opaque, cooked through, and lightly golden at the edges, 10 to 12 minutes.

PALLOTTE IN SUGO FINTO (BREAD BALLS IN TOMATO-VEGETABLE SAUCE)

MAKES 24 TO 30 BALLS

If you are an Italian American of the first or second generation, perhaps these are familiar to you. *Pallotte* are an example of *cucina povera* (poor man's cuisine), from the Abruzzi. They are meatless meatballs made of stale bread, eggs, and cheese. Like meatballs, they can be fried (see Variation) or they can be simmered as dumplings in a loose vegetable-tomato sauce called *sugo finto*. These are a wonderful starter. They are so delicious and addictive you'll want to make a meal of them and eat a dozen. Don't. Like doughnuts, they will expand in your stomach and you'll end up in a food coma for the rest of the night. Try and limit yourself to two or three.

PALLOTTE:

3 cups packed stale crustless peasant-style white bread cubes

Water or milk, for moistening the bread

¼ cup finely chopped fresh flat-leaf parsley leaves

4 large free-range organic eggs, beaten

2 large cloves garlic, finely chopped or grated

2 tablespoons EVOO

⅛ teaspoon freshly grated nutmeg

1½ cups freshly grated Pecorino Romano cheese

SUGO FINTO (TOMATO-VEGETABLE SAUCE):

3 tablespoons olive oil

1 carrot, finely chopped or grated

1 rib celery with leafy top, finely chopped

1 medium onion, finely chopped

2 large cloves garlic, finely chopped or thinly sliced

2 or 3 large fresh bay leaves

Salt and pepper

1½ cups chicken or vegetable stock

4 cups passata or tomato puree

Make the pallotte: In a shallow bowl, sprinkle the bread with a little water or milk to moisten the cubes—no need to fully cover them, just keep adding water or milk little by little until the cubes soften up. Squeeze as much excess liquid out of the bread as possible; the bread should feel almost dry.

With your fingers, rub the bread into large bread crumbs and drop them into a large bowl. Add the parsley, eggs, garlic, EVOO, nutmeg, and pecorino and combine well. Chill the mixture for 30 minutes.

Meanwhile, make the sugo finto: In a wide pot, heat the oil (3 turns of the pan) over medium heat. Add the carrot, celery, onion, garlic, bay leaves, salt, and pepper. Partially cover and sweat the vegetables, stirring occasionally, for 10 minutes. Add the stock and cook, uncovered, until it has reduced by about half. Add the passata and bring the sauce to a gentle bubble. Reduce the heat to keep at a gentle simmer.

Roll the chilled bread mixture into balls 1½ to 2 inches in diameter. Add them to the simmering sauce and cook until firm and cooked through, 10 to 15 minutes. Fish out and discard the bay leaves.

Serve the pallotte in bowls with some of the sauce ladled over the top.

VARIATION

Fried Pallotte in Sugo Finto

You can fry the pallotte before simmering in the sugo finto. In a Dutch oven, heat 3 to 4 inches of vegetable or canola oil to 350°F (use a deep-fry thermometer). Roll the balls as directed and add 7 or 8 at a time to the hot oil and brown for 2 minutes. Drain on a rack placed over paper towels to catch the drippings. Add the fried balls to the sauce and simmer for 10 to 15 minutes before serving.

EGGPLANT BALLS

MAKES 24 TO 30 BALLS

If you love eggplant Parm (and who doesn't?), wait until you try these! Serve the meatballs with a tomato-based pasta sauce (such as marinara or pizza sauce) for dipping.

2 medium-large eggplants

3 tablespoons olive oil

Salt and pepper

1 small onion, grated

2 cloves garlic, finely chopped or grated

2 tablespoons fresh thyme leaves, chopped

¼ cup fresh mint leaves, finely chopped

¼ cup fresh flat-leaf parsley leaves, finely chopped

Grated zest of 1 organic lemon

2 cups fine dry bread crumbs

1 cup freshly grated Parmigiano-Reggiano cheese

4 large free-range organic eggs

Salt and pepper

Canola, vegetable, or sunflower oil, for frying

12 ounces fresh mozzarella cheese, cut into ¼-inch cubes

1 cup flour

Warmed tomato sauce, store-bought or homemade (see Tip), for dipping

Preheat the oven to 400°F.

Halve the eggplants lengthwise, brush with the oil, and season with salt and pepper. Place cut side down on a baking sheet and roast until tender, about 30 minutes. Let the eggplants cool until you can comfortably handle them, then scoop the flesh out of the skins into a food processor. Pulse until finely chopped and transfer to a bowl.

Add the onion, garlic, thyme, mint, parsley, lemon zest, 1 cup of the bread crumbs, ½ cup of the Parm, and 1 of the eggs. Season with salt and pepper and pulse to combine. Refrigerate the mixture for 30 minutes to make it easier to work with.

Fill a countertop fryer with oil or pour a few inches of oil into a large Dutch oven. Heat the oil to 350°F (on a deep-fry thermometer if using a Dutch oven).

Use a 2-ounce scoop or spoon out about 2 rounded tablespoons of the chilled eggplant mixture per ball. Nest a cube of mozzarella in the center of each ball.

Set up a breading station: Line up 3 shallow bowls on the counter. Spread the flour out in one and season with salt and pepper. Beat the remaining 3 eggs in the second. Mix the remaining ½ cup Parm and 1 cup bread crumbs in the third. Coat the balls in the flour, then in the egg, and finally in the cheesy crumbs.

Fry the eggplant balls in small batches until deep golden. Drain on paper towels and serve with warm tomato sauce for dipping.

 TIP Lots of choices for tomato sauces for dipping. Try one of these: Pomodoro Sauce (page 121), Marinara Sauce (page 121), Roasted Tomato Sauce (page 122), Roasted Garlic, Tomato, and Red Pepper Sauce (page 142), Cherry Tomato Sauce (page 122), 'Nduja Arrabbiata with Fresh Tomatoes (page 123), Pizza Sauce with Balsamic Vinegar (page 88), or Naples Pizza Sauce (page 88).

TUNA POLPETTE

1¼ pounds fresh tuna, cut into chunks

3 or 4 flat anchovy fillets (to taste)

2 to 3 tablespoons capers (to taste), drained

A small handful of fresh flat-leaf parsley leaves

½ cup fresh bread crumbs

Grated zest and juice of 1 organic lemon

1 scant teaspoon crushed red pepper flakes

Salt and black pepper

3 large free-range organic eggs

Canola, vegetable, or sunflower oil, for frying

1 cup flour

1 cup fine dry bread crumbs

Lemon wedges, for serving

In a food processor, combine the tuna, anchovies, capers, and parsley and pulse-chop until very fine. Transfer to a bowl and add the fresh bread crumbs, lemon zest and juice, red pepper flakes, salt, black pepper, and 1 of the eggs. Mix well and refrigerate for 30 minutes.

Fill a countertop fryer with oil or pour 3 inches of oil into a large Dutch oven. Heat the oil to 350°F (on a deep-fry thermometer if using a Dutch oven).

Use a 2-ounce scoop or spoon out about 2 rounded tablespoons of the tuna mixture and roll balls like oversize walnuts.

Set up a breading station: Line up 3 shallow bowls on the counter. Spread the flour out in one and season with salt and black pepper. Beat the remaining 2 eggs in the second and season with salt and black pepper. Place the dry bread crumbs in the third. Coat the tuna balls in the flour, then in the egg, and finally in the bread crumbs.

Fry the balls in small batches until deep golden. Serve with lemon wedges and toothpicks.

THE 7 BALLS OF CHRISTMAS

I'm sure you've heard of the traditional Italian Christmas Feast of the 7 Fishes, but if you know me, you've also heard of the 7 Balls of Christmas, a party I threw once where I served 7 different polpette (meatballs).

For the pescatarians: Swordfish Polpette (page 49) and Tuna Polpette (page 52).

For kids and traditionalists: Chicken and Rice Balls (page 53) and Broken Spaghetti Meatballs (page 54).

For vegetarians: Bread Balls in Tomato-Vegetable Sauce (page 50) and Eggplant Balls (page 51)—they're both hugely popular with meat eaters as well.

And my personal favorite: Veal and Sage Meatballs with Gorgonzola (page 53). But at the end of the day, here's the bottom line: Balls are fun to make, fun to eat, fun to say.

VEAL AND SAGE MEATBALLS WITH GORGONZOLA

MAKES 30 TO 36 BALLS

1¼ pounds ground veal

⅓ to ¾ cup fresh bread crumbs

2 tablespoons heavy cream

⅛ teaspoon freshly grated nutmeg

Salt and pepper

4 ounces dry Gorgonzola cheese crumbles or blue cheese crumbles

7 or 8 fresh sage leaves, finely chopped

2 cloves garlic, finely chopped or grated

1 large free-range organic egg, beaten

3 tablespoons pignoli (pine nuts), toasted and finely chopped

2 to 3 tablespoons freshly grated Parmigiano-Reggiano cheese

2 teaspoons grated lemon zest (from an organic lemon)

Preheat the oven to 375°F. Line a baking sheet with parchment paper.

Place the veal in a bowl. Add ½ cup of the bread crumbs and moisten with the cream. Season the meat and bread with the nutmeg and salt and pepper. Add the Gorgonzola, sage, garlic, egg, pine nuts, Parm, and lemon zest and mix, adding another ¼ cup bread crumbs if the mixture seems too wet.

Use a 2-ounce scoop or spoon out about 2 rounded tablespoons of the veal mixture and roll one test ball (about the size of an oversize walnut). Roast for 15 to 18 minutes to taste for seasoning. Adjust the seasonings, if necessary, then roll the remaining balls and roast until very light golden and just cooked through, 15 to 18 minutes.

CHICKEN AND RICE BALLS

MAKES 24 TO 28 MEATBALLS

Toasting the pasta is key here; it gives the balls a nutty flavor. You could also make this with leftover cold rice or rice pilaf. If using leftover rice or pilaf, you'll need a little over 1 cup cooked rice, and you can skip the first step (and also omit the pasta).

1 tablespoon butter

3 tablespoons orzo pasta or finely broken spaghetti

⅓ cup long-grain white rice

Salt and pepper

¾ to 1 cup chicken stock

A small handful of fresh flat-leaf parsley tops, chopped

1 large free-range organic egg, beaten

1 to 1¼ pounds ground chicken (whatever the package size is)

½ cup freshly grated Parmigiano-Reggiano cheese

⅛ teaspoon freshly grated nutmeg

EVOO, for drizzling

In a small saucepan, melt the butter over medium heat. Add the pasta and toast until deep golden. Add the rice, season with salt and pepper, and stir. Add ¾ cup stock and bring to a low boil. Cover and reduce the heat to low. Cook, stirring occasionally, until the rice and pasta are tender, 15 to 18 minutes. Add an additional ¼ cup stock if the pan gets dry before the rice cooks through. Fluff the rice pilaf with a fork and transfer to a bowl to cool completely.

Preheat the oven to 400°F. Line the baking sheet with parchment paper.

Add the parsley, egg, ground chicken, Parm, nutmeg, salt, and pepper to the cooled rice, along with a drizzle of EVOO. Mix everything to combine. Roll the chicken-and-rice mixture into balls like oversize walnuts and arrange them on the prepared baking sheet.

Roast the meatballs until light golden, cooked through, and crispy, 18 to 20 minutes.

BROKEN SPAGHETTI MEATBALLS

MAKES ABOUT 28 BALLS

Serve the meatballs with a tomato-based pasta sauce (such as marinara or pizza sauce) for dipping.

⅔ cup broken (2- to 3-inch pieces) spaghetti or linguine

Salt

2 rounded tablespoons tomato paste

¼ cup hot water

½ to ¾ cup fresh bread crumbs

1¼ pounds ground beef or a mix of ground beef, pork, and veal

2 large cloves garlic, grated or finely chopped

3 to 4 tablespoons grated onion (to taste)

A small handful of fresh flat-leaf parsley tops, finely chopped

A fat handful of freshly grated Pecorino Romano or Parmigiano-Reggiano cheese

EVOO, for drizzling

Pepper

1½ to 2 cups warmed tomato sauce, store-bought or homemade (see Tip, page 51), for dipping (optional)

In a saucepan, bring a quart of water to a rolling boil. Add the pasta, salt the water, and cook to al dente. Drain, run under cold water to cold-shock, and drain well. Set aside to cool.

Preheat the oven to 400°F. Line a baking sheet with parchment paper.

In a large bowl, combine the tomato paste and hot water and stir to loosen the paste. Add ½ cup of the bread crumbs to moisten them. Add the cooled pasta, ground beef, garlic, onion, parsley, cheese, a drizzle of EVOO, salt, and pepper and mix well to combine. Add another ¼ cup bread crumbs if the mixture seems too wet.

Roll the mixture into 1½- to 2-inch balls. It's fine if pieces of cooked spaghetti stick out of the meatballs—they'll get crispy in the oven. Arrange the balls on the prepared baking sheet and bake until cooked through, browned, and crispy at the edges, 18 to 20 minutes. Serve with warm tomato sauce for dipping, if desired.

CLASSIC ARANCINI

The name of these fried rice balls, *arancini*, which translates to "little oranges," comes from their round shape and bread crumb coating. The classic recipe is made with cold, cooked Arborio rice mixed with a meat sauce and lots of peas. I prepare Risi e Bisi (page 184), which is rice with peas already in it, and set aside 1½ cups to use in this dish the next day.

2 tablespoons butter

½ pound ground beef

½ small onion, finely chopped

¼ cup grated carrot

1 small rib celery from the heart, finely chopped

2 cloves garlic, chopped

1 tablespoon fresh thyme leaves, chopped

Salt and pepper

1 rounded tablespoon tomato paste

½ cup dry white wine

½ cup chicken or beef stock

3 large free-range organic eggs

1½ cups fine dry bread crumbs, plus more as needed

1½ cups cold Risi e Bisi (rice and peas; page 184)

8 ounces fresh mozzarella cheese, cut into ¼-inch cubes

Canola, vegetable, or sunflower oil, for frying

Flour, for dredging

½ cup freshly grated Pecorino Romano or Parmigiano-Reggiano cheese

In a large skillet, melt the butter over medium to medium-high heat. Add the beef, breaking it up into fine crumbles as it browns. Add the onion, carrot, celery, garlic, thyme, salt, and pepper and stir for 5 to 6 minutes. Add the tomato paste and cook for 1 or 2 minutes. Add the wine and let it absorb. Add the stock and stir to combine, then adjust the seasonings. Transfer to a bowl to cool.

Add 1 of the eggs and ½ cup of the bread crumbs to the cooled beef mixture. Add the cold rice and peas and mix to combine. Add a little more bread crumbs if the mixture seems too wet. Roll the mixture into balls about 2 inches in diameter. Nest a cube of mozzarella in the center of each ball.

Fill a countertop fryer with oil or pour a few inches of oil into a large Dutch oven. Heat the oil to 350° to 360°F. (The oil is ready when a 1-inch cube of white bread cooks to golden brown in 40 seconds.)

Set up a breading station: Line up 3 shallow bowls on the counter. Spread the flour out in one and season with salt and pepper. Beat the remaining 2 eggs in the second. Mix the grated cheese and the remaining 1 cup bread crumbs in the third. Coat the balls in the flour, then in the egg, and finally in the cheesy bread crumbs, pressing to make sure the coating sticks.

Fry the rice balls in batches until deep golden and hot through. Drain on butcher paper and serve warm.

VARIATIONS

Limoncini

Use 2 cups cold Lemon Risotto (page 187) and omit the beef sauce (first step) and the Risi e Bisi. To make the rice mixture, mix the cold risotto with 1 egg and ½ cup dry bread crumbs. Roll, stuff with cheese, bread, and fry as described (see left). Serve with lemon wedges.

Limoncini with Peas

Add 1 cup blanched fresh peas to the rice mixture.

Butternut Arancini

Butternut risotto makes a great base for arancini, because the "little oranges," or fried rice balls, are bright orange on the inside as well as on the outside. Use 1½ to 2 cups cold Risotto Milanese with Roasted Butternut Squash (page 186). Garnish with a gremolata of orange zest, fresh flat-leaf parsley, and garlic chopped together.

CARCIOFI ALLA GIUDIA
(TWICE-FRIED ARTICHOKES)

SERVES 8

Like proper crispy Belgian/French *frites* (fries), the secret to perfect Roman fried artichokes from the Jewish quarter in Rome is frying the artichokes twice at two different temperatures. This dish is labor-intensive, but not difficult, and quite frankly, more worth it than any potato chip or fry. Fried artichokes have such a distinct flavor, a real individual among peers.

3 lemons
8 medium tight-leaved firm globe
    artichokes
Canola, vegetable, or sunflower
    oil, for frying
Fine sea salt and pepper

Fill a bowl with water and a little ice and the juice and juiced shell of 1 lemon. Trim the artichokes down to the pale green leaves. Peel the stems, reserving as much as possible, 1 to 3 inches. Trim off the top 1 to 2 inches of the pointy leaves. As you work, put the artichokes in the cold lemon water.

Fill a countertop fryer with oil or pour 3 inches of oil into a large Dutch oven. Heat the oil to 325°F (on a deep-fry thermometer if using a Dutch oven).

Invert the artichokes on kitchen towels to drain and pat the outsides very dry as well.

Fry 2 or 3 of the artichokes at a time until the stem and heart are fork-tender, 12 to 15 minutes per batch (be sure to let the oil come back to temp between batches). Remove and season the artichokes liberally with sea salt and pepper while warm. Invert on a cooling rack set over layered paper towels to cool. Remove the spiny center leaves and scrape out the chokes. (I use a serrated grapefruit spoon for this job.)

Open the artichokes flat, like sunflowers, and press on the countertop to bend all the leaves outward.

Bring the oil in the Dutch oven or countertop fryer to 350° to 365°F (on a deep-fry thermometer if using a Dutch oven).

Meanwhile, heat a small skillet over medium-high heat. Halve the remaining 2 lemons. Lightly brush the cut side of the lemons with a little of the oil and place them in the hot skillet, cut side down. Caramelize the lemon halves to golden on their cut sides, 1 to 2 minutes. (Caramelizing the lemons mellows their bitterness and gets the juices flowing.)

When the oil is up to temp, fry the artichokes in small batches until deep golden and very crisp. Transfer to a platter lined with butcher paper, season with more salt and pepper, and douse with the juice of the caramelized lemons. Eat with your fingers, like potato chips.

FRIED GIARDINIERA

This is a snack that will go very fast once it hits the table. If you, the cook, want to get any, you'd better keep a plate for yourself in the kitchen and guard it well.

Canola, vegetable, or sunflower oil, for frying
¾ cup flour
1 cup freshly grated Parmigiano-Reggiano cheese
2 large free-range organic eggs
1 teaspoon dried thyme, lightly crushed in your palm
½ teaspoon ground piment d'Espelette, pepperoncini, or other ground red chile
3 to 4 cups drained giardiniera, homemade (page 31) or store-bought
Fine or flaky sea salt

Fill a countertop fryer with oil or pour a few inches of oil into a large Dutch oven. Heat the oil to 350° to 365°F (on a deep-fry thermometer if using a Dutch oven).

In a bowl, whisk the flour, Parm, eggs, thyme, and ground chile. Dip the giardiniera pieces into the batter, letting the excess drip off. Add a few pieces at a time to the hot oil and fry until deep golden. Drain on a rack or butcher paper or paper towels and sprinkle with sea salt while still hot.

VARIATION

Fried Cauliflower

Trim the cauliflower leaves from 1 small head cauliflower, then cut a deep cross into the cauliflower stem. In a wide pot, bring 4 to 5 inches of water to a boil. Generously salt the water and add the cauliflower. Cook, partially covered, at a rolling simmer until tender but still firm (not mushy), 7 to 8 minutes. Drain very well and let cool. Cut into generous florets. Proceed with the battering and frying as above. Serve on its own or with Classic Salsa Verde (page 262).

SAUSAGE-STUFFED SPICY OLIVES

These olives can be breaded then frozen so you always have some on hand. If you fry them from room temperature, they take about 3 minutes. Frying them frozen will take 5 to 6 minutes. Always fry in small batches and bring your oil back to temp before frying the next batch.

48 large pitted green Sicilian olives (2 cups)
2 tablespoons fruity EVOO
Canola, vegetable, or sunflower oil, for frying
1 cup flour
4 large free-range organic eggs
1 cup fine dry bread crumbs
¼ cup finely grated pecorino cheese
2 tablespoons very finely chopped fresh flat-leaf parsley leaves
1 tablespoon finely chopped fresh thyme leaves
½ pound Hot Italian Sausage, homemade (page 237) or store-bought

Rinse the olives in water twice, then dry them very well, put them in a bowl, and toss with the EVOO.

Fill a countertop fryer with oil or pour a few inches of oil into a large Dutch oven. Heat the oil to 350°F (on a deep-fry thermometer if using a Dutch oven).

Set up a breading station: Line up 3 shallow bowls on the counter. Spread the flour out in one, beat the eggs in the second, and mix the bread crumbs, pecorino, parsley, and thyme in the third.

Use a chopstick or wooden dowel to stuff the olives with sausage. Coat the olives in the flour, then in the egg, and finally in the herbed bread crumb mix, pressing to make sure the coating sticks.

Working in batches, fry the olives until deep golden, about 3 minutes. Drain.

SHALLOW-FRYING ZUCCHINI FLOWERS OR GREEN TOMATOES

The coating on my shallow-fried green tomatoes is identical to that on my stuffed shallow-fried zucchini flowers, so learn one method, get two uses out of it. I treat fried tomato slices as sort of a tangy piece of toast and use it as a jumping-off point for a number of different dishes. A zucchini flower, on the other hand, is like nature's dumpling wrapper, and I stuff it with all sorts of things. The toppings and fillings for either are only limited by the imagination of the cook.

Breading Mixture

=== MAKES ENOUGH TO BREAD 12 ZUCCHINI FLOWERS OR TOMATO SLICES ===

1 cup flour
Salt and pepper
3 large free-range organic eggs
1 cup fine dry bread crumbs or a combination of fine bread crumbs and panko bread crumbs
½ cup fine-grind cornmeal, or ⅔ cup medium-grind cornmeal
1 cup freshly grated Pecorino Romano, Parmigiano-Reggiano cheese, or a combination
A handful of fresh flat-leaf parsley tops, finely chopped

1 tablespoon finely grated lemon zest (from an organic lemon)
1 rounded teaspoon fennel pollen or ground fennel
1 teaspoon granulated garlic
1 teaspoon granulated onion

Set up a breading station: Line up 3 shallow bowls on the counter. Spread the flour out in one and season with salt and pepper. Beat the eggs in the second and season with salt and pepper. In the third, mix the bread crumbs, cornmeal, cheese, parsley, lemon zest, fennel pollen, garlic, and onion.

Fried Green Tomatoes

=== MAKES 12 SLICES ===

Salt
3 large green tomatoes, each cut into four (¼- to ½-inch-thick) slices
Canola, vegetable, or sunflower oil, for frying
Breading mixture (see left)
Lemon wedges or topping of choice (list follows)

Salt the tomatoes on each side and let them weep on a kitchen towel for 20 minutes.

Meanwhile, pour ½ inch of oil into a large cast-iron skillet or shallow heavy-bottomed pan and heat the oil to 350°F. Set up a breading station with the breading mixture.

Pat the tomato slices dry. Coat the tomatoes in the flour, then the egg, and finally in the bread crumb mixture. Working in batches, fry the tomatoes for 2 to 3 minutes per side. Drain on a cooling rack.

Serve warm or room temperature, with lemon wedges or with one of the toppings listed.

Toppings:

■ Parmigiano-Style Fried Green Tomatoes: Top the fried tomatoes with tomato sauce or cherry tomato sauce. Top with shaved Parmigiano-Reggiano and/or thinly sliced fresh mozzarella and run under the broiler to melt.

■ Ricotta-Thyme: Top fried green tomatoes with dollops of fresh ricotta and garnish with thyme, honey, salt, and pepper.

■ Ricotta Ranch Tomatoes: Serve tomatoes topped with Ricotta Ranch Dressing: 1 cup fresh ricotta, ¼ cup heavy cream, 1½ tablespoons fresh lemon juice, 1 teaspoon Tabasco (or to taste), 1 clove garlic (pasted), 6 tablespoons chopped mixed fresh herbs (such as chives, flat-leaf parsley, thyme, and/or tarragon), a drizzle of EVOO, and salt and pepper.

■ BLFGT: Layer tomatoes with bacon and lettuce and top with minced giardiniera and a dollop of Garlicky Mixed Herb Aioli (page 33) or Sweet Basil Aioli (page 33).

Battered-Fried Zucchini Flowers

SERVES 8

I love raw zucchini flowers, filled with fresh ricotta and cherry tomatoes or fresh corn and herbs, or simply tossed with any garden salad. But beer-batter anything and it becomes better—these fried zucchini flowers are special because of the egg whites. YUM. They go fast and are best served hot.

Canola, vegetable, or sunflower oil, for frying
20 to 24 large zucchini flowers
1¼ cups flour
1 teaspoon kosher salt
12 ounces chilled lager beer, pilsner, or club soda
3 large egg whites
Flaky sea salt (such as Maldon)
Lemon wedges, for serving

Fill a countertop fryer with oil or pour a few inches of oil into a large Dutch oven. Heat the oil to 350° to 365°F (on a deep-fry thermometer if using a Dutch oven).

Remove the stamens from the zucchini flowers and trim the stems to 1 to 2 inches.

In a bowl, whisk the flour and salt. Stir in the chilled beer. In a separate bowl, whisk the egg whites to soft peaks, then fold them into the beer batter.

Dip the flowers in the batter and shake off the excess. Fry in small batches and drain on butcher paper or a cooling rack set over paper towels to catch the oil. Sprinkle with flaky sea salt and serve with lemon wedges.

Breaded Stuffed Zucchini Flowers

MAKES 12 PIECES

12 large zucchini flowers
1 to 1½ cups filling of choice (see right)
Canola, vegetable, or sunflower oil, for frying
Breading mixture (page 58)
Lemon wedges, for serving

Remove the stamens from the zucchini flowers and leave 1 inch of stem intact. Fill the zucchini flowers with the filling of your choice. Twist the ends of the blossoms to trap the filling inside.

Pour 1 inch of oil into a large cast-iron skillet or other shallow heavy-bottomed pan and heat the oil to 350°F. Set up a breading station with the breading mixture.

Coat the stuffed flowers in the flour, then in egg, and finally in the bread crumb mix, pressing to make sure the coating sticks.

Working in small batches, shallow-fry the flowers until deep golden brown and hot throughout, 3 to 4 minutes. Drain on a cooling rack. Serve with lemon wedges.

Fillings (Choose One):
- Finely diced fresh mozzarella with finely chopped cherry or grape tomatoes and chopped fresh basil
- Finely diced fresh mozzarella with chopped anchovy fillets and minced fresh flat-leaf parsley
- Finely diced fresh mozzarella with fresh corn kernels, chopped cherry tomatoes, chopped fresh basil, and fresh thyme
- Finely diced fresh mozzarella with finely chopped zucchini, lemon juice, fresh mint, garlic, and fresh parsley
- Fresh ricotta with blanched peas and chopped fresh mint and flat-leaf parsley
- Fresh ricotta with chopped fresh thyme and honey

MOZZARELLA IN CARROZZA WITH HAM

MAKES 8 TO 16 PIECES

Fried, egg-battered grilled cheese and ham? Yes, please. Halve or quarter these as a party snack or serve one per person for a *primi piatti*.

8 slices good-quality white bread, crusts trimmed, or bread cut into 3-inch rounds
8 slices (¼ to ½ inch thick) fior di latte cheese (fresh mozzarella)
4 slices prosciutto cotto (cooked ham)
½ cup flour
½ teaspoon granulated garlic
½ teaspoon granulated onion
Salt and pepper
3 large free-range organic eggs
A handful of freshly grated Parmigiano-Reggiano cheese
1 tablespoon fresh lemon juice
Olive, sunflower, or canola oil, for shallow-frying

Make 4 sandwiches by layering the ingredients as follows: a slice of bread, a slice of mozzarella, a slice of ham folded to fit inside the edges of the bread, another slice of mozzarella, and another slice of bread. Pinch the edges of the bread slices together to seal the sandwiches.

Set up a breading station: Line up 2 shallow bowls on the counter. Spread the flour out in one and stir in the garlic, onion, and salt and pepper. In the second bowl, beat the eggs, Parm, lemon juice, salt, and pepper.

Pour ¼ inch of oil into a large skillet and heat over medium to medium-high heat.

Coat the sandwiches in the flour, then in the egg batter. Add the sandwiches to the skillet and fry until deeply golden, 3 minutes on each side.

Halve or quarter the sandwiches to serve.

MOZZARELLA IN CARROZZA OF EGGPLANT OR GREEN TOMATO

MAKES 8 PIECES

Mozzarella in carrozza is a fried breaded grilled cheese sandwich. In this recipe, eggplant or green tomatoes replace the bread to serve as "little carriages" for the buttery, thick slices of mozzarella.

SAUCE:
2 tablespoons butter
1 large clove garlic, smashed
½ small onion, peeled
1 (28- to 32-ounce) can San Marzano tomatoes (look for DOP on the label)
A couple of fresh basil leaves, torn
Salt

SANDWICHES:
Flour, for dredging
3 large free-range organic eggs
1 cup panko bread crumbs
½ cup freshly grated Parmigiano-Reggiano cheese
½ cup cornmeal
1 teaspoon granulated onion
1 teaspoon granulated garlic
3 tablespoons finely chopped fresh flat-leaf parsley leaves
Olive, sunflower, or canola oil, for shallow-frying
Salt
16 slices (¼ inch thick) eggplant or green tomatoes
8 slices (½ inch thick) fresh mozzarella cheese

Make the sauce: In a saucepan, melt the butter over medium heat. When it foams, add the garlic and stir for 1 minute. Add the onion and tomatoes, crushing up the tomatoes a bit; stir in the basil and a little salt. Simmer for 20 minutes, then remove the onion.

Set up a breading station: Line up 3 shallow bowls on the counter. Spread the flour out in one and beat the eggs in the second. In the third, mix the panko, Parm, cornmeal, granulated onion, granulated garlic, and parsley.

Pour ¼ inch of oil into a large skillet and heat over medium to medium-high heat.

Make the sandwiches: Salt the eggplant and drain on paper towels for 20 minutes, turning once. Put each mozzarella slice between two eggplant slices. Coat in the flour, then in the egg, and finally in the bread crumb mix, pressing to make the coating stick. Fry the sandwiches until golden, about 3 minutes on each side. Serve hot, with the sauce alongside.

Lentil Soup with Sausage
and Kale (page 82) served
with Focaccia (page 102);
Shaved Raw Artichoke
Salad (page 24).

CHAPTER 3

SOUPS

Some people remember me from a show on Food Network called $40 *a Day*, a travel challenge. In real life, for a few years after I first moved to New York City, $40 was my entire weekly budget for food. As you can imagine, I ate a lot of soup. There are so many things I love about soup: the promise of comforting you when you are sick and the promise of always being enough to feed a big family or group, like a "Stone Soup." Soups are very forgiving, and they are a big hug at the end of any long day, especially if you are dining alone!

STOCKS

The most important part of soup is the stock. I worked for over a year on the flavor and quality of my own boxed chicken, beef, and vegetable stocks. I am very proud of our product, and many nights of the week, our boxed stocks are my handy solution for long-cooked flavor in quick-cooking dishes. However, over the weekend or on a day off, I always take the time and the dollar- and flavor-stretching exercise of making homemade stock. I make chicken and vegetable stocks most often, since beef and veal stock require heavy bags of bones to slow-roast in preparation. So, quite frankly, for veal, lamb, or beef stock, I use store-bought.

CHICKEN STOCK (AND POACHED CHICKEN)

MAKES 2 TO 2½ POUNDS MEAT
AND ABOUT 3 QUARTS STOCK

The nice side benefit to this recipe is that you end up with cooked chicken meat that you can slice, dice, or pull into bite-size pieces to use in recipes of your choice or as an addition to salads.

1 whole chicken (4 to 5 pounds)
2 carrots, coarsely chopped
1 large leek, halved lengthwise, quartered crosswise, and washed well
2 ribs celery with leafy tops, quartered crosswise
2 or 3 large cloves garlic, smashed
1 large fresh bay leaf
Herb bundle: a few sprigs of fresh flat-leaf parsley, thyme, and rosemary, tied together with kitchen twine
6 to 8 black peppercorns
1 small unpeeled organic lemon, cut crosswise into ¼-inch slices
1 piece of rind from Parmigiano-Reggiano or Grana Padano cheese (optional)
Kosher salt

Set the chicken in a large pot and add the carrots, leek, celery, garlic, bay leaf, herb bundle, peppercorns, lemon, and cheese rind (if using). Add water to just cover the chicken. Bring to a low rolling boil. Once the water comes to a boil, season with salt and reduce the heat to keep the bubbling lightly rolling. Poach the chicken for 30 to 40 minutes. Turn the bird and poach for 30 minutes more. Here is the key: Turn off the heat, cover, and let the chicken cool in its own liquid for 1 to 2 hours to room temperature.

Remove the chicken from the poaching liquid. Strain the stock and store in the refrigerator; it keeps for up to 1 week (or freeze for longer storage). Separate the chicken meat from the skin and bones, and store the white and dark meat in separate containers in the refrigerator for up to 1 week.

VEGETABLE STOCK

This stock is a bit odd in that I add tomato. I find it helps with the color, consistency, and sweetness of vegetable stocks. If you peel tomatoes for fresh tomato sauce or gazpachos in the summer months, you can use the leftover skins for this recipe.

3 large carrots with tops, coarsely chopped

4 ribs celery with leafy tops, quartered crosswise

1 large onion, unpeeled, quartered

1 large leek (white and light green parts), halved lengthwise and washed

2 overripe vine tomatoes, halved, or 2 cups tomato skins

4 cloves garlic, smashed

1 unpeeled organic lemon, cut crosswise into ¼-inch slices

Herb bundle: a few sprigs of fresh flat-leaf parsley, thyme, and bay leaf, tied together with kitchen twine

6 black peppercorns

Kosher or sea salt

In a large pot, combine all the ingredients with 4 quarts water. Bring to a boil, reduce the heat to a simmer, and cook for 1 hour. Let cool to room temperature, then strain the stock and discard the solids in the strainer.

KEEPING A STASH of stock (or just good-quality stock in a box) is a key tool in the kitchen. It's important for soups, or course, as well as stock-dependent dishes like risotto, but you can also use it for any sauce that gets too "tight." Just go ahead and add some chicken or vegetable stock. It will loosen up the sauce and add flavor—not dilute flavor as water might.

MUSHROOM STOCK

Adding earthy, beefy dried mushrooms makes the flavor of this stock rich and unique, especially for a vegetable stock. It makes vegetarian and vegan recipes taste heartier and more fulfilling—"beefier."

1 ounce dried porcini mushrooms

1 small celery root, peeled and thickly sliced, or 4 ribs celery with leafy tops, quartered crosswise

2 large carrots with tops, coarsely chopped

2 leeks (white and light green parts), halved lengthwise and washed well

1 large onion, unpeeled, quartered

4 cloves garlic, smashed

Herb bundle: a few sprigs of fresh flat-leaf parsley, thyme, and bay leaf, tied together with kitchen twine

6 black peppercorns

Kosher or sea salt

In a large pot, combine all the ingredients with 4 quarts water. Bring to a boil, reduce the heat to a simmer, and cook for 1 hour. Let cool to room temperature, then strain the stock and discard the solids in the strainer.

SOUP AND SANDWICH, ITALIAN-STYLE

The combo of tomato soup and a grilled cheese sandwich is comfort reinvented. You have your choice of two cream of tomato soups: one made with roasted end-of-summer tomatoes and the other made with canned tomatoes, vodka, and heavy cream.

Eggplant-Parm Grilled Cheese
SERVES 4 TO 6

1 medium eggplant
Salt
⅓ cup olive oil
2 cloves garlic, very thinly sliced
Leaves from 1 sprig fresh
    rosemary, finely chopped
A fat pinch of crushed red
    pepper flakes
8 to 12 slices good-quality
    white bread or firm Italian
    semolina bread
Softened butter or mayo, for
    spreading on the bread
1 to 1½ cups freshly grated
    Parmigiano-Reggiano cheese
1 pound fresh mozzarella
    cheese (I use fior di latte),
    thinly sliced
2 vine or plum tomatoes,
    thinly sliced
A handful of fresh basil leaves,
    torn

Preheat the broiler to high.

Trim the skin off two opposite sides of the eggplant, then very thinly slice the eggplant into ⅛- to ¼-inch planks. Season the eggplant with salt and drain on paper towels for a few minutes.

In a small skillet, heat the oil over medium heat. Add the garlic and cook until light golden in color. Remove from the heat. Remove the garlic with a fork and let cool. Chop the cooled garlic and set aside. Add the rosemary and red pepper flakes to the oil.

Pat the eggplant dry, brush with the flavored oil, and arrange on a baking sheet. Broil for 2 to 3 minutes per side, or until charred and tender.

Heat a griddle or nonstick skillet over medium heat.

Lightly butter one side of each slice of bread and press it into or sprinkle with the Parm.

Build the sandwiches: Place half the bread Parm side down on a work surface. Top each slice with mozzarella, grilled eggplant, tomato, chopped crispy garlic, basil, and more mozzarella. Top with a second slice of bread, Parm side facing up.

Grill the sandwiches until golden brown and the cheese has melted, 3 to 4 minutes per side.

Roasted Tomato Soup
SERVES 4

If you don't have fresh tomatoes, sub in a 28- to 32-ounce can of San Marzano tomatoes. Keep the soup at a low bubble (before adding the cream) while you make the grilled cheese. Then put the finishing touches on the soup and serve.

1 tablespoon EVOO
2 tablespoons butter
2 onions, chopped
4 cloves garlic, sliced or
    chopped
2 tablespoons fresh thyme
    leaves, chopped
1 rounded tablespoon sweet
    paprika
1 teaspoon ground fennel or
    fennel pollen (optional)
Salt and pepper
2 tablespoons tomato paste
4 cups chicken or vegetable
    stock, preferably homemade
    (pages 64 and 65)
3 to 4 pounds assorted
    tomatoes, roasted (see box,
    page 77)
½ cup fresh basil leaves, torn or
    thinly sliced
¼ cup heavy cream

Heat a medium soup pot over medium-high heat. Add the EVOO (1 turn of the pan) and melt the butter into it. Add the onions, garlic, thyme, paprika, fennel (if using), salt, and pepper. Partially cover the pot and cook to soften the onions, about 10 minutes. Add the tomato paste and stir until fragrant, about 2 minutes. Add 2 cups of the stock and stir to deglaze the pan. Transfer the mixture to a food processor, add the roasted tomatoes, and process until smooth. Return to the pot and add the remaining 2 cups stock. (Alternatively, use an immersion blender to combine the tomatoes and stock directly in the pot itself.) Stir in half the basil.

Finish the soup by stirring the cream into the soup. (Do not return the soup to a boil after adding the cream.) Top with the remaining basil to garnish.

Tomato-Vodka Soup

SERVES 4

You could use 3 to 4 pounds roasted tomatoes instead of the canned tomatoes in this soup (see box, page 77). We sometimes serve this soup at parties in a fun way: In shot glasses or cocktail glasses rather than soup cups.

4 cups chicken stock, preferably homemade (page 64)
A handful of dry-pack sun-dried tomatoes
2 tablespoons EVOO
1 onion, finely chopped
1 carrot, grated or finely chopped
4 cloves garlic, finely chopped
1 bay leaf
2 tablespoons chopped fresh thyme leaves
Salt and pepper
1 cup vodka
1 (28- to 32-ounce) can San Marzano tomatoes (look for DOP on the label)
A few fresh basil leaves, torn
1 cup heavy cream

In a small saucepan, combine 1½ cups of the stock and the sun-dried tomatoes and bring the stock to a low boil. Reduce the heat and simmer until the tomatoes have softened, 6 to 7 minutes.

Meanwhile, in a large saucepan, heat the EVOO (2 turns of the pan) over medium-high heat. Add the onion, carrot, garlic, bay leaf, thyme, salt, and pepper. Cook until the veggies have softened, about 5 minutes. Add the vodka, stir to deglaze the pan, and cook for a minute to reduce. Hand-crush the tomatoes as you add them to the pan and add the juices from the can. Cook for 15 to 18 minutes to reduce and thicken a bit.

Add the remaining 2½ cups stock, the reconstituted sun-dried tomatoes and their stock, and the basil. Fish out and discard the bay leaf. Puree the soup directly in the pan with an immersion blender, return to a bubble, and stir in the cream. (Do not return to a boil after adding the cream.)

PAPPA AL POMODORO

SERVES 6

Stale bread and tomato soup, also called *pappa col pomodoro*, is a simple dish with very few ingredients—and it is all about the tomatoes. Make this when tomatoes are at their sweetest and fullest flavor in the summer and into early fall. If you garden and have more tomatoes than you know what to do with, this is the perfect recipe for you.

3 to 4 pounds tomatoes, peeled (see Tip)
2 ribs celery, finely chopped
4 large cloves garlic, chopped
¼ cup good-quality olive oil
2 quarts chicken or vegetable stock, preferably homemade (pages 64 and 65)
6 slices (1 inch thick) stale peasant-style white bread, cut into cubes
1 cup loosely packed fresh basil leaves, torn
EVOO, for serving
Shaved Parmigiano-Reggiano cheese, for serving

Chop the tomatoes (you should have 5 to 6 cups total) and transfer to a soup pot. Add the celery, garlic, oil, and stock. Bring to a low rolling boil, then reduce to a simmer and cook for 1 hour.

Add the bread and stir to thicken the soup, then add the torn basil. Serve in shallow bowls, passing EVOO and shaved Parm at the table.

TIP

TO PEEL tomatoes: Fill a bowl with ice and water. Heat a pot of water to a low rolling boil. With a sharp paring knife, score the skins of the tomatoes with an "X." Add the tomatoes to the boiling water a few at a time and blanch for 30 seconds to loosen the skins. Cold-shock the tomatoes in the prepared ice bath and then pull off the skins.

ITALIAN-STYLE GAZPACHO

MAKES ABOUT 15 DOUBLE-SHOTS,
OR SERVES 8 AS A FIRST COURSE

My mom requests this soup every year as the first course for her birthday. I prefer a high-powered blender over a food processor for making this. Reserve a few of the chopped peppers, onions, and cucumber pieces to garnish your soup and give it texture.

¼ cup EVOO

Juice of 1 lemon, or 2 tablespoons white balsamic vinegar

1 thick slice stale peasant-style white bread, crust removed, torn

Salt and pepper

2½ to 3 pounds plum tomatoes, peeled (see Tip, page 67) and chopped, or 1 (28- to 32-ounce) can San Marzano tomatoes (look for DOP on the label) with their juices

2 cups passata, tomato puree, or tomato-vegetable juice (spicy or regular)

A few fresh basil leaves, torn

2 tablespoons grated fresh horseradish

2 ribs celery with leafy tops, chopped

1 cubanelle or red frying pepper, chopped

1 fresh chile, seeded and ribs removed

1 small red onion, coarsely chopped

¼ seedless cucumber, peeled and diced

2 cloves garlic, smashed

Basically, pile the ingredients into a high-speed blender and puree. Adjust the seasonings, chill, and serve in small shot glasses for a sip or chilled mugs or small bowls for a first course.

TIP

On a really hot day, add a few ice cubes to the blender to really chill that soup.

WHITE GAZPACHO

MAKES 12 TO 14 SHOT GLASS PORTIONS,
OR SERVES 6 AS A FIRST COURSE

This soup is refreshing and unusual. It makes a great starter for summer parties. You may want to reserve some of the vegetables, finely chopped, for garnish. I love serving gazpachos with grilled jumbo shrimp alongside for dipping (see box, page 217).

¼ cup EVOO

Juice of 1 lemon, or 2 tablespoons white balsamic vinegar

1 thick slice stale peasant-style white bread, crusts removed, torn

1 small bulb fennel, cored and coarsely chopped

2 green tomatoes, chopped

1 small romaine lettuce heart, coarsely chopped

½ seedless cucumber, peeled and coarsely chopped

1 medium white onion, chopped

1 mild green pepper (such as a cubanelle), coarsely chopped

2 cloves garlic, chopped

1 fresh jalapeño or other green chile

A handful of fresh flat-leaf parsley tops

A handful of fresh mint leaves, plus shredded mint for garnish

Leaves from a few sprigs fresh thyme

A few fresh basil or tarragon leaves, chopped

Salt and pepper

Combine all the ingredients in a high-speed blender and puree until smooth, adjusting the consistency with water as needed. Serve garnished with fresh mint.

MUSHROOM SOUP WITH MARSALA

This soup is so fast and amazing. We love it as a lunch or late supper. The fried bread makes it.

1 ounce dried porcini or mixed wild mushrooms

1 quart chicken or vegetable stock, preferably homemade (pages 64 and 65)

¼ cup EVOO

1 pound fresh mushrooms (such as cremini, shiitake, button, wood ear—whatever varieties look best and have a fair price per pound), sliced

1 large fresh bay leaf

4 shallots, chopped

4 cloves garlic, chopped

2 tablespoons fresh thyme leaves, chopped

Salt and pepper

1 cup Marsala

½ cup fresh flat-leaf parsley leaves, finely chopped

Juice of ½ lemon

Good-quality peasant-style white or Italian bread, sliced and pan-toasted (lightly fried) in EVOO or butter

Grated Parmigiano-Reggiano cheese, for serving

In a saucepan, combine the dried mushrooms and stock and bring to a low simmer to reconstitute the mushrooms.

In a soup pot, heat the EVOO (4 turns of the pan) over medium-high heat. When it ripples, add the fresh mushrooms and cook until lightly browned and tender, 12 to 15 minutes. Add the bay leaf, shallots, garlic, and thyme and season with salt and pepper. Stir for 2 to 3 minutes to soften. Add the Marsala, stir to deglaze the pan, and cook until the liquid has reduced by half.

Scoop the reconstituted dried mushrooms from the soaking liquid, chop them, and add to the soup pot. Carefully pour in the soaking liquid, leaving the last few spoonfuls in the pan as grit may have settled there. Add 2 cups water and simmer for a few minutes, then taste and adjust the seasonings. Discard the bay leaf.

To serve, stir in the parsley and lemon juice. Place a small round of toast in each bowl, sprinkle with cheese, and top with soup.

CREAMY CELERY SOUP WITH GARLIC TOAST

I love the grassy flavor of this soup, especially as a starter to heavy meals featuring roast turkey or roast beef. The garlic toasts really make the dish (as they do for anything they're served with).

4 tablespoons (½ stick) butter, diced

1 bunch organic celery with leafy tops, chopped (about 6 cups)

2 onions, chopped

6 cloves garlic: 4 chopped, 2 halved

2 large fresh bay leaves

Celery salt

Pepper

2 large potatoes, peeled and diced

2 medium celery root, peeled and diced

6 cups chicken stock, preferably homemade (page 64)

2 cups heavy cream

6 slices ciabatta or peasant-style white bread

EVOO, for drizzling

Flaky sea salt

In a soup pot, melt the butter over medium heat. When it begins to foam, add the celery, onions, chopped garlic, and bay leaves. Season with celery salt and pepper. Partially cover and cook, stirring occasionally, until the vegetables are very tender and soft, about 20 minutes.

Add the potatoes, celery root, and stock and bring to a boil. Reduce the heat to a low rolling boil and simmer, partially covered, for 20 minutes more. Fish out and discard the bay leaves. Stir in the cream and puree with an immersion blender. Taste and adjust the seasonings.

Char or toast the bread and rub with the cut garlic. Drizzle with EVOO and season with flaky sea salt.

Serve the soup in shallow bowls with the charred garlic toasts alongside.

ROASTED SQUASH SOUP

This soup is my fall favorite and is usually served by the cup on Thanksgiving Day.

1 butternut squash or other orange-fleshed squash or pumpkin, peeled and sliced
EVOO, for drizzling
Freshly grated nutmeg
Salt and pepper
3 tablespoons butter
2 carrots, thinly sliced
1 rib celery, finely chopped
1 onion, chopped
2 Honeycrisp apples, peeled and chopped
1 tablespoon grated lemon zest (from an organic lemon)
1 tablespoon grated orange zest (from an organic orange)
2 pinches saffron threads
1 tablespoon honey
1 quart water or chicken stock, preferably homemade (page 64), plus more as needed
Chopped toasted pistachios, for garnish
Toasted pumpkin seeds, for garnish

Preheat the oven to 400°F.

Drizzle the squash with EVOO, season with a few grates of nutmeg, salt, and pepper and toss to evenly coat. Roast until golden at the edges and very tender, about 25 minutes.

In a soup pot, heat a drizzle of EVOO over medium to medium-high heat. Melt in the butter. Add the carrots, celery, onion, apples, and citrus zest. Season with salt and pepper. Partially cover and cook until the vegetables begin to soften, about 10 minutes. Add the saffron, honey, and water or stock. Bring to a boil, then reduce to a simmer and cook to soften the vegetables, about 20 minutes.

Puree the vegetables directly in the pot with an immersion blender. Add the roasted squash and blend to combine, thinning the soup with extra water or stock if necessary. Adjust the seasonings.

Serve topped with toasted pistachios and pumpkin seeds.

CHICKPEA AND POTATO SOUP

So fast, yet so filling—this soup will send you into a food coma pretty quickly.

3 tablespoons olive oil
2 large potatoes, peeled and chopped
Salt and pepper
1 large onion, chopped
3 or 4 cloves garlic (to taste), chopped
1 (28-ounce) can chickpeas, or 2 (15-ounce) cans, drained and rinsed
1 quart chicken or vegetable stock, preferably homemade (pages 64 and 65)
1 cup ditalini pasta
1 (10-ounce) box frozen chopped spinach, thawed and drained
Grated Parmigiano-Reggiano cheese, for serving

In a soup pot or Dutch oven, heat the oil (3 turns of the pan) over medium to medium-high heat. Add the potatoes, season with salt and pepper, and cook to lightly brown the potatoes, 5 to 6 minutes. Add the onion and garlic, partially cover the pan, and cook to wilt the onions, 5 to 6 minutes more.

Add the chickpeas, stock, and 3 cups water and bring to a low boil. Add the pasta and cook to al dente. Add the spinach, separating it with your fingers as you stir it in. Adjust the seasonings and serve the soup in shallow bowls topped with grated Parm.

RIBOLLITA

What makes my *ribollita* a bit different from the rest is that I always toast my torn, stale bread until it is deep golden brown, very nutty, and fragrant. Also, I add a rind of Parmigiano-Reggiano cheese to the stock or the soup itself, and (as I do with minestra and minestrone) I puree half the beans to give the broth some weight. The total weight of the dried beans for this soup should be ¾ pound.

½ cup dried borlotti beans

½ cup dried cannellini beans

½ cup dried chickpeas

2 onions: 1 halved, 1 quartered and thinly sliced

4 cloves garlic: 1 smashed, 3 chopped

2 bay leaves

2 sprigs fresh rosemary

Salt

¼ cup olive oil

1 bulb fennel, trimmed, cored, quartered, and thinly sliced

1 leek (white and light green parts only), halved lengthwise, cut crosswise into half-moons

2 carrots, chopped

2 medium or 3 small ribs celery with leafy tops, chopped

2 tablespoons chopped fresh thyme leaves

Pepper

3 quarts chicken stock, preferably homemade (page 64)

½ small head green or savoy cabbage, chopped (2 to 3 cups)

1 bunch lacinato kale (also called black, Tuscan, or dinosaur kale) or Swiss chard, stemmed and chopped

2 cups passata or tomato puree (see Tip)

Rind from a small wedge of Parmigiano-Reggiano cheese

Freshly grated nutmeg

6 slices (1 inch thick) peasant-style white bread, cut into coarse cubes or torn

Thinly sliced yellow or white onion, for serving

EVOO, for serving

Grated Parmigiano-Reggiano cheese, for serving

Soak all the beans overnight in a large bowl with enough water to cover. (Or, quick-soak the beans: Place them in a heatproof bowl and cover with boiling water by 3 inches. Let stand for 1 hour.) Rinse the beans and transfer them to a pot. Add fresh water to cover the beans by 3 to 4 inches. Add the halved onion, smashed garlic, bay leaves, and rosemary and bring to a boil. Salt the water, reduce the heat to a low boil, and cook until tender, 35 to 45 minutes.

Discard the rosemary and bay leaves. Measure out and set aside half the beans. With an immersion blender, puree the remaining beans and cooking liquid in the pot (or transfer the beans to a blender and puree in batches).

Meanwhile, in a large soup pot, heat the oil (4 turns of the pan) over medium to medium-high heat. Add the fennel, leek, carrots, celery, sliced onion, chopped garlic, thyme, salt, and pepper. Cover and cook, stirring occasionally, until the vegetables have softened, about 10 minutes.

Add the stock, cabbage, kale, passata, reserved beans, bean puree, Parm rind, and some nutmeg. Adjust the seasonings. Bring to a bubble, then reduce to a simmer.

Preheat the oven to 350°F. Spread the bread on a baking sheet and toast until deep golden. Add the bread to the soup.

Serve in warmed shallow bowls topped with sliced onion, a generous drizzle of EVOO, and grated Parm.

INSTEAD OF store-bought passata or tomato puree, you could make this with 2 pounds of tomatoes, peeled (see Tip, page 67) and diced.

ZUCCHINI AND FENNEL SOUP WITH GARLIC CROUTONS

Fennel is so sweet and has a slightly licorice flavor that I find it pairs beautifully with zucchini. I love basil or tarragon with zucchini, so why not the related flavor of fennel?

CROUTONS:

4 slices good-quality white or
    peasant-style bread
1 clove garlic, halved
EVOO, for drizzling
Sea salt and pepper
Small handful of freshly grated
    pecorino cheese

SOUP:

3 tablespoons olive oil
1 large bulb fennel, trimmed,
    cored, and chopped, plus a fat
    handful of the fronds
2 medium zucchini (about
    1½ pounds total), diced
1 large onion, chopped
4 cloves garlic, sliced
Salt and pepper
2 quarts vegetable or chicken
    stock, preferably homemade
    (pages 65 and 64)
3 or 4 overripe tomatoes, grated,
    with their juices
1 cup chopped mixed fresh herbs:
    basil, tarragon, parsley, mint,
    or any combination

Preheat the oven to 400°F or preheat the broiler.

Make the croutons: Toast or char the bread in the hot oven or under the broiler. Rub the bread with the cut garlic, then cut the bread into cubes and transfer to a bowl. Drizzle with a little EVOO, season with salt and pepper, and toss with the pecorino.

Spread the bread cubes on a rimmed baking sheet and return to the oven/broiler to crisp the edges. Keep an eye on them; it can take as little as 30 seconds to 1 minute under the broiler, but longer in the oven.

Make the soup: In a medium soup pot, heat the oil (3 turns of the pan) over medium heat. Add the chopped fennel, zucchini, onion, and garlic. Season with salt and pepper. Partially cover the pot and cook to soften the fennel and onion, 10 to 12 minutes.

Add the stock and grated tomatoes with their juices and bring to a boil. Reduce to a simmer and cook to combine the flavors. Just before serving, stir in the herbs and fennel fronds.

Divide the croutons among the bowls and top with the soup. Let stand for 2 to 3 minutes to soften the bread, then serve.

MINESTRA

John makes this for me when I am sick or feeling blue. It was one of the first meals I ever had as a child, and I love it today because it cures me when I am homesick. There are a couple of choices to make for the soup: canned beans (for a quick soup) or dried beans cooked from scratch; pancetta or anchovies for the salty component that starts off the soup; pasta or potatoes for the starch (other than the beans).

3 tablespoons olive oil

¼ pound pancetta, diced or finely chopped, or 4 good-quality flat anchovy fillets

1 onion, chopped

4 cloves garlic, thinly sliced

½ teaspoon crushed red pepper flakes

8 cups chopped escarole

Salt and black pepper

Freshly grated nutmeg

2 quarts chicken stock, preferably homemade (page 64), plus more as needed

Rind from a small wedge of grating cheese (such as Parmigiano-Reggiano)

1 cup dried cannellini beans, cooked from scratch (see box), or 1 (28-ounce) can cannellini beans, rinsed and drained

Leaves from 1 sprig fresh rosemary (optional)

1 long strip of lemon zest

¾ cup ditalini pasta, or 1 large or 2 medium potatoes, peeled and chopped

Juice of 1 lemon

Grated Parmigiano-Reggiano cheese, for serving

In a soup pot, heat the oil (3 turns of the pan) over medium heat. Add the pancetta and cook for 3 minutes to render (or add the anchovies and melt them into the oil; see Tip). Add the onion, garlic, and red pepper flakes and stir and sweat for 5 minutes or so. Wilt the escarole into the pan and season with a little salt, some pepper, and nutmeg. Add the stock and cheese rind and bring to a boil, then reduce the heat to keep the soup at a low rolling boil.

Measure out and set aside half the beans. If using scratch beans, discard the onion, bay leaf, and rosemary stem and puree the remaining beans with 2 cups of the cooking liquid. If using canned beans, puree the remaining beans with the rosemary leaves and 2 cups of stock.

Add the bean puree, whole beans, and lemon zest to the soup. Bring to a low rolling boil and add the pasta. Simmer until firm-tender, 5 to 6 minutes. (If adding potatoes, cook until firm-tender, 10 to 12 minutes.) Add a few cups of water if the soup gets too thick.

Just before serving, stir in the lemon juice. Serve in shallow bowls topped with grated Parm.

TO MELT anchovies, add the anchovies to the pan, cover the pan with a splatter screen or lid, and shake until the anchovies begin to break up. Reduce the heat a bit, uncover, and stir until the anchovies melt into the oil.

SCRATCH BEANS

MAKES ABOUT 3 CUPS

1 cup dried beans
1 small onion, halved
1 large bay leaf
1 large sprig fresh rosemary
Salt

Soak the beans in a bowl with water to cover overnight. (Alternatively, quick-soak the beans: Place them in a heatproof bowl and cover with boiling water by 3 inches. Let stand for 1 hour.) Rinse the soaked beans and transfer them to a pot. Add fresh water to cover the beans by 3 to 4 inches, the onion, bay leaf, and rosemary. Bring the water to a boil, salt the water, and cook the beans until tender, 30 to 40 minutes. Discard the onion halves, bay leaf, and rosemary stem.

SPRING MINESTRA

I love beans and greens. In spring, I make a version that is lighter than my cannellini-based minestra. Here, fresh favas and peas, both signs of spring, make a soup that is comforting on cool days or nights, yet light enough for the warmer seasons.

CROUTONS:

2 tablespoons olive oil
2 tablespoons butter
4 flat anchovy fillets
3 cups cubed or torn stale
    peasant-style white bread

SOUP:

3 tablespoons olive oil
¼ pound pancetta, finely chopped
1 onion, chopped
4 cloves garlic, chopped
8 cups chopped escarole (about
    2 heads) or mixed greens and
    lettuces
Freshly grated nutmeg
Salt and pepper
6 to 8 cups chicken stock,
    preferably homemade
    (page 64)
1 cup peeled shelled fresh fava
    beans (see Tip)
1 cup shelled fresh peas
1 cup packed fresh mint and flat-
    leaf parsley leaves, chopped
Juice of 1 lemon
Grated Parmigiano-Reggiano
    cheese, for serving (optional)

Make the croutons: In a skillet, heat the oil (2 turns of the pan) over medium heat. Melt in the butter. When it foams, add the anchovies, cover the pan with a splatter screen or lid, and shake until the anchovies begin to break up. Reduce the heat a bit, uncover, and stir until the anchovies melt into the oil. Add the bread, toss to coat, and cook until deep golden and fragrant.

Make the soup: In a soup pot, heat the oil (3 turns of the pan) over medium to medium-high heat. Add the pancetta and stir for 2 to 3 minutes. Add the onion and garlic and cook to soften, a few minutes more. Wilt the greens into the pot and season with a few grates of nutmeg, salt, and pepper. Add the stock (use the larger amount if serving 6 people) and bring to a low rolling boil. Add the favas and peas and cook to heat through.

Just before serving, stir in the herbs and lemon juice. To serve, place a few croutons in a shallow bowl and ladle the soup over top. Serve with Parm, if desired.

TIP

To peel fresh favas, pop the beans out of the pods, then blanch the beans in boiling water for 3 to 4 minutes. Run under cold water to stop the cooking. Pinch the bright green favas out of their skins.

MINESTRONE WITH ROASTED TOMATO

There are so many beans in this soup that you could leave out the pasta, but if you do cook pasta for the soup, cook it separately and dress it lightly with EVOO. Then, when it comes time to serve the soup, put some of the pasta in the soup bowl and ladle the soup on top.

1½ cups mixed dried beans (such as cannellini, chickpeas, and borlotti), cooked from scratch (see box, page 75)

3 to 4 pounds assorted tomatoes (I use some vine, plum, and cherry tomatoes)

5 cloves garlic: 3 smashed, 2 chopped

3 tablespoons fresh thyme leaves, chopped

2 tablespoons olive oil, plus more for drizzling

1 large bulb fennel, trimmed, cored, and cut into ¼- to ½-inch cubes

1 onion, chopped

2 ribs celery with leafy tops, chopped

2 carrots, chopped

1 potato, peeled and chopped

2 to 3 cups chopped green cabbage

1 large fresh bay leaf

Salt and pepper

1 quart chicken stock, preferably homemade (page 64)

Rind from a small wedge of Parmigiano-Reggiano cheese

1½ cups small-cut pasta, such as ditalini or pennette (optional)

Grated Parmigiano-Reggiano cheese, for serving

Measure out half the cooked beans and puree them. Reserve the remaining beans, leaving them whole, plus 2 cups of their cooking liquid.

Roast the tomatoes (see box), adding the smashed garlic and thyme before roasting.

In a soup pot, heat the oil (2 turns of the pan) over medium to medium-high heat. Add the chopped garlic, fennel, onion, celery, carrots, potato, cabbage, bay leaf, salt, and pepper. Cook, stirring, until the vegetables begin to soften, 8 to 10 minutes. Add the stock, cheese rind, pureed beans, whole beans, reserved bean cooking liquid, and roasted tomatoes (discard the garlic). Simmer the soup gently for 15 to 20 minutes to soften the vegetables and combine the flavors, adding water as needed if the soup is too thick. Discard the bay leaf.

If including pasta in the soup, just before serving, cook the pasta in boiling salted water to al dente. (If making ahead, dress it with a little olive oil.) Place a little pasta in each bowl, top with soup, sprinkle with Parm, and serve.

ROASTING TOMATOES

Position a rack in the center of the oven and preheat the oven to 375°F. Fill a rimmed baking sheet with assorted tomatoes—coarsely chop larger tomatoes; leave small or cherry tomatoes whole. Season with salt and pepper, coat lightly with EVOO, and toss. Roast until the pieces have browned at the edges or the small tomatoes have burst, 45 minutes to 1 hour. The tomatoes should be slumped and saucy, but not dried out. Transfer to a large bowl and mash with a wooden spoon or potato masher.

BROKEN TOASTED SPAGHETTI SOUP WITH ESCAROLE

SERVES 4

This is a kid-friendly soup like chicken and rice, as it has lots of toasted pasta in it. Grown-ups love it, too, but they might prefer (as I do) Toasted Spaghetti Minestra with Tuscan Kale (see right).

3 tablespoons butter
¾ pound spaghetti, broken in thirds
2 tablespoons olive oil
1 large onion, chopped
4 cloves garlic, chopped
Herb bundle: a few sprigs of fresh thyme and flat-leaf parsley, tied together with kitchen twine
Salt and pepper
1 large head escarole, chopped
Freshly grated nutmeg
2 quarts chicken stock, preferably homemade (page 64)
Grated zest and juice of 1 organic lemon
Grated Parmigiano-Reggiano cheese, for serving

In a medium soup pot, melt 2 tablespoons of the butter over medium heat. When it foams, add the pasta and cook until nutty, fragrant, and deep golden brown, 3 to 4 minutes. Scoop out and set aside until closer to serving time.

Add the oil (2 turns of the pan) to the pot. Melt in the remaining 1 tablespoon butter. Add the onion, garlic, and herb bundle. Season with salt and pepper and sweat until tender, about 5 minutes. Wilt in the escarole and season with a few grates of nutmeg.

Add the stock and bring the soup to a low boil. Add the toasted pasta and cook to al dente. Stir in the lemon zest and juice. Serve in shallow bowls topped with Parm.

TOASTED SPAGHETTI MINESTRA WITH TUSCAN KALE

SERVES 4

This is the grown-up version of Broken Toasted Spaghetti Soup with Escarole (see left). I like either white beans or chickpeas stirred into this soup.

2 quarts chicken or vegetable stock, preferably homemade (pages 64 and 65)
1 ounce dried porcini mushrooms
2 tablespoons olive oil
2 tablespoons butter
½ pound whole wheat or farro spaghetti, broken into 2- to 3-inch pieces
1 onion, finely chopped
1 carrot, finely chopped
2 ribs celery, finely chopped
4 cloves garlic, finely chopped
Salt and pepper
1 bunch Tuscan kale (also called lacinato, black, or dinosaur kale), stemmed and thinly sliced
Freshly grated nutmeg
1 (15-ounce) can cannellini beans or chickpeas, rinsed and drained
Grated Pecorino Romano cheese, for serving

In a saucepan, heat the stock along with the mushrooms to soften, 10 to 15 minutes. Set aside.

In a soup pot, heat the oil (2 turns of the pan) over medium to medium-high heat. Melt the butter into the oil and add the pasta. Toast the pasta until nutty and very fragrant, 3 to 4 minutes. Scoop out and set aside until closer to serving time.

Add the onion, carrot, celery, and garlic to the soup pot. Season with salt and pepper. Partially cover the pan and cook to sweat the vegetables, 7 to 8 minutes. Wilt in the kale and season with a few grates of nutmeg.

Scoop the mushrooms out of the stock and chop them. Add to the kale and vegetables. Carefully pour in the stock, leaving the last few spoonfuls in the pan as grit may have settled there.

Bring the soup to a simmer and add the beans. Add the toasted pasta and cook the pasta to al dente. Ladle the soup into shallow bowls and top with grated pecorino.

ITALIAN-STYLE CHICKEN NOODLE SOUP

I love chicken noodle soup. As a lover of it, I have a technique to eating it: I slurp up the broth and leave myself a giant bowl of the good stuff hoarded off to one side. But with this soup, there's no need to ration or hoard: It's full of extra everything. As with any soup I add noodles to, I cook the noodles separately so they don't get too bloated or soft in the soup itself.

2 tablespoons EVOO, plus more for drizzling

2 carrots, cut into ½-inch cubes

2 ribs celery, chopped

2 medium leeks, chopped and washed well

1 small onion, chopped

1 bulb fennel, trimmed, cored, and chopped

2 large cloves garlic, grated or finely chopped

Salt and pepper

1 (14.5-ounce) can diced tomatoes

2 quarts chicken stock, preferably homemade (see Tip)

1 to 1½ pounds cooked chicken (see Tip), diced

1 (3- to 4-inch) rind of Parmigiano-Reggiano cheese

⅓ pound green beans, halved lengthwise then cut into thirds on an angle

1 pound pici (fat spaghetti) or bucatini (if you use bucatini, break it into 3- to 4-inch pieces)

In a soup pot, heat the EVOO (2 turns of the pan) over medium heat. Add the carrots, celery, leeks, onion, fennel, and garlic. Season with salt and pepper. Cover and cook, stirring occasionally, to sweat the vegetables, about 10 minutes. Add the tomatoes, stock, chicken, and cheese rind and bring the soup to a low boil. Add the green beans and simmer until they are tender, about 5 minutes.

Meanwhile, bring a large pot of water to a boil. Salt the water and cook the pasta to al dente. Drain and toss with a drizzle of EVOO.

When ready to serve, stir the noodles into the soup just long enough to reheat them.

IF YOU USE THE recipe for chicken stock (page 64), you will end up with the stock and chicken meat that you need for this soup. In fact, you will end up with a little more than you need, so just save the extra chicken for salads and freeze the stock. You could also make the soup with good-quality store-bought stock and meat from a rotisserie chicken.

CHICKEN AND ORZO (BARLEY) SOUP

⸻ SERVES 6 ⸻

In Italian, orzo does not refer to the little pasta shape but to barley, a staple for cold salads and hot soups. Barley is wonderfully filling, mild in flavor, and has a great chew to it. I cook barley, farro, and pasta separately for soups and add them at the last minute. I do not care for soggy/bloated grains or pasta.

Chicken stock and poached chicken (page 64)
Salt
1 cup pearl barley (orzo perlato)
1 small onion, halved
¼ cup olive oil, plus more for drizzling
¾ pound cremini mushrooms, sliced
2 ribs celery with leafy tops, chopped
4 cloves garlic, grated or chopped
4 large shallots, or 1 onion, chopped
2 tablespoons chopped fresh thyme
Salt and pepper
½ cup dry sherry or Marsala
1 (5- to 6-ounce) package spinach or baby kale

Make the chicken stock. Dice the chicken meat so you have 2½ to 3 cups and measure out 2 quarts of the stock (see Tip).

In a medium pot, bring 2 quarts water to a boil. Salt the water. Add the barley and onion halves and cook until the barley is tender, about 25 minutes. Drain and discard the onion. Return the barley to the pot and toss with a tiny drizzle of oil to keep it from sticking. Set aside.

In a medium soup pot, heat the oil (4 turns of the pan) over medium to medium-high heat. Add the mushrooms and brown. Add the celery, garlic, shallots, thyme, salt, and pepper. Cook to soften the garlic and shallots, 7 to 8 minutes. Add the sherry, stir to deglaze the pan, and cook until reduced by half. Stir in the chicken stock and diced poached chicken. Wilt in the spinach.

When ready to serve, add the barley to the soup and heat through.

WHEN YOU MAKE the stock, you'll get more meat and stock than you need for the soup. Reserve the rest of the chicken meat for another meal or to add to a salad. Refrigerate or freeze the extra stock.

STRACCIATELLA WITH MINI CHICKEN MEATBALLS

⸻ SERVES 4 ⸻

When the eggs are stirred into the soup, they become "rags" (*stracci* in Italian). The mini meatballs make this a fun and easy lunch or light dinner if you are fighting off a little cold.

2 quarts chicken stock, preferably homemade (page 64)
½ cup fresh bread crumbs
3 tablespoons milk
1 pound ground chicken
¼ teaspoon freshly grated nutmeg
Salt and pepper
3 tablespoons grated onion
2 cloves garlic, finely chopped or grated
6 large free-range organic eggs
½ cup freshly finely grated Parmigiano-Reggiano cheese
2 tablespoons very finely chopped fresh flat-leaf parsley
1 bunch scallions (white and light green parts), chopped
Juice of ½ lemon

In a soup pot, bring the stock to a simmer.

In a large bowl, moisten the bread crumbs with the milk. Add the chicken and season with the nutmeg, salt, and pepper. Add the onion, garlic, and 1 of the eggs. Mix the ingredients thoroughly but gently. Roll into walnut-size meatballs and drop into the simmering stock. Simmer until cooked through, 7 to 8 minutes.

In a bowl, whisk the remaining 5 eggs, the Parm, and parsley. Season with salt and pepper. Pour the egg mixture into the soup in ribbons, streaming the eggs across the broth. The eggs will turn into "rags."

Remove from the heat, add the scallions and lemon juice, and serve in shallow bowls.

LENTIL SOUP WITH SAUSAGE AND KALE

SERVES 6

Lentils are good luck, especially when eaten around New Year's, as they signify prosperity for the year to come: the lentils symbolize coins.

2 tablespoons olive oil

1 pound Sweet Italian Sausage with Fennel or Hot Italian Sausage, homemade (page 237) or store-bought, casings removed

2 carrots, chopped

2 medium or 3 small ribs celery, chopped

1 onion, chopped

4 cloves garlic, chopped

Herb bundle: a few sprigs of fresh flat-leaf parsley, rosemary, and thyme, plus 2 bay leaves, tied together with kitchen twine

Salt and pepper

2 potatoes, peeled and cut into ¼-inch cubes

3 tablespoons tomato paste

2 quarts chicken stock, preferably homemade (page 64)

1½ cups Norcia lentils (see box, page 38) or brown lentils

1 bunch kale, stemmed and shredded or chopped

In a soup pot, heat the oil (2 turns of the pan) over medium-high heat. Add the sausage, breaking it up into crumbles as it browns.

Add the carrots, celery, onion, garlic, herb bundle, and salt and pepper. Cover the pot and cook, stirring occasionally, for 5 minutes. Stir in the potatoes and cook for 4 to 5 minutes more. Add the tomato paste and stir until fragrant, about 1 minute. Add the stock and lentils and bring the soup to a boil. Reduce to a low rolling simmer and cook until the lentils are tender, about 40 minutes. Add a few cups of water if the soup gets too thick.

Fish out and discard the herb bundle and wilt in the kale. Taste and adjust the seasonings.

VARIATION

'Nduja and Lentil Soup

'Nduja is a spicy pork paste (see box, page 123) that I sometimes substitute for the sausage in my lentil soup. Use ¼ pound 'nduja in place of the 1 pound Italian sausage; the spicy paste is intense, so a little goes a long way. Substitute shredded zucchini for the kale, stirring it in just before serving.

WHITE ZUPPA DI PESCE

I grew up (and continue to live part-time) in the mountains of the Adirondack Park. It can be cold, especially at night, even in August. This soup is perfect and comforting for chilly nights, but light enough for any season. This is a fish soup, but feel free to add scallops, clams, or shrimp to the mix if you wish.

SOUP:

3 tablespoons good-quality olive oil

1 bulb fennel, trimmed, cored, quartered, and thinly sliced, small handful of fronds reserved (see Tip)

1 onion, quartered and thinly sliced

2 leeks (white and light green parts), halved lengthwise, thinly sliced crosswise into half-moons, and washed well

1½ pounds potatoes, peeled and very thinly sliced

4 cloves garlic, thinly sliced

2 tablespoons fresh thyme leaves, chopped

1 large fresh bay leaf

1 (2- to 3-inch) strip of lemon zest (from an organic lemon)

1 cup dry vermouth or white wine

1 quart chicken stock, preferably homemade (page 64), or a blend of chicken and seafood stock

2 to 2½ pounds black cod, cod, haddock, or flounder, cut into chunks

Salt and pepper

1 cup peas

½ cup crème fraîche

¼ cup fresh tarragon leaves, chopped

BRUSCHETTA:

4 slices ciabatta or peasant-style white bread

1 clove garlic, halved

EVOO, for drizzling

Flaky sea salt

Make the soup: In a large soup pot, heat the oil (3 turns of the pan) over medium heat. Add the sliced fennel, onion, leeks, potatoes, garlic, thyme, bay leaf, and lemon zest. Cover and cook, stirring occasionally, until all the vegetables are beginning to soften, 10 to 12 minutes.

Uncover and increase the heat a bit. Add the vermouth and cook until it has evaporated. Add the stock and bring to a low rolling boil. Add the fish and season with salt and pepper. Cover the pan to cook through, 6 to 7 minutes. Uncover and stir in the peas and crème fraîche. Remove from the heat and stir in the tarragon and fennel fronds. Discard the bay leaf.

Make the bruschetta: Char or toast the bread and rub it with the cut garlic. Drizzle with EVOO and season with flaky sea salt.

Serve the soup in shallow bowls with the bruschetta alongside.

TIP

Save a small handful of the fennel fronds to chop and then stir into the soup just before serving.

Left to right: White Clam
Pizza (page 93); Naples-
Style Calzone with Ham
and Salami (page 104);
Sicilian Pizza (page 89);
Ricotta, Walnut, and
Zucchini Pizza (page 90).

CHAPTER 4

PIZZA, CALZONES, AND FOCACCIA

I started working in kitchens when I was twelve years old. I never planned to have TV shows or cookbooks, never dreamed of designing my own pots and dishes. I loved working with food because it made people happy and it was a way to make a living that centered around sharing. I did daydream that one day I could save enough money to have a big gas stove and a wood-burning oven. After thirty years of hard work I got my life's wish. Pizza baking in what seems like moments is exciting. But I am here to tell you that I can make a smoky and delicious pizza without that oven. In my tiny NYC apartment, I get pizza that tastes almost identical to the pizza from my wood-burning oven.

HOW TO BAKE PIZZA AND CALZONES

Buy a large pizza stone, 14 x 16 inches (about $40). Preheat the stone for at least 1 hour at the highest temp you can set your oven to, around 550°F. Buy an inexpensive short-handled wooden pizza peel to build your pizzas on and to slide them on and off your stone. (Note: Sicilian-style pizza is baked on a baking sheet rather than on a stone; see Sfincione, page 89, for details.)

- Thin-crust pizza: Bake for 5 to 6 minutes, then switch on the broiler for 1 to 2 minutes to char the edges.
- Thick-crust pizza: Bake for 9 to 10 minutes, then switch on the broiler for 1 to 2 minutes to char the edges.
- Calzones: Bake for 7 to 8 minutes until golden and the bottom is firm, then broil for 1 to 2 minutes to char the edges.

IF YOU HAVE A PIZZA OVEN

Turning the pizzas every 30 to 45 seconds is the key. John prepares the oven early in the day and by nightfall he has it up to 800° to 900°F.

- Bake thin-crust pizza 2 to 3 minutes, but turn it a quarter-turn every 30 seconds or so.
- Bake pizzas made with Naples Pizza Dough (page 87) up to a minute longer.
- We cook thick-crust Sicilian pizza or calzones right at the edge of the oven, at the opening, where the temp runs more in the neighborhood of 650° to 700°F. Calzones cook in 5 to 6 minutes, and John often bastes them with a little additional EVOO if they start to look a bit dry on top.

SAME-DAY DOUGH

MAKES 2 POUNDS (ENOUGH FOR EIGHT 12-INCH INDIVIDUAL PIZZAS)

Use this recipe for thin-crust pizzas (or adapt it for thicker pizzas—see Variation).

- 1½ cups warm water (105° to 115°F)
- 1 envelope active dry yeast
- 2 teaspoons kosher salt
- 1½ teaspoons sugar or acacia honey
- 1 tablespoon EVOO
- 4 cups "00" flour or all-purpose flour, plus more for dusting

In a large bowl, stir the water, yeast, salt, sugar, and EVOO and let stand for 5 to 10 minutes. Stir in the flour to form a wet dough. Cover and let stand for 2 hours. Refrigerate the dough for 2 to 3 hours more.

Remove the dough from the refrigerator, sprinkle with flour, and cut into balls or portions using a bench scraper or kitchen scissors. Cut 8 small balls for thin-crust pizza: 10- to 12-inch individual pies. (The dough can be cut, dated, and frozen for up to 3 weeks; refrigerate overnight to thaw.)

Cut and pull the dough into smooth rounds and let the dough stand under a clean kitchen towel for 1 hour. Flour a work surface and your hands a bit, knead each round for 6 to 10 turns, and roll out with a lightly floured pin to ¹⁄₁₆ to ⅛ inch thick, about 12 inches across. Slide onto a pizza peel and top as you like or as directed in the recipe.

VARIATION

Sicilian-Style Pizza

To adapt the dough for thick-crust Sicilian-style pizza, use half all-purpose flour and half "00" flour for a thicker, heartier dough. Cut the dough into two portions for two Sicilian-style pizzas and use one 13 x 18-inch rimmed baking sheet plus one square or round pan up to 12 inches for baking. For the smaller pizza, cut off one-quarter to one-third of the dough. For the larger pie, use the remainder of the dough, about 1½ pounds. To bake this type of pizza, lightly oil the rimmed baking sheet and the round or square pan. Roll the dough on a floured surface with a floured pin to get it going, then transfer to the baking pans and press the dough all the way into the corners of the pans.

ONE-HOUR DOUGH

MAKES 1 POUND (ENOUGH FOR FOUR 10- TO 12-INCH INDIVIDUAL PIZZAS OR CALZONES)

This dough is actually my husband John's favorite, and it is the fastest and easiest dough to make of those included in this section. He likes the chew and flavor the best. I use half "00" flour and half all-purpose flour, which yields dough that's thin and crispy enough for pizza but sturdy enough to be used for an overstuffed calzone. If you like dough with "crispy, bubbly bumps"—which John especially loves—this dough is for you. My personal favorite is the two- to three-day slow-rise Naples Pizza Dough (see right), but this processor dough is so easy and quick that it has become a go-to.

1 envelope active dry yeast
¾ cup warm water (105° to 115°F)
2 tablespoons EVOO, plus more for the bowl
1 cup "00" flour, plus more for dusting
1 cup all-purpose flour
1 teaspoon sugar
1 teaspoon kosher salt

In a small bowl, stir the yeast, warm water, and EVOO and let stand for about 5 minutes.

In a food processor with the dough blade, combine the flours, sugar, and salt and pulse a few times. With the machine running, stream in the yeast mixture to form a sticky dough. Turn the dough out onto a "00"-floured surface and knead just until smooth, a minute or so. Oil a bowl, put the dough in the bowl, cover with a kitchen towel, and let stand for 1 hour.

Cut the dough into 4 pieces with a bench scraper and knead each piece a few turns on a floured surface, then roll out to 10- to 12-inch rounds and place on a "00"-floured peel for topping. (Or if you want to make the dough ahead, wrap and refrigerate or freeze the 4 pieces of dough. Thaw the frozen dough in the refrigerator overnight, or let the chilled dough come to room temp for 40 to 45 minutes before using.)

NAPLES PIZZA DOUGH (PASTA DA PIZZA)

MAKES ABOUT 2 POUNDS (ENOUGH FOR FOUR 10- TO 12-INCH INDIVIDUAL PIZZAS)

This is a slow-rise (2 to 3 days) dough for traditional Naples-style pizza.

2 cups warm water (105° to 115°F)
¾ teaspoon active dry yeast
2 tablespoons sugar or acacia honey
2 tablespoons EVOO, plus more for brushing
5½ cups "00" flour, or half "00" flour and half all-purpose flour, plus more for dusting
2 teaspoons kosher salt

In a stand mixer fitted with the dough hook, combine the water, yeast, sugar, and EVOO and let stand for 10 minutes.

In a separate bowl, combine the flour and salt. With the mixer running, slowly add the flour to the yeast mixture until a dough forms, 7 to 8 minutes.

Transfer the dough to an oiled baking sheet, cover with a towel, and let stand for 1 hour. Cut the dough into 4 pieces and roll into balls. Place them back on the baking sheet and brush lightly with oil, cover tightly with plastic wrap, and refrigerate for 2 to 3 days before using.

"00" FLOUR

Also called tipo "00" flour, this is a type of Italian flour that is favored for making pizza dough. It is very finely milled (the "00" is a measure of that). Very fine flour like this tends to need a little less liquid to hydrate it, so if you substitute all-purpose flour for "00" flour, you might have to use a little more water.

PIZZA SAUCE WITH BALSAMIC VINEGAR

This sweet, tangy sauce is fantastic on pizzas topped with meats and/or mushrooms. It also makes a great dipper (warm and let simmer for a few minutes) for garlic toast or bruschetta as well.

1 (28- to 32-ounce) can San Marzano tomatoes (look for DOP on the label)
2 small cloves garlic, smashed
1 tablespoon EVOO
2 teaspoons aged balsamic vinegar (the thicker and sweeter, the better)
1 teaspoon fresh oregano leaves
Salt and pepper
A few fresh basil leaves

In a food processor, combine the tomatoes, garlic, EVOO, vinegar, oregano, salt, pepper, and 2 basil leaves. Puree. Transfer to a small saucepan and simmer gently to thicken a bit, about 15 minutes. Transfer to a bowl, let cool to room temp, and add a few torn basil leaves.

NAPLES PIZZA SAUCE

Simmering is an optional step here, and gives you, obviously, a sauce that's a little thicker, but many *pizzaioli* (pizza professionals) use the tomatoes straight from the can once the tomatoes have been hand-crushed or put through a food mill.

1 (28- to 32-ounce) can San Marzano tomatoes (look for DOP on the label)
1 teaspoon kosher salt
EVOO

Hand-crush the tomatoes into a saucepan and add the juices from the can. Stir in the salt and a drizzle of EVOO. Simmer until thickened, about 15 minutes. Let cool to room temp.

PIZZA MARGHERITA

The ingredients here are for an individual 10- to 12-inch pizza. For more pizzas, just multiply the ingredients by the number of people you are serving.

1 ball Naples Pizza Dough (page 87) or One-Hour Dough (page 87)
Flour, for dusting
Fine semolina, for dusting the peel
¼ to ⅓ cup Naples Pizza Sauce (see left)
4 ounces fresh mozzarella cheese (buffalo or fior di latte), thinly sliced
A handful of fresh basil leaves, torn
EVOO, for drizzling

Make the dough. When you're ready to make the pizza, preheat the oven and a pizza stone (see How to Bake Pizza and Calzones, page 86).

Roll the dough out on a floured surface to a 10- to 12-inch round and transfer to a semolina-dusted pizza peel. Slather the sauce over the dough with the back of a spoon, leaving a 1-inch border. Top with the mozzarella.

Bake or broil according to the directions. When you remove the pizza from the oven, top with basil and a few turns of EVOO.

VARIATION

Fresh Tomato Margherita

When the garden is bursting with cherry and grape tomatoes, we sprinkle a few fresh quartered tomatoes over the sauce before the pizza goes in the oven. Cherry and grape tomatoes are always in season at the grocery store, so try this add-in if you want to add sweetness and more texture. Also, we often drizzle our homemade spicy pepperoncini oil rather than EVOO on the pizza, and we all like a sprinkle of flaky sea salt.

SFINCIONE (SICILIAN PIZZA)

This recipe makes a 13 x 18-inch rectangular pizza. When you make the Same-Day Dough for this, you will end up with an extra portion of dough that will make a small (12-inch) round or square pizza. If you want to make a second smaller pizza, so you can use all the dough, just make 1½ times the topping ingredients. Otherwise, just wrap and freeze the additional dough for another day or use.

1½ pounds Same-Day Dough (page 86)

¼ cup EVOO, plus more for oiling the pan

4 flat anchovy fillets

A fat pinch of crushed red pepper flakes

2 large onions, halved and thinly sliced

4 cloves garlic, sliced or chopped

1 (28- to 32-ounce) can San Marzano tomatoes (look for DOP on the label)

1 scant teaspoon sugar

1 teaspoon dried oregano

Salt and black pepper

1 pound caciocavallo or fior di latte cheese (fresh mozzarella), thinly sliced

½ cup freshly grated Pecorino Romano cheese

Make the dough. When you're ready to make the pizza, portion out the 1½ pounds you need for this recipe according to the directions in the Sicilian-Style Pizza variation on page 86.

In a Dutch oven, heat the EVOO (4 turns of the pan) over medium heat. Add the anchovies, cover the pot with a splatter screen or lid, and shake until the anchovies begin to break up. Reduce the heat a bit, uncover, and stir until the anchovies melt into the oil. Stir in the red pepper flakes, then add the onions and stir for 15 minutes to soften and sweeten them. Add the garlic and cook, stirring, for 5 minutes more. Hand-crush the tomatoes as you add them to the pot, then add the juices from the can. Add the sugar, oregano, and a bit of salt and black pepper and simmer to cook the tomatoes down, about 15 minutes more. Taste the sauce and adjust the seasonings. Remove from the heat.

Preheat the oven to 425°F. Lightly oil a 13 x 18-inch rimmed baking sheet.

Roll out the dough and press it into the pan. Arrange the sliced cheese evenly over the dough. Top the cheese with the tomato-onion sauce and sprinkle with the pecorino.

Bake until crispy and browned on the bottom and bubbling at the edges, about 25 minutes. Let cool for 5 to 10 minutes, then cut and serve.

BASICS

FRESH MOZZARELLA AND PIZZA

Fresh mozzarella cheese is so buttery and delicate, but it can be a little wet on pizzas. So I remove mine from its container or liquid or pouch the day before I make the pizza and wrap it in plain paper towels, then let it dry out a bit in the fridge overnight. It makes it easier to handle and slice or shred or dice (for any recipe, not just pizza). For our pizzas, I use fior di latte (fresh cow's milk mozzarella) from an Italian market.

RICOTTA, WALNUT, AND ZUCCHINI PIZZA

SERVES 1

1 ball Naples Pizza Dough
(page 87) or One-Hour Dough
(page 87), or 2 balls very thin
Same-Day Dough (page 86)

½ cup fresh ricotta cheese

¼ cup walnuts, toasted

¼ cup milk

2 tablespoons freshly grated
Parmigiano-Reggiano cheese

Freshly grated nutmeg

3 tablespoons olive oil

1 small firm zucchini, or 6 to 8
baby zucchini, thinly sliced

2 large cloves garlic, chopped or
thinly sliced

½ teaspoon ground fennel or
fennel pollen

Salt and pepper

A handful of fresh flat-leaf parsley
tops, chopped

Flour, for dusting

Fine semolina or cornmeal, for
dusting the peel

¼ to ⅓ pound thinly sliced
smoked mozzarella or
fior di latte cheese

4 zucchini flowers, stamens
removed, halved (optional)

Make the dough. When you're ready to make the pizza, preheat the oven and a pizza stone (see How to Bake Pizza and Calzones, page 86).

In a food processor, combine the ricotta, walnuts, milk, Parm, and a few grates of nutmeg. Puree into a thick sauce. Add another splash of milk if the sauce is too thick to spread on the dough.

In a medium skillet, heat the oil (3 turns of the pan) over medium-high heat. When the oil smokes, add the zucchini and lightly brown, 2 to 3 minutes on each side. Add the garlic, fennel, salt, and pepper and stir for a minute. Remove from the heat and add the parsley.

Roll the dough out on a floured surface to a 10- to 12-inch round and transfer to a semolina-dusted pizza peel. Top with the walnut-ricotta cream, mozzarella, zucchini, and zucchini flowers (if using).

Bake or broil according to the directions.

PUTTANESCA PIZZA

SERVES 1

The secret of this pizza is the anchovy oil that's brushed all over the dough before baking. The same method is also the base for my White Clam Pizza (page 93). I like to bake the tomatoes and mozzarella on the pizza, except for in the summer when I just bake the dough simply with the anchovy oil and then top with cold tomatoes and cheese for a refreshing but hearty raw sauce.

ANCHOVY OIL:

2 tablespoons olive oil

4 flat anchovy fillets

2 cloves garlic, sliced or chopped

Pinch of crushed red pepper
flakes

PIZZA:

1 ball Same-Day Dough (page 86),
One-Hour Dough (page 87), or
Naples Pizza Dough (page 87)

Flour, for dusting

Fine semolina or cornmeal, for
dusting the peel

½ pint cherry or grape tomatoes,
quartered

¼ pound fresh mozzarella cheese
(buffalo or fior di latte), finely
diced

A small handful of oil-cured olives,
pitted and chopped

1 tablespoon capers, drained

A small handful of thinly sliced or
chopped red onion

A fat handful of fresh flat-leaf
parsley leaves, chopped

4 to 6 marinated white anchovies

2 or 3 fresh basil leaves, torn

Make the anchovy oil: In a small skillet, heat the oil (2 turns of the pan) over medium heat. Add the anchovies, cover the pan with a splatter screen or lid, and shake until the anchovies begin to break up. Reduce the heat a bit, uncover, and stir until the anchovies melt into the oil. Stir in the garlic and red pepper flakes and cook for 1 minute. Remove from the heat.

Make the pizza: Make the dough. When you're ready to make the pizza, preheat the oven and a pizza stone (see How to Bake Pizza and Calzones, page 86).

Roll the dough out on a floured surface to a 12-inch round and transfer to a semolina-dusted pizza peel. Brush the dough with the anchovy oil and top with the tomatoes and mozzarella.

Bake or broil according to the directions. When you remove the pizza from the oven, top with the olives, capers, onion, parsley, white anchovies, and basil.

CARAMELIZED LEMON PIZZA

My mother loves lemons so much that her nickname is "Mamacello," based on her affection for *limoncello*, a lemon liqueur. She loves this pizza. The trick is to develop the sugars in the sliced lemons before the pizza goes into the oven. It's a tart, sweet, and delicious mix of flavors. Sometimes I add a few dollops of fresh ricotta spiked with thyme to this pizza as well.

1 ball Same-Day Dough (page 86), One-Hour Dough (page 87), or Naples Pizza Dough (page 87)

1 tablespoon olive oil

6 slices organic lemon

Flour, for dusting

Fine semolina or cornmeal, for dusting the peel

¼ pound smoked fresh mozzarella cheese (buffalo or fior di latte), sliced

2 tablespoons freshly grated Pecorino Romano cheese

2 teaspoons grated lemon zest (from an organic lemon)

6 to 8 fresh basil leaves

EVOO, for drizzling

Make the dough. When you're ready to make the pizza, preheat the oven and a pizza stone (see How to Bake Pizza and Calzones, page 86).

In a small skillet, heat the oil (1 turn of the pan) over medium-high heat. When it ripples, add the lemon slices and cook, turning occasionally, until tender and caramelized, about 3 minutes.

Roll the dough out on a floured surface to a 12-inch round and transfer to a semolina-dusted pizza peel. Top with both cheeses and the lemon zest. Arrange the caramelized lemon slices and basil on top and drizzle with EVOO to protect them in the oven.

Bake or broil according to the directions.

THE RACHAEL

Since I was 11 or 12 years old, I have been eating pizza at the bar in a family run Italian American restaurant, called the Harvest, in Queensbury, New York. After I'd been ordering the same pizza for a couple of decades, they named it after me on their menu. Their crust is a secret recipe and tastes more like a crispy biscuit than traditional dough. When I make a version of it at home (they do close once a year so everyone can take a vacation), I make a cracker-thin Same-Day Dough or One-Hour Dough, but a deep-dish pan pizza dough or focaccia would make a tasty base as well.

1 ball Same-Day Dough (page 86) or One-Hour Dough (page 87)

Flour, for dusting

Fine semolina or cornmeal, for dusting the peel

⅓ cup Pizza Sauce with Balsamic Vinegar (page 88)

1½ cups shredded low-moisture supermarket mozzarella cheese

A sprinkle of dried Italian seasoning or oregano

A sprinkle of granulated garlic

½ cup thinly sliced green bell pepper

½ cup thinly sliced red onions

¼ cup sliced pickled Italian cherry peppers, or sliced banana peppers if you can't find hot cherry peppers

Make the dough. When you're ready to make the pizza, preheat the oven and a pizza stone (see How to Bake Pizza and Calzones, page 86).

Roll the dough out on a floured surface to a 10- to 12-inch round and transfer to a semolina-dusted pizza peel. Top with the pizza sauce, spreading it to the edge of the dough. Top with the mozzarella, oregano, garlic, bell pepper, onion, and cherry peppers.

Bake or broil according to the directions.

CAPRICCIOSA PIZZA

This pizza has a little something for every taste or mood, all on one pizza: mushrooms, artichokes, ham, and olives. When in season, you can use freshly shaved baby artichokes (cut with a mandoline) rather than packaged artichoke hearts. You can layer the toppings evenly around the pizza or section them into four quadrants: plain cheese and basil, ham, mushroom, and artichoke and olive.

1 ball One-Hour Dough (page 87) or Naples Pizza Dough (page 87)

Flour, for dusting

Fine semolina or cornmeal, for dusting the peel

⅓ cup Naples Pizza Sauce (page 88)

¼ pound fresh mozzarella cheese, thinly sliced

A few fresh basil leaves, torn

EVOO, for drizzling

4 thin slices prosciutto cotto (cooked ham)

⅓ cup Marsala Mushrooms (page 331)

⅓ cup sliced artichoke hearts (see Tip)

A small handful of olives, oil-cured or another variety, pitted

Make the dough. When you're ready to make the pizza, preheat the oven and a pizza stone (see How to Bake Pizza and Calzones, page 86).

Roll the dough out on a floured surface to a 12-inch round and transfer to a semolina-dusted pizza peel. Top with the pizza sauce, mozzarella, and basil. If arranging in quadrants, leave one-quarter of the pie as is (Margherita-style) and drizzle with a little EVOO. In the next quadrant, layer the ham. In the next quadrant, top with the mushrooms. In the final quadrant, arrange the artichokes and olives. If you combine the toppings, simply distribute them evenly.

Bake or broil according to the directions.

LOOK FOR packages of grilled artichoke hearts in the produce section or use frozen artichoke hearts, thawed or steamed and sliced. In season, use fresh baby artichokes. Shave them with a mandoline and dress them with lemon juice, EVOO, salt, and pepper.

│ VARIATION │

Capricciosa with Egg

Scatter a chopped hard-boiled egg over the pizza once it comes out of the oven. Or top the pizza with an over-easy egg and mix the creamy yolk into the toppings with your fork and knife.

BUTTERNUT PIZZA WITH SAGE AND GORGONZOLA

I love this pizza because of its earthy, layered flavors and texture. It reminds me of my Butternut Squash Galette (page 16), which I make often for brunch. If you like this pizza, try that galette some Sunday brunch, soon.

1 ball Same-Day Dough (page 86), One-Hour Dough (page 87), or Naples Pizza Dough (page 87)

1 tablespoon olive oil

1 tablespoon butter

¼ small-medium butternut squash, peeled and thinly sliced

½ small onion, thinly sliced

Salt and pepper

Freshly grated nutmeg

5 or 6 fresh sage leaves, thinly sliced

Flour, for dusting

Fine semolina or cornmeal, for dusting the peel

¼ cup crumbled dry Gorgonzola cheese, or a few dollops of Gorgonzola dolce cheese

¼ pound Fontina Val d'Aosta cheese, shredded on the large holes of a box grater

EVOO, for drizzling

Make the dough. When you're ready to make the pizza, preheat the oven and a pizza stone (see How to Bake Pizza and Calzones, page 86).

In a medium skillet, heat the oil (1 turn of the pan) over medium heat. Melt in the butter. Add the sliced squash and the onion. Season with salt, pepper, and nutmeg and cook until tender-crisp, 7 to 8 minutes. Add the sage and toss.

Roll the dough out on a floured surface to a 10- to 12-inch round and transfer to a semolina-dusted pizza peel.

Top the dough with the butternut mixture, dot with Gorgonzola, and cover with Fontina. Drizzle with EVOO.

Bake or broil according to the directions.

WHITE CLAM PIZZA

I use the same anchovy oil to brush this pizza as I use on my Puttanesca Pizza (page 90).

1 ball Same-Day Dough (page 86), One-Hour Dough (page 87), or Naples Pizza Dough (page 87)

Anchovy Oil (from Puttanesca Pizza; see page 90)

Flour, for dusting

Fine semolina or cornmeal, for dusting the peel

¼ pound fresh mozzarella cheese (buffalo or fior di latte)

1 (6.5-ounce) can clams, drained, 2 tablespoons of juice reserved

½ tablespoon fresh thyme leaves, chopped

1 teaspoon grated lemon zest (from an organic lemon)

Pepper

A small handful of fresh flat-leaf parsley tops, chopped

Lemon wedge

EVOO, for drizzling

Make the dough. When you're ready to make the pizza, preheat the oven and a pizza stone (see How to Bake Pizza and Calzones, page 86).

Make the anchovy oil.

Roll the dough out on a floured surface to a 10- to 12-inch round and transfer to a semolina-dusted pizza peel. Brush the dough with the anchovy oil. Top with the mozzarella, clams, clam juice, thyme, lemon zest, and a few grinds of pepper.

Bake or broil according to the directions. When you remove the pizza from the oven, top with the parsley, the juice of a lemon wedge, and a drizzle of EVOO.

PIZZA WITH ROASTED GARLIC, POTATO, SAGE, FONTINA, AND TRUFFLE

SERVES 1

1 head garlic, top cut off to expose the cloves

3 tablespoons EVOO, plus more for drizzling

Salt and pepper

1 ball Same-Day Dough (page 86) or One-Hour Dough (page 87)

Flour, for dusting

Fine semolina or cornmeal, for dusting the peel

2 or 3 baby potatoes, thinly sliced with a mandoline

5 or 6 fresh sage leaves, thinly sliced

¼ pound Fontina Val d'Aosta cheese, shredded on the large holes of a box grater

3 tablespoons freshly grated Parmigiano-Reggiano cheese

Real truffle oil or freshly shaved truffles, when in season

Preheat the oven to 400°F. Drizzle the garlic with some EVOO and season with salt and pepper. Wrap in foil and roast until tender and caramel in color, about 40 minutes. Squeeze the roasted garlic from the skins and paste the cloves with the side of your knife. In a small bowl, combine the garlic paste with 3 tablespoons EVOO.

Make the dough. When you're ready to make the pizza, preheat the oven and a pizza stone (see How to Bake Pizza and Calzones, page 86).

Roll the dough out on a floured surface to a 10- to 12-inch round and transfer to a semolina-dusted pizza peel. Slather the dough evenly with the roasted garlic paste, top with a thin layer of potatoes, season with salt and pepper, scatter the sage over the top, and sprinkle evenly with the Fontina and Parm.

Bake or broil according to the directions. When you remove the pizza from the oven, top with a little truffle oil (or EVOO and shaved truffles).

MONTANARA (FRIED PIZZA DOUGH)

MAKES 2 FRIED PIZZAS; SERVES 4

Montanara, aka *pizza fritta*, is fried Neapolitan-style pizza. This needs no sales pitch, right? The title sells it: fried dough. In addition to the gremolata-and-burrata-topped version, you could also make it Margherita-style (see Variation).

1 pound Same-Day Dough (page 86) or One-Hour Dough (page 87), cut into 2 pieces

Flour, for dusting

Canola or sunflower oil, for frying

¼ cup chopped fresh flat-leaf parsley

1 garlic clove, minced

Grated zest of 1 organic lemon

Crushed red pepper flakes

Burrata cheese

Make the dough. Roll each piece of dough out on a floured surface into a 10- to 12-inch round.

Fill a cast-iron skillet with ½ inch of oil and heat the oil to 365° to 375°F (use a deep-fry thermometer). Flash-fry the dough for 90 seconds on each side until deep golden. Drain on a cooling rack lined with paper towels.

Make the gremolata: On a cutting board, chop the parsley, garlic, and lemon zest. Top each fried dough with gremolata and a sprinkle of red pepper flakes while still hot. Place the burrata in the center of the dough and break it open at the table. Serve with a serrated knife for cutting off pieces of fried dough.

VARIATION

Margherita-Style Fried Pizza

Make the dough. When ready to make the pizza, preheat the oven and a pizza stone in the lower third of the oven (see How to Bake Pizza and Calzones, page 86). Roll out and fry the dough as described above. Transfer to a pizza peel. Top the dough with ¼ to ⅓ cup tomato-basil sauce and ¼ pound thinly sliced fresh mozzarella cheese. Turn the oven to broil and broil until the cheese is bubbling. When the pizza comes out of the oven, top with torn fresh basil leaves.

RICOTTA, FRIED GREEN TOMATO, AND ZUCCHINI FLOWER PIZZA

For this pizza, we typically use leftover fried green tomatoes from a weekend brunch or lunch, especially when we are up to our ears in green tomatoes. But in case you don't happen to be like us, with extra fried green tomatoes on hand, I've included instructions for making just enough for this pizza.

FRIED GREEN TOMATOES:

Salt

1 large green tomato, cut into four slices (¼ to ½ inch thick)

Canola, vegetable, or sunflower oil, for frying

Flour, for dredging

1 large free-range organic egg

⅓ cup fine dry bread crumbs or panko bread crumbs

3 tablespoons fine-grind cornmeal

3 tablespoons grated pecorino cheese

A pinch of ground fennel

A pinch of crushed red pepper flakes

PIZZA:

1 ball Same-Day Dough (page 86), One-Hour Dough (page 87), or Naples Pizza Dough (page 87)

½ cup fresh cow or sheep's milk ricotta cheese

1 tablespoon fresh thyme leaves

½ teaspoon grated lemon zest (from an organic lemon)

EVOO, for drizzling

Flour, for dusting

Fine semolina or cornmeal, for dusting the peel

A few fresh basil leaves

A few zucchini flowers, stamens removed, halved lengthwise

¼ pound smoked fresh mozzarella cheese (buffalo or fior di latte)

Make the fried green tomatoes: Salt the tomatoes on each side and let them weep on a kitchen towel for 20 minutes.

Meanwhile, pour ½ inch of oil into a large cast-iron skillet or other shallow heavy-bottomed pan and heat the oil to 350°F (use a deep-fry thermometer).

Set up a breading station: Line up 3 shallow bowls on the counter. Put the dredging flour in one. Beat the egg in the second. In the third, mix the bread crumbs, cornmeal, pecorino, fennel, and red pepper flakes.

Pat the tomato slices dry. Coat the tomatoes in the flour, then the egg, and finally in the bread crumb mixture. Fry the tomatoes for 2 to 3 minutes per side. Drain on a cooling rack.

Make the pizza: Make the dough and when ready to make the pizza, preheat the oven and a pizza stone (see How to Bake Pizza and Calzones, page 86).

In a bowl, combine the ricotta, thyme, lemon zest, and a drizzle of EVOO.

Roll the dough out on a floured surface to a 10- to 12-inch round and transfer to a semolina-dusted pizza peel. Spread the ricotta mixture over the dough. Scatter the basil and zucchini flowers over the dough and top with the fried green tomatoes and mozzarella.

Bake or broil according to the directions.

GRILLED PIZZA BIANCA

This is a white pizza that we grill outdoors in the summer, usually rounding out a buffet of stuffed and grilled vegetables and multiple salads from the garden. I make this dough with all-purpose flour, as it produces dough that stands up better on the grill. The pizza dough is smoky from the grill and the toppings are buttery and tangy. Truffle honey gives it a sweet finish. Amazing.

DOUGH:
1 envelope active dry yeast
2 cups warm water (105° to 115°F)
5 cups all-purpose flour, plus more for dusting
1 tablespoon flaky sea salt
¼ cup EVOO, plus more for the bowl
2 to 3 tablespoons fresh rosemary leaves, chopped

PIZZA:
Oil, for the grill grates
2 cups fresh cow or sheep's milk ricotta cheese
¾ pound ripe Taleggio cheese
2 cups freshly grated young pecorino or Pecorino Romano cheese (about ⅓ pound)
Truffle honey or acacia honey and/ or freshly shaved truffle, if in season
Sea salt
A few baby arugula leaves (optional)

Make the dough: In a bowl, combine the yeast and warm water and let stand for a few minutes. In the bowl of a stand mixer fitted with the dough hook, combine the yeast mixture with the flour, salt, EVOO, and rosemary and mix on medium speed to form a sticky dough. Turn out onto a floured surface and knead for 10 minutes. Place in an oiled bowl and cover with a kitchen towel. Let stand for 3 hours.

Make the pizza: Heat an outdoor grill to medium-high or prepare coals. When ready to grill, brush the grill grates with oil.

Stretch the dough into 2 large or 4 small ovals. Grill the pizza bases for about 2 minutes. Flip and top with the ricotta, dollops of Taleggio, and grated pecorino. Close the lid to melt the toppings, then transfer to a cutting board, drizzle with honey and/or add shaved truffles, sprinkle with sea salt, cut, and serve, scattered with a few baby arugula leaves, if desired.

FINOCCHIONA (FENNEL SALAMI) PIZZA

SERVES 1

In New York, my favorite pizza place is Motorino on 12th Street. They named a white pizza with fennel salami after me, but it's my husband, John, who is addicted to this one. (I like spicy soppressata; see Hot Soppressata Pizza, page 101.) I dress the arugula used to top the pizza with a little lemon and EVOO to brighten things up.

1 ball Naples Pizza Dough (page 87) or One-Hour Dough (page 87)

Flour, for dusting

Fine semolina or cornmeal, for dusting the peel

¼ pound fresh mozzarella cheese (buffalo or fior di latte), thinly sliced

2 tablespoons freshly grated pecorino cheese

4 to 6 slices finocchiona (sweet fennel salami), enough to cover the pizza (it will depend on the diameter of the salami)

A fat handful of arugula

Juice of 1 lemon wedge

EVOO, for drizzling

Make the dough. When you're ready to make the pizza, preheat the oven and a pizza stone (see How to Bake Pizza and Calzones, page 86).

Roll the dough out on a floured surface to a 10- to 12-inch round and transfer to a semolina-dusted pizza peel. Top with the mozzarella and pecorino. Arrange the salami in a single layer over the cheeses.

Bake or broil according to the directions.

Meanwhile, lightly dress the arugula with lemon juice and EVOO.

When you remove the pizza from the oven, top it with the dressed arugula.

REGINA PIZZA (TUNA AND TOMATO)

SERVES 1

Whenever I travel to Rome, my very first stop is a pizza place on via Della Croce near the Spanish Steps. I always order the same thing: Regina Pizza with tuna, tomatoes, and white onions. Make this with the Same-Day Dough and roll it as thin as possible, ¹⁄₁₆ inch. Regina pizza is cracker-thin, and for me, it is a perfect thing.

1 ball Same-Day Dough (page 86)

Flour, for dusting

Fine semolina or cornmeal, for dusting the peel

¼ pound fior di latte cheese (fresh mozzarella), thinly sliced

2 tablespoons freshly grated Pecorino Romano cheese

6 very thin slices beefsteak or vine tomato

4 ounces good-quality line-caught canned tuna, flaked

1 small or ½ medium white onion, thinly sliced

EVOO, for drizzling

A fat sprinkle of crushed red pepper flakes

A small handful of fresh flat-leaf parsley tops, chopped

6 fresh basil leaves torn

Make the dough. When you're ready to make the pizza, preheat the oven and a pizza stone (see How to Bake Pizza and Calzones, page 86).

Roll the dough out cracker-thin (¹⁄₁₆ inch) on a floured surface and transfer to a semolina-dusted pizza peel. Top the dough with the mozzarella and pecorino. Arrange the tomatoes, tuna, and onion on top. Drizzle with EVOO to protect them in the oven.

Bake or broil according to the directions for thin-crust pizza on page 86. When you remove the pizza from the oven, top it with red pepper flakes, parsley, and basil.

HOT SOPPRESSATA PIZZA

SERVES 1

This is spicy and delicious. It's my at-home version of another Motorino (12th Street and First Avenue, NYC) favorite. I always order a side of flat-leaf parsley and red onions when I order this, so I added it to my recipe.

1 ball Naples Pizza Dough (page 87) or One-Hour Dough (page 87)

Flour, for dusting

Fine semolina or cornmeal, for dusting the peel

⅓ cup Pizza Sauce with Balsamic Vinegar (page 88)

¼ pound fresh mozzarella cheese, sliced

2 to 3 tablespoons freshly grated pecorino cheese

6 to 8 slices hot soppressata

Thinly sliced red onion

Coarsely chopped fresh flat-leaf parsley tops

Make the dough. When you're ready to make the pizza, preheat the oven and a pizza stone (see How to Bake Pizza and Calzones, page 86).

Roll the dough out on a floured surface to a 10- to 12-inch round and transfer to a semolina-dusted pizza peel. Spread the pizza sauce over the dough in a thin layer using the back of a spoon. Cover the sauce with mozzarella, pecorino, and soppressata.

Bake or broil according to the directions. When you remove the pizza from the oven, top with red onion and parsley.

MORTADELLA PIZZA WITH PISTACHIO PESTO

SERVES 1

Serve this pizza with spicy mustard. That's what my husband, John, does.

1 ball Naples Pizza Dough (page 87) or One-Hour Dough (page 87)

¼ cup pistachios

1 clove garlic, smashed

2 to 3 tablespoons freshly grated pecorino cheese

¼ cup fresh mint leaves

½ cup fresh flat-leaf parsley tops

Juice of ½ lemon

3 tablespoons EVOO, plus more for drizzling

Salt and pepper

Flour, for dusting

Fine semolina or cornmeal, for dusting the peel

2 or 3 slices mortadella, quartered

3 or 4 fresh basil leaves

¼ pound fresh mozzarella cheese, sliced

Make the dough. When you're ready to make the pizza, preheat the oven and a pizza stone (see How to Bake Pizza and Calzones, page 86).

In a food processor, combine the pistachios, garlic, pecorino, mint, parsley, lemon juice, EVOO, salt, and pepper and pulse into a pesto. Add a small splash of water if the pesto seems too thick to spread.

Roll the dough out on a floured surface to a 10- to 12-inch round and transfer to a semolina-dusted pizza peel. Spread the pesto in a thin layer over the dough. Top with the mortadella, then the basil and mozzarella. Drizzle with EVOO to protect it in the oven.

Bake or broil according to the directions.

FOCACCIA

Focaccia is delicious on its own but makes wonderful sandwiches, panini, and even buns for burgers. Additionally, stale focaccia makes a great instant pizza: just split, toast in a pan on each side, top with sauce and cheese or topping of choice, and broil for 1 to 2 minutes.

1 envelope active dry yeast

1½ cups warm water (112° to 115°F)

1 tablespoon sugar

4 cups all-purpose flour, plus more for dusting

1½ teaspoons kosher salt, plus more for sprinkling

Leaves from 2 large sprigs fresh rosemary

⅔ cup olive oil

In a bowl, combine the yeast, warm water, and sugar and let stand for 10 minutes.

In the bowl of a stand mixer fitted with the dough hook, combine the flour, salt, and rosemary. With the mixer on medium speed, slowly add half the oil and the yeast mixture and mix to form a dough. Turn the dough out onto a floured surface and knead the dough for 5 to 6 minutes. Place the dough in an oiled bowl, cover, and set aside in a warm place to rise for 1 hour.

Knead the dough a second time, then stretch or roll it into a large flatbread. Use your fingers to push dimples into the dough, literally making small holes here and there. Place the dough on an oiled rimmed baking sheet. Using what oil you have left, lightly brush the top of the dough as well. Cover with a kitchen towel and let stand for 45 minutes.

Preheat the oven to 425°F. Sprinkle what should be well-dimpled dough with a bit of salt.

Bake until light golden and even in color, about 30 minutes. Let cool, then cut into large squares, which can be halved to make sandwiches.

CHICAGO-STYLE PIZZA

Fresh focaccia dough makes the most insane deep-dish pizza crust. Brush a cast-iron skillet liberally with EVOO, line with the dough, fill with your toppings, and heat on the stovetop to start the bottom crust. Then transfer to a preheated 400°F oven to bake through.

VARIATION

Cherry Focaccia

When cherries are in season, this focaccia is a delicious addition to any brunch or lunch. Prepare the dough as directed. Just before baking, top with a couple handfuls of halved pitted cherries, brush the dough with more oil, and sprinkle lightly with coarse sugar and a little sea salt. Bake as directed.

GARLIC LOVERS' CALZONE SAUCE

MAKES ABOUT 2 CUPS

3 tablespoons EVOO
3 large cloves garlic, finely chopped or grated
1 small sprig fresh oregano
1 (28- to 32-ounce) can San Marzano tomatoes (look for DOP on the label)
2 or 3 fresh basil leaves, torn
1 teaspoon sea salt or kosher salt

In a saucepan, heat the EVOO (3 turns of the pan) over medium-low heat. Add the garlic and oregano and stir for 1 or 2 minutes. Hand-crush the tomatoes as you add them to the pan, then add the juices from the can. Stir in the basil and salt. Partially cover, bring to a bubble, then reduce the heat and simmer for 20 minutes. Let cool to room temperature.

NAPLES-STYLE CALZONE WITH HAM AND SALAMI

MAKES 4 CALZONES (SERVES 4)

John loves this calzone. He can devour one in less than 3 minutes, then looks up longingly at me when it's gone, asking for a second. This calzone is topped with sauce then baked, but John likes additional warm, garlicky sauce on the side for dipping.

1 pound Naples Pizza Dough (page 87) or One-Hour Dough (page 87)
Flour, for dusting
Fine semolina or "00" flour, for dusting the peel
1½ to 2 cups fresh cow or sheep's milk ricotta cheese, drained
¾ pound fior di latte cheese (fresh mozzarella), cut into small cubes
Leaves from a couple sprigs fresh thyme
8 slices prosciutto cotto (cooked ham), cut into ½-inch-wide strips
16 slices (½ inch thick) finocchiona (sweet fennel salami) or salami of your choice, finely diced
1 cup Naples Pizza Sauce (page 88)
½ to ¾ cup freshly grated Pecorino Romano cheese
A few fresh basil leaves, torn
Garlic Lovers' Calzone Sauce (see left), for serving

Make the dough. When you're ready to make the calzones, preheat the oven and a pizza stone (see How to Bake Pizza and Calzones, page 86).

Cut the dough into 4 portions. On a floured surface, roll out each portion of dough into an oval or rectangle 7 to 8 inches by 10 to 12 inches, and transfer to a semolina-dusted pizza peel.

Spread the ricotta over half the surface of the dough, leaving a small border. Dot the mozzarella over the ricotta and top with thyme. Arrange the ham and salami over the cheese. Brush the edges of the dough with a little water, fold the calzone in half, and press the edges to seal. Prick the top of the calzone 2 or 3 times with the tines of a fork. Spread the top of the calzone with a thin layer of pizza sauce and sprinkle with the pecorino.

Bake or broil according to the directions. Garnish with torn basil. Serve with the garlic sauce for dipping.

RICOTTA, MUSHROOM, AND SAUSAGE CALZONES

MAKES 4 CALZONES (SERVES 4)

This is another favorite of my husband's. What's not to like? Homemade sausage, sherry-laced sliced mushrooms, cheese? All good. He loves a big side of warm, garlicky sauce for dipping—with any calzone. My favorite? I actually make a weird mash-up of this recipe and the recipe for spinach calzone: I make it with these sherry mushrooms, some spinach, a few crumbles of sausage, and a blend of ricotta, pecorino, Parm, and fior di latte (fresh mozzarella).

1 pound Naples Pizza Dough (page 87) or One-Hour Dough (page 87)

2 tablespoons EVOO, plus more for the dough

1 pound Sweet Italian Sausage with Fennel, homemade (page 237) or store-bought, casings removed

12 large cremini mushrooms, thinly sliced

2 large cloves garlic, chopped

1 tablespoon fresh thyme leaves, chopped

Salt and pepper

¼ cup dry sherry

Fine semolina or "00" flour, for dusting the peel

1½ to 2 cups fresh cow or sheep's milk ricotta cheese, drained

½ to ¾ cup freshly grated Pecorino Romano cheese

¾ pound fior di latte cheese (fresh mozzarella), cut into small cubes

1 cup Garlic Lovers' Calzone Sauce (page 104), for serving

Make the dough. When you're ready to make the calzones, preheat the oven and a pizza stone (see How to Bake Pizza and Calzones, page 86).

In a medium skillet, heat 1 tablespoon of the EVOO (1 turn of the pan) over medium-high heat. Add the sausage, breaking it up into crumbles as it browns. Remove from the skillet and set aside. Add the remaining 1 tablespoon EVOO to the pan. Add the mushrooms and cook to brown. Add the garlic, thyme, and salt and pepper and stir for a minute more. Add the sherry and stir until it has evaporated.

Cut the dough into 4 portions. On a floured surface, roll each portion of dough into an oval or rectangle 7 to 8 inches by 10 to 12 inches, and transfer to a semolina-dusted pizza peel.

Spread the ricotta over about half the surface of the dough, leaving a small border. Scatter the pecorino on top. Dot with the mozzarella. Arrange the mushrooms and crumbled sausage over the cheese. Brush the edges of the dough with a little water, fold the calzone in half, and press to seal the edges. Prick the top of the calzone 2 or 3 times with the tines of a fork, then brush the calzone with EVOO.

Bake or broil according to the directions. Pass the garlic sauce at the table for dipping.

CALZONE WITH SPINACH, CAPERS, AND GARLIC

This calzone can be topped with tomato sauce, Naples-style, or simply brushed with a dab of oil and baked. I love to make these in early spring or around Easter because my mom and I enjoyed them on our first trip to Rome many years ago. The mixture of greens is called *verdure del primo maggio*, "greens of the first of May."

1 pound Naples Pizza Dough (page 87) or One-Hour Dough (page 87)

2 tablespoons EVOO, plus more for brushing

3 or 4 flat anchovy fillets (optional, but recommended)

1 bunch scallions or spring onions (white and light green parts), finely chopped

2 or 3 large cloves garlic, finely chopped or grated

A pinch of crushed red pepper flakes

6 to 8 cups stemmed chopped greens: rainbow or Swiss chard, spinach, and/or baby kale

2 tablespoons capote capers, drained

Salt and pepper

Freshly grated nutmeg

Fine semolina or "00" flour, for dusting the peel

1½ to 2 cups fresh cow or sheep's milk ricotta cheese, drained

1 cup shaved pecorino or Parmigiano-Reggiano cheese

¾ pound fior di latte cheese (fresh mozzarella), cut into small cubes

Naples Pizza Sauce (page 88) or Garlic Lovers' Calzone Sauce (page 104), for dipping (optional)

Make the dough. When you're ready to make the calzones, preheat the oven and a pizza stone (see How to Bake Pizza and Calzones, page 86).

In a skillet, heat the EVOO (2 turns of the pan) over medium heat. Add the anchovies, cover the pan with a splatter screen or lid, and shake until the anchovies begin to break up. Reduce the heat a bit, uncover, and stir until the anchovies melt into the oil. Add the scallions, garlic, and red pepper flakes and stir for 1 minute. Add the greens. Stir in the capers and season with salt, pepper, and nutmeg.

Cut the dough into 4 pieces. On a floured surface, roll each piece of dough into an oval or rectangle 7 to 8 inches by 10 to 12 inches, and transfer to a semolina-dusted pizza peel.

Spread the ricotta over about half the surface of the dough, leaving a small border. Scatter a bit of grated pecorino over the ricotta and dot with the mozzarella. Top with the greens (drained of excess liquid).

Brush the edges of the dough with a little water, fold the calzone in half, and pinch the edges to seal. Prick the top of the calzone 2 or 3 times with the tines of a fork and brush lightly with EVOO.

Bake or broil according to the directions. If desired, pass pizza sauce or garlic sauce at the table for dipping.

VARIATION

Spinach and Ricotta Calzone

For a simplified and more traditional calzone with greens, omit the anchovies, red pepper flakes, and capers from the recipe. For the greens, you can use all spinach or, as my family prefers, a half-and-half mix of chopped Swiss chard and spinach. Cook the onions (or small leeks) and garlic in oil. Wilt in the greens and season with salt, pepper, and nutmeg. Drain off the excess liquid from the cooked greens. Roll out, fill, and bake the calzones as directed. Serve with Garlic Lovers' Calzone Sauce (page 104) for dipping.

UN-PIZZAS

Enjoy pizza even when you hold the dough. These two pizzas use polenta instead of pizza dough. (And you can even build a "pizza" on a thin grilled chicken cutlet; see Chicken Paillard, Pizzette-Style, page 297.)

Deep-Dish Polenta "Pizza" with Mushrooms and Sausage

=== SERVES 4 ===

3 tablespoons EVOO, plus more
  for the pan
3 cups chicken stock
1 cup quick-cooking polenta
½ cup freshly grated
  Parmigiano-Reggiano cheese
⅛ teaspoon freshly grated
  nutmeg
Salt and pepper
¾ pound Sweet Italian Sausage
  with Fennel, homemade
  (page 237) or store-bought,
  casings removed
½ pound cremini mushrooms,
  sliced
2 tablespoons fresh thyme
  leaves, chopped
2 large cloves garlic, chopped
1½ cups fresh ricotta cheese,
  drained well
½ pound fresh mozzarella
  cheese, shredded

Preheat the oven to 425°F. Brush a 9-inch cake pan, 9-inch springform pan, or 8-inch square pan with EVOO.

In a saucepan, bring the stock to a low boil. Whisk in the polenta and let it get very thick and fairly tight, 3 to 4 minutes. Stir in the Parm and season with the nutmeg, salt, and pepper. When the polenta is cool enough to handle, use it to line the bottom and sides of the pan, forming a deep-dish crust.

In a large skillet, heat 1 tablespoon of the EVOO (1 turn of the pan) over medium-high heat. Add the sausage, breaking it up into crumbles as it browns. Remove from the skillet and set aside. Add the remaining 2 tablespoons oil (2 turns of the pan) to the skillet. Add the mushrooms and cook until browned. Sprinkle with the thyme and season with salt and pepper. Add the garlic and stir for a minute more.

Fill the "pizza shell" with the ricotta and top with half the sausage and mushrooms. Top with the mozzarella, then top that with the remaining sausage and mushrooms. Bake until browned and bubbling, 20 to 25 minutes.

Deep-Dish Polenta "Pizza" with Spinach and Artichokes

=== SERVES 4 ===

Olive oil, for the pan
3 cups chicken stock
1 cup quick-cooking polenta
½ cup freshly grated
  Parmigiano-Reggiano cheese
⅛ teaspoon freshly grated
  nutmeg
Salt and pepper
1½ cups fresh ricotta cheese,
  drained well
1 cup chopped grilled, canned,
  or frozen artichoke hearts
  (see Tip)
2 tablespoons fresh thyme
  leaves, chopped
2 cloves garlic, grated or pasted
1 teaspoon grated lemon zest
  (from an organic lemon)
1 (10-ounce) box frozen
  chopped spinach, thawed
  and wrung dry in a kitchen
  towel
¾ pound fior di latte cheese
  (fresh mozzarella), shredded

Preheat the oven to 425°F. Brush a 9-inch cake pan, 9-inch springform pan, or 8-inch square pan with oil.

In a saucepan, bring the stock to a low boil. Whisk in the polenta and let it get very thick and fairly tight, 3 to 4 minutes. Stir in the Parm and season with the nutmeg, salt, and pepper. When the polenta is cool enough to handle, use it to line the bottom and sides of the pan, forming a deep-dish crust.

In a bowl, stir the ricotta, artichokes, thyme, garlic, and lemon zest. Pull the spinach into shreds as you add it to the bowl. Season with salt and pepper and stir to combine.

Fill the "pizza shell" with the ricotta mixture and top with the mozzarella. Bake until browned and bubbling, about 20 minutes.

TIP

LOOK FOR packages of grilled artichoke hearts in the produce section or use water-packed canned artichoke hearts or frozen artichoke hearts, thawed or steamed and chopped.

Short Rib Ragu with
Pappardelle (page 135);
Broccoli Rabe and Ricotta
Salata (page 314); and
Marinated Eggplant
(page 32).

CHAPTER 5

PASTA,
GNOCCHI, POLENTA, AND THEIR SAUCES

In my family on big holidays or special occasions, pasta and gnocchi are served as they are in Italy, as *primi piatti*, first courses. But on any given weeknight throughout the year, we have simple pastas and a salad as a quick supper. And the big, rich pasta dishes, like ziti and lasagna, are favorites for Sundays.

For most meals, I use dried pasta, but when I get the time, though, it is hard to top the rich, delicate but comforting appeal of homemade egg tagliatelle with Bolognese.

Whether you have ten minutes or all day to prepare your meals, this section of the book will become the most-used and covered with flour and sauce droplets. These are not recipes—these are translations of hugs, kisses, and pure love. (A word of advice: Only prepare lasagna with homemade pasta for diners you wish to have around for decades. They will never be able to get enough of it.)

EGG PASTA

3 cups "00" flour
1 teaspoon kosher or fine sea salt
3 large free-range organic eggs
1 large free-range organic egg
    yolk
About 2 tablespoons warm water
A fat drizzle of EVOO (1 to
    1½ tablespoons)

On a large work surface, mound the flour and make a well at the center. Sprinkle the flour with the salt. Add the whole eggs, egg yolk, water, and EVOO to the well and mix with a fork. Using the fork, start pulling the flour into the well to make a sticky dough, then work in the flour a little at a time with your hands to fully incorporate. Knead the dough in one direction away from your body, turning it into a smooth and elastic dough, 5 to 10 minutes. Cover with a kitchen towel and let stand for about 30 minutes.

Cut the dough into 4 equal pieces with a bench scraper. Working with one piece of dough at a time (keep the dough that you are not working with under a clean kitchen towel to keep it from drying out), set your pasta machine to the widest setting and pass the dough through. Fold the dough over on itself in thirds and pass through the pasta machine again. Pass the dough through the pasta machine

three more times. Next, pass the dough through the machine decreasing the width with each pass until the dough is at the second to last setting, forming a ¹⁄₁₆-inch-thick sheet. Cut the long sheet in half crosswise and place the sheets on parchment paper dusted with "00" flour. Repeat this process with each piece of dough.

FOR LASAGNA: Use the whole sheet or cut each sheet crosswise into thirds if it is easier to layer them this way.

FOR MALTAGLIATI: This is a hand-torn pasta typically made from dough scraps. I don't actually tear the pasta; I use a small, sharp knife to cut the dough into irregular diamond shapes. I love this shape with White Ragu (page 127) and as the pasta in Pulled Pork with Arugula, Meyer Lemon, and Pasta (page 231).

FOR TAGLIATELLE: Starting at a short end of each sheet, roll it up tightly, then slice the roll crosswise into ribbons between ¼ and ½ inch wide. Separate the bunches into small loose nests and cook in boiling water for 3 minutes. Use a spider to carefully transfer the pasta to a warm serving dish.

FOR PAPPARDELLE: Roll up the sheets as you did for tagliatelle, but cut the ribbons 1 to 1½ inches wide. Cook by the same method.

FOR FILLED PASTA: Cut the dough lengthwise into 3 or 4 extra-wide strips with a small pasta wheel. Then cut squares as wide as you like and fill. Work in batches, filling the pasta completely before cutting another sheet of dough so the sheets do not dry out before you can get them filled. Check out Pear and Pecorino Ravioli (page 171) and Ravioli with Spinach and Four Cheeses (page 172).

A NOTE ON CHEESE
To cheese or not to cheese is really a question for you. Most Italian restaurants will not even give you cheese for a dish made with seafood. However, when you're cooking at home, you're the boss. If you want to put cheese on something like Linguine con Vongole (page 151) or a puttanesca, that's your prerogative.

FLOUR AND WATER PASTA FOR PICI OR STROZZAPRETI

SERVES 6

My favorite pasta, pici (or *pinci* in dialect), which is a hand-rolled fat spaghetti, is made at Taverna del Grappolo Blu in Montalcino, Italy. I can only get there once a year, on our anniversary. The rest of the year, we make our own pici or use dried. If we cut the pasta shorter, 2 to 3 inches, and give a twist to each piece, it becomes a favorite of my husband John's—*strozzapreti*. This is not because the shape tastes or chews any differently, but because he enjoys saying the name—it means "strangle the priest." Ouch!

I love fresh pici with Cherry Tomato Sauce (page 122) and Etruscan-Style Pesto (page 115). My family enjoys dried pici with Roasted Garlic, Tomato, and Red Pepper Sauce (page 142) and in Christmas Pasta (page 135). The dried pasta comes in little nest shapes.

4 cups "00" flour, plus more
    for dusting
1 cup semolina
1½ teaspoons salt
1 fat tablespoon olive oil
About 1 cup warm water

Place the flour and semolina in a large bowl. Stir in the salt and oil and add ⅔ to ¾ cup warm water, stirring to form a sticky dough. Then continue to work in a splash of water more until a big ball forms and you can no longer stir by hand. Transfer the dough to a large work space and knead for 5 to 10 minutes, working in one direction away from your body. Let the dough rest under a kitchen towel for at least 30 minutes and up to a few hours.

FOR PICI: Cut the dough in half and keep half under a towel. Using a floured rolling pin, roll the dough into a large rectangle ⅛ to ¼ inch thick and about 10 inches across. Cut lengthwise into strips ⅛ to ¼ inch wide. Roll the strips into irregular fat spaghetti-like strands and arrange on a large kitchen towel or parchment paper sheets lightly dusted with flour.

FOR STROZZAPRETI: After you roll the pici, cut the pasta dowels into 3-inch pieces and give each one a twist at the middle. Set aside on a kitchen towel or flour-dusted parchment paper.

If not using immediately, the pasta can be frozen for 6 to 8 weeks.

Cook the pasta in salted boiling water for about 5 minutes, or until floating and tender. Do not crowd the pot, cooking in batches if necessary, and use a slotted spoon or spider to transfer the cooked pasta to a warm serving platter.

GNOCCHI

Gnocchi are "gno" big deal to make. I've read countless recipes that make the process sound daunting, difficult, and only for skilled cooks. It's all hype. You'll make it once or twice and get the feel for the right amount of flour for you, but even first time out it will work. It will take less time than you imagined, and the time will pass fast; the repetitive nature of rolling and pinching or cutting the gnocchi is so relaxing it becomes Italian Zen. These little pillows are a hug from the inside out. Serve with Pomodoro Sauce (page 121), any of the pestos on pages 115 to 118, or Brown Butter and Crispy Sage (page 114).

4 large russet (baking) potatoes, unpeeled
Salt
4 large free-range organic egg yolks
½ cup freshly grated Parmigiano-Reggiano cheese
Pepper
Freshly grated nutmeg
2 to 2½ cups "00" flour, plus more for dusting (see Tip)

Depending on how you'd like to cook the potatoes, either preheat the oven to 425°F or bring a pot of water to a boil. Cook the potatoes until very tender, either roasting them for 45 minutes or boiling for 25 to 30 minutes. Let cool completely.

Bring a pot of salted water to a boil. Line a baking sheet with parchment paper.

Peel the potatoes and pass them through a ricer onto a large work surface. Mound the riced potatoes and make a well at the center. Place the egg yolks and Parm in the well. Season the potatoes with salt, pepper, and a little nutmeg. Work the eggs and cheese into the potatoes. Sprinkle 2 cups flour over the potatoes and work it in. If the dough is sticky, sprinkle in a little more flour until the dough is firm enough to roll.

On a floured surface, roll the dough into ropes about ¾ inch in diameter. Cut the ropes into 1-inch lengths (or pillows) or use a gnocchi tool to roll and mark the dumplings. Transfer the gnocchi to the prepared baking sheet.

Cook the gnocchi in small batches of 2 to 3 serving portions in the boiling water until they float and are cooked through. Use a spider or slotted spoon to transfer the cooked gnocchi to a warm serving bowl.

VARIATION

Spinach Gnocchi

Thaw 8 ounces (half a 16-ounce bag) of frozen chopped spinach. Wring dry in a kitchen towel and very finely chop. Measure out ½ cup. Work the spinach into the gnocchi dough after adding the 2 cups flour. Add more flour if the dough is too sticky. Roll, cut, and cook as directed.

TIP

I prefer the lighter texture of "00" flour, but all-purpose flour would work, and has a more familiar bite.

EGG-FREE GNOCCHI

SERVES 6 TO 8

I prefer gnocchi made with egg for many reasons, including flavor and texture, but this recipe made with "00" flour is a delicious alternative when I am cooking for friends who are allergic to eggs.

1 medium large Yukon Gold
    potatoes
Salt
1½ cups "00" flour or all-purpose
    flour, plus more for dusting
1 teaspoon fine sea salt
⅛ teaspoon freshly grated
    nutmeg

In a deep pot, combine the potatoes and cold water to cover. Cover and bring to a boil. Uncover and keep at a low rolling boil until the potatoes are tender, about 30 minutes. Drain and let cool completely. Peel the potatoes.

Bring a pot of salted water to a boil. Line a baking sheet with parchment paper.

Mix the flour, sea salt, and nutmeg on a work surface and make a well in the center. Pass the potatoes through a ricer into the well and work the riced potatoes through the flour, adding a bit more from the well as you work.

On a floured surface, roll the dough into ropes about ¾ inch in diameter. Cut the ropes into 1-inch lengths (or pillows) or use a gnocchi tool to roll and mark the dumplings. Transfer the gnocchi to the prepared baking sheet.

Cook the gnocchi in small batches of 2 to 3 serving portions in the boiling water until they float and are cooked through. Use a spider or slotted spoon to transfer the cooked gnocchi to a warm serving bowl.

BUTTERNUT GNOCCHI

SERVES 6 TO 8

These gnocchi are best with Brown Butter and Crispy Sage (page 114)—a marriage made in food heaven.

1 (3-pound) butternut squash or
    red kurl squash (Hokkaido),
    peeled, halved, and seeded
Olive oil, for drizzling
Salt and pepper
⅛ teaspoon freshly grated
    nutmeg
2 large free-range organic egg
    yolks
2 cups all-purpose flour

Preheat the oven to 400°F.

Cut the squash into thin wedges and dress lightly with oil. Season with salt, pepper, and the nutmeg. Spread on a baking sheet and roast until tender, about 30 minutes. Let cool.

Bring a pot of salted water to a boil. Line a baking sheet with parchment paper.

Pass the squash through a ricer onto a work surface and make a well in the squash. Add the egg yolks to the well and sprinkle the flour over the top, 1 cup at a time, working it into the squash.

Roll the dough into short, 1-inch-diameter ropes, then cut them crosswise into 1-inch pillows. Transfer the gnocchi to the prepared baking sheet.

Cook the gnocchi in small batches of 2 to 3 serving portions in the boiling water until they float and are cooked through. Use a spider or slotted spoon to transfer the cooked gnocchi to a warm serving bowl.

GNUDI

Pronounced "nudie," these are "naked ravioli," or fresh ricotta dumplings—fun to make and even more fun to say. I like to use fresh sheep's milk ricotta in gnudi because it is so tangy. But sheep's milk ricotta can be hard to find. If I'm in Manhattan, I can get it from a wonderful market called Buon Italia in the Chelsea Market. But when I am in upstate New York, I cannot get it, so then I use fresh cow's milk ricotta, which is delicious and buttery in flavor. If you have a little extra time, you can make your own ricotta (see box, page 40); it's easy to do, and the result is simply delicious. Serve with Walnut-Anchovy Sauce (page 118), Mushroom Ragu (page 128), or Prosciutto, Sage, and Mushroom Sauce (page 128).

Salt
1 cup fresh ricotta cheese, homemade (see box, page 40) or store-bought
1 large free-range organic egg
1 large free-range organic egg yolk
⅛ teaspoon freshly grated nutmeg
About ⅓ cup fine dry bread crumbs
¾ cup "00" flour or all-purpose flour
Pepper
½ cup freshly grated Parmigiano-Reggiano or Grana Padano cheese
Semolina or all-purpose flour, for dredging

Bring a pot of salted water to a boil. Line a baking sheet with parchment paper.

In a bowl, combine the ricotta, whole egg, egg yolk, and nutmeg. Add the bread crumbs and flour, season with salt and pepper, and mix well. Work in the grated cheese. Roll the dough into dumplings about the size of golf balls and dredge to lightly coat in semolina or all-purpose flour. Transfer to the prepared baking sheet.

Cook the gnudi in small batches of 2 to 3 serving portions in the boiling water until they float and are cooked through. (Take one out and taste to be sure.) Use a spider or slotted spoon to transfer the cooked gnudi to a warm platter.

BROWN BUTTER AND CRISPY SAGE

Serve with gnocchi, gnudi, or spaghetti squash.

6 ounces (1½ sticks) cold butter, diced
36 fresh sage leaves
Freshly grated nutmeg
Grated Parmigiano-Reggiano cheese, for serving

In a small pan, melt the butter over medium heat and cook until browned, nutty, and fragrant. The butter will foam and then you will see brown bits on the bottom of the pan. When it starts to smell nutty and turn light brown, add the sage leaves, about 12 at a time, and fry until crispy. Drain on paper towels. Pour the browned butter over the pasta or spaghetti squash, crumble crispy leaves of sage over top, season with nutmeg, and top with some Parm.

SPAGHETTI SQUASH

If you want to lighten up the calories a little—or if you have guests who have issues with gluten—spaghetti squash is a great solution. You'll need 1 large spaghetti squash per every two entrée servings. Top with your choice of Brown Butter and Crispy Sage (see above), Mushroom Ragu (page 128), Roasted Tomato Sauce (page 122), Cacio e Pepe (page 140), Warm Spinach-Walnut Pesto (page 118), or Romesco Sauce with Hazelnuts (page 120).

Preheat the oven to 400°F. Halve the squash lengthwise and pull out the seeds. Season the squash with salt and pepper and place cut side down on a baking sheet or sheets, if roasting several squash. Roast the squash until very tender, 45 minutes to 1 hour. Holding the squash with a potholder, use a fork to scrape the squash "spaghetti" strands into a bowl and toss with the sauce of your choice. When a recipe calls for tossing a sauce with a little of the starchy cooking water, you can toss the squash noodles with a little stock instead.

For a nice presentation, save the squash shells and use them as pasta bowls.

PESTO GENOVESE

SERVES 6

If you own a mortar and pestle, it is really fun to produce this sauce the old-fashioned way by hand-grinding the oil, nuts, and leaves. However, the food processor is fast, efficient, and much less work. Pesto freezes so well that I usually make 2 to 6 deli tubs of it at a time, especially when we are up to our knees in basil from our backyard garden patch. If the basil accidentally goes to flower or survives a cold night and starts to become bitter, drop the basil into low-boiling water for 15 seconds, then cold-shock it in ice water, drain, and dry it before making your sauce. It will mellow it out and sweeten up the leaves.

3 cups fresh basil leaves
⅓ cup pignoli (pine nuts), toasted
1 or 2 cloves garlic, pasted or grated
Juice of ½ lemon
½ cup freshly grated Parmigiano-Reggiano cheese
Salt and pepper
⅓ to ½ cup EVOO

In a food processor, pulse the basil, pine nuts, and garlic into a finely chopped, almost pastelike consistency. Transfer to a bowl and stir in the lemon juice, Parm, and salt and pepper. Stream in the oil to a slow count of 6. Adjust the seasonings.

TO SERVE: Cook 1 pound pasta to al dente. Drain, reserving some of the starchy cooking water. Toss together the pesto, starchy water, and pasta.

VARIATION

Tarragon Pesto

Tarragon is very closely related to basil in flavor, and we often mix some into basil pesto (about two parts basil to one part tarragon, along with a handful of parsley). But when we make a tarragon-based pesto, we use mostly parsley and then a small amount of mint and tarragon.

ETRUSCAN-STYLE PESTO

SERVES 6

This sauce is especially delicious on pici (*pinci*) or *strozzapreti*, but is good with any long- or short-cut pasta. It also works as a topper for fish or meat (broiled or grilled). I prefer it to traditional Genovese pesto because it has more complexity of flavor.

1 large hard-boiled egg, coarsely chopped
1 or 2 cloves garlic, pasted with salt or pasted with 2 flat anchovy fillets
1 cup packed fresh basil leaves
1 cup packed mixed fresh mint leaves and flat-leaf parsley tops
⅓ to ½ cup freshly grated pecorino cheese
⅓ to ½ cup olive oil
Pepper

In a food processor, combine the egg, garlic (or garlic and anchovies), basil, and mint/parsley and pulse to very finely chop. Transfer to a bowl and stir in the pecorino, then the oil. Season with pepper.

TO SERVE: Cook 1 pound pasta to al dente. Drain, reserving some of the starchy cooking water. Toss together the pesto, starchy water, and pasta.

GARLIC SCAPE PESTO

Scapes are the green curly flower stalks that the garlic plant sends above ground as the bulb matures below. They are delicious and mild in flavor, a cross between grass, onion, and garlic. You can find them in late spring at farmers' markets.

1½ cups loosely packed coarsely chopped garlic scapes (8 to 10)
1 cup packed fresh basil leaves or any combination of mixed fresh herbs: basil, tarragon, parsley, and mint
3 to 4 tablespoons pistachios or pignoli (pine nuts), toasted
A couple of handfuls of grated pecorino or Parmigiano-Reggiano cheese or a combination of the two
About ⅓ cup EVOO
Juice of 1 small lemon
Salt and pepper

In a food processor, pulse the garlic scapes, basil, pistachios, and cheese. Add enough EVOO to make a thick sauce. Add the lemon juice for brightness and pulse to combine. Season with salt and pepper.

TO SERVE: Cook 1 pound pasta to al dente. Drain, reserving 1 cup of the starchy cooking water. Toss together the pesto, starchy water, and pasta.

KALE PESTO

This is a delicious four-season pesto. I enjoy it with fat ribbons of pappardelle, but it is also delicious with short- or long-cut farro pasta.

5 to 6 cups coarsely chopped stemmed lacinato kale (also called black, Tuscan, or dinosaur kale)
Juice of 1 lemon
¼ cup pignoli (pine nuts) or chopped hazelnuts, toasted
¼ to ⅛ teaspoon freshly grated nutmeg (to taste)
½ cup freshly grated pecorino cheese
Salt and pepper
⅓ to ½ cup EVOO

In a food processor, pulse the kale to finely chop. Add the lemon juice, pine nuts, nutmeg, cheese, salt, and pepper. Pulse to combine, then transfer to a bowl. Stir in the EVOO, in a slow stream to a count of 6. Taste and adjust the seasonings.

TO SERVE: Cook 1 pound pasta to al dente. Drain, reserving 1 cup of the cooking water. Toss together the pesto, starchy water, and pasta.

WARM SPINACH-WALNUT PESTO

⅓ to ½ cup vegetable or chicken stock

1½ cups loosely packed fresh flat-leaf parsley

1 large shallot, coarsely chopped

2 or 3 cloves garlic, peeled

½ cup walnut pieces, toasted

1 (16-ounce) bag frozen chopped or leaf spinach, thawed and wrung dry in a kitchen towel

¼ cup olive oil

Salt and pepper

Freshly grated nutmeg

Grated Parmigiano-Reggiano cheese

In a food processor, combine ⅓ cup of the stock, the parsley, shallot, garlic, and walnuts. Pull the spinach apart with your fingertips to loosen it up as you add it to the processor. Pulse into a pesto sauce, adding a bit more stock if it seems too dry.

In a large skillet, heat the oil (4 turns of the pan) over medium heat. Add the pesto and stir for 2 to 3 minutes to warm and combine the flavors. Season with salt, pepper, and nutmeg.

TO SERVE: Cook 1 pound pasta to al dente. Drain, reserving some of the cooking water. Add the pasta to the skillet and toss it with the pesto and starchy water. Stir in Parm a small handful at a time, to taste. Serve warm.

WALNUT-ANCHOVY SAUCE

Toss with gnudi or short-cut pasta.

1 cup walnuts

About ¼ cup olive oil

4 ounces (1 stick) butter

12 flat anchovy fillets

1 teaspoon pepper

1 cup milk

Preheat the oven to 325°F.

Spread the walnuts on a rimmed baking sheet and toast in the oven until fragrant and browned, 8 to 10 minutes. Let cool, then finely chop.

In a deep large skillet, heat the oil (4 turns of the pan) over medium heat. Melt the butter into the oil. Add the anchovies, cover the pan with a splatter screen or lid, and shake until the anchovies begin to break up. Reduce the heat a bit, uncover, and stir until the anchovies melt into the oil. Add the pepper, toasted walnuts, and milk and simmer for 10 minutes to thicken a bit.

TO SERVE: Cook 1 pound pasta to al dente. Drain, reserving some of the cooking water. Add the pasta to the skillet and toss it together with the walnut sauce and starchy water. Serve warm.

BASICS

PARMIGIANO-REGGIANO VS. PARMESAN

I most often use Parmigiano-Reggiano over Parmesan. Places like Wisconsin make great Parmesan cheese and if it is more budget-friendly, feel free to use it any place I write Parmigiano-Reggiano. For me, I would get kicked out of my family if I didn't use Parmigiano-Reggiano. When I was growing up, my mom always bought a hunk from the local Italian grocer. Parmigiano-Reggiano comes from certain provinces of Italy and is made a certain way. But if you have Parmesan, go ahead and use it, there's nothing wrong with it . . . as long as you don't buy it in a can.

WALNUT-ORANGE SAUCE

1 organic blood orange or navel orange
¼ cup olive oil, plus more for drizzling
4 large cloves garlic, finely chopped
1 fresh or dried red chile, finely chopped, or 1 teaspoon crushed red pepper flakes
1 cup chopped walnuts
½ cup fresh flat-leaf parsley tops, chopped
Salt and black pepper
Grated Parmigiano-Reggiano, for serving

Grate the zest from the orange and set aside. Cut the orange in half.

In a large skillet, heat a drizzle of oil over medium heat. Add the orange halves, cut side down, and cook to caramelize the fruit. Remove and set aside.

Add the ¼ cup of oil (4 turns of the pan) to the skillet. Add the garlic and chile and stir for 1 to 2 minutes. Add the walnuts and orange zest and stir until the nuts are toasted, fragrant, and golden. Squeeze in the juice from the caramelized orange halves. Add the parsley and season with salt and black pepper. Remove from the heat.

TO SERVE: Cook 1 pound pasta to al dente. Drain, reserving 1 cup of the cooking water. Toss together the sauce, starchy water, and pasta. Pass Parm for topping at the table.

ROASTED EGGPLANT SAUCE

This sauce is amazing, and it combines two of my favorites: roasted eggplant and gremolata (a mixture of lemon zest, herbs, and garlic). It also makes a delicious side to my famous (among friends and family) Swordfish Cutlets (page 204).

1 large heavy eggplant
1 cup packed fresh flat-leaf parsley leaves
½ cup packed fresh mint leaves
2 cloves garlic, peeled
1 rounded tablespoon grated lemon zest (from an organic lemon)
2 flat anchovy fillets (optional)
Salt and pepper
Grated pecorino or Parmigiano-Reggiano cheese, for serving

Preheat the oven to 425°F.

Poke a few holes in the skin of the eggplant with a small, sharp knife. Roast the eggplant until it begins to look like a flat tire, very tender and beginning to collapse, 30 to 40 minutes, depending on the size of the eggplant.

Meanwhile, in a food processor or by hand, finely chop the parsley, mint, garlic, lemon zest, and anchovies (if using). Transfer the gremolata to a bowl.

When the eggplant is cool enough to handle, peel and transfer the flesh to the food processor (no need to clean the work bowl). Puree the flesh, then add it to the bowl with the gremolata and stir to combine. Season with salt and pepper.

TO SERVE: Cook 1 pound pasta to al dente. Drain, reserving ½ cup of the cooking water. Toss together the sauce, starchy water, and pasta. Pass cheese at the table.

GORGONZOLA SAUCE

SERVES 6

Serve this sauce with gnudi, gnocchi, or short-cut pasta.

1 large clove garlic, peeled
1 rib celery with leafy top, chopped
½ small onion, chopped
2 cups half-and-half or heavy cream
4 fresh sage leaves
1 hard-boiled free-range organic egg yolk
Pepper
6 ounces Gorgonzola dolce cheese

In a food processor, combine the garlic, celery, onion, half-and-half, sage, egg yolk, and pepper to taste and blend until smooth. Pour into a small pot and simmer for 15 minutes. Stir in the Gorgonzola to melt.

TO SERVE: Cook 1 pound pasta to al dente. Drain, reserving some of the cooking water. Return the pasta to the cooking pot, add the sauce, and toss together, adding some of the starchy water if necessary to loosen up the sauce. Serve warm.

ROMESCO SAUCE WITH HAZELNUTS

SERVES 6

Use this sauce on gnocchi or spaghetti squash. It's also great on cheese, vegetables, and cooked proteins (see Variation). Delish!

3 large roasted red peppers, homemade (see box, page 334) or store-bought, or 10 to 12 water-packed piquillo peppers, drained
⅓ cup olive oil
2 tablespoons sherry vinegar
½ cup loosely packed fresh flat-leaf parsley tops
⅓ cup Marcona almonds, toasted
¼ cup skinned hazelnuts, toasted
1½ teaspoons regular or smoked paprika
1 teaspoon black pepper
1 teaspoon acacia honey
Sea salt

In a blender or food processor, combine the roasted peppers, oil, vinegar, parsley, almonds, hazelnuts, paprika, black pepper, and honey. Process to blend. Taste and season with sea salt.

TO SERVE: Cook 1 pound pasta to al dente. Drain, reserving ½ cup of the cooking water. Toss together the sauce, starchy water, and pasta.

VARIATION

If you want to use this sauce as a dip or as an accompaniment for vegetables or cooked proteins, add 1 slice stale bread, softened with a few tablespoons water. Tear the bread up a bit before adding it to the food processor or blender with the other ingredients.

POMODORO SAUCE

This is our basic family recipe for sweet tomato sauce and is used often in casseroles and cutlet dishes, and on hot sandwiches. Our favorite use is, of course, on spaghetti.

1 tablespoon olive oil
2 tablespoons butter
1 small onion, finely chopped
4 cloves garlic, finely chopped
Salt
1 cup chicken stock
2 (28- to 32-ounce) cans San Marzano tomatoes (look for DOP on the label)
A few leaves fresh basil, torn
Rind from a small wedge of Parmigiano-Reggiano or Grana Padano cheese (optional)

In a pot, heat the oil (1 turn of the pan) over medium heat. Melt in the butter, add the onion and garlic, season with salt, and cook, partially covered, until very soft. Add the stock. Hand-crush the tomatoes as you add them to the pot, then add the juice from the cans. Stir in the basil and add the cheese rind (if using). Reduce the heat, partially cover, and simmer gently, stirring occasionally, for 20 to 30 minutes. Adjust the salt. Remove the cheese rind before serving.

TO SERVE: See Spaghetti with Pomodoro Sauce, below.

TIP **FOR A THINNER** sauce or to stretch the yield, add 2 cups passata or tomato puree.

SPAGHETTI WITH POMODORO SAUCE

Bring a large pot of water to a boil, salt the water, and cook 1 pound spaghetti to al dente. Reserve ½ cup of the starchy cooking water just before draining. Combine the pasta with 2 tablespoons butter, the starchy water, and half the sauce and toss together for about 1 minute. Sprinkle with a little Parm and toss. Serve in shallow bowls, topped with the remaining sauce and more Parm.

MARINARA SAUCE

We like a little fennel seed and some heat in our marinara, so we add fresh or dried chiles. My mom finds oregano too floral for the sauce, so we add thyme, which I love with tomatoes. Use this sauce not only on pasta but with meatballs as a dipper and to dress sandwiches and panini as well.

¼ cup olive oil
8 cloves garlic, chopped
1 teaspoon fennel seeds
1 fresh or dried pepperoncino (Italian chile pepper), finely chopped, or 1 teaspoon crushed red pepper flakes
2 (28- to 32-ounce) cans San Marzano tomatoes (look for DOP on the label)
2 tablespoons chopped fresh thyme
Salt and pepper
A handful of fresh basil leaves, torn

In a medium saucepan, heat the oil (4 turns of the pan) over medium heat. Add the garlic and stir for 2 minutes. Add the fennel and chile and stir for a minute more. Hand-crush the tomatoes as you add them to the pan, then add the juices from the cans. Add the thyme, season with salt and pepper, and bring to a bubble. Reduce the heat and simmer for 20 minutes or so. Add the basil and simmer for 5 to 10 minutes more.

TO SERVE: Cook 1 pound pasta to al dente. Drain, reserving 1 cup of the cooking water. Toss the pasta with half the sauce and some of the starchy water. Serve topped with the remaining sauce.

ROASTED TOMATO SAUCE

Fresh tomatoes are tasty for such a short time in each calendar year. One way to add flavor to out-of-season tomatoes is to concentrate their juices in a roasted tomato sauce. The roasting process makes the tomatoes taste more like their in-season selves, but tangier, with a slightly smoky and earthy flavor that is particularly comforting. Serve with short- or long-cut pasta, spaghetti squash, gnocchi, or gnudi.

24 plum tomatoes (4 to 5 pounds), halved
6 cloves garlic, sliced
About 4 tablespoons olive oil
¼ cup fresh thyme leaves, chopped
Salt and pepper
8 to 10 fresh basil leaves, torn
Grated Parmigiano-Reggiano or Grana Padano cheese, for serving

Preheat the oven to 400°F.

Place the tomatoes on two large rimmed baking sheets and scatter the garlic over them. Drizzle each baking sheet with about 2 tablespoons of the oil. Toss to coat, sprinkle with the thyme, and season with salt and pepper.

Roast until the tomatoes are browned at the edges and slumped, 30 to 40 minutes. Slide the tomatoes and any liquid in the baking sheets into a bowl, add the basil, and mash.

TO SERVE: Cook 1 pound pasta to al dente. Drain, reserving 1 cup of the cooking water. Toss the pasta with half the sauce and some of the starchy water. Serve topped with the remaining sauce and cheese.

CHERRY TOMATO SAUCE

Like roasted tomato sauces, cherry tomato sauce allows us to enjoy the flavor of perfect summer tomatoes outside of the super-short growing season. Cherry tomatoes and grape tomatoes are quick-cooking, sweet, and burst with flavor, more so in the summer but even in the cold days of fall and winter.

3 tablespoons olive oil
1 small red or white onion, or
   1 bunch scallions or spring onions (white parts only), finely chopped
4 cloves garlic, chopped or thinly sliced
2 pints cherry or grape tomatoes
A handful of fresh basil leaves, torn
Salt and pepper
Grated ricotta salata, Parmigiano-Reggiano, or pecorino cheese, for serving

In a skillet with a tight-fitting lid, heat the oil (3 turns of the pan) over medium-high heat. Stir in the onion and garlic, cover the pan, and cook, stirring occasionally, for 5 minutes to sweat the onions. Add the tomatoes, shake the pan, cover, and cook until the tomatoes begin to burst, 8 to 10 minutes. Mash and stir the sauce. Add the basil. Season with salt and pepper.

TO SERVE: Cook 1 pound pasta to al dente. Drain, reserving 1 cup of the cooking water. Toss together the sauce, starchy water, and pasta. Top with cheese and serve.

VARIATIONS

Marinara-Style Cherry Tomato Sauce

Add ½ cup dry white wine and 2 tablespoons fresh thyme leaves or the finely chopped leaves from 1 sprig fresh oregano.

Arrabbiata-Style Cherry Tomato Sauce

Add 1 or 2 small fresh or dried chiles, finely chopped.

'NDUJA ARRABBIATA
WITH FRESH TOMATOES

SERVES 4 TO 6

When tomatoes are not perfect (most of the year), I make this sauce as a use-up for cherry tomatoes, plum tomatoes, and vine tomatoes. And because of the color and flavor of the 'nduja (see box), the sauce comes out rosy red, juicy, and full of huge flavor and heat. As he does with Carbonara (page 158), John likes both nutty Parm and tangy Romano grated on top of this pasta dish.

2 tablespoons olive oil

3 to 4 tablespoons 'nduja

1 small onion, finely chopped

4 cloves garlic, thinly sliced

1 cup dry white wine

1½ to 2 pints cherry or grape tomatoes

2 vine tomatoes, chopped (overripe is fine, just trim any spots before chopping)

4 to 6 plum tomatoes, chopped

A couple of fresh basil leaves, torn

A handful of fresh flat-leaf parsley tops, chopped

Grated Parmigiano-Reggiano and Pecorino Romano cheese, for serving

In a large skillet with a tight-fitting lid, heat the oil (2 turns of the pan) over medium to medium-high heat. Add the 'nduja and "melt" it into the oil. Stir in the onion and garlic, cover the pan, and cook, stirring occasionally, for 3 to 4 minutes to sweat the onion. Uncover, add the wine, and cook to reduce the wine by half. Stir in all of the tomatoes, cover the pan, and cook, shaking occasionally, until the cherry tomatoes all burst, 10 to 15 minutes. Stir in the basil and reduce the heat to low.

TO SERVE: Cook 1 pound pasta to al dente. Drain, reserving 1 cup of the cooking water. Toss together the sauce, parsley, starchy water, and pasta. Top with cheese and serve.

'NDUJA

'Nduja is listed on many websites as a sausage, but it's really more of a chile paste. It's made of chile peppers, pork fat, and pork, and it has a spreadable consistency. 'Nduja is extremely versatile, packs a real flavor punch, and adds a depth of flavor you cannot get from chiles alone. You can source 'nduja online. I get mine from Buon Italia, in New York City's Chelsea Market.

PUTTANESCA

Puttanesca sauce, or "streetwalkers' sauce," is a favorite in our house, but the women who made this sauce famous (or infamous) probably didn't have to walk too many streets to lure in their customers. They simply put the ingredients for this sauce in clay pots and let the sauce bake in the windows of their houses all day before tossing the tomatoes and anchovies with pasta. No one knows if the men came in for the ladies or the sauce—my bet is they had hopes of getting truly lucky and enjoying both. Regardless of its history, you do feel naughty when you eat this spicy, salty, wildly delicious concoction.

¼ cup olive oil

8 to 12 good-quality anchovy fillets (see Tip)

6 large cloves garlic, thinly sliced or chopped

2 small dried or fresh red chiles, finely chopped

½ cup dry vermouth

1 (28- to 32-ounce) can San Marzano tomatoes (look for DOP on the label)

A few fresh basil leaves, torn

½ cup pitted oil-cured black olives, chopped

1 cup loosely packed fresh flat-leaf parsley tops, finely chopped

In a large skillet, heat the oil (4 turns of the pan) over medium heat. Add the anchovies, cover the pan with a splatter screen or lid, and shake until the anchovies begin to break up. Reduce the heat a bit, uncover, and stir until the anchovies melt into the oil.

Add the garlic and chiles and stir for 2 minutes. Add the vermouth. Hand-crush the tomatoes as you add them to the skillet, then add the juices from the can. Add the basil and olives and simmer over medium-low heat for 20 minutes to break down the tomatoes.

TO SERVE: Cook 1 pound spaghetti or linguine to al dente. Drain, reserving 1 cup of the cooking water. Toss together the sauce, starchy water, parsley, and pasta.

TIP

USE OIL-PACKED Spanish l'Escala anchovy fillets, drained, or 4 to 6 salted whole anchovies, soaked to remove some of the salt and separated from their spines into 8 to 12 fillets.

Cherry Tomato Puttanesca

Substitute 2 pints cherry tomatoes for the canned tomatoes. Add them to the pan after adding the vermouth. Cover the pan and cook, shaking occasionally, until the tomatoes have burst, about 10 minutes. Continue with the recipe as directed.

SPAGHETTATA DI MEZZANOTTE

Spaghettata di mezzanotte translates to "midnight spaghetti," and how appropriate that it is served in the middle of the night, because the base recipe is streetwalkers' sauce (puttanesca). This dish and Carbonara (page 158) are both late-night bites in our lives. My husband, John, often plays late gigs with his rock band. When he does, we eat late, after the show. Carbonara and puttanesca are his favorites, so this is a go-to. To serve puttanesca midnight-style, just toast a couple of pieces of ciabatta or peasant bread or char them under a hot broiler on both sides to make bruschetta. Rub the toasted or charred bread with cut garlic and dress with olive oil and flaky sea salt. Tear the bread into pieces and pulse-chop in a food processor (or finely chop by hand) to make garlicky bread crumbs. You can either top the pasta with the crumbs or toss them in with the pasta and sauce.

BOLOGNESE

I have tried many versions of this buttery meat sauce, which can take literally all day to prepare (Marcella Hazan's recipe is a favorite of mine, but it does take a good 6 to 7 hours). My own recipe for Bolognese has taken me years to develop and tweak—I can be very fickle when it comes to this sauce. It takes just over 2 hours to prepare and to date it has received the best response from those who have dined on it. I prefer ribbon pasta such as tagliatelle or pappardelle with this sauce, but some in my family prefer heavy pasta such as rigatoni or pici.

2 tablespoons EVOO
¼ pound pancetta, finely diced
1 carrot, finely chopped
1 rib celery with leafy top, finely
    chopped
1 small onion, finely chopped
4 cloves garlic, finely chopped
1 pound ground beef, at room
    temperature
½ pound ground veal, at room
    temperature
1 fresh bay leaf
⅛ teaspoon freshly grated
    nutmeg
A good pinch of ground cloves
Salt and pepper
1 cup dry white wine
5 tablespoons tomato paste
3 cups chicken or veal stock
Rind from a small wedge of
    Parmigiano-Reggiano cheese

1½ cups milk or half-and-half,
    warmed (do not boil)
Butter
Grated Parmigiano-Reggiano
    cheese, for serving

In a Dutch oven, heat the EVOO (2 turns of the pan) over medium heat. When it ripples, add the pancetta and render for 2 to 3 minutes. Add the carrot, celery, onion, and garlic and cook, partially covered, for 7 to 8 minutes to soften the vegetables. Add the beef, veal, bay leaf, nutmeg, and cloves; season with salt and pepper. Cook the meat, breaking it into fine crumbles (a pastry cutter or potato masher works) as it browns. Add the wine and allow it to be absorbed completely by the meat at a low simmer. Stir in the tomato paste until incorporated, then add the stock and cheese rind. Reduce the heat to low, partially cover, and simmer, stirring occasionally, for 1¼ hours.

Add the milk and simmer gently for 30 to 45 minutes more. Remove and discard the bay leaf and cheese rind.

TO SERVE: Cook 1 to 1½ pounds pasta to al dente. Drain, reserving ½ cup of the cooking water. Toss the pasta with a few pats of butter, salt, pepper, the starchy water, and a few ladles of the sauce. Top the pasta with additional sauce and cheese.

TUSCAN MEAT SAUCE

This is a slight variation of Bolognese sauce with the rich addition of chicken livers. I love the earthy flavor of this wildly delicious sauce, and the minced rosemary makes it even better. If you enjoy this sauce as much as I do, try my mom's Tuscan Chicken Liver Spread (page 43), which you can make with the remainder of the chicken livers if you were forced to buy a full 1-pound tub of them. If you try both recipes within the same week, spend a little extra time at the gym and eat lots of oatmeal before your next cholesterol checkup, but it will be worth it.

2 tablespoons olive oil

2 tablespoons butter

3 chicken livers (about ¼ pound), trimmed, patted dry, and very finely chopped

Leaves from 2 sprigs fresh rosemary, very finely chopped

1 carrot, finely chopped

1 rib celery with leafy top, finely chopped

1 small onion, finely chopped

4 cloves garlic, finely chopped

1½ pounds mixed ground beef, pork, and veal, at room temperature

1 fresh bay leaf

⅛ teaspoon freshly grated nutmeg

Salt and pepper

1 cup dry white wine

¼ cup tomato paste

3 cups chicken stock

Rind from a small wedge of Parmigiano-Reggiano cheese

1½ cups milk or half-and-half, warmed (do not boil)

Butter

Grated Parmigiano-Reggiano cheese, for serving

In a Dutch oven, heat the oil (2 turns of the pan) over medium-high heat. When it ripples, melt in the butter. Add the chicken livers, sprinkle with the rosemary, and cook until browned, about 5 minutes. Add the carrot, celery, onion, and garlic and cook, partially covered, for 7 to 8 minutes to soften the vegetables. Add the meat, bay leaf, and nutmeg; season with salt and pepper. Cook the meat, breaking it into fine crumbles (a pastry cutter or potato masher works) as it browns. Add the wine and allow it to be absorbed completely into the meat at a low simmer. Stir in the tomato paste until incorporated, then add the stock and cheese rind. Reduce the heat to low, partially cover, and simmer, stirring occasionally, for 1¼ hours.

Add the milk and simmer gently for 45 minutes more. Fish out and discard the bay leaf and cheese rind.

TO SERVE: Cook 1 to 1½ pounds pasta (such as tagliatelle or pappardelle) to al dente. Drain, reserving ½ cup of the cooking water. Toss the cooked pasta with a few pats of butter, salt, pepper, the starchy water, and a few ladles of sauce. Top the pasta with additional sauce and cheese.

WHITE RAGU

White ragu is not really white in color. Thanks to tomato paste, it's blush pink and similar to a hearty Bolognese, but made with chicken rather than red meat as the base. When I have the time, I start this sauce by poaching a chicken. I use half the cooked chicken in this ragu, and then reserve the rest of the meat and 2 quarts of homemade stock for making a soup—such as Italian-Style Chicken Noodle Soup (page 79) or Chicken and Orzo (Barley) Soup (page 80)—for later in the week. For a delicious and fast version that can be made on any weeknight, use store-bought stock and ground chicken instead of the poached chicken.

My mom and husband love this sauce when I serve it tossed with maltagliati (irregular-shaped torn pasta), either freshly homemade (see page 110) or store-bought dried. You can also toss it with any short-cut pasta like penne rigate.

---

2 tablespoons olive oil

1 teaspoon fennel seeds

1 small bulb fennel, finely chopped

2 small ribs celery with leafy tops, finely chopped

1 small onion, finely chopped

3 cloves garlic, finely chopped

Salt and pepper

½ cup dry white wine

1 tablespoon tomato paste

1½ pounds finely chopped cooked dark and white meat chicken, from chicken stock (page 64), or 1¼ pounds ground chicken

2 cups chicken stock

Rind from a small wedge of Parmigiano-Reggiano cheese (optional)

1 cup milk

Grated Grana Padano or Parmigiano-Reggiano cheese, for serving

Minced fennel fronds and celery tops, for garnish (optional)

In a deep large skillet, heat the oil (2 turns of the pan) over medium-high heat. Stir in the fennel seeds, then add the fresh fennel, celery, onion, and garlic. Season with salt and pepper, partially cover, and cook to soften, 8 to 10 minutes. Add the wine, stir to deglaze the pan, and cook until it has evaporated completely. Add the tomato paste and stir for 1 minute. Add the chicken and stock and bring to a low boil. (If you happen to have a piece of cheese rind, add that, too.) Add the milk, reduce the heat, and cook at a low bubble for 35 to 45 minutes.

TO SERVE: Cook 1 pound penne rigate or 6 "portions" (see Tip) maltagliati or broken lasagna to al dente. Drain, reserving ½ cup of the cooking water. Transfer the starchy water to a warm serving dish along with half the ragu and the drained pasta and toss gently to combine.

Sprinkle in a little cheese. Serve in shallow bowls topped with the remaining sauce and garnish with more cheese and/or minced fennel fronds and celery greens.

 IT'S DIFFICULT TO put a weight on a "portion" of maltagliati, which is irregular-shaped torn pasta, as it varies depending on how thin it has been rolled. When I buy dried maltagliati, the brand I use is so thin that 250 grams (about 8 ounces) would easily feed 4 to 6 people. When I use homemade pasta sheets or broken pieces of dried flat lasagna sheets, it takes 12 ounces for 4 to 6 portions. Here is a good rule of thumb: For dried maltagliati or broken lasagna, measure a "portion" by taking 1 fat handful; for fresh maltagliati, measure out a pile as wide as the full palm of your hand.

PROSCIUTTO, SAGE, AND MUSHROOM SAUCE

SERVES 4 TO 6

Toss this sauce with gnudi, gnocchi, or egg tagliatelle. Top with crispy ham and sage leaves.

1½ cups chicken stock
½ ounce dried porcini mushroom slices
⅓ cup olive oil
12 slices prosciutto di Parma
36 fresh sage leaves
1 pound cremini mushrooms, sliced
Salt and pepper
3 tablespoons fresh thyme leaves, chopped
4 shallots, chopped
4 cloves garlic, chopped
½ cup dry white wine

In a small saucepan, heat the stock with the dried porcini to soften the mushrooms, 10 to 15 minutes. Scoop out the mushrooms, reserving the soaking liquid, and chop.

In a skillet, heat the oil over medium to medium-high heat. Working in batches of a few slices at a time, crisp the prosciutto for 2 minutes on each side. Drain on paper towels and chop or tear into pieces. Working in two batches, add the sage leaves to the oil and fry until crisp. Drain on paper towels.

Add the fresh mushrooms to the skillet and brown well. Season with salt and pepper. Add the thyme, shallots, and garlic and stir for 2 to 3 minutes. Add the wine and porcini. Carefully pour in the porcini soaking liquid, leaving the last few spoonfuls in the pan as grit may have settled there.

TO SERVE: Cook 1 to 1½ pounds pasta. Drain, reserving ½ cup of the cooking water. Toss the cooked pasta with the sauce and the starchy cooking water. Season with salt and pepper.

MUSHROOM RAGU

SERVES 6

This is a meatless alternative to Bolognese sauce, and yet it is every bit as beefy in flavor due to the rich combination of meaty cremini and dried porcini. Serve the sauce over pappardelle, egg tagliatelle, spaghetti squash, gnocchi, or gnudi.

4 cups chicken stock
A fat handful of dried porcini mushroom slices (about ½ cup)
¼ cup olive oil
1¼ pounds cremini mushrooms, chopped
3 tablespoons fresh thyme leaves, chopped
1 small carrot, finely chopped
2 shallots, chopped
1 small onion, finely chopped
4 large cloves garlic, chopped
Salt and pepper
3 rounded tablespoons tomato paste
½ cup dry sherry or Marsala
1 fresh bay leaf
1 cup milk
Rind from a small wedge of Parmigiano-Reggiano or Grana Padano cheese
Grated Parmigiano-Reggiano or Grana Padano cheese, for serving

In a small saucepan, heat the stock with the dried porcini to soften the mushrooms, 10 to 15 minutes. Scoop out the porcini, reserving the soaking liquid, and chop.

In a large pot, heat the oil (4 turns of the pan) over medium-high heat. Add the fresh mushrooms and brown well, 15 minutes or so. Add the thyme, carrot, shallots, onion, garlic, salt, and pepper and cook until the vegetables are tender, 5 to 8 minutes. Stir in the tomato paste and cook for 1 minute. Add the sherry, bay leaf, and porcini. Carefully pour in the porcini soaking liquid, leaving the last few spoonfuls in the pan as grit may have settled there. Add the milk and cheese rind, reduce the heat to low, and simmer for 30 minutes to reduce. Discard the bay leaf and cheese rind.

TO SERVE: Cook 1 pound pasta to al dente. Drain, reserving ½ cup of the cooking water. Toss the cooked pasta with the starchy water and a few ladles of the ragu. Top the pasta with additional ragu and cheese.

QUICK BEAN AND PORCINI RAGU

This dish feeds an army for little to no money and can be made easily with items kept on hand: canned beans, root vegetables, garlic, and dried mushrooms. Serve the sauce over spaghetti or bucatini.

2½ cups vegetable stock

A fat handful of dried porcini mushroom slices (about ½ cup)

3 tablespoons EVOO

2 ribs celery with leafy tops, finely chopped

1 onion, finely chopped

1 carrot, finely chopped

3 or 4 cloves garlic (to taste), finely chopped

1 large fresh bay leaf

Salt and pepper

2 (15-ounce) cans cannellini beans or Roman beans, rinsed and drained

½ cup dry white wine

Grated pecorino cheese

In a small saucepan, heat 1½ cups of the stock with the porcini to soften the mushrooms, 10 to 15 minutes. Scoop out the porcini, reserving the soaking liquid, and chop.

In a deep large skillet, heat the EVOO (3 turns of the pan) over medium-high heat. Add the celery, onion, carrot, garlic, bay leaf, and salt and pepper. Partially cover and sweat the vegetables for 10 minutes to soften.

In a food processor, puree half the beans with the remaining 1 cup stock.

Add the wine to the skillet and stir to deglaze the pan. Stir in the bean puree and the whole beans. Add the chopped porcini and carefully pour in the soaking liquid, leaving the last few spoonfuls in the pan as grit may have settled there. Reduce the heat to low to keep the sauce warm. Discard the bay leaf.

TO SERVE: Cook 1 pound pasta to al dente. Drain, reserving ½ cup of the cooking water. Toss together the sauce, starchy water, and pasta. Toss in some cheese and serve.

VARIATION

Slightly-Less-Quick Bean and Porcini Ragu

Only less quick because you cook your own beans. Instead of the canned beans, cover ¾ cup dried cannellini or borlotti beans with boiling water and quick-soak for 1 hour. Drain, cover with fresh water, and add 1 bay leaf, 1 small halved onion, and salt. Bring to a boil and cook until just tender, 35 to 40 minutes. Drain, reserving 1 cup of the cooking liquid. (Fish out and discard the bay leaf and onion halves.) Puree the beans as directed, using 1 cup of the cooking liquid in place of the stock called for. The rest of the recipe is the same.

CINGHIALE (WILD BOAR) RAGU

In Tuscany, wild boar sauce is sold everywhere—even at rest stop restaurants. I rarely get the chance to cook with boar when I'm at home in New York State, but you can order it from many butcher shops or even order it online. Pork shoulder, hand-cut into small pieces, also makes a tasty sauce that's very similar in flavor. Serve the sauce over polenta, with pici, or with bucatini. You can also add tangy freshly grated pecorino cheese or nutty grated Grana Padano or Parmigiano-Reggiano

2 pounds wild boar, cut into 1-inch cubes (substitute mature pork shoulder if you cannot get boar)

Milk, as needed to cover the meat

Kosher salt

4 tablespoons olive oil

8 to 10 juniper berries

2 teaspoons fennel seeds

1 teaspoon pink or black peppercorns

2 carrots, coarsely chopped

3 or 4 small ribs celery with leafy tops, coarsely chopped

2 small to medium onions, chopped

4 cloves garlic, chopped

3 tablespoons fresh rosemary leaves, coarsely chopped

1 large bay leaf

½ teaspoon ground allspice, or ⅛ teaspoon ground cloves

2 cups veal or chicken stock

2 to 3 cups dry red wine (such as Barolo or Rosso di Montalcino)

1 (28- to 32-ounce) can San Marzano tomatoes (look for DOP on the label)

Grated pecorino or Parmigiano-Reggiano or Grana Padano cheese, for serving

Pat the meat very dry and place it in a shallow bowl or dish of cold milk diluted with some water, just enough to cover the meat, and let sit for several hours to tenderize. Drain the meat and pat dry. Cut the meat into small pieces, then season with salt.

In a large Dutch oven, heat 2 tablespoons of the oil (2 turns of the pan) over medium-high heat. Add half of the meat and brown to caramelize. Transfer to a plate. Repeat with the remaining 2 tablespoons oil and the remaining meat.

Meanwhile, in a small skillet, toast the juniper, fennel seeds, and peppercorns. Grind in a spice grinder or wrap in cheesecloth to make a sachet.

Once all the meat is evenly browned, add the carrots, celery, onions, garlic, rosemary, and bay leaf to the pan and season with a little salt. Partially cover and cook for 10 minutes to soften. Add the meat, juniper mixture (or sachet), allspice, stock, and wine (enough to cover the meat). Cover the pan and cook over low heat until the meat is tender, about 2 hours.

Hand-crush the tomatoes as you add them to the pan, then add the juices from the can. Simmer, uncovered, to cook down the tomatoes, 20 to 30 minutes. Fish out and discard the bay leaf (and the spice sachet, if you used one).

TO SERVE: Cook 1 pound pici or bucatini to al dente. Drain, reserving ½ cup of the starchy cooking water. Toss together the sauce, starchy water, and pasta. Adjust the seasonings and top with grated cheese.

SPICY LAMB RAGU

This is a great sauce to make when the seasons are transitioning from winter to spring. It's warm, rich, and comforting, but the flavor of the lamb and all the fresh and dried herbs hint at spring, especially when topped with fresh creamy ricotta cheese to mix in. If you like the combination of lamb and pasta, check out the recipe for Lamb Ragu with Potatoes (page 250); it can just as easily be served over pasta. Serve this ragu tossed with bucatini, pici, pappardelle, or tagliatelle.

2 tablespoons olive oil

1½ teaspoons fennel seeds

1½ pounds ground lamb

1 teaspoon dried marjoram or oregano, lightly crushed

1 teaspoon ground pepperoncini or crushed red pepper flakes

Salt and black pepper

1 onion, finely chopped

1 carrot, grated or finely chopped

4 cloves garlic, chopped

2 tablespoons fresh thyme leaves, chopped

3 tablespoons fresh rosemary leaves, minced

1 large fresh bay leaf

1 small cinnamon stick (optional)

1 large strip of blood orange or navel orange zest (from an organic orange)

1½ cups milk

2 tablespoons tomato paste

1½ cups dry white or red wine

2 cups lamb or chicken stock

1 (28- to 32-ounce) can San Marzano tomatoes (look for DOP on the label), or 8 to 10 in-season plum tomatoes, peeled (see Tip, page 67) and chopped

Fresh ricotta or grated pecorino cheese, for serving

A handful of fresh mint leaves, finely chopped, for serving

A handful of fresh flat-leaf parsley tops, finely chopped, for serving

Grated orange zest (from an organic orange), for serving

In a large Dutch oven, heat the oil (2 turns of the pan) over medium-high heat. Add the fennel seeds and stir for 30 seconds. Add the lamb, marjoram, pepperoncini, salt, and black pepper and cook, breaking the meat into crumbles as it browns. Add the onion, carrot, garlic, thyme, rosemary, bay leaf, cinnamon stick (if using), and orange zest strip and cook to soften the onion, 7 to 8 minutes. Add the milk, reduce the heat to low, partially cover, and simmer to let the meat absorb the milk, 35 to 45 minutes.

Stir in the tomato paste until fragrant, 1 to 2 minutes. Stir in the wine, partially cover, and cook for 15 minutes to reduce. Add the stock. Hand-crush the canned tomatoes as you add them to the pot and add the juices from the can (or add the fresh tomatoes), partially cover, and simmer for 30 minutes to cook down the tomatoes and thicken the sauce. Fish out and discard the orange zest strip, bay leaf, and cinnamon stick. Adjust the seasonings.

TO SERVE: Cook 1 to 1½ pounds pasta to al dente. Drain, reserving 1 cup of the cooking water. Toss together the sauce, starchy water, and pasta. Serve in bowls topped with fresh ricotta. Mix the mint, parsley, and grated orange zest and sprinkle over the top to garnish.

PAPPARDELLE WITH LAMB RAGU

SERVES 6

You can also braise the lamb in a 300°F oven instead of on the stovetop. Put it into the oven after you add the stock and return the lamb to the pan.

2 tablespoons olive oil
1½ to 2 pounds lamb stew meat (lamb shoulder), cubed
Salt and pepper
1 carrot, finely chopped or grated
1 rib celery with leafy tops, finely chopped
1 onion, finely chopped
4 cloves garlic, chopped
1 small dried or fresh red chile, finely chopped, or 1 teaspoon crushed red pepper flakes
1 large bay leaf
1 teaspoon dried marjoram or oregano
Leaves from 1 sprig rosemary, finely chopped
5 or 6 sage leaves, thinly sliced
1 cup white wine
2 cups lamb or chicken stock
1 (28- to 32-ounce) can San Marzano tomatoes (look for DOP on the label)
1 (3- to 4-inch) strip of orange or lemon zest (from organic citrus)
12 large Brussels sprouts
1 pound whole wheat pappardelle, fettuccine, buckwheat pasta, or rigatoni

2 tablespoons butter
½ cup finely chopped fresh mint
¼ cup finely chopped flat-leaf parsley
Freshly grated pecorino cheese

In a Dutch oven, heat the oil (2 turns of the pan) over medium-high to high heat. Pat the meat dry and add to the pan in batches, cooking to brown all sides and seasoning with salt and pepper. Transfer the lamb to a plate as you cook it.

Add the carrot, celery, onion, garlic, chile, bay leaf, marjoram, rosemary, sage, and salt and pepper to taste. Partially cover and cook until the vegetables soften, 5 to 7 minutes. Add the wine and cook until the liquid reduces to about ¼ cup.

Add the stock and return the lamb to the pan. Cover and braise over low heat until tender, 1 hour to 1 hour 30 minutes.

Shred the meat with two forks right in the pan. Hand-crush the tomatoes as you add them to the pot, then add the juices from the can. Add the citrus zest, partially cover the pan, and simmer 30 minutes longer. Remove the citrus zest.

Bring a large pot of water to a boil. Set up a big bowl of ice and water.

Trim the Brussels spouts and separate into leaves. Salt the boiling water, add the Brussels sprouts leaves, and cook for 2 to 3 minutes. Scoop out with a strainer or spider and cold-shock in the ice bath.

Bring the salted water back to a boil. Add the pasta and cook to al dente. Reserve about ½ cup of starchy cooking water, drain the pasta and return to the pot.

Add the ragu, Brussels sprouts leaves, butter, and reserved starchy water and toss to combine. Adjust the seasonings.

Serve in shallow bowls and garnish with mint, parsley, and pecorino.

TAGLIATELLE WITH LAMB RAGU WITH MEYER LEMON AND OLIVES

SERVES 6 TO 8

If lemon and olives are among your favorite flavors, try this delicious delivery system. If time is limited, this is a great alternative to the other slower-cooking lamb ragu.

2 tablespoons olive oil

1½ pounds ground lamb

1 large onion, finely chopped

3 or 4 cloves garlic (to taste), finely chopped

1 large bay leaf

2 Meyer lemons: 1 zested (to get 2 tablespoons zest) and juiced, 1 thinly sliced

Salt and pepper

1 cup good-quality green Sicilian olives, pitted and coarsely chopped

3 tablespoons tomato paste

1 cup dry white wine

2 to 3 cups lamb or chicken stock

1 to 1½ pounds egg tagliatelle or fettuccine (see Tip)

2 tablespoons butter

½ cup finely chopped fresh flat-leaf parsley and/or mint

Fresh ricotta cheese or freshly grated pecorino cheese, for serving

In a Dutch oven, heat the oil (2 turns of the pan) over medium-high heat. Pat the meat dry, add to the pan, and cook, breaking it up into crumbles as it browns. Add the onion, garlic, bay leaf, Meyer lemon zest, salt, and pepper. Cook for 5 minutes to soften, then add the olives and tomato paste and stir for 1 minute. Add the wine and stir to deglaze the pan. Stir in 2 cups of the stock, reduce the heat to low, and simmer for 30 minutes for the flavors to combine; add more stock if the pan gets too dry.

Bring a large pot of water to a boil for the pasta. Salt the water and cook the pasta to al dente. Before draining, ladle out about ½ cup of the starchy pasta cooking water.

Meanwhile, in a small skillet, melt the butter. Add the lemon slices and cook until lightly browned on both sides. Sprinkle with a pinch of salt.

Add the lemon juice to the ragu. Drain the pasta and add it to the sauce along with the starchy water and half the chopped herbs. Toss with tongs for 1 to 2 minutes for the flavors to be absorbed.

Serve in shallow bowls, topped with the caramelized lemon slices, cheese, and the remaining herbs.

TIP

Use the larger amount of pasta if serving 8.

SHORT RIB RAGU

Make this dish at least 1 day before serving. We love this rich sauce in the winter months. I serve it three slightly different ways: over Rachael's Polenta (page 179), with Drunken Pasta (see box, at right), and for Christmas I add homemade sausage to the ragu and it becomes Christmas Pasta (see Variation, below). If serving with pasta, toss the cooked, drained pasta with a little butter and a few ladles of the sauce, then top with meat and grated pecorino (tangy) or Parm (nutty).

6 meaty short ribs (about 4 inches long), at room temperature
Kosher salt and pepper
2 tablespoons olive or canola oil
2 small ribs celery with leafy tops, chopped
1 carrot, chopped
1 onion, chopped
2 large shallots, chopped
4 cloves garlic, thinly sliced
1 large bay leaf
A few juniper berries (optional)
3 cups Barolo wine
6 cups veal or beef stock
1 (28- to 32-ounce) can San Marzano tomatoes (look for DOP on the label)
Herb bundle: a few sprigs of fresh flat-leaf parsley, sage, and 1 sprig rosemary, tied together with kitchen twine

Position a rack in the center of the oven and preheat the oven to 325°F.

Pat the meat dry and season with salt and pepper. Heat a large Dutch oven over medium to medium-high heat. Add the oil (2 turns of the pan). Working in two batches, add the ribs and cook to brown on all sides. Color is flavor, so take care to get a good crust on the meat. Transfer the ribs to a plate and repeat with the second batch.

Reduce the heat a bit and add the celery, carrot, onion, shallots, garlic, bay leaf, and juniper berries (if using); season with salt and pepper. Partially cover and cook, stirring occasionally, to soften the vegetables, 8 to 10 minutes. Add the wine, stir to deglaze the pan, and cook until it has reduced by half. Add the stock, then hand-crush the tomatoes as you add them to the pot and add the juices from the can. Slide the ribs into the sauce and bring to a low boil. Add the herb bundle, cover, and transfer to the oven. Roast until very tender, 2½ to 3 hours. Let the meat cool to room temperature in the sauce. Refrigerate to chill and solidify the fat.

Skim the fat from the top and remove the meat from the bones, discarding the connective tissue. Shred the meat with two forks and return the meat to the sauce. Reheat the sauce, partially covered, over medium heat. Remove and discard the bay leaf and herb bundle.

VARIATION

Christmas Pasta

This is basically the Short Rib Ragu with these changes: Before browning the short ribs, brown and crumble Sweet Italian Sausage with Fennel (page 237) or Hot Italian Sausage (page 237), whichever you prefer. Transfer the cooked sausage to a plate and continue with the recipe as written. Store the sausage separately until the sauce is skimmed and the meat pulled. Add the sausage when you reheat the ragu to serve it.

DRUNKEN PASTA

This is a method more than a recipe. Bring a large pot of water to a boil for the pasta. Salt the water, add the pasta, boil for 5 minutes, and drain. Remove and set aside the pasta. Return the pot to the heat. Add 1 bottle of dry red wine for every pound of pasta you cooked. Bring the wine to a boil and then cook for 2 to 3 minutes to reduce. Add the pasta to the wine and cook over medium-high heat, tossing frequently with tongs until most of the liquid has evaporated. The pasta should be cooked to al dente. Drain the pasta, reserving the starchy cooking wine. Toss the pasta with a little of the starchy wine and whatever sauce you are serving the drunken pasta with.

RIGGIES WITH HOT SAUSAGE RAGU

2 tablespoons olive oil

1 pound Hot Italian Sausage, homemade (page 237) or store-bought, casings removed

1 onion, finely chopped

2 cloves garlic, sliced

1 tablespoon fresh rosemary leaves, finely chopped

1 cup chestnuts (roasted or from a jar or vacuum pack), finely diced

½ cup dry red or white wine

1 cup chicken or veal stock

1 (28- to 32-ounce) can San Marzano tomatoes (look for DOP on the label)

1 pound short-cut ridged pasta (such as rigatoni, mostaccioli rigate, or medium-large shells)

Grated Parmigiano-Reggiano cheese, for serving

In Dutch oven or deep large skillet, heat the oil (2 turns of the pan) over medium-high heat. Add the sausage and cook, breaking it up into crumbles as it browns. Add the onion, garlic, and rosemary and cook to soften the onion, 5 to 6 minutes. Add the chestnuts and stir for 1 or 2 minutes. Add the wine, stir to deglaze the pan, and cook until almost evaporated. Add the stock. Hand-crush the tomatoes as you add them to the pan, then add the juices from the can. Reduce the heat and simmer for 20 to 30 minutes at a low bubble.

Bring a large pot of water to a boil for the pasta. Salt the water and cook the pasta to al dente. Before draining, ladle out about a cup of the starchy pasta cooking water and add it to the sauce. Drain the pasta and return it to the same pot. Add the sauce, tossing with tongs for 1 to 2 minutes for the flavors to be absorbed.

Serve in shallow bowls, topped with Parm.

GNOCCHI WITH VEAL AND SAGE RAGU

I love making homemade gnocchi, but grocery stores also have amazing quality plain and vegetable gnocchi in both the fresh and frozen food sections—such a great fallback to serve with this quick-cooking ragu.

1 tablespoon EVOO

2 tablespoons butter

8 fresh sage leaves

1 pound ground veal

1 small to medium onion, finely chopped

2 large cloves garlic, finely chopped

Freshly grated nutmeg

Salt and pepper

½ cup Sancerre or other Sauvignon Blanc

1 cup whole milk

4 to 5 ounces Gorgonzola dolce cheese

1 pound good-quality frozen or fresh gnocchi or butternut gnocchi, homemade (pages 112 and 113) or store-bought

Grated Parmigiano-Reggiano or Grana Padano cheese, for serving

Finely chopped toasted hazelnuts, for garnish

Bring a large pot of water to a boil for the gnocchi.

In a deep large skillet or saucepan, heat the EVOO (1 turn of the pan) over medium heat. Melt in the butter. When the foam subsides and the butter begins to smell nutty, add the sage leaves and cook until crisp. Drain on paper towels.

Add the veal to the skillet and cook, breaking it up into crumbles as it browns. Add the onion, garlic, nutmeg, salt, and pepper. Cook to soften the onion, about 5 minutes. Add the wine and cook to absorb into the meat. Add the milk, reduce the heat to medium-low, and simmer for 15 minutes to thicken. Add the Gorgonzola and stir to melt in. Chop the crispy sage and add it to the sauce.

Salt the boiling water and cook the gnocchi until they float. Drain and toss with the sauce.

Serve the gnocchi topped with cheese and hazelnuts.

PICI WITH VEAL AND EGGPLANT RAGU

If you love veal chops with sage, here is a hearty pasta dish to share the love of the flavors without the cost of the chops. You could also serve this with any sturdy pasta cut such as strozzapreti.

1 medium eggplant, half the skin peeled (in stripes) and cut into ¼- to ½-inch cubes
Salt
2 tablespoons olive oil
1 tablespoon butter
1½ pounds ground veal
10 to 12 fresh sage leaves, thinly sliced
Freshly grated nutmeg
Pepper
1 small onion, finely chopped
2 to 3 cloves garlic (to taste), chopped
2 tablespoons tomato paste
½ cup dry white wine
1½ cups veal or chicken stock
¼ to ⅓ cup heavy cream
1 pound pici
Grated Parmigiano-Reggiano cheese, for serving

Season the eggplant with salt and let drain on a kitchen towel.

Heat a Dutch oven or deep large skillet over medium to medium-high heat. Add the oil (2 turns of the pan) and melt the butter into the oil. Add the veal, breaking it into crumbles as it browns. Add the sage and a few grates of nutmeg and season with salt and pepper. Increase the heat to medium-high and stir in the onion, garlic, and eggplant. Partially cover and cook, stirring occasionally, until the vegetables are tender, 8 to 10 minutes. Add the tomato paste and cook for 1 minute. Add the wine and stir to deglaze the pan. Add the stock and bring to a bubble. Stir in the cream and simmer over low heat for 10 minutes.

Bring a large pot of water to a boil for the pasta. Salt the water, add the pasta, and cook to al dente. Drain, reserving ½ cup of the starchy cooking water. Toss together the sauce, starchy water, and pasta. Adjust the seasonings and top with grated cheese.

SICILIAN LEMON SPAGHETTI

My mom is a little Sicilian with a mighty personality. She loves lemons; they have a lot in common because they both make everything better, always. I make this spaghetti for my mom on her birthday, July 18.

Grated zest of 2 organic lemons
Juice of 6 lemons (about 1 cup)
½ cup EVOO
Salt and black pepper
1 teaspoon crushed red pepper flakes (optional)
1 pound spaghetti
1 cup fresh basil leaves, torn
2 to 3 cups baby arugula
Finely chopped toasted pistachios, for serving
Grated pecorino cheese, for serving (optional)

Bring a large pot of water to a boil for the pasta.

In a serving bowl, whisk the lemon zest, lemon juice, and EVOO. Season with salt and black pepper and add the red pepper flakes (if using).

Salt the boiling water, add the spaghetti, and cook to al dente. Before draining, ladle out about 1 cup of the cooking water.

Combine the starchy water, spaghetti, and torn basil in the serving bowl with the lemon dressing and toss to coat. Adjust the seasonings. Add the arugula and toss to combine.

Serve in shallow bowls topped with pistachios and pecorino, if desired.

AGLIO E OLIO

Acciughe (anchovies) are actually the main ingredient in our recipe for garlic and oil spaghetti. If you think you don't like anchovies, you may be surprised. When you add heat to anchovies, they break down so completely that they actually disappear, melting into warm oil. Once the anchovies disintegrate, their flavor changes and mellows; the flavor is less fishy and more that of toasted, salted nuts.

When I was a little girl, this dish was a favorite of mine, and I loved sharing it with my grandpa Emmanuel. He loved anchovies, and his recipe for artichokes with anchovy bread crumbs (see page 44) is our favorite holiday dish each Christmas.

A friend of mine, the very talented photographer Melanie Dunea, asked me to participate in a project of hers in which she collected photographs of, and essays by, cooks and chefs about what their last meal would be. I told her that I would be so upset it was my last meal that I would not be hungry for anything at all. However, when I die and there turns out to be a heaven, and if I get to eat a first meal when I get there, I would share Aglio e Olio with extra anchovies with my grandpa Emmanuel and some roasted butternut squash with my first dog, Boo. (Squash was her favorite.) I miss them both so very much.

¼ cup olive oil

12 good-quality anchovy fillets (see Tip)

6 large cloves garlic, thinly sliced or chopped

2 small dried or fresh red chiles, finely chopped

½ cup dry vermouth

Salt

1 pound spaghetti or linguine

1 cup loosely packed fresh flat-leaf parsley tops, finely chopped

Black pepper (optional)

Bring a large pot of water to a boil for the pasta.

Meanwhile, in a large skillet, heat the oil (4 turns of the pan) over medium heat. Add the anchovies, cover the pan with a splatter screen or lid, and shake until the anchovies begin to break up. Reduce the heat a bit, uncover, and stir until the anchovies melt into the oil. Reduce the heat a bit more, add the garlic

and chiles, and stir for 2 minutes more. Add the vermouth.

Salt the boiling water, add the spaghetti, and cook to al dente. Before draining, ladle out about 1 cup of the starchy pasta cooking water and add it to the sauce along with the parsley. Drain the pasta and return it to the pot. Add the sauce, season with black pepper (if using), and toss with tongs for 1 to 2 minutes for the flavors to be absorbed.

TIP

Use oil-packed Spanish l'Escala anchovy fillets, drained, or 6 salted whole anchovies, soaked to remove some of the salt, and separated from their spines into 12 fillets.

VARIATION

Pasta con Mollica Siciliana

Aglio e Olio is made richer with the addition of toasted homemade bread crumbs and almonds. The nuts really add something special to the nutty flavor of the anchovies. Before beginning the Aglio e Olio recipe, use a medium skillet to toast ½ cup sliced almonds in ⅓ cup olive oil over medium heat until golden. Transfer to a board to cool, then chop and set aside. Return the skillet to the stove and heat 3 tablespoons olive oil over medium heat. When the oil ripples, add 1 cup homemade bread crumbs and toast until deep golden and nutty. Combine with the chopped nuts and 1 cup chopped fresh flat-leaf parsley. Set aside while you make the Aglio e Olio sauce, adding 3 tablespoons capers when you add the garlic. Cook the pasta as directed and add about two-thirds of the almond bread crumbs when you toss the pasta with the sauce. Transfer to a serving dish and scatter the remaining crumbs over the top. Pass EVOO for drizzling at the table.

CACIO E PEPE

SERVES 6 TO 8

Serve tossed with long- or short-cut pasta, egg tagliatelle, gnocchi, or gnudi.

Salt
1½ pounds pasta
4 ounces (1 stick) butter
2 teaspoons coarsely ground pepper
1 cup freshly grated Pecorino Romano cheese
½ cup freshly grated Grana Padano or Parmigiano-Reggiano cheese

Bring a large pot of water to a boil for the pasta. Salt the water and cook the pasta to al dente.

Meanwhile, in a small saucepan, combine the butter and pepper and melt the butter over low heat.

Before draining the pasta, ladle out about 1 cup of the starchy pasta cooking water. Drain the pasta and return it to the pot. Add the sauce, starchy water, and cheeses and toss with tongs for 1 to 2 minutes for the flavors to be absorbed.

VARIATION

Cacio e Pepe with Spaghetti Squash

Roast the spaghetti squash as directed on page 114. When you remove the squash from the oven, melt the butter with the pepper. In a small saucepan, warm up 1 cup chicken stock. Toss the pepper butter, warm stock, and both cheeses together and serve over the spaghetti squash.

PENNE WITH PEAS AND MINT

SERVES 4 TO 6

This is a lovely light lunch or supper that I often make in late spring when peas are sweet and fresh. It's a meal that can be made in less than 10 minutes.

1 cup chicken or vegetable stock
1 clove garlic, smashed
1 (16-ounce) bag frozen peas, or 3 cups shelled fresh peas
½ cup fresh mint leaves
¼ cup fresh dill leaves
¼ cup fresh flat-leaf parsley tops
Juice of 1 lemon or Meyer lemon
1 to 2 tablespoons EVOO
Salt and pepper
1 pound penne rigate
½-pound ricotta salata cheese, crumbled or shaved
1 cup grape tomatoes, quartered

Bring a large pot of water to a boil for the pasta.

In a deep skillet or medium pot, combine the stock and garlic and bring to a simmer. Add the peas, cook for 3 minutes, and remove from the heat. Scoop out and set aside 1 cup of the peas. In a blender or food processor, combine the remaining peas, the stock and garlic, the mint, dill, parsley, lemon juice, EVOO, salt, and pepper and puree.

Salt the boiling water and cook the pasta to al dente. Before draining, ladle out about ½ cup of the starchy pasta cooking water. Drain the pasta and return it to the pot. Add the pea puree, starchy water, and whole peas and toss with tongs for 1 to 2 minutes for the flavors to be absorbed. Adjust the seasonings.

Serve in shallow bowls topped with lots of crumbled or shaved ricotta salata and garnish with grape tomatoes.

FETTUCCINE WITH ASPARAGUS, MUSHROOMS, AND HERBS

SERVES 4 TO 6

This dish is made with tempered egg yolks, like a carbonara. I use Araucana eggs, which are organic eggs with greenish-blue shells. Because the chickens are fed marigolds, the yolks are bright orange rather than yellow, giving this sauce a lot of color and great flavor. Pasteurized egg product can be substituted if you're worried about using raw egg yolks.

3 tablespoons olive oil

½ pound purple or green asparagus, thinly sliced on an angle

Salt and pepper

2 tablespoons butter

½ pound cremini mushrooms, thinly sliced

¼ pound hen-of-the-woods mushrooms (maitake), root cut away and mushrooms separated

2 shallots, chopped

3 or 4 cloves garlic (to taste), chopped

2 tablespoons fresh thyme leaves

¼ cup sherry or Marsala

1 pound fettuccine

4 large free-range organic egg yolks

½ cup freshly grated Pecorino Romano cheese

½ cup freshly grated Parmigiano-Reggiano cheese

¼ cup fresh flat-leaf parsley tops, chopped

¼ cup fresh tarragon leaves, chopped

¼ cup minced fresh chives

Bring a large pot of water to a boil for the pasta.

In a large skillet, heat 1 tablespoon of the oil (1 turn of the pan) over medium-high heat. Add the asparagus, season with salt and pepper, and toss for 2 to 3 minutes until tender-crisp. Transfer to a plate. Add the remaining 2 tablespoons oil (2 turns of the pan) and melt the butter into the oil. Add the mushrooms and brown well, 7 to 8 minutes. Add the shallots, garlic, thyme, salt, and pepper and stir for 2 minutes. Add the sherry and reduce the heat to low.

Salt the boiling water and cook the pasta to al dente. Before draining, ladle out about 1 cup of the starchy pasta cooking water and beat it into the egg yolks to warm them (temper them). Drain the pasta and add it to the skillet along with the asparagus and toss. Remove from the heat and toss with the tempered egg yolks and cheeses for 1 to 2 minutes to form a silky sauce. Add the parsley, tarragon, and chives and adjust the seasonings.

SPAGHETTI WITH RAW SAUCE

SERVES 6

Summer love! Serve this dish hot or cold.

RAW SAUCE:

4 cloves garlic, very thinly sliced or chopped

1 Vidalia or red onion, quartered and very thinly sliced

1 small fresh red chile, thinly sliced

2½ pounds red and yellow or orange tomatoes, chopped, with their juices

About ⅓ cup EVOO

½ cup green Sicilian olives, pitted and chopped

3 tablespoons capers, drained

A handful of fresh basil leaves, torn

½ cup fresh flat-leaf parsley tops, chopped

Salt and pepper

PASTA:

Salt

1 to 1½ pounds spaghetti

½ pound fior di latte cheese (fresh mozzarella), diced

Grated Parmigiano-Reggiano cheese, for serving

Make the raw sauce: In a large shallow serving bowl, combine the garlic, onion, chile, tomatoes, EVOO, olives, capers, basil, parsley, salt, and pepper. Let stand for 15 to 20 minutes for the juices to be drawn out and combine.

Make the pasta: Bring a large pot of water to a boil. Salt the water and cook the pasta to al dente. Before draining, ladle out about ½ cup of the starchy pasta cooking water and add it to the sauce. Drain the pasta and return it to the pot. Add the sauce, tossing with tongs for 1 to 2 minutes for the flavors to be absorbed. Add the mozzarella and transfer the pasta to a serving bowl. Serve topped with Parm.

PICI WITH ROASTED GARLIC, TOMATO, AND RED PEPPER SAUCE

SERVES 8

Serve this sauce with pici (*pinci* in dialect), which is a thick, long-cut pasta predominantly used in Tuscan cooking. We call it fat spaghetti. Dried pici can be purchased in Italian markets or from online suppliers. A good alternative, which is easy to find in most markets, is bucatini—fat, hollow spaghetti.

2 heads garlic, roasted (see box, page 312)

24 plum tomatoes (4 to 5 pounds), halved

Olive oil, for drizzling

Leaves from 10 to 12 sprigs fresh thyme

Salt and pepper

2 red field peppers or large bell peppers, roasted (see box, page 334)

4 fresh basil leaves

1½ pounds pici or bucatini

2 tablespoons butter (optional)

Grated Parmigiano-Reggiano cheese, for serving

Roast the garlic, then reduce the oven temperature to 350°F.

Place the tomatoes on two large baking sheets and drizzle liberally with oil. Toss to coat, sprinkle with the thyme, and season with salt and pepper. Roast until well slumped, about 1 hour.

Meanwhile, roast, peel, and seed the peppers.

Bring a large pot of water to a boil for the pasta.

Working in two batches, in a high-powered blender, combine half the tomatoes, half the peppers, and 2 basil leaves. Squeeze in the garlic from one of the heads. Puree and transfer to a saucepan. Repeat with the remaining tomatoes, pepper, basil, and garlic. Bring the sauce to a low simmer to keep warm.

Salt the boiling water and cook the pasta to al dente. Before draining, ladle out about a cup of the starchy pasta cooking water. Drain the pasta, return it to the pot with the butter (if using), half the sauce, and some of the starchy water, tossing with tongs for 1 to 2 minutes for the flavors to be absorbed.

Serve in shallow bowls or family-style on a large platter, topped with the remaining sauce. Pass lots of Parm at the table.

SPAGHETTI WITH PEPPERS AND ONIONS

SERVES 4 TO 6

When I make this for my husband and myself or my mom, I serve it with sweet and hot Italian sausage links. However, this sauce is now a family classic because of my sister, Maria. Maria doesn't like pork or sausage, so one night I had to adapt a sausage ragu my mom and husband really liked for Maria. The result was this sauce, which has become a staple. With fennel seeds, fresh fennel, chiles, peppers, and onions, you honestly do not miss the sausage; all the same flavors are there.

¼ cup good-quality olive oil

4 cloves garlic, very thinly sliced

1 teaspoon fennel seeds

1 teaspoon crushed red pepper flakes

1 bulb fennel, or 3 to 4 bulbs baby or wild fennel, trimmed and thinly sliced

1 large yellow or red onion, quartered and thinly sliced

2 cubanelle peppers, halved and thinly sliced

2 tablespoons tomato paste

½ cup dry vermouth or dry white wine

1 cup chicken stock

1 (28- to 32-ounce) can San Marzano tomatoes (look for DOP on the label)

A few fresh basil leaves, torn

1 pound spaghetti

2 tablespoons butter

Grated Parmigiano-Reggiano cheese, for serving

In a large skillet, heat the oil (4 turns of the pan) over medium heat. Add the garlic and stir for 2 minutes. Add the fennel seeds and red pepper flakes and stir for 30 seconds. Add the fresh fennel, onion, and peppers, partially cover, and cook to soften the vegetables, 8 to 10 minutes. Add the tomato paste and stir for 1 minute, until fragrant. Stir in the vermouth to deglaze the pan and add the stock. Hand-crush the tomatoes as you add them to the pan, then add the juices from the can and the basil. Simmer for 15 to 20 minutes to thicken.

Meanwhile, bring a large pot of water to a boil. Salt the water and cook the pasta to al dente. Before draining the pasta, ladle out about a cup of the starchy pasta cooking water. Drain the pasta and return it to the pot. Add the starchy water and butter, tossing with tongs to melt the butter. Add half the sauce and toss to combine.

Serve in shallow bowls and top the pasta with the remaining sauce and lots of Parm.

SPAGHETTI WITH RAMPS

Ramps (wild leeks) are wildly delicious in every form: pickled, wilted on pizza, placed on over-easy or poached eggs and toast, and on and on. But for my money, winding up with as many ramps as possible in the arms of perfectly cooked spaghetti—well, that is as good as it gets.

¼ cup olive oil

3 bunches ramps (about 36), white parts finely chopped or thinly sliced, green tops cut into 1-inch pieces

Salt and pepper

½ cup dry crisp white wine or dry vermouth

1 to 1½ pounds spaghetti, Sicilian Lemon Spaghetti (page 138), or egg tagliatelle

Juice of 1 lemon

3 tablespoons butter

A fat handful of fresh flat-leaf parsley or a combination of parsley and fresh mint, chopped

Grated pecorino cheese, for tossing and serving

Bring a large pot of water to a boil for the pasta.

In a large skillet, heat the oil (4 turns of the pan) over medium heat. Add the ramp whites, season with salt and pepper, and stir for 2 to 3 minutes, until very fragrant. Add the wine and reduce the heat to low.

Meanwhile, salt the boiling water and cook the pasta to al dente. Before draining, ladle out about a cup of the starchy pasta cooking water.

Add the lemon juice and butter to the sauce in the skillet, swirling to melt the butter. Add the starchy water. Drain the pasta and add it to the sauce along with the ramp greens, parsley, and a couple handfuls of pecorino and toss with tongs for 1 or 2 minutes for the flavors to be absorbed. Adjust the seasonings.

Serve in shallow bowls with more pecorino at the table.

PASTA ALLA NORMA

This is a family favorite, so much so that we call it Pasta Normal, because we make it so often. What's not to love? Eggplant, tomatoes, pasta, ricotta—you can see why anyone would want to eat it on a regular, "normal" basis.

1 heavy medium-large eggplant, half the skin peeled (in stripes)

Salt

About ⅓ cup olive oil

6 large cloves garlic, thinly sliced or chopped

1 small dried or fresh red chile, finely chopped

1 (28- to 32-ounce) can San Marzano tomatoes (look for DOP on the label), 2 pints cherry tomatoes, or 12 plum or vine tomatoes, peeled (see Tip, page 67) and chopped

A fat handful of fresh basil leaves, torn

1 pound spaghetti or linguine

½ cup loosely packed fresh flat-leaf parsley tops, chopped

½ pound ricotta salata cheese, crumbled or grated on the large holes of a box grater

Cut the eggplant into ½-inch-thick planks, then into batons ½ inch wide and about 2 inches long. Salt the eggplant and arrange it in a single layer on a kitchen towel. Set aside to sweat for 30 minutes. Gently press out excess water.

In a large skillet, heat 3 table-spoons of the oil (3 turns of the pan) over medium-high heat. When the oil smokes, add half the eggplant and lightly brown all over. Set the first batch aside and repeat with the remaining eggplant, adding more oil if necessary. Add the garlic and chile to the eggplant in the pan and stir for 2 to 3 minutes. Return the first batch of eggplant to the pan, along with the tomatoes (if using canned tomatoes, hand-crush them as you add them). If you are using cherry tomatoes, cover the pan and cook, shaking occasionally, until they burst, about 10 minutes. Canned or fresh tomatoes should simmer at a low bubble for 20 minutes. Stir in the basil.

Meanwhile, bring a large pot of water to a boil for the pasta. Salt the water and cook the pasta to al dente. Before draining, ladle out about a cup of the pasta water. Drain the pasta and return it to the pot. Add the sauce, pasta water, and parsley and toss for 1 to 2 minutes for the flavors to be absorbed. Adjust the seasonings.

Serve the pasta in shallow bowls and top with ricotta salata.

ORECCHIETTE WITH RAPINI

This is a unanimous family favorite. If you want to make it even heartier, add 1 pound homemade sweet or hot sausage (see page 237), browned and crumbled, to the dish.

1 bunch rapini (broccoli rabe), trimmed

Salt

¼ cup olive oil

4 to 6 flat anchovy fillets

1 small red onion, quartered and sliced

4 cloves garlic, chopped or sliced

1 sweet red frying pepper, sliced

2 red Italian cherry peppers, seeded and sliced

Freshly grated nutmeg

½ cup chicken or vegetable stock

1 pound orecchiette or farfalle

2 tablespoons chopped sweet or hot Italian pickled peppers, with a splash of their brine (optional)

Ricotta salata cheese, crumbled or grated, for serving

Fill a large bowl with ice and water. Cut the broccoli rabe into 2-inch pieces, halving any thick stems lengthwise. Bring a large pot with a few inches of water to a rolling boil, season with salt, add the broccoli rabe, and cook for 2 to 3 minutes to cook out the bitterness. Cold-shock in the ice bath and drain well.

Fill the pot with water and bring to a boil for the pasta.

In a large skillet, heat the oil (4 turns of the pan) over medium heat. Add the anchovies, cover the pan with a splatter screen or lid, and shake until the anchovies begin to break up. Reduce the heat a bit, uncover, and stir until the anchovies melt into the oil. Stir in the onion, garlic, frying pepper, and cherry peppers and stir for 3 to 4 minutes to soften. Add the chopped broccoli rabe and season with salt and a little nutmeg. Add the stock and reduce the heat to keep warm.

Salt the boiling water and cook the pasta to al dente. Before draining, ladle out about a cup of the starchy pasta cooking water and add it to the sauce. Drain the pasta and return it to the pot. Add the sauce, tossing with tongs for 1 to 2 minutes for the flavors to be absorbed. Add the pickled peppers (if using) and toss.

Serve topped with ricotta salata.

DRUNKEN SPAGHETTI WITH SWEET ROASTED BEETS AND RICOTTA SALATA

SERVES 4 TO 6

This is a dish I often make for friends because of its color, but it's the flavors that make return guests request it again and again. If you love the combination of sweet and salty, this dish is for you.

1 bunch beets with large leafy tops

3 tablespoons olive oil, plus more for the beets

Salt and pepper

1 pound spaghetti

1 (750ml) bottle red Zinfandel or Barolo wine

4 large shallots, or 1 small red onion, finely chopped

4 cloves garlic, finely chopped

1 teaspoon sugar

2 tablespoons aged balsamic vinegar

½ cup fresh flat-leaf parsley tops, finely chopped

½ pound ricotta salata cheese, crumbled or grated

Preheat the oven to 400°F.

Trim the beet greens, wash well, and cut into 1-inch-wide ribbons. Trim the beets, but leave unpeeled. Rub the beets with oil, season with salt and pepper, and place in a baking dish. Cover with foil and roast until tender, 50 minutes to 1 hour. When cool enough to handle, rub off the skins with a paper towel. (Rub your hands with a little oil to keep them from being stained.) Chop into small bite-size pieces (use a plastic cutting board so you don't stain your wooden board).

Bring a large pot of water to a boil for the pasta. Salt the water and cook the pasta for 5 minutes, then drain. Return the empty pot to the stove, add the wine, bring to a boil, and cook for 2 to 3 minutes to reduce. Add the parcooked pasta and cook over medium-high heat, tossing frequently with tongs, until most of the liquid has evaporated and the pasta is al dente. Add the beet greens when the pasta is just about al dente.

Meanwhile, in a skillet, heat the oil (3 turns of the pan) over medium-high heat. Add the shallots and garlic, season with salt and pepper, and cook until tender, 7 to 10 minutes. Sprinkle with the sugar. Add the vinegar and some of the wine sauce from the pasta pot and stir to deglaze the pan.

Scrape the onion mixture into the pasta pot and toss to combine with the pasta. Add the beets and parsley and toss well.

Serve topped with ricotta salata.

BROKEN SPAGHETTI RISOTTO WITH MUSHROOMS, WALNUTS, AND GORGONZOLA

I love rice pilaf, and it's not because of the rice—it's because of the nutty broken spaghetti. One day I decided to make a pot of rice pilaf, but hold the rice. Good idea.

½ cup walnuts
2 tablespoons butter
1 tablespoon olive oil
1 small onion, finely chopped
½ pound cremini mushrooms, sliced
2 cloves garlic, grated
1 pound spaghetti, broken into bite-size pieces
Salt and pepper
½ cup white wine
4 cups chicken or vegetable stock, preferably homemade (pages 64 and 65)
10 fresh sage leaves, sliced
1 cup crumbled Gorgonzola cheese

Preheat the oven to 325°F.

Spread the walnuts on a rimmed baking sheet and toast in the oven, 10 to 12 minutes (your nose will know when they are done).

In a medium skillet, melt 1 tablespoon of the butter with the oil (1 turn of the pan) over medium heat. Add the onion and cook until tender, 2 to 3 minutes. Add the mushrooms and garlic and brown, about 4 minutes. Add the spaghetti and toast until golden brown, about 5 minutes. Season with salt and pepper and stir in the wine. Stir constantly as the wine evaporates, then add a ladleful of stock. Keep stirring as that evaporates. Continue the process until the spaghetti is tender and cooked through. Stir in the sage, remaining 1 tablespoon butter, and half the Gorgonzola.

Serve topped with the rest of the Gorgonzola and the toasted walnuts.

BROKEN SPAGHETTI RISOTTO WITH KALE AND HAZELNUTS

½ ounce dried mixed wild mushrooms or dried porcini
6 to 7 cups chicken or mushroom stock, preferably homemade (pages 64 and 65)
2 tablespoons olive oil
1 small onion, finely chopped
2 large cloves garlic, grated or finely chopped
¾ pound spaghetti, broken into 1½-inch pieces
Salt and pepper
1 cup dry white wine
2 cups packed baby kale or spinach, coarsely chopped
3 tablespoons butter
½ cup freshly grated Parmigiano-Reggiano cheese
¾ cup hazelnuts, toasted and chopped
Freshly grated nutmeg
½ lemon

In a saucepan, combine the dried mushrooms and stock and keep warm over low heat.

In a risotto pot (see box, page 184) or other round-bottomed pan, heat the oil (2 turns of the pan) over medium to medium-high heat. Add the onion and garlic and stir until tender, 3 to 4 minutes. Add the spaghetti, season with salt and pepper, and toast until deeply golden in color and very nutty in fragrance, 3 to 4 minutes. Stir in the wine and let it cook away, 1 minute. Add a couple of ladles of stock every few minutes, stirring for a good minute with each addition of stock to develop the starches. Evaporate almost all of the liquid before each addition of stock. Pasta will cook more quickly than rice; start tasting after about 9 minutes of cooking, once you begin to add stock.

When you are down to the last addition of your liquids, scoop out the reconstituted mushrooms, chop, and add to the pasta. Wilt in the greens and stir in the butter, Parm, and hazelnuts. Adjust the seasonings and add nutmeg to taste. Remove from the heat and finish the dish with a squeeze of lemon juice.

FARRO SPAGHETTI WITH SHALLOTS, KALE, AND HAZELNUTS

For this recipe I start with my That's Shallot-a-Pasta (see box) and add shredded kale and some toasted hazelnuts. Wow! Great nutrition and great idea! Even tastier than the original.

2 tablespoons EVOO

3 tablespoons butter

12 to 14 large shallots, halved and thinly sliced

3 or 4 cloves garlic (to taste), finely chopped

Salt and pepper

1 pound farro spaghetti or whole wheat spaghetti

1 small bunch lacinato kale (also called black, Tuscan, or dinosaur kale), stemmed and shredded

½ cup fresh flat-leaf parsley tops, chopped

1 cup freshly grated pecorino or Parmigiano-Reggiano cheese, plus more for serving

½ cup chopped hazelnuts, toasted

In a deep skillet, heat the EVOO (2 turns of the pan) over medium-low heat. Melt in the butter. When it foams, add the shallots and garlic, season with salt and pepper, and cook, stirring occasionally, until the shallots are lightly caramelized, about 20 minutes.

Bring a large pot of water to a boil for the pasta. Salt the water and cook the pasta to al dente, adding the kale about 30 seconds before the pasta is al dente. Before draining, ladle out 1 cup of the starchy pasta cooking water and stir it into the shallots. Drain the pasta and kale and toss it with the shallots, parsley, and cheese. Adjust the pepper and toss for 1 minute for the liquid to be absorbed.

Serve topped with more cheese and the hazelnuts.

THAT'S SHALLOT-A-PASTA!

For years I have made a dish I call That's Shallot-a-Pasta! I've taught it on air several times, and once I make it for friends, they always request it on return visits. The recipe is so easy it's barely a recipe at all. It's just tons of shallots cooked in a combo of EVOO and butter until lightly caramelized. Then you toss the cooked pasta with the shallots, some pasta water, parsley, salt, pepper, and grated Parm or pecorino. Done. Then you're addicted, converted, if you will—a member of the club.

FARRO SPAGHETTI WITH CHICKPEAS AND ROASTED CAULIFLOWER

SERVES 4 TO 6

This is a high-protein, nutty, quick pasta dinner that is deeply satisfying.

1 head cauliflower, cut into florets
¼ cup olive oil, plus more for drizzling
3 tablespoons fresh rosemary leaves, chopped
Salt and black pepper
4 flat anchovy fillets
5 to 6 cloves garlic (to taste), grated
1 teaspoon crushed red pepper flakes
1 (28-ounce) can chickpeas or 2 (15-ounce) cans, rinsed and drained
1 cup chicken stock
½ cup fresh flat-leaf parsley tops, chopped
1 pound farro spaghetti or whole wheat spaghetti
Grated Grana Padano or Parmigiano-Reggiano cheese, for serving

Preheat the oven to 425°F.

In a bowl, drizzle the cauliflower with a little oil, sprinkle with the rosemary, and season with salt and black pepper. Toss everything together, spread on a baking sheet, and roast until tender and caramelized at the edges, about 25 minutes.

Meanwhile, bring a large pot of water to a boil for the pasta.

In a large skillet, heat the oil (4 turns of the pan) over medium heat. Add the anchovies, cover the pan with a splatter screen or lid, and shake until the anchovies begin to break up. Reduce the heat a bit, uncover, and stir until the anchovies melt into the oil. Add the garlic and reduce the heat a bit, then stir in the red pepper flakes. In a food processor or blender, puree half the chickpeas with the stock and add to the pan along with the whole chickpeas and parsley.

Salt the boiling water and cook the pasta to al dente. Before draining, ladle out about ½ cup of the starchy pasta cooking water and add it to the sauce. Drain the pasta and return it to the pot. Add the sauce and toss with tongs for 1 to 2 minutes for the flavors to be absorbed. Add the roasted cauliflower and toss.

Serve on warm dishes topped with cheese.

ROASTED PEA AND CARROT PASTA

SERVES 8

This is a delicious room-temperature side dish for spring or summer. We like it for Easter buffets. The pesto is so sweet we wipe our bowls with our fingers.

2 bunches baby carrots with leafy tops, or 2 or 3 regular carrots
⅓ cup olive oil, plus more for drizzling
Salt and pepper
1½ pounds sugar snap peas, strings removed
1 cup packed fresh flat-leaf parsley tops
¼ cup packed fresh mint leaves
¼ cup packed fresh tarragon
1 clove garlic, chopped
¼ cup pignoli (pine nuts), toasted
¼ cup sliced almonds, toasted
Juice of 1 lemon
About ½ cup water or vegetable stock
1 cup freshly grated Parmigiano-Reggiano cheese
1½ pounds fusilli or other short-cut pasta

Preheat the oven to 425°F.

Cut off the carrot tops and set aside. Trim the stems and any brown edges and cut the carrots on an angle or into bite-size cubes. Spread on a rimmed baking sheet and toss with a drizzle of oil and salt and pepper.

Spread the sugar snaps on a separate large rimmed baking sheet, drizzle lightly with oil, and season liberally with salt and lots of pepper.

Roast the carrots and peas until tender and crispy at the edges but not browned all over, 15 to 20 minutes.

Meanwhile, bring a large pot of water to a boil for the pasta.

In a food processor, combine the reserved carrot tops, the parsley, mint, tarragon, garlic, pine nuts, almonds, lemon juice, half the roasted peas, and the water or stock. Pulse until finely chopped. Add the ⅓ cup oil and pulse to combine. Transfer the pesto to a large bowl and stir in the Parm. Season with salt and pepper.

Salt the boiling water and cook the pasta to al dente. Before draining, ladle out about a cup of the starchy pasta cooking water and add it to the pesto. Drain the pasta and return it to the pot. Add the sauce along with the carrots and remaining peas. Toss with tongs for 1 to 2 minutes for the flavors to be absorbed.

STRAW AND HAY PASTA WITH VEGETABLES IN BAGNA CAUDA SAUCE

SERVES 4 TO 6

Bagna cauda is a wonderful dip for vegetables. One day I decided to turn it into a pasta sauce for a primavera-style dish— lots of vegetables and color.

Salt and pepper
1½ to 2 pounds assorted farm-fresh vegetables: asparagus, baby golden beets, baby carrots, baby zucchini, cauliflower or purple cauliflower, haricots verts, pattypan squash, and/or sugar snap peas
Bagna Cauda (page 37)
½ pound egg tagliatelle
½ pound spinach tagliatelle
¼ cup finely chopped fresh flat-leaf parsley leaves

In a large pot, bring a few inches of water to a boil. Salt the water. Fill a large bowl with ice and water. Cut the vegetables into similar shapes and sizes but keep them separate. Blanch the vegetables in the boiling water until tender-crisp: Delicate vegetables like asparagus and thin beans will take 1 to 2 minutes, firmer vegetables will take 3 minutes. After each batch, transfer them to the ice bath to cool using a spider or a small strainer. Drain well.

Make the Bagna Cauda.

Bring a large pot of water to a boil for the pasta. Salt the water and cook the pasta to al dente. Add the vegetables to the water with the pasta in the last minute of cooking to reheat them. Drain the pasta and vegetables and return them to the pot. Add the bagna cauda and parsley, season with salt and pepper, and toss with tongs for 1 to 2 minutes for the flavors to be absorbed.

LINGUINE CON VONGOLE

SERVES 4

The trick to this clam sauce is starting with Aglio e Olio with plenty of anchovies. It's the extra-nutty, salty something in the background that makes everyone ask, "What's in this?"

2½ to 3 pounds littleneck or Manila clams, scrubbed
¼ cup olive oil
6 flat anchovy fillets
4 large cloves garlic, thinly sliced
1 tablespoon grated lemon zest (from an organic lemon)
1 teaspoon crushed red pepper flakes
2 tablespoons chopped fresh thyme
1 cup chicken stock
½ cup dry vermouth
Black pepper
A fat handful of fresh flat-leaf parsley tops, finely chopped
Leaves from 2 sprigs oregano, chopped
Salt
1 pound linguine
Juice of 1 lemon
4 tablespoons (½ stick) butter, melted (optional)
½ cup sliced almonds, toasted
½ cup grated Parmiggiano-Reggiano cheese
EVOO, for drizzling (see Tip)

In a bowl, cover the clams with water and soak for 1 hour. Lift the clams out of the bowl to leave behind any grit.

Bring a large pot of water to a boil for the pasta.

In a large skillet with a lid, heat the oil (4 turns of the pan) over medium heat. Add the anchovies and stir until they melt into the oil. Add the garlic, lemon zest, red pepper flakes, thyme, stock, vermouth, black pepper, parsley, and oregano. Cook to reduce by half, then add the clams. Cover and cook until the clams open, 5 to 7 minutes. Discard any unopened clams.

Salt the boiling water and cook the pasta until just shy of al dente.

Drain the pasta and add it to the clam sauce. Douse with lemon juice and butter (if using) and gently toss for 1 to 2 minutes to allow the pasta to finish cooking and soak up the flavor of the sauce. Remove the pot from the heat and toss the pasta with the cheese. If butter wasn't added earlier, then you can add a fat drizzle of EVOO.

Serve in warm shallow bowls topped with toasted almonds.

 WITH ANY PASTA dish, you can always finish with a good-quality olive oil and cheese. When you toss the EVOO and cheese with the hot liquids, they will emulsify and become part of the sauce.

LINGUINE WITH HOT SAUSAGE AND CLAM SAUCE

I was a guest on *Good Morning America* one morning, and while chatting with fellow foodie and cohost Josh Elliott, this recipe was born. It was more of an early-morning daydream the two of us came up with. Tasty dream.

2 pounds Manila clams or cockles, scrubbed

3 tablespoons EVOO

1 pound Hot Italian Sausage, homemade (page 237) or store-bought, casings removed

1 onion, finely chopped

6 cloves garlic, finely chopped

1 fresh red or green chile, thinly sliced

2 tablespoons fresh thyme leaves, chopped

½ cup dry vermouth

1 cup chicken stock or clam broth

1 pound linguine

3 tablespoons butter

½ cup fresh flat-leaf parsley tops, finely chopped

Salt and pepper

½ cup grated Parmiggiano-Reggiano cheese (optional)

EVOO, for drizzling (optional)

In a bowl, cover the clams with salted water and soak for 1 hour. Lift the clams out of the bowl to leave behind any grit.

Bring a large pot of water to a boil for the pasta.

Meanwhile, in a deep large skillet with a tight-fitting lid, heat the EVOO (3 turns of the pan) over medium-high heat. Add the sausage and cook, breaking it up into crumbles as it browns. Add the onion, garlic, chile, and thyme; partially cover and cook for 5 minutes to soften. Add the vermouth and stock. Cook to reduce the stock by about half. Add the clams, cover, and cook until the clams open. Discard any unopened clams.

Salt the boiling water and cook the pasta to al dente. Before draining, ladle out about a cup of the starchy pasta cooking water.

Add the butter and parsley to the clams and season with salt and pepper. Drain the pasta and add to the skillet along with the starchy water and toss to combine.

If desired, remove the pan from the heat, add the cheese and a fat drizzle of EVOO, and toss.

LINGUINE WITH CHERRY TOMATO–RED CLAM SAUCE

2½ to 3 pounds Manila clams, scrubbed

3 tablespoons EVOO

6 flat anchovy fillets

1 small red onion, finely chopped

4 cloves garlic, chopped

1 teaspoon crushed red pepper flakes

Leaves from 2 sprigs fresh oregano, finely chopped, or 1 teaspoon dried oregano

A handful of fresh flat-leaf parsley tops, finely chopped

Black pepper

1 pint cherry tomatoes

Salt

1 pound linguine

1 cup dry white wine

3 tablespoons butter, cut into small pieces

½ cup grated Parmiggiano-Reggiano cheese (optional)

½ cup fresh basil leaves, torn

In a bowl, cover the clams with salted water and soak for 1 hour. Lift the clams out of the bowl (to leave behind any grit).

Bring a large pot of water to a boil for the pasta.

In a deep large skillet with a tight-fitting lid, heat the EVOO (3 turns of the pan) over medium to medium-high heat. Add the anchovies, cover the pan with a splatter screen or lid, and shake until the anchovies begin to break up. Reduce the heat a bit, uncover, and stir until the anchovies melt into the oil. Add the onion, garlic, red pepper flakes, oregano, parsley, and black pepper. Stir for 2 to 3 minutes, then add the tomatoes, cover the pan, and shake occasionally until the tomatoes burst, 7 to 8 minutes.

Meanwhile, salt the boiling water and cook the pasta to just shy of al dente.

Add the wine to the skillet and let it reduce for a minute, then melt in the butter. Add the clams, cover, and cook until the clams open, about 5 minutes. Discard any unopened clams.

Drain the pasta and add it to the pan. Toss the linguine with the sauce for 2 to 3 minutes to let the pasta finish cooking and allow it to absorb the flavors. If using Parm, remove the pan from the heat, add the cheese, and toss. Add the basil and adjust the seasonings.

LINGUINE WITH WHITE CLAM SAUCE FROM THE CUPBOARD

SERVES 2

Other than lemon, garlic, and parsley, this sauce is made straight from the cupboard. Serve with crusty bread for mopping up the juices.

¼ cup olive oil
4 to 6 cloves garlic (to taste), finely chopped
6 flat anchovy fillets
1 teaspoon dried thyme
½ cup dry vermouth or dry white wine
1 (15-ounce) can whole baby clams
Grated zest and juice of 1 organic lemon
Salt
½ pound linguine, thin linguine, or thin spaghetti
2 tablespoons chopped fresh flat-leaf parsley
Pepper

Bring a large pot of water to a boil for the pasta.

Heat a deep large skillet over medium heat. Add the oil (4 turns of the pan), garlic, and anchovies. Cook until the anchovies melt into the oil. Add the thyme and vermouth. Simmer for about 1 minute to reduce the vermouth. Stir in the clams with their juice and the lemon zest.

Salt the boiling water and cook the pasta to just shy of al dente. Drain the pasta and add it to the sauce. Toss with tongs for 2 to 3 minutes to finish cooking the pasta and for the flavors to be absorbed. Add the lemon juice and parsley and season with salt and pepper.

LINGUINE WITH CRAB

SERVES 4

This is one of many dishes we serve on Christmas Eve, but it is a quick go-to dinner year-round. You can make this meal in just minutes, and it is addictively sweet, spicy, and simply delicious.

2 tablespoons olive oil
¼ pound pancetta, finely diced
4 large shallots, chopped
4 large cloves garlic, thinly sliced
2 red Holland or Fresno chiles, thinly sliced
3 tablespoons fresh thyme leaves, chopped
Salt and pepper
1 cup dry vermouth or dry white wine
2 tablespoons butter
1 pound linguine
1 pound lump, king, or snow crabmeat
Grated zest and juice of 1 organic lemon
¼ cup chopped fresh flat-leaf parsley
¼ cup minced fresh chives

Bring a large pot of water to a boil for the pasta.

In a deep large skillet, heat the oil (2 turns of the pan) over medium-high heat. When it ripples, add the pancetta and render for 2 to 3 minutes. Add the shallots, garlic, chiles, thyme, salt, and pepper and stir for 2 to 3 minutes. Add the vermouth and cook until it has reduced by half. Swirl in the butter, then reduce the heat to low to keep warm while the pasta cooks.

Salt the boiling water and cook the pasta to just shy of al dente. Before draining, ladle out about a cup of the starchy pasta cooking water and add it to the sauce along with the crabmeat, lemon zest, and lemon juice. Drain the pasta and add it to the sauce. Toss with tongs for 1 to 2 minutes for the pasta to finish cooking and to allow the flavors to be absorbed. Toss in the parsley and chives and adjust the seasonings.

LINGUINE WITH SHRIMP FRA DIAVOLO

SERVES 4

This is a sexy date-night dish. There is something so exciting about the sweetness of shrimp combined with the slightly painful burn of chiles and the afterburn of good sherry. Eat by candlelight when possible. (To scale this down to serve just two for date night, reduce all the amounts in this recipe by half.)

4 tablespoons olive oil
1½ pounds large shrimp, peeled (tails left on) and deveined
1 tablespoon fresh lemon juice
4 large shallots, or 1 small onion, finely chopped
4 large cloves garlic, chopped
2 tablespoons fresh thyme leaves, finely chopped
2 small dried red chiles, finely chopped, 2 fresh red chiles, thinly sliced, or 1½ to 2 teaspoons crushed red pepper flakes
Salt and black pepper
½ cup dry sherry
2 tablespoons butter
1 (28- to 32-ounce) can San Marzano tomatoes (look for DOP on the label)
A handful of fresh flat-leaf parsley tops, finely chopped
A few fresh basil leaves, torn
1 pound linguine or thin linguine
2 tablespoons finely chopped pickled peppers (bottled Greek pepperoncini or hot cherry peppers), plus 2 tablespoons of their brine

In a large skillet, heat 2 tablespoons of the oil (2 turns of the pan) over medium-high heat. When it begins to smoke, add half the shrimp and lightly brown but do not cook all the way through, 1 to 2 minutes on each side. Transfer to a bowl. Repeat with the remaining shrimp. Add the lemon juice to the shrimp, toss, and set aside.

Add the remaining 2 tablespoons oil to the pan. Add the shallots, garlic, thyme, and chiles and season with salt and black pepper. Stir for 2 to 3 minutes. Add the sherry, stir to deglaze the pan, and cook for 1 minute to reduce. Melt in the butter. Hand-crush the tomatoes as you add them to the pan, then add the juices from the can. Add the parsley and basil, reduce the heat to low, and simmer for 15 minutes to cook down the tomatoes.

Meanwhile, bring a large pot of water to a boil for the pasta. Salt the water and cook the pasta to al dente. Before draining, ladle out about ½ cup of the starchy pasta cooking water. Drain the pasta and return it to the pot.

Five minutes before draining the pasta, return the shrimp to the sauce and cook for 5 minutes, or until cooked through.

Combine the drained pasta, sauce, and starchy water and toss with tongs for 1 to 2 minutes for the flavors to be absorbed. Just before serving, stir in the pickled peppers and their brine.

Serve in shallow bowls.

FAT SPAGHETTI WITH FRUTTI DI MARE

You can use any mix of seafood that catches your eye or simply the freshest catches of the day for this dish. If you cook the lobster or crab yourself, toast the shells in a skillet, then throw them in with your saffron stock as it warms.

2 cups chicken stock

A fat pinch of saffron threads

4 tablespoons olive oil

1 onion, finely chopped

1 small carrot, grated

2 small ribs celery with leafy tops, finely chopped

1 small bulb fennel, trimmed, cored, quartered, and very thinly sliced

1 leek (white and light green parts), halved lengthwise, thinly sliced crosswise

6 cloves garlic, thinly sliced

2 tablespoons fresh thyme leaves, chopped

1 large fresh bay leaf

1 teaspoon crushed red pepper flakes

Salt and black pepper

1 cup dry white wine or dry vermouth

1 (28- to 32-ounce) can San Marzano tomatoes (look for DOP on the label)

1 pound bucatini or perciatelli

1 pound large shrimp, peeled (tails left on) and deveined

1½ pounds Manila clams (see Tip) or cockles, scrubbed

8 to 10 calamari/squid, cut into 1-inch slices

1 pound cooked lobster or king crabmeat

Juice of 1 lemon

Bring a large pot of water to a boil for the pasta.

In a small saucepan, combine the stock and saffron, bring to a gentle simmer, and let simmer for 10 to 15 minutes.

In a large saucepan, heat 2 tablespoons of the oil (2 turns of the pan) over medium-high heat. Add the onion, carrot, celery, fennel, leek, half the garlic, the thyme, bay leaf, red pepper flakes, salt, and black pepper. Cover and sweat, stirring occasionally, for 8 to 10 minutes. Add ½ cup of the wine and cook to reduce for 1 minute. Hand-crush the tomatoes as you add them to the pan, then add the juices from the can. Bring to a bubble, add the warm saffron stock, and simmer the sauce while you cook the seafood and pasta.

Salt the boiling water and cook the pasta to al dente. Before draining, ladle out about a cup of the starchy pasta cooking water.

Meanwhile, in a large skillet with a lid, heat the remaining 2 tablespoons oil (2 turns of the pan). Add the shrimp, clams, squid, and remaining garlic; season with salt and pepper. Cover and cook, shaking the pan occasionally, until the clams open, 5 to 7 minutes. Discard any unopened clams. Stir in the remaining ½ cup wine and the lobster. Douse with the lemon juice.

Drain the pasta and return it to the pot. Add half of the sauce and all of the seafood, tossing with tongs for 1 to 2 minutes for the flavors to be absorbed. If the mixture looks a little dry, add the starchy cooking water and toss.

Serve in shallow bowls topped with a little more sauce. Pass more sauce at the table.

TIP

To clean the clams, place them in a bowl, cover with salted water and soak for 1 hour. Lift the clams from the bowl to leave behind the grit.

PASTA CON SARDE

I LOVE SARDINES! This dish is quick to prepare, inexpensive, and has a totally unique flavor. I have worked on my recipe for this classic for years—a lot of love and thought went into developing this into the balanced and layered sauce it's become. We are addicted and hope you will be, too. It is so much fun to slurp and suck up with this sweet and savory sauce with perciatelli—hollow strands, like fountain straws—or the slightly smaller bucatini (also a hollow strand). Though these hollow spaghettis are our favorite cuts for this pairing, we have also used chitarra (square spaghetti) or regular spaghetti in a pinch. You can also make this dish with fresh sardines (see Variations).

¼ cup olive oil

2 (6.4-ounce) jars sardines, drained

2 ribs celery from the heart with leafy tops, very finely chopped

1 small onion, very finely chopped

½ small bulb fennel or 1 baby fennel, finely chopped (½ to ¾ cup)

4 large cloves garlic, finely chopped or grated

2 tablespoons dried currants

A fat pinch of crushed red pepper flakes

⅓ cup Pernod

1 cup chicken stock

Salt and black pepper

1 pound perciatelli, bucatini, or spaghetti

1 cup mixed fresh flat-leaf parsley tops, celery tops, and fennel fronds, chopped

⅓ cup sliced almonds or pignoli (pine nuts), toasted

Bring a large pot of water to a boil for the pasta.

In a deep large skillet, heat the oil (4 turns of the pan) over medium to medium-high heat. Add the sardines and crumble the fish into bits as it melts down into the hot oil, remove large spine pieces and large pieces of shiny skin/fin as you break down the fishes. Small bits of skin and spine will melt away.

Add the celery, onion, fennel, garlic, currants, and red pepper flakes to the skillet. Stir and arrange in an even layer. Cook, turning occasionally, for 7 to 8 minutes. The fish will lightly brown and the celery, fennel, and onion will become tender. Add the Pernod, stir to deglaze the pan, and stir for a minute to almost evaporate the liquid. Add the stock and season with salt and black pepper. Reduce the heat to low while you cook the pasta.

Salt the boiling water and cook the pasta to al dente. Before draining, ladle out 1 to 1½ cups of the starchy pasta cooking water and add it to the sauce. Drain the pasta, return it to the pot, and add the sauce, tossing with tongs for 1 to 2 minutes for the flavors to be absorbed. Stir in the mixed parsley, fennel fronds, and celery tops. Adjust the seasonings and serve with nuts scattered on top.

VARIATIONS

Pasta with Fresh Sardines

Instead of the jars of sardines, use 2 pounds fresh sardine fillets. Before you add the sardines to the hot oil, melt in 4 anchovy fillets. Then add half the sardines and break them up. Let them cook down as you would do with the jarred ones. Once the fennel and onions are cooked, add the remaining sardine fillets, let them cook through, then gently break them into larger pieces. Continue with the recipe as directed.

Summer Pasta con Sarde

When you add the vegetables, throw in 2 garden-ripe tomatoes, peeled (see Tip, page 67) and chopped.

PENNE ALLA VODKA WITH PROSCIUTTO AND PEAS

SERVES 6

This is a nice spring twist on a classic. We make this often when peas are at their best in late spring. I also love Peas with Prosciutto as a side dish (page 333).

¼ cup olive oil

¼ pound prosciutto di Parma (or ask for the "ends," see Tip), cut into ¼-inch cubes

1 small onion, finely chopped

1 small rib celery from the heart with leafy top, finely chopped

4 cloves garlic, finely chopped

Salt and pepper

1 cup vodka (I like Tito's Handmade)

1 (28- to 32-ounce) can San Marzano tomatoes (look for DOP on the label)

1 cup passata, tomato puree, or tomato sauce

1 pound penne

½ cup heavy cream

A handful of fresh tarragon leaves, chopped, or a few fresh basil leaves, torn

1 cup shelled fresh or thawed frozen peas

Grated Grana Padano or Parmigiano-Reggiano cheese, for serving

In a deep large skillet, heat the oil (4 turns of the pan) over medium heat. Add the prosciutto and render for 2 minutes. Add the onion, celery, garlic, salt, and pepper. Partially cover and cook until the vegetables are very tender, 10 to 12 minutes. Add the vodka and cook until reduced by half. Hand-crush the tomatoes as you add them to the pan, then add the juices from the can and the passata. Simmer for 20 minutes to cook down the tomatoes.

Meanwhile, bring a large pot of water to a boil for the pasta. Salt the water and cook the pasta to al dente. Before draining, ladle out about ½ cup of the starchy pasta cooking water.

Add the cream and tarragon to the simmering sauce and reduce the heat to low. Add the peas and cook to heat through. Add the starchy water. Drain the pasta and add to the sauce, tossing with tongs for 1 to 2 minutes for the flavors to be absorbed. Adjust the seasonings.

Serve the penne in shallow bowls and top with cheese.

JUST AS THE name suggests, the "ends" are the pieces at the end of a ham (prosciutto di Parma or prosciutto cotto) that are too small to be cut into lovely slices. If your recipe calls for dicing or chopping the prosciutto and you don't need slices, ask the counterperson at the deli or your Italian market for the ends, which they should sell to you at a lower price.

CARBONARA

The only trick to carbonara is tempering the egg yolks to ensure you do not end up with scrambled eggs. I use Araucana eggs (look for them at Whole Foods or farmers' markets) to get the brightest color in the sauce: The hens that lay these blue-tinted eggs are often fed marigolds, which makes the yolks intensely bright yellow-orange. Many recipes for carbonara include cream—but I never add cream. The creamy quality of the sauce should come from the tempered eggs emulsifying with the cheeses and pasta.

3 tablespoons olive oil

⅓ pound pancetta or guanciale, finely diced

5 or 6 cloves garlic (to taste), chopped

Pepper

½ cup dry white wine

3 large free-range organic egg yolks

Salt

1 pound pasta (such as linguine, spaghetti, or egg tagliatelle)

½ cup freshly grated Pecorino Romano cheese, plus more for serving

½ cup freshly grated Parmigiano-Reggiano cheese, plus more for serving

½ cup fresh flat-leaf parsley tops, finely chopped

Bring a large pot of water to a boil for the pasta.

In a deep large skillet, heat the oil (3 turns of the pan) over medium heat. Add the pancetta and cook until browned, 3 to 4 minutes. Add the garlic and some pepper and stir for 2 minutes more. Add the wine and reduce the heat to low.

In a heatproof bowl, whisk the egg yolks, season with salt and pepper, and have at the ready.

Salt the boiling water and cook the pasta to al dente. Before draining, ladle out 1½ cups of the starchy pasta cooking water. Whisking constantly, add 1 cup of the starchy water in a slow stream to the egg yolks to temper them.

Drain the pasta and add it to the skillet with the pancetta and garlic. Remove from the heat and add the tempered egg yolks, pecorino, Parm, and parsley, tossing to coat and melt the cheeses. If the sauce seems tight, add some more starchy water. Adjust the seasonings.

VARIATION

Carbonara con Zafferano

In this variation, use warm saffron-scented stock—rather than the starchy cooking water from the pasta—to temper the egg yolks. This is a favorite of mine, as it tastes like Risotto Milanese, but is ready even quicker and with less effort. Start by heating 1½ cups chicken stock with a fat pinch of saffron threads to infuse the stock with saffron flavor. Continue with the recipe as written. When you would whisk the hot cooking water into the egg yolks, use 1 cup of the saffron stock instead. Save the remaining stock to loosen up the sauce if it's too tight.

CELEBRATION CARBONARA

The first year my husband, John, and I celebrated his birthday together, I asked him what he wanted me to make for his special dinner. I listed options from veal Oscar to lobster thermidor. He stopped me and replied firmly, "Carbonara. I want some spaghetti carbonara!" Bacon and egg "coal miner's spaghetti" is simple, inexpensive, and hands down my husband's number one favorite meal. I have to prepare carbonara for every special occasion throughout every calendar year. To keep it interesting, sometimes I give it a Milanese twist by using saffron (see Variation), or I'll add seasonal ingredients like garlic scapes or ramps or spring onions and lemon. Sometimes I add homemade fennel sausage crumbles, making it into bacon, sausage, and egg pasta. . . . Recently, for Valentine's Day, I added artichokes (see page 160).

CARBONARA WITH ARTICHOKES

SERVES 6

This was my 2014 Valentine's Day plan for John's carbonara. I thought artichokes would be appropriate, as we were going to be in California on Valentine's Day, and they grow a hearty arti! Every year on Valentine's Day I also send John a bouquet of salumi . . . 12 different flavors of salami and sausages. Some Valentines get armfuls of flowers—John prefers armfuls of salumi.

1 large lemon

3 medium artichokes (the size of a lightly clenched fist), with healthy stems attached

3 cups chicken stock

3 tablespoons olive oil

¼ to ⅓ pound pancetta or guanciale, finely diced

3 cloves garlic, sliced or chopped

½ cup dry white wine

Pepper and salt

1 pound spaghetti

3 large free-range organic egg yolks

1 cup freshly grated Parmigiano-Reggiano cheese

3 tablespoons chopped mixed fresh herbs: tarragon and/or parsley

Bring a large pot of water to a boil for the pasta.

Fill a bowl with water and a little ice and the juice and juiced shell of 1 lemon. Trim the artichokes down to the pale leaves. Peel the tough outer layer of the stems. Halve the artichokes lengthwise and scrape out the spiny chokes with a spoon (I use a serrated grapefruit spoon for this). Cut lengthwise into thin wedges. Add them to the lemon water as you work.

Meanwhile, in a small saucepan, warm the stock.

In a deep large skillet, heat the oil (3 turns of the pan) over medium to medium-high heat. Add the pancetta and render the fat. Transfer to a plate. With a spider or slotted spoon, remove the artichokes from the water and lightly dry on a kitchen towel. Add to the hot oil and lightly brown on each side, about 5 minutes.

Add the garlic and stir for 2 to 3 minutes. Add the wine and stir. Add half the warmed stock, partially cover, and cook, stirring occasionally, until the artichokes are tender-crisp, 8 to 10 minutes. Add a few grinds of pepper and return the pancetta to the pan. Reduce the heat to a low simmer while you cook the pasta.

Salt the boiling water and cook the pasta to al dente.

In a heatproof bowl, whisk the egg yolks and season with salt and pepper. Whisking constantly, add the remaining warm stock to the egg yolks in a slow stream to temper them.

Drain the pasta and add it to the skillet with the artichokes. Remove the pan from the heat and add the tempered egg yolks, Parm, and herbs, tossing to coat and melt the cheese. Adjust the salt.

FARFALLE WITH 'NDUJA AND ZUCCHINI

SERVES 4

'Nduja is a spicy sausage-like paste (see box, page 123) that I use in everything from lentil soup (see page 82) to deviled eggs (see page 34) to this simple pasta supper for nights when time is tight and we have too many zucchini to use up.

1½ pounds zucchini (2 to 3 medium)
2 tablespoons olive oil
3 to 4 tablespoons 'nduja
1 small white onion, finely chopped
3 or 4 cloves garlic, finely chopped
Salt
1 pound farfalle
½ cup fresh flat-leaf parsley tops, chopped
1 cup freshly grated Pecorino Romano or Parmigiano-Reggiano cheese

Bring a large pot of water to a boil for the pasta.

Halve the zucchini lengthwise, gently scoop out the seeds, and grate on the large holes of a box grater.

In a deep large skillet, heat the oil (2 turns of the pan) over medium-high heat. Add the 'nduja and "melt" it into the oil. Add the onion and garlic, stir, and cook for 2 to 3 minutes. Add the grated zucchini and toss to combine.

Salt the boiling water and cook the pasta to al dente. Before draining, ladle out about a cup of the starchy pasta cooking water and add it to the sauce along with the parsley. Drain the pasta and return it to the pot. Add the sauce, tossing with tongs for 1 to 2 minutes for the flavors to be absorbed.

Serve in shallow bowls and top with cheese.

PASTA WITH BACON, RAMPS, AND RICOTTA

SERVES 6

About 2 tablespoons olive oil
⅓ pound pancetta or center-cut bacon, diced
3 bunches ramps (about 36), whites finely chopped or thinly sliced, green tops cut into 1-inch pieces
4 cloves garlic, chopped
2 tablespoons fresh thyme leaves, chopped
1 tablespoon grated lemon zest (from an organic lemon)
Salt and pepper
½ cup crisp dry white wine
1 to 1½ pounds spaghetti or Sicilian Lemon Spaghetti (page 138)
1 cup fresh sheep's milk ricotta cheese
A fat handful of fresh flat-leaf parsley tops, chopped
Grated pecorino cheese, for tossing and serving

Bring a large pot of water to a boil for the pasta.

In a deep large skillet, heat the oil (2 turns of the pan) over medium-high heat. When the oil is hot, add the pancetta and cook until crisp. Reduce the heat to medium-low and add the ramp whites, garlic, thyme, and lemon zest. Season with salt and pepper and stir for 2 to 3 minutes, until very fragrant. Stir in the white wine.

Salt the boiling water and cook the pasta to al dente. Before draining, ladle out about a cup of the starchy pasta cooking water and add it to the sauce along with the ricotta. Drain the pasta and add it to the sauce along with the ramp greens, parsley, and a couple handfuls of pecorino, tossing with tongs for 1 to 2 minutes for the flavors to be absorbed. Adjust the seasonings.

Serve in shallow bowls with more pecorino at the table.

BUCATINI ALL'AMATRICIANA

Amatriciana, or bacon and onion sauce, has real crowd appeal. We make ours with black pepper and bay leaf; the pepper highlights the pork and the bay leaf brings out the sweetness of the onion. The wine sweetens the dish even more, balancing the pepper, and the stock gives it a slow-cooked taste.

3 tablespoons olive oil

¼ to ⅓ pound pancetta or guanciale, finely diced

1 large onion, chopped

4 large cloves garlic, thinly sliced or chopped

1 teaspoon coarsely ground pepper

1 large fresh bay leaf

½ cup white wine

½ cup chicken stock

1 (28- to 32-ounce) can San Marzano tomatoes (look for DOP on the label), or 12 fresh plum or vine tomatoes, peeled (see Tip, page 67) and chopped

A few fresh basil leaves, torn

½ cup loosely packed fresh flat-leaf parsley tops, chopped

Salt

1 pound bucatini

Grated Parmigiano-Reggiano or pecorino cheese, for serving

In a deep large skillet, heat the oil (3 turns of the pan) over medium-high heat. When the oil smokes, add the pancetta and render for 3 minutes. Add the onion, garlic, pepper, and bay leaf. Reduce the heat to medium-low, partially cover, and cook until the onion is very soft, about 15 minutes.

Add the wine and cook until almost evaporated. Add the stock and hand-crush the canned tomatoes as you add them to the pan, then add the juices from the can (if using fresh tomatoes, simply add them to the pan).

Stir in the basil and parsley and simmer for 20 minutes.

Meanwhile, bring a large pot of water to a boil for the pasta. Salt the water and cook the pasta to al dente. Before draining, ladle out about a cup of the starchy pasta cooking water and add it to the sauce.

Drain the pasta and return it to the pot. Add the sauce, tossing with tongs for 1 to 2 minutes for the flavors to be absorbed. Discard the bay leaf. Adjust the seasonings.

Serve the pasta in shallow bowls and top with Parm or pecorino.

BACON, CORN, AND MASCARPONE TAGLIATELLE

This combination of bacon, corn, and mascarpone is a fantastic celebration of one of my favorite vegetables. I can't get enough of it. So if I'm not in the mood for pasta (which is rare, of course), I just serve this combo as a side dish.

2 tablespoons EVOO

⅓ pound thickly sliced center-cut bacon or pancetta, cut into ¼-inch cubes

1 medium onion, chopped

4 cloves garlic, finely chopped

2 tablespoons fresh thyme leaves, chopped

Kernels from 4 ears corn (see Tip)

1 cup chicken stock

½ cup mascarpone cheese

Black pepper, piment d'Espelette, or cayenne pepper

Salt

1 pound egg tagliatelle or fettuccine

A handful of freshly grated Parmigiano-Reggiano cheese, plus more for serving

Chopped fresh flat-leaf parsley and chives, for serving

Bring a large pot of water to a boil for the pasta.

In a deep large skillet, heat the EVOO (2 turns of the pan) over medium-high heat. Add the bacon and cook until crisp. Transfer to a plate. Add the onion, reduce the heat a bit, and cook to soften. Add the garlic, thyme, and corn and cook until the corn just begins to lightly brown. Add the stock, bring to a bubble, and cook for a minute or so to reduce slightly. Stir in the mascarpone and pepper and reduce the heat to low.

Salt the boiling water and cook the pasta to al dente. Before draining, ladle out about a cup of the starchy pasta cooking water and add it to the sauce. Drain the pasta and add it to the sauce along with the Parm, tossing with tongs for 1 to 2 minutes for the flavors to be absorbed.

Serve in shallow bowls with bacon, parsley, and chives on top, and pass extra Parm at the table.

 TO REMOVE THE kernels from corncobs, invert a small bowl inside a large, shallow bowl. Balance the stem end of the cob on the smaller bowl and scrape the kernels from the cob. The kernels and "milk" from the corn will fall into the larger bowl beneath.

RIDICULOUSLY GOOD CHICKEN RIGGIES

A pink-blushed, quick adaptation of chicken cacciatore and an Italian American, western New York State specialty, Chicken Riggies is a crowd-pleaser. This is my updated version of an oldie but a goodie.

2 red frying peppers or bell peppers, roasted (see box, page 334)

4 tablespoons EVOO

1 pound boneless, skinless chicken thigh or breast, cut into bite-size pieces

Salt and black pepper

½ pound cremini mushrooms, thinly sliced

1 onion, chopped

4 cloves garlic, chopped or thinly sliced

2 green cubanelle peppers, halved lengthwise and thinly sliced crosswise

2 fresh Italian hot cherry peppers or Fresno chiles, seeded and finely chopped

¼ to ⅓ cup Marsala or dry sherry

1 (28- to 32-ounce) can San Marzano tomatoes (look for DOP on the label)

A few fresh basil leaves, torn

1 cup half-and-half or milk

1 pound rigatoni or whole wheat rigatoni

Grated Parmigiano-Reggiano cheese

Roast and peel the peppers, then quarter them lengthwise and slice them crosswise.

Bring a large pot of water to a boil for the pasta.

In a deep large skillet, heat 1 tablespoon of the EVOO (1 turn of the pan) over medium-high heat. Season the chicken liberally with salt and black pepper. Add the chicken to the skillet in a single layer and brown evenly on both sides, 5 to 6 minutes. Transfer to a plate. Add the remaining 3 tablespoons EVOO (3 turns of the pan) and then the mushrooms. Cook the mushrooms until browned, 5 to 6 minutes. Add the onion, garlic, cubanelle peppers, and hot peppers. Season with salt and black pepper and cook to soften the onion and peppers, 6 to 7 minutes. Add the Marsala and stir to deglaze the pan. Hand-crush the tomatoes as you add them to the pan, then add the juices from the can. Reduce the heat to a simmer, add the basil, sliced roasted peppers, and chicken and stir in the half-and-half. Cook the sauce to reduce and thicken while you cook the pasta.

Salt the boiling water and cook the pasta to al dente. Before draining, ladle out about a cup of the starchy pasta cooking water. Drain the pasta and return it to the pot. Add the sauce, a small handful of Parm, and a splash or two of the starchy water as needed to help the sauce combine. Toss with tongs for 1 to 2 minutes for the flavors to be absorbed.

Serve in shallow bowls and pass more Parm at the table.

SPAGHETTI AND MEATBALLS

SERVES 6

Spaghetti and meatballs always make us smile. Eating spaghetti and meatballs can make us silly with the twirling and sucking up of the pasta. Equally true—thanks to *Lady and the Tramp*—it can be a very romantic menu for a candlelit evening at home. I always bake my meatballs to keep their integrity. Fried meatballs tend to be unevenly cooked and can easily rip or break apart. As an exception, I like to cook veal *polpette* (meatballs) directly in a light tomato sauce, as you would cook dumplings.

MEATBALLS:

4 slices stale peasant-style white bread, crusts trimmed, coarsely chopped

Milk, to moisten the bread

2 pounds mixed ground beef, pork, and veal

¼ cup finely chopped fresh flat-leaf parsley

A fat handful of freshly grated Pecorino Romano cheese

A fat handful of freshly grated Parmigiano-Reggiano cheese

¼ cup pignoli (pine nuts), toasted and chopped

3 to 4 tablespoons grated onion

2 tablespoons EVOO

1 large egg

2 cloves garlic, grated or pasted

2 teaspoons ground sage

1 teaspoon crushed red pepper flakes

1 teaspoon fennel seeds

Salt and black pepper

SAUCE:

1 tablespoon olive oil

2 tablespoons butter

1 onion, chopped

2 cloves garlic, finely chopped

Salt

1 cup dry white wine

1 cup chicken or veal stock

3 (28- to 32-ounce) cans San Marzano tomatoes (look for DOP on the label)

10 to 12 fresh basil leaves, torn

Rind from a small wedge of Parmigiano-Reggiano cheese

PASTA:

Salt

1½ pounds spaghetti

2 tablespoons butter

Grated pecorino and/or Parmigiano-Reggiano cheese, for serving

Preheat the oven to 400°F. Line a baking sheet with parchment paper.

Make the meatballs: In a small bowl, sprinkle the bread with milk to soak and soften. Squeeze out the excess milk and transfer the bread to a large bowl.

Add the meat, parsley, pecorino, Parm, pine nuts, onion, EVOO, egg, garlic, sage, red pepper flakes, fennel seeds, salt, and black pepper. Gently but thoroughly combine all the ingredients. Roll the mixture into 2½-inch balls and arrange them on the prepared baking sheet. Bake for 15 minutes to partially cook and lightly brown.

Meanwhile, make the sauce: In a large Dutch oven, heat the oil (1 turn of the pan) over medium heat. Melt in the butter and add the onion, garlic, and salt to taste. Partially cover and sweat, stirring frequently, until very tender, about 20 minutes; reduce the heat if the onion starts to brown.

Add the wine and cook until reduced by half. Add the stock. Hand-crush the tomatoes as you add them to the pan, then add the juices from the cans. Bring to a bubble, reduce to a simmer, add the basil and cheese rind, and cook gently for 30 minutes to thicken.

Add the meatballs to the sauce and keep at a low simmer while you cook the pasta.

Make the pasta: Bring a large pot of water to a boil for the pasta. Salt the water and cook the pasta to al dente. Before draining, ladle out about a cup of the starchy pasta cooking water and add it to the sauce. Drain the pasta, return it to the pot, and add the butter and half the sauce, tossing with tongs for 1 to 2 minutes for the flavors to be absorbed.

Serve in shallow bowls and top with more sauce and the meatballs. Pass extra cheese at the table.

SPAGHETTI WITH SALAMI AND FENNEL

SERVES 4 TO 6

This is a tasty—salty-sweet-spicy all at once—weeknight supper if you get home late from work. John loves it (a fact that goes without saying if the ingredient list includes salami, a major food group for him).

3 tablespoons EVOO, plus more for drizzling

⅓ pound mixed sliced salami (a combo of mild and spicy), cut into ⅛-inch-wide strips

1 bulb fennel, trimmed, cored, quartered, and very thinly sliced, fronds chopped and reserved

1 onion, thinly sliced

4 cloves garlic, thinly sliced

2 tablespoons chopped fresh thyme leaves

1 teaspoon fennel seeds

Salt and pepper

1 organic lemon

¼ cup Pernod, dry vermouth, or white wine

½ cup chicken stock

1 (14-ounce) can cannellini beans, rinsed and drained

1 pound spaghetti

Grated Parmigiano-Reggiano cheese, for serving

Bring a large pot of water to a boil for the pasta.

In a large skillet, heat the EVOO (3 turns of the pan) over medium-high heat. Separate the strips of salami as you scatter them into the pan. Cook, tossing with tongs, until crisp, 2 to 3 minutes, then transfer to a plate. Reduce the heat to medium and stir in the sliced fennel, onion, garlic, thyme, and fennel seeds; season with salt and pepper. Grate the zest of the lemon over the fennel mixture. Cook, tossing occasionally, until the fennel and onion are very tender, about 12 minutes. Add the Pernod and stir to deglaze the pan. Add the stock and beans and heat through.

Salt the boiling water and cook the pasta to al dente. Before draining, ladle out about a cup of the starchy pasta cooking water and add it to the sauce. Drain the pasta and add it to the sauce along with the salami, tossing with tongs for 1 to 2 minutes for the flavors to be absorbed.

Toss in the reserved fennel fronds and squeeze in 1 table-spoon fresh lemon juice. Adjust the seasonings.

Serve in shallow bowls with grated Parm.

PENNE WITH LENTILS AND SAUSAGE

SERVES 6

If you're really looking for a super comfort food, there is no stronger one-two punch than legumes and pasta combined. Enjoy the dish . . . and your nap.

1 cup Norcia lentils (see box, page 38) or Puy lentils

2 small onions: 1 halved, 1 finely chopped

1 large bay leaf

Salt

2 tablespoons olive oil

1 pound Norcia-Style Sausage (page 237)

1 carrot, finely chopped

1 rib celery with leafy top, finely chopped

2 cloves garlic, finely chopped

Pepper

1 cup chicken stock

¼ cup finely chopped fresh flat-leaf parsley

1 pound penne rigate

Grated Parmigiano-Reggiano or pecorino cheese, for serving

In a small pot, combine the lentils, water to cover by a few inches, the halved onion, and the bay leaf. Bring to a boil, salt the water, and cook until the lentils are just tender, 30 to 35 minutes. Drain and discard the bay leaf and onion halves.

Meanwhile, bring a large pot of water to a boil for the pasta.

In a deep large skillet, heat the oil (2 turns of the pan) over medium-high heat. Add the sausage and cook, breaking it into crumbles as it browns. Add the chopped onion, carrot, celery, and garlic and season with salt and pepper. Cook for 5 minutes to soften the vegetables. Add the stock, lentils, and parsley. Reduce the heat to low and keep at a simmer while you cook the pasta.

Salt the boiling water and cook the pasta to al dente. Before draining, ladle out about ½ cup of the starchy pasta cooking water. Drain the pasta and add it to the sausage and lentils along with some of the starchy water, tossing with tongs for 1 to 2 minutes for the flavors to be absorbed. Adjust the seasonings.

Serve with cheese to pass at the table.

SWEET SAUSAGE AND EGGPLANT WITH SAFFRON CREAM AND PASTA

SERVES 6

John and I were married in Montalcino, Italy. The village is so beautiful and special to us for so many reasons. We love to eat lunch in town. Our favorite spot is Taverna del Grappolo Blu, where we have the *pinci* (fat spaghetti) with tomato sauce or ribollita, and for sure their fantasy salad. However, one afternoon they had no room for us at Grappolo, so we ate at a little wine bar up a side street. We had the special pasta and a few salads to share. The pasta was actually a tiny gnocchi-shaped dried pasta, traditional in Sardinia. The chef prepared it with sausage and eggplant, and it was wonderful. This is our home version and it rivals the original, which is hard to do.

Salt

1 heavy medium-large eggplant, half the skin peeled (in stripes), finely diced

1½ cups chicken stock

A fat pinch of saffron threads

3 tablespoons olive oil

1 pound Sweet Italian Sausage with Fennel, homemade (page 237) or store-bought, casings removed

1 small onion, finely chopped

4 cloves garlic, chopped

2 tablespoons fresh thyme leaves, chopped

½ cup dry white wine

¼ cup heavy cream

1 pound gnocchetti sardi or other short-cut pasta

A fat handful of freshly grated pecorino or Parmigiano-Reggiano cheese

Salt the eggplant and spread it on a kitchen towel to sweat water for 20 to 30 minutes.

Bring a large pot of water to a boil for the pasta.

In a small saucepan, combine the stock and saffron and bring to a low simmer to infuse the stock with flavor and color.

In a large skillet, heat the oil (3 turns of the pan) over medium-high heat. When the oil ripples, add the sausage and cook, breaking it up into crumbles as it lightly browns. Add the onion, garlic, and thyme. Partially cover and sweat the onions until tender. Add the eggplant, partially cover, and cook, stirring occasionally, until very tender, 8 to 10 minutes. Add the wine and cook to absorb into the eggplant and sausage. Add the warm saffron stock and cream and reduce the heat to low while you cook the pasta.

Salt the boiling water and cook the pasta to al dente. Before draining, ladle out about ½ cup of the starchy pasta cooking water and add it to the sauce. Drain the pasta and return it to the pot. Add the sauce and cheese, tossing with tongs for 1 to 2 minutes for the flavors to be absorbed.

Serve in shallow bowls.

PENNE WITH SQUASH AND SAUSAGE

If you're making your own homemade sausage, make it with plenty of time ahead of serving (as long as overnight) to give the sausage a little time for the flavors to combine.

2 to 3 pounds red kuri squash (Hokkaldo) or butternut squash, peeled, seeded, and cut into ¾-inch cubes

1 tablespoon olive oil, plus more for drizzling

¼ teaspoon freshly grated nutmeg

Salt and pepper

3 cups chicken or vegetable stock

1 small onion, halved

1 large fresh bay leaf

1 large clove garlic, smashed

4 tablespoons (½ stick) butter

12 to 16 fresh sage leaves (see Tip)

1 pound Sweet Italian Sausage with Fennel, homemade (page 237) or store-bought, casings removed

1 to 1½ pounds penne rigate or whole grain penne rigate

½ cup crème fraîche

Grated Parmigano-Reggiano cheese, for serving

Preheat the oven to 400°F.

Toss half the squash with a drizzle of oil and season with the nutmeg and salt and pepper. Spread on a baking sheet and roast until tender, about 20 minutes. Set aside.

Meanwhile, in a medium saucepan, combine the remaining squash, the stock, onion, bay leaf, garlic, and salt to taste. Bring to a simmer and cook until very tender, 15 to 20 minutes. Fish out and discard the onion halves and bay leaf and puree the squash mixture with an immersion blender. The sauce should be loose and just coat the back of a spoon.

Bring a large pot of water to a boil for the pasta.

In a small skillet, melt the butter over medium heat. When the foam subsides, working in two batches, add the sage leaves and fry until crisp. Drain on paper towels. Pour the brown butter into the squash puree and stir to combine.

In a large skillet, heat the oil (1 turn of the pan) over medium-high heat. Add the sausage and cook, breaking it up into crumbles as it browns. Add the squash puree to the sausage.

Salt the boiling water and cook the pasta to al dente. Before draining, ladle out about ½ cup of the starchy pasta cooking water and add it to the sauce along with the crème fraîche. Remove from the heat. Drain the pasta and return it to the pot. Add the sauce, tossing with tongs for 1 to 2 minutes for the flavors to be absorbed. Toss in the roasted squash.

Serve in shallow bowls, topped with crispy fried sage leaves and Parm.

TIP

Use the larger amount of squash, sage, and pasta if serving 8.

FLORENTINE PENNE WITH CHICKEN

There are many popular recipes for this dish, and they are basically red sauces with baby spinach wilted in. For me, Florentine as a descriptor brings to mind white sauce and spinach. My family especially loves this creamy, green penne on cold nights.

2 tablespoons olive oil

1 to 1½ pounds boneless, skinless chicken thigh or breast, diced

Salt and pepper

4 tablespoons (½ stick) butter

¾ pound cremini or button mushrooms, sliced

1 small onion, finely chopped

4 cloves garlic, finely chopped

2 rounded tablespoons flour

1 cup dry white wine

1 cup chicken stock

1½ to 2 cups milk

Freshly grated nutmeg

1 (16-ounce) bag frozen chopped spinach, thawed and wrung dry in a kitchen towel

1 pound penne or mostaccioli rigate

A handful of freshly grated Parmigiano-Reggiano cheese, plus more for serving

Bring a large pot of water to a boil for the pasta.

In a deep large skillet, heat the oil (2 turns of the pan) over medium-high heat. Season the chicken with salt and pepper. Add the chicken to the pan and brown on all sides. Transfer to a plate. Melt in the butter, add the mushrooms, and lightly brown, 5 to 6 minutes. Add the onion and garlic, season with salt and pepper, reduce the heat a bit, and cook to soften the onion, 5 to 6 minutes.

Sprinkle in the flour and stir for 1 minute. Add the wine and cook until reduced by half. Add the stock and milk and cook until the sauce is thick enough to coat the back of a spoon. Season with a few grates of nutmeg. Pull the spinach apart with your fingers as you add it to the pan, and stir to heat it through. Adjust the seasonings.

Meanwhile, salt the boiling water and cook the pasta to al dente.

Stir the Parm into the sauce, return the chicken to the sauce, and cook to heat through. Drain the pasta and toss it with the sauce and chicken.

Serve in shallow bowls and top with more Parm.

PEAR AND PECORINO RAVIOLI

This is a common Tuscan combination: salty, tangy sheep's milk cheese and sweet pears. I dress these in a light butter and white wine sauce and I add a little sage if I have it on hand. It is a very special first course, and a unique and comforting main course to follow with a light salad.

2 ½ to 3 cups grated young to mid-aged pecorino cheese

1 cup mascarpone cheese or fresh sheep's milk ricotta cheese

4 or 5 pears (see Tip), peeled and grated

⅛ to ¼ teaspoon freshly grated nutmeg

Egg pasta (page 110)

4 ounces (1 stick) butter

8 to 10 fresh sage leaves, thinly sliced (optional)

1 cup crisp, lightly fruity white wine

Salt

In a bowl, combine the pecorino, mascarpone, pears, and nutmeg.

Make the egg pasta, following the recipe and then rolling the dough into thin sheets 10 x 24 inches. Keep covered with a slightly damp kitchen towel so they don't dry out. Line baking sheets with parchment paper. Place a small pastry brush in a bowl of water at your workstation and have a small, sharp knife or pasta cutter ready.

Working with one sheet of pasta at a time, set it on the work surface with one long side facing you. Make 2 rows of 6 mounds (1½ to 2 tablespoons each) of filling on the top half of the sheet. Space the mounds evenly, leaving space so you can press and cut between them. Paint with water around the filling mounds. Carefully fold the dough over and press around each mound to seal, then cut into 12 ravioli. Transfer the ravioli to the prepared baking sheets. Repeat with the remaining sheets of dough and filling. You should end up with a total of 48 ravioli.

In a large skillet, melt the butter over medium heat. When the foam subsides, add the sage (if using) and swirl. Add the wine and cook until reduced by half, then reduce the heat to low while you cook the ravioli.

Bring a large, wide pot of water to a low rolling boil. Salt the water. Working in batches, cook the ravioli for 4 minutes and use a spider to transfer them to the butter and wine sauce.

Serve in warm bowls.

TIP

I prefer crisp, slightly underripe Bosc pears, but for a sweeter filling, use Bartlett pears.

RAVIOLI WITH SPINACH AND FOUR CHEESES

2 cups fresh cow or sheep's milk ricotta cheese, homemade (see box, page 40) or store-bought

1 cup grated fresh mozzarella cheese

½ cup mascarpone cheese

½ cup freshly grated Parmigiano-Reggiano or pecorino cheese (see Tip)

¼ teaspoon freshly grated nutmeg

1 (16-ounce) bag frozen chopped spinach, thawed and wrung dry in a kitchen towel

Salt and pepper

Egg pasta (page 110)

Pomodoro Sauce (page 121) or Marinara Sauce (page 121), for serving

In a bowl, combine the ricotta, mozzarella, mascarpone, and grated Parm. Add the nutmeg. With your fingers, separate the spinach as you add it to the bowl. Season with salt and pepper. Stir well to combine.

Make the egg pasta, following the recipe and then rolling the dough into thin sheets 10 x 24 inches. Keep covered with a slightly damp kitchen towel so they don't dry out. Line baking sheets with parchment paper. Place a small pastry brush in a bowl of water at your workstation and have a small, sharp knife or pasta cutter ready.

Working with one sheet of pasta at a time, set it on the work surface with one long side facing you. Make 2 rows of 6 mounds (1½ to 2 tablespoons each) of filling on the top half of the sheet. Space the mounds evenly, leaving space so you can press and cut between them. Paint with water around the filling mounds. Carefully fold the dough over and press around each mound to seal, then cut into 12 ravioli. Transfer the ravioli to the prepared baking sheets. Repeat with the remaining sheets of dough and filling. You should end up with a total of 48 ravioli.

Bring a large, wide pot of water to a low rolling boil. Salt the water. Working in batches, cook the ravioli for 4 minutes and use a spider to transfer them to a warm platter.

TO SERVE: Toss the ravioli with a little of their starchy cooking water and your sauce of choice.

TIP

If you use sheep's milk ricotta, then match it by using pecorino, which is made from sheep's milk. If you use cow's milk ricotta, use Parmesan.

STUFFED SHELLS

SERVES 6

When I was a little girl, we rarely went out for Italian food because we made so much of it at home. But there was a little Italian American place in South Glens Falls, New York, that had jukeboxes in every booth. Once in a while, Mom would take us there for stuffed shells. I liked to listen to Frank Sinatra songs. My sister loved Barry Manilow and Air Supply. We all loved the shells.

2 tablespoons olive oil
2 tablespoons butter
1 onion, finely chopped
4 cloves garlic, chopped
1 sprig fresh oregano
Salt and pepper
2 tablespoons tomato paste
½ cup dry white wine
1 (28- to 32-ounce) can San Marzano tomatoes (look for DOP on the label)
A few fresh basil leaves, torn
24 large pasta shells
1 (10-ounce) box frozen chopped spinach, thawed and wrung dry in a kitchen towel, or 1 cup loosely packed fresh flat-leaf parsley, finely chopped
2 cups fresh ricotta cheese, drained well
½ pound fresh mozzarella cheese, cut into ¼-inch cubes
1 cup freshly grated Parmigiano-Reggiano cheese

1 large free-range egg, beaten
1 teaspoon grated lemon zest (from an organic lemon)
⅛ teaspoon freshly grated nutmeg

In a saucepan, heat the oil (2 turns of the pan) over medium heat. Melt in the butter. Add the onion, garlic, and oregano and season with salt and pepper. Partially cover and cook, stirring occasionally, until softened, 7 to 8 minutes. Add the tomato paste and stir for a minute. Add the wine and stir to loosen up the tomato paste. Hand-crush the tomatoes as you add them to the pan, then add the juices from the can. Stir in the basil, reduce the heat to low, and simmer for 20 minutes.

Bring a large pot of water to a boil for the pasta. Salt the boiling water and cook the pasta for 5 to 6 minutes. Drain the shells and cold-shock under cold running water. Drain well.

Preheat the oven to 375°F.

In a bowl, combine the spinach (pull it apart with your fingers as you add it to the bowl), ricotta, mozzarella, Parm, egg, lemon zest, nutmeg, salt, and pepper.

Pour half the sauce into a baking dish big enough to fit all the stuffed shells in a single layer. Fill the shells with the ricotta mixture and place open side up in the baking dish. Dot the tops with more sauce and bake until golden at the edges and hot through, about 45 minutes.

MACARONI AND CHEESE PRIMAVERA

Mac and cheese is more all-American than Italian, but this dish is a light, delicious, Italian twist on the traditionally heavy, rich side dish. This mac is worthy of center plate. The ingredient list of vegetables below is just a guideline; you can use any mix of veg you like. Just use 3 to 4 cups of very thinly sliced fresh baby vegetables.

VEGETABLES:

2 tablespoons olive oil
5 or 6 baby carrots, vey thinly sliced on an angle
5 or 6 baby zucchini or a mix of baby zucchini and pattypan squash, thinly sliced
2 or 3 baby fennel, very thinly sliced
A fat handful of sugar snap peas, thinly sliced on an angle, or shelled fresh peas or thawed frozen peas
3 or 4 green Vidalia or fat spring onions, or 2 leeks (white and light green parts), thinly sliced and washed well
¼ cup chopped garlic scapes, or 2 large cloves garlic, thinly sliced
Salt and pepper
Lemon wedge
¼ cup fresh tarragon leaves, coarsely chopped

CHEESE SAUCE AND MAC:

4 tablespoons (½ stick) butter
¼ cup flour
1 cup chicken stock
2 cups milk, warmed
Freshly grated nutmeg
Salt and pepper
2 cups grated Fontina Val d'Aosta or Gruyère cheese
1 cup grated Asiago cheese
1 pound macaroni with ridges, cavatappi (hollow corkscrew pasta), or penne rigate
1 cup freshly grated Parmigiano-Reggiano cheese

Preheat the oven to 350°F.

Bring a large pot of water to a boil for the pasta.

Make the vegetables: In a large skillet, heat the oil (2 turns of the pan) over medium to medium-high heat. Add the carrots, zucchini, fennel, peas, onions, and garlic scapes and season with salt and pepper. Cook until tender-crisp, about 5 minutes. Remove from the heat, douse with a squeeze of lemon juice, and stir in the tarragon.

Make the cheese sauce and mac. In a saucepan, melt the butter over medium heat. Whisk in the flour and cook for 1 minute. Whisk in the stock and cook for 1 or 2 minutes to thicken. Slowly whisk in the warm milk. Season with the nutmeg and salt and pepper. Cook until thickened enough to lightly coat the back of a spoon. Add the Fontina and Asiago a handful at a time and stir with a wooden spoon in a figure-8 motion to incorporate.

Salt the boiling water and cook the pasta 2 to 3 minutes shy of al dente. Drain the pasta and return it to the pot. Add the cheese sauce and vegetables and stir. Adjust the seasonings.

Transfer to a large baking dish (at least 9 x 13 inches) and cover evenly with the Parm. Bake until browned and bubbling, 20 to 25 minutes.

BAKED ZITI

My mom calls any baked pasta with ricotta mixed in "Scuderi kids' pasta." There were 10 kids around her table growing up, so the idea of "kids' pasta" paints the mental picture of 20 hungry hands vying for the largest helping.

Everyone loves baked ziti. It doesn't have to be made with ziti (lots of us make it with any short-cut pasta, like penne, mostaccioli, or rigatoni), but the words "baked ziti" create the anticipation. "Baked penne." What's that? Baked ziti, everyone knows and expects a mozzarella-topped pasta casserole—with creamy ricotta, meaty red sauce, and those worth-fighting for crispy corners—that can feed an army of hungry mouths.

Though I use homemade sausage—it's a leaner way to go—a quick shortcut is store-bought sausage. (I cheat, too, occasionally.)

Good on any day of the week when you are feeding a crowd, this is a game-day go-to. Keep it in mind every Super Bowl, which is always on a Sunday. Remember, no matter the team you root for, everyone is Italian on Sunday.

---

2 tablespoons olive oil

1 pound Sweet Italian Sausage with Fennel, homemade (page 237) or store-bought

1 pound ground beef (80% lean)

4 cloves garlic, finely chopped

1 onion, finely chopped

1 teaspoon dried marjoram or oregano, lightly crushed in your palm

1 teaspoon crushed red pepper flakes (optional)

Salt and black pepper

1 cup veal or beef stock

2 cups passata, tomato puree, or tomato sauce

2 (28- to 32-ounce) cans San Marzano tomatoes (look for DOP on the label)

A few fresh basil leaves, torn

1 pound ziti rigate or any short-cut pasta with ridges

2 cups fresh ricotta cheese

1 cup freshly grated Parmigiano-Reggiano cheese

1 large free-range organic egg, beaten

12 to 16 ounces fior di latte cheese (fresh mozzarella), grated on the large holes of a box grater (see Tip)

A small handful of fresh flat-leaf parsley tops, finely chopped

In a large Dutch oven, heat the oil (2 turns of the pan) over medium-high heat. Add the sausage, breaking it up into chunks, then add the beef and cook, breaking up both meats into crumbles as they brown. Add the garlic, onion, marjoram, and red pepper flakes (if using) and season with salt and black pepper. Cook to soften the onions, 8 to 10 minutes. Add the stock and passata. Hand-crush the canned tomatoes as you add them to the pan, then add the juices from the cans. Bring to a bubble, reduce the heat to a low simmer, add the basil, and simmer for 30 minutes.

Bring a large pot of water to a boil for the pasta. Salt the water and cook the pasta about 3 minutes shy of al dente. Before draining, ladle out about ½ cup of the starchy pasta cooking water. Drain the pasta.

Preheat the oven to 375°F.

In a large bowl, combine the ricotta and ½ cup of the Parm. Stir in the egg, the starchy water, the pasta, and half the sauce. Transfer the pasta to a large baking dish (at least 9 x 13 inches) and top with the remaining sauce. Cover the pasta and sauce evenly with mozzarella and the remaining ½ cup Parm. Top with the parsley and bake until browned and bubbling on top and hot through, about 30 minutes.

TIP

If the mozzarella is very wet or packed in water, pat it dry, wrap it in paper towels, and refrigerate overnight to firm it up for grating.

LASAGNA WITH MEAT RAGU

SERVES 8 TO 12

For the meat sauce in this lasagna, I use a slightly lighter version of a Bolognese that uses more veal than beef and omits the milk (since the lasagna is layered with a rich white sauce). It's an all-day labor of love to make and prepare fresh pasta for this (and so worth it), but a legitimate shortcut is the no-boil thin lasagna sheets made by Barilla. They're fantastic. If you don't want to make a large lasagna, you can a): divide all the ingredients in half to make just one 8-inch square pan, or—better yet—b): bake two pans and save the second one to freeze for a rainy day, or to gift to a friend.

RAGU:
2 tablespoons olive oil
1 tablespoon butter
1 carrot, finely chopped
1 small rib celery with leafy top, finely chopped
1 small onion, finely chopped
4 cloves garlic, finely chopped
1 pound ground veal
½ pound ground beef
1 tablespoon chopped fresh sage leaves
1 tablespoon rosemary leaves, finely chopped
1 bay leaf
⅛ teaspoon ground cloves
Salt and pepper
3 tablespoons tomato paste
½ cup dry white wine
3 cups chicken or veal stock

BESCIAMELLA:
5 tablespoons butter
5 tablespoons flour
4 cups milk, warmed
Salt and pepper
Freshly grated nutmeg

Salt
8 sheets fresh egg pasta (page 110), or 16 no-boil lasagna sheets (I use Barilla)
1½ to 2 cups freshly grated Parmigiano-Reggiano or Grana Padano cheese
Chopped fresh flat-leaf parsley, for garnish

Make the ragu: In a large skillet or Dutch oven, heat the oil (2 turns of the pan) over medium heat. When it ripples, melt in the butter. Add the carrot, celery, onion, and garlic; partially cover and cook until the vegetables are softened, 7 to 8 minutes. Add the meat, sage, rosemary, bay leaf, and cloves and season with salt and pepper. Cook, breaking up the meat into crumbles as it browns. Add the tomato paste and stir for 1 minute. Add the wine to loosen up the tomato paste and cook until it has been absorbed. Add the stock and simmer for 30 minutes. Discard the bay leaf.

Preheat the oven to 375°F.

Make the besciamella: In a saucepan, melt the butter over medium heat. Whisk in the flour and cook for 1 minute. Whisk in the milk and season with salt and pepper and a little nutmeg. Cook the sauce until thick enough to coat the back of a spoon.

If using fresh pasta sheets, heat a large and wide pot of water to a low rolling boil. Fill a pan with ice and water. Salt the boiling water and cook the pasta sheets 2 at a time for about 2 minutes. Cold-shock the sheets in the ice water to stop the cooking process. Drain on a clean kitchen towel and transfer to parchment paper. Stack the sheets neatly (you can do this ahead and freeze or store in the fridge until ready to use).

Coat the bottom of a 9 x 13-inch lasagna pan or two 8-inch square pans with a thin layer of besciamella. Add a pasta sheet or sheets, top with besciamella and ragu in thin layers, and sprinkle with cheese. Repeat the layering to the top of the pan(s), ending with besciamella and cheese. Bake until browned and bubbling, 30 to 35 minutes (1 hour if using dried pasta). Top with parsley and let stand for 20 minutes before cutting and serving.

BUTTERNUT SQUASH AND ESCAROLE LASAGNA

This is a quick-and-easy make-ahead meal. I usually make it with no-boil dried pasta sheets for super-quick assembly, but if I am making fresh pasta, I make and freeze extra sheets to have them on hand for lasagna season (which, in upstate New York, can last from November to early May). If you don't want to make two lasagnas, you can a): divide all the ingredients in half to make just one 8-inch square pan, or—better yet—b): save the second lasagna to freeze for a rainy day or to gift to a friend.

Salt

16 no-boil lasagna sheets (I use Barilla), or 8 sheets fresh egg pasta (page 110)

2 small or 1 large butternut squash, halved, peeled, and seeded

5 ounces (1¼ sticks) butter

½ cup plus 2 tablespoons flour

5 cups chicken stock, warmed

4 cups milk, warmed

Pepper

Freshly grated nutmeg

2 tablespoons olive oil

1 onion, finely chopped

4 cloves garlic, finely chopped or thinly sliced

2 heads escarole, trimmed and coarsely chopped

¼ cup very thinly sliced fresh sage leaves, plus 12 small whole leaves for garnish

3 cups grated mixed cheeses (such as Fontina Val d'Aosta, Gruyère, and/or Parmigiano-Reggiano)

If using fresh pasta sheets, heat a large and wide pot of water to a low rolling boil. Fill a pan with ice and water. Salt the boiling water and cook the pasta sheets 2 at a time for about 2 minutes. Cold-shock the sheets in the ice water to stop the cooking process. Drain on a clean kitchen towel and transfer to parchment paper. Stack the sheets neatly (you can do this ahead and freeze or store in the fridge until ready to use).

Cut the squash into very thin slices (no thicker than ⅛ inch) with a very sharp knife or using a mandoline or the slicer blade on a box grater.

In a large saucepan, melt the butter over medium heat. Whisk in the flour and cook for 1 minute. Whisk in 4½ cups of the stock, then the milk. Bring the sauce to a low simmer, whisking occasionally until the sauce thickens enough to lightly coat the back of a spoon. Season the white sauce with salt and pepper and a little nutmeg.

In a deep large skillet, heat the oil (2 turns of the pan) over medium heat. Add the onion and garlic and cook to soften, 5 to 6 minutes. Wilt the escarole into the pan and season with salt and pepper. Add the remaining ½ cup stock and simmer the greens for 3 to 5 minutes to cook out the liquids and bitterness.

Preheat the oven to 350°F.

Coat the bottoms of two 8-inch square pans with a little sauce. Add 2 sheets of no-boil lasagna (or the equivalent of fresh) to each of the pans and top with a layer of sliced squash. Season with salt and pepper and scatter with a little sliced sage. Top the squash with a thin layer of greens and white sauce. Layer on more lasagna sheets—facing the opposite direction. Each pan of lasagna should contain 4 layers of pasta and 3 layers of filling, ending with the white sauce on top. Scatter the grated cheese blend over each lasagna and arrange 6 sage leaves on top, spaced to indicate where portions should be cut.

Cover with foil and bake for 1 hour (30 minutes if using fresh pasta). Uncover and bake until the cheese has browned, 10 to 15 minutes. Let cool for 20 minutes before cutting and serving.

BASIC POLENTA

SERVES 8

Use a bain-marie (a water bath or double boiler) to slow-cook the polenta. This method is by far the easiest and most foolproof. Most recipes use water to cook polenta, but I always cook my polenta in stock, a blend of stock and milk, or water and milk in a pinch. If you keep the liquids-to-cornmeal ratio at 4 to 1, the choice of liquids used is up to you. Serve the polenta topped with sauce or ragu, sautéed mushrooms, braised vegetables, or another topping of your choice.

2 quarts chicken or vegetable stock
2 cups polenta (coarse yellow cornmeal)
Salt
2 tablespoons butter

If you have a double boiler, use it. Otherwise, choose a medium pot that fits comfortably in a shallow, wider pan to make a bain-marie. Pour about ¾ inch water in the bottom of the wider pan. Bring the water to a simmer and keep at a simmer over medium-low heat, adding more water as necessary.

In the medium pot (the top of the double boiler), bring the stock to a low rolling boil. Whisking constantly in a single direction, pour the polenta in slowly. Bring to a bubble, then transfer the pan to the bain-marie, cover, and cook, stirring occasionally, about 1¼ hours. Season with salt. Stir in the butter and remove from the heat.

Serve in shallow bowls.

CHECK THIS OUT

Other recipes in the book that call for polenta:

- Deep-Dish Polenta "Pizza" with Mushrooms and Sausage (page 107)
- Deep-Dish Polenta "Pizza" with Spinach and Artichokes (page 107)
- Polenta with Tipsy Mushrooms, Poached Eggs, and Green Salad (page 10)
- Quick Polenta with Asparagus, Leeks, and Poached Eggs (page 10)

RACHAEL'S POLENTA

SERVES 8

This is my go-to polenta. It has a terrific balance of salty and sweet. Serve the polenta with your sauce of choice (my favorite sauce is Mushroom Ragu, page 128). If you're making this ahead, keep the polenta warm and covered in a bain-marie (see Basic Polenta, at left, for how to set up a bain-marie)

6 cups chicken stock
2 cups milk
2 cups polenta (coarse yellow cornmeal)
1 teaspoon coarsely ground pepper
Freshly grated nutmeg
3 tablespoons butter
2 tablespoons acacia honey
½ cup freshly grated Parmigiano-Reggiano cheese
Salt

In a medium pot, bring the stock and milk to a low rolling boil. Whisking constantly in a single direction, pour the polenta in slowly. Add the pepper and a few grates of nutmeg and bring to a bubble. Reduce the heat to medium-low to keep the polenta at a delayed bubble, just a burp every 2 seconds or so. Cook for 45 minutes, whisking every 10 minutes or so.

Stir in the butter, honey, and Parm. Remove from the heat and season with salt. Serve in warm shallow bowls.

BAKED POLENTA

Line a rimmed medium baking sheet with parchment paper. Pour the cooked polenta out in an even layer about 1 inch thick. Dot with pats of butter. Bake in a preheated 375°F oven until firm and tender. Let cool, then cut into any shape you like for grilling or stacking.

Risotto Milanese (page 185) and Mixed Citrus Salad (page 25).

CHAPTER 6

RISOTTO AND GRAINS

As I write this section, it occurs to me how trendy and popular grains and rice are today. I suppose it began with a growing awareness of gluten intolerance—and the serious celiac disease. Thankfully, we have no history of this condition in our family (a good thing, since we eat more than our share of bread, pizza, and pasta). I love whole grains because of their nutty quality and because, when cooked properly, they have a great chew to them. Grains are filling and nutritious and are real dollar-stretchers when you prepare them at home.

And of course there could be no discussion of Italian food and grains without the classic risotto. Although lots of people are intimidated by risottos, they shouldn't be. Just check out my basic intro to the subject on page 184.

RICE PILAF

Broken spaghetti toasted in butter is what makes rice pilaf so good. I don't understand why people buy packages of rice with powdered stock and so little rice and pasta. If you make your own, you get more of everything, including flavor. The rice is great as is, but my mom always added smoked almonds to our rice pilaf when we were children. Toasted pine nuts are great, too.

CHECK THIS OUT

Here are some other grain recipes including whole grain pasta sprinkled throughout the book:

- Classic Arancini (page 55)
- Chicken and Orzo (Barley) Soup (page 80)
- Toasted Spaghetti Minestra with Tuscan Kale (page 78)
- Farro Spaghetti with Chickpeas and Roasted Cauliflower (page 150)
- Farro Spaghetti with Shallots, Kale, and Hazelnuts (page 149)

3 tablespoons butter
½ cup broken spaghetti
1½ cups long-grain white rice
Salt and pepper
3½ to 4 cups chicken stock, preferably homemade (page 64)
½ cup smoked almonds, chopped, or ¼ cup pignoli (pine nuts), toasted (optional)

In a large skillet with a tight-fitting lid, melt the butter over medium heat. Add the pasta and toast until deep golden in color and very nutty in smell. Add the rice and stir for a minute. Season with salt and pepper, add 3½ cups of the stock, and bring to a low boil. Reduce the heat to low, cover, and cook until the rice is just tender, about 18 minutes, adding extra stock as necessary if the pan gets too dry. Fluff with a fork. Add the nuts (if using) and serve.

VARIATION

Rice Primavera

Add sautéed vegetables to the rice pilaf rather than the nuts. Use any vegetables you like. Sometimes I add a little freshly grated cheese to the rice as well. This is our colorful mix of chopped vegetables sautéed in 3 tablespoons olive oil: 1 small zucchini, 1 small red bell pepper, 1 small red onion, 1 cup peas or peeled shelled favas, and 2 cloves garlic. Season with salt and pepper and stir in ½ cup chopped fresh herbs such as tarragon, parsley, and chives.

ROSEMARY AND ROASTED GARLIC WILD RICE BLEND

SERVES 4

This very basic side is great as an earthy contrast to citrusy chicken or pork dishes. You can also buy a good wild and brown rice blend instead of putting together your own.

2 heads garlic, roasted
    (see box, page 312)
1½ cups brown rice
½ cup wild rice
2 tablespoons EVOO
4½ to 5 cups chicken stock,
    preferably homemade
    (page 64)
¼ cup fresh rosemary leaves,
    finely chopped
Salt and pepper
½ cup pignoli (pine nuts), toasted

Squeeze the roasted garlic from the skins into a bowl and mash.

In a soup pot, combine the brown rice, wild rice, EVOO, and 4½ cups of the stock. Whisk in the garlic paste, rosemary, salt, and pepper. Bring to a boil, reduce the heat, cover, and simmer, stirring occasionally, for 30 minutes. If the rice gets a little dry before it's fully cooked, add the remaining ½ cup stock. Turn off the heat and let stand for 10 to 15 minutes. Fluff with a fork and stir in the pine nuts. Season the rice with salt and pepper.

RICE SALAD WITH GOLDEN BEETS

SERVES 6 TO 8

This is a great side for smoked chicken. It is shockingly bright yellow in color because the grated golden beets are cooked with the rice.

SALAD:
1½ cups basmati or long-grain
    white rice
2 cups chicken or vegetable stock,
    preferably homemade (pages
    64 and 65)
4 small yellow or golden beets,
    peeled and grated
3 oranges, supremed (see box,
    page 221) and chopped
2 carrots, grated
1 red onion, chopped
1 small red or yellow bell pepper,
    chopped
1 bunch scallions, thinly sliced
    or chopped
Salt and black pepper

DRESSING:
Juice of 1 orange
3 tablespoons white balsamic
    vinegar
2 teaspoons Tabasco sauce
2 teaspoons sugar
1 teaspoon ground coriander
1 teaspoon paprika
⅓ cup EVOO
Salt and pepper

Make the salad: In a saucepan, combine the rice and stock and bring to a boil. Reduce the heat, cover, and simmer for 10 minutes. Add the beets, cover, and simmer for 5 minutes. Turn off the heat and let stand, covered, for 10 minutes. Uncover and fluff, then spread on a baking sheet to cool.

In a large bowl, combine the cooled rice and beets, oranges, carrots, onion, bell pepper, and scallions. Season with salt and black pepper.

Make the dressing: In a small bowl, whisk the orange juice, vinegar, Tabasco, sugar, coriander, and paprika. Whisk in the EVOO in a slow stream to emulsify. Season with salt and pepper.

Add the dressing to the salad and toss. Adjust the seasonings.

RISOTTO

Many people steer clear of risottos because they consider them labor intensive. Unless a stirring motion causes you great physical pain, these are the keys to successful risottos:

- *Most important:* Start with a really flavorful stock! (Check out the homemade stocks, pages 64 and 65.)
- Prepare risotto over medium-high heat.
- Use a round-bottomed pot or risotto pot (see box, at right).
- Stir with a round wooden paddle or spoon.
- Add warm liquids in stages, a few ladles at a time.
- Allow liquids to be almost completely absorbed before adding more, stirring frequently.
- Finish risotto by stirring in butter and cheese to completely emulsify with the starchy rice.
- The perfect risotto should be porridgelike, creamy, and pourable.
- From the first addition of warm liquids, a risotto takes 18 to 20 minutes. Done, simple math.

RISI E BISI

SERVES 6

In Italian families, rice with peas is a common memory of childhood and one of our first solid food memories. I make this basic risotto as a *primi* or light supper anytime I want to make arancini (see page 55), fried rice balls that look like "little oranges."

6 cups chicken stock, preferably homemade (page 64)
2 tablespoons olive oil
¼ pound pancetta, finely chopped
1 small onion, finely chopped
2 large cloves garlic, finely chopped
1½ cups Arborio or carnaroli rice
1 bay leaf
Salt and pepper
2 to 3 cups shelled fresh peas
3 tablespoons butter, cut into pieces
½ cup freshly grated Parmigiano-Reggiano cheese
A fat handful of fresh flat-leaf parsley tops, finely chopped
A small handful of fresh mint leaves, finely chopped

In a saucepan, bring the stock to a simmer and keep warm.

In a risotto pot (see box, at right) or other round-bottomed pan, heat the oil (2 turns of the pan) over medium-high heat. Add the pancetta and stir for 1 to 2 minutes. Add the onion and garlic and stir for 1 to 2 minutes more. Stir in the rice and bay leaf and season with salt and pepper. Begin adding the hot chicken stock, a few ladles at a time, stirring constantly and cooking until the liquid has been absorbed before adding more. Continue adding stock this way until the rice is al dente, about 18 minutes total. Add the peas in the last 3 to 4 minutes with the last addition of stock. Fish out and discard the bay leaf.

Stir in the butter and Parm to finish the dish, and garnish with parsley and mint.

RISOTTO POT

When I cook risotto, I use a wide pot with a long handle, somewhat like a deep skillet, and a rounded bottom. The key feature here is the rounded bottom. It makes it much easier to stir the rice and keep it from sticking. If you use a conventional pan with a squarish bottom, you are guaranteed to have rice sticking in the corners.

RISOTTO PRIMAVERA

SERVES 6

My mom and I went to Harry's Bar in Venice for lunch to celebrate our first trip there together. We had risotto primavera for lunch—rice and vegetables—and each dish cost $54. We never ate rice with vegetables away from home again.

6 cups chicken or vegetable stock, preferably homemade (pages 64 and 65)
A fat pinch of saffron threads
4 tablespoons olive oil
½ bunch purple or green asparagus, thinly sliced on an angle
Salt and pepper
1 small carrot, finely chopped
1 small rib celery with leafy top, finely chopped
1 small onion, finely chopped
1 small zucchini, seeded and finely chopped
2 large cloves garlic, finely chopped
1½ cups Arborio or carnaroli rice
1 cup dry white wine
1 cup shelled fresh peas
3 tablespoons butter, cut into pieces
½ cup freshly grated Parmigiano-Reggiano cheese
½ cup chopped mixed fresh herbs: tarragon, flat-leaf parsley, and chives
Juice of ½ lemon

In a saucepan, combine the stock and saffron, bring to a simmer, and keep warm over low heat.

In a risotto pot (see box, page 184) or other round-bottomed pan, heat 2 tablespoons of the oil (2 turns of the pan) over medium to medium-high heat. Add the asparagus, season with salt and pepper, and stir for 2 to 3 minutes to lightly brown. Transfer to a plate. Add the remaining 2 tablespoons oil (2 turns of the pan), the carrot, celery, onion, zucchini, and garlic, season with salt and pepper, and stir for 1 or 2 minutes more. Add the rice, season with salt and pepper, and stir to combine. Add the wine and stir to evaporate. Begin adding the hot stock, a few ladles at a time, stirring constantly and cooking until the liquid has been absorbed before adding more. Continue adding stock this way until the rice is al dente, about 18 minutes total. Add the peas in the last 2 to 3 minutes.

Stir in the butter, Parm, asparagus, herbs, and lemon juice to finish the dish. Serve in shallow bowls.

RISOTTO MILANESE

SERVES 4 TO 6

This recipe is a great base for many risotto dishes (see Variations, page 186). It is a basic risotto with one important feature that makes it Milanese: The stock is steeped like tea with a fat pinch of saffron, which gives this risotto its rich golden-orange color and extra layer of elegant flavor

6 cups chicken stock, preferably homemade (page 64)
A fat pinch of saffron threads
2 tablespoons olive oil
¼ pound pancetta, finely chopped
1 small onion, finely chopped
2 large cloves garlic, finely chopped
1½ cups Arborio or carnaroli rice
Salt and pepper
1 cup dry white wine
3 tablespoons butter, cut into pieces
½ cup freshly grated Parmigiano-Reggiano cheese
A fat handful of fresh flat-leaf parsley tops, finely chopped

In a saucepan, combine the stock and saffron, bring to a simmer, and keep warm over low heat.

In a risotto pot (see box, page 184) or other round-bottomed pan, heat the oil (2 turns of the pan) over medium-high heat. Add the pancetta and stir for 1 to 2 minutes. Add the onion and garlic and stir for 1 to 2 minutes more. Add the rice, season with salt and pepper, and stir to combine. Add the wine and cook to evaporate. Begin adding the hot chicken stock, a few ladles at a time, stirring constantly and cooking until the liquid has been absorbed before adding more. Continue adding stock this way until the rice is al dente, about 18 minutes total.

Stir in the butter and Parm, and garnish with parsley.

Risotto Milanese with Asparagus

Thinly slice 12 to 15 asparagus spears on an angle. In a skillet, heat 1 tablespoon EVOO over medium-high heat, add the asparagus, season with salt and pepper, and cook until tender-crisp. Make the risotto and stir half of the asparagus into the risotto just before serving. Garnish with the remaining asparagus and some chopped fresh tarragon.

Risotto Milanese with Shrimp

In a skillet, heat 1 tablespoon EVOO over medium-high heat. Add 12 to 18 large peeled and deveined shrimp, season with salt and pepper, and cook until the shrimp are opaque. Add ½ cup dry vermouth to the pan to deglaze. Douse the shrimp with the juice of ½ lemon. Serve the risotto with the shrimp on top.

Risotto Milanese with Crab

When you cook the onion and garlic for the risotto, add 2 ribs finely chopped celery from the heart, 1 bay leaf, and 1 small fresh or dried split chile. Use dry vermouth rather than dry white wine. At the very end, remove the risotto from the heat, discard the bay leaf and chile, and stir in 8 ounces crabmeat (from a plastic tub, not a can), picked over for shell and cartilage. Garnish with minced fresh chives.

Risotto Milanese with Scapes

Omit the garlic from the recipe. When the risotto is about 5 minutes from being done, stir in 5 or 6 finely chopped garlic scapes.

Risotto Milanese with Ramps

Omit the onion from the recipe and replace with the chopped whites of 2 bunches ramps. Cut the ramp greens into 1-inch-wide slices and stir them in just before serving, along with the juice of ½ lemon.

Risotto Milanese with Roasted Butternut Squash

Halve and seed 1 small butternut squash, drizzle with a little EVOO, and season with salt, pepper, and freshly grated nutmeg. Place on a baking sheet, cut side down, and roast in a preheated 400°F oven until very tender, about 35 minutes. Puree the squash flesh with a bit of water or stock. Cook the risotto to al dente. Just before adding the butter and cheese, stir in the butternut puree. Garnish with fried sage leaves. This butternut risotto is great for arancini (see page 55).

LEMON RISOTTO

My mom's nickname is "Mamacello" because she loves *limoncello* (lemon liqueur) so much. She loves lemon spaghetti and lemon risotto, and expects one of them every Mother's Day or on her birthday. This dish is great with sautéed shrimp on top (follow the directions for the Risotto Milanese with Shrimp, page 186). I often make enough risotto to have leftovers, because I love making arancini—"little oranges," Italian rice balls (see page 55).

6 cups chicken stock, preferably homemade (page 64)

3 tablespoons olive oil

Grated zest and juice of 2 organic lemons

3 cloves garlic, finely chopped

1 small onion, chopped

2 baby or wild fennel, or ½ bulb fennel, very finely chopped

1 small bay leaf

1½ cups Arborio fresh rice

Salt and pepper

1 cup dry white wine

3 tablespoons butter, cut into small pieces

½ cup freshly grated Parmigiano-Reggiano cheese

½ cup chopped fresh flat-leaf parsley

¼ cup chopped fresh mint, tarragon, or basil

In a saucepan, bring the stock to a simmer and keep warm.

In a risotto pot (see box, page 184) or other round-bottomed pan, heat the oil (3 turns of the pan) over medium to medium-high heat. Add the lemon zest, garlic, onion, fennel, and bay leaf and stir for 2 to 3 minutes. Add the rice, season with salt and pepper, and stir to coat with the oil. Cook for 1 minute to toast the rice. Add the wine and stir to evaporate. Begin adding the hot stock, a few ladles at a time, stirring constantly and cooking until the liquid has been absorbed before adding more. Continue adding stock this way until the rice is al dente, about 18 minutes total.

Stir in the butter, Parm, lemon juice, parsley, and herbs. Discard the bay leaf. Adjust the seasonings and serve in shallow bowls.

WALNUT RISOTTO WITH WHITE TRUFFLE AND GORGONZOLA DOLCE

This is a really earthy, deep, sexy dish.

6 cups chicken stock, preferably homemade (page 64)

2 tablespoons olive oil

1 small onion, finely chopped

1 or 2 cloves garlic (to taste), finely chopped

2 tablespoons thinly sliced fresh sage leaves

1½ cups Arborio or carnaroli rice

Salt and pepper

1 cup dry white wine

1 to 2 tablespoons natural truffle oil (to taste)

1½ cups walnuts, toasted and finely chopped

1 to 2 tablespoons butter (to taste)

4 to 5 ounces ripe Gorgonzola dolce cheese

Fresh white truffle, shaved

Grated Parmigiano-Reggiano cheese, for serving

In a saucepan, bring the stock to a simmer and keep warm.

In a risotto pot (see box, page 184) or other round-bottomed pan, heat the oil (2 turns of the pan) over medium to medium-high heat. Add the onion and garlic and stir until fragrant. Add the sage and rice, season with salt and pepper, and cook for 1 to 2 minutes. Add the wine and cook until completely evaporated. Begin adding the hot stock, a few ladles at a time, stirring constantly and cooking until the liquid has been absorbed before adding more. Continue adding stock in this way until the rice is al dente, about 18 minutes total.

Add the truffle oil (start with the smaller amount), walnuts, butter, and Gorgonzola and stir to melt the cheese into the rice. Adjust the seasonings. Serve in shallow bowls, topped with shaved truffle and Parm.

RISOTTO WITH PORCINI AND CELERY

SERVES 4 TO 6

When in season, garnish this dish with freshly shaved white truffles. Wow! I serve this most often at holidays and as the *primi* course to Braised Whole Veal Shank (page 273).

6 cups mushroom stock (page 65) or chicken stock, preferably homemade (page 64)

1 ounce dried porcini mushrooms (see Tip)

2 tablespoons olive oil

1 small onion, finely chopped

2 ribs celery from the heart with leafy tops, finely chopped

2 large cloves garlic, finely chopped

1½ cups Arborio or carnaroli rice

Salt and pepper

1 cup dry white wine

1 cup walnut halves, toasted and chopped

3 tablespoons butter, cut into small pieces

1 cup freshly grated pecorino cheese

Freshly grated nutmeg

Finely chopped celery tops, for serving

Freshly shaved white truffle and/or natural truffle oil, for serving

In a saucepan, heat the stock along with the mushrooms to soften, 10 to 15 minutes. Scoop out the mushrooms and chop. Keep the stock warm.

In a risotto pot (see box, page 184) or other round-bottomed pan, heat the oil (2 turns of the pan) over medium to medium-high heat. Add the onion, celery, and garlic and stir for 1 to 2 minutes to soften. Add the rice and cook for 1 minute to toast. Season with salt and pepper. Add the wine and stir to evaporate. Begin adding the hot stock, a few ladles at a time, stirring constantly and cooking until the liquid has been absorbed before adding more. Continue adding the stock this way until the rice is al dente, about 18 minutes total.

Stir in the chopped porcini, walnuts, butter, pecorino, and nutmeg to taste. Adjust the seasonings.

Serve in shallow bowls and garnish with celery tops, shaved truffle, and/or truffle oil.

USE THE DRIED porcini even if you are starting with the mushroom stock.

DRUNKEN RISOTTO

Smoky speck, starchy rice simmered in wine scented with rosemary and juniper berries, tangy, freshly grated pecorino cheese—what's not to love? I serve this as a starter, but everyone prefers it to anything I serve for dinner, so I think this dish will have to graduate to entrée. Sometimes I add chopped or sliced roasted beets to the dish. The sweetness balances the speck.

1 (750ml) bottle fruity, spicy red wine

2 cups veal or beef stock

2 bay leaves

5 or 6 juniper berries

2 sprigs fresh rosemary

2 tablespoons EVOO

¼ to ⅓ pound speck (smoky ham) or smoky bacon, finely chopped

1 onion, chopped

4 cloves garlic, finely chopped

1½ cups Arborio or carnaroli rice

Salt and pepper

3 cups baby kale or spinach, coarsely chopped

Freshly grated nutmeg

3 tablespoons butter, cut into pieces

1 cup freshly grated Pecorino Romano cheese

In a medium saucepan, combine the wine, stock, bay leaves, juniper berries, and rosemary and heat over low heat. Let steep for a few minutes before beginning the risotto.

In a risotto pot (see box, page 184) or other round-bottomed pan, heat the EVOO (2 turns of the pan) over medium to medium-high heat. Add the speck and render for 2 to 3 minutes. Add the onion and garlic and cook for 1 to 2 minutes to soften. Add the rice, season with salt and more liberally with pepper, and cook for 1 to 2 minutes to toast the rice. Begin adding the wine-stock mixture, a few ladles at a time, stirring constantly and cooking until the liquid has been absorbed before adding more. Continue adding the stock mixture this way until the rice is al dente, about 18 minutes total. Wilt in the greens. Fish out and discard the bay leaf, juniper berries, and rosemary sprigs. Season with nutmeg to taste and adjust the seasonings.

Stir in the butter and pecorino to finish, and serve in shallow bowls.

BARLEY RISOTTO WITH CRAB AND PINK PEPPERCORNS

When I'm in L.A., my first stop is always at Wa Sushi for crispy rice spicy tuna and barley risotto with crab. TT, the chef, is an inventive cook, and he is my inspiration for this Italian-Japanese risotto.

6 cups mushroom stock (page 65)
3 tablespoons olive or canola oil
½ pound mixed fresh mushrooms: shiitake, cremini, and/or hen-of-the-woods (maitake), thinly sliced
1 leek (white and light green parts only), quartered lengthwise, thinly sliced crosswise, and washed well
1 rib celery with leafy top, finely chopped
2 large cloves garlic, finely chopped
1 large fresh bay leaf
1½ cups pearl barley (orzo perlato)
2 tablespoons fresh thyme leaves, chopped
1½ teaspoons pink peppercorns, cracked

Salt
½ cup dry sherry
1 pound lump crabmeat, picked over
Juice of ½ lemon
2 tablespoons butter, cut into pieces
1 cup freshly grated Parmigiano-Reggiano cheese
A few drops of natural truffle oil, for serving

In a saucepan, bring the stock to a simmer and keep warm.

In a risotto pot (see box, page 184) or other round-bottomed pan, heat the oil (3 turns of the pan) over medium to medium-high heat. Add the mushrooms and lightly brown. Add the leek, celery, garlic, and bay leaf and cook for 1 to 2 minutes to soften. Add the barley, thyme, pink peppercorns, and salt to taste. Stir for 1 to 2 minutes to toast the barley. Add the sherry and stir until almost completely evaporated. Add the stock a few cups at a time and simmer, stirring occasionally, until the barley is tender, 40 to 45 minutes. Add a little water if you run out of stock and the pan gets too dry. Stir in most of the crabmeat, then the lemon juice.

Remove from the heat and stir in the butter and Parm. Adjust the seasonings. Fish out and discard the bay leaf.

Serve immediately in shallow bowls, garnished with the remaining crabmeat and the truffle oil.

ORZO (BARLEY)

In my family, when we say *orzo* we mean barley (*not* the little rice-shaped pasta). It's a staple for cold salads and hot soups (see Chicken and Orzo (Barley) Soup, page 80) and a basic first food for children in Italian culture. Barley is filling, but innocuous and mild in flavor, yet it retains a great chew. When used in risottos, it does not get as creamy or starchy as Arborio rice, but it has a wonderful pop to it that gives it a virtue of its own.

"GREEN" BARLEY RISOTTO WITH ROASTED CARROTS

SERVES 4

This dish is terrific in spring and early summer because it is brightly colored and very flavorful. There are carrot tops in the puree, so pick carrots with nice-looking greens attached to them.

1¼ cups pearl barley (orzo perlato)

1 bunch baby carrots or small carrots, thinly sliced on an angle, 1 cup tops reserved

4 tablespoons olive oil

Salt and pepper

7 cups vegetable or chicken stock, preferably homemade (pages 65 and 64)

2 cups packed spinach or baby kale

1 cup fresh flat-leaf parsley tops

1 small onion, finely chopped

2 cloves garlic, finely chopped

2 tablespoons fresh thyme leaves, chopped

3 tablespoons butter, cut into pieces

1 cup freshly grated Parmigiano-Reggiano cheese

½ cup sliced almonds, toasted

1 lemon, halved

Preheat the oven to 375°F. Spread the barley on a rimmed baking sheet and bake until golden and nutty, about 10 minutes. Leave the oven on for the carrots.

Spread the carrots on a baking sheet, dress with 2 tablespoons of the oil, and season with salt and pepper. Roast until tender and golden, 20 to 25 minutes.

Meanwhile, in a saucepan, bring the stock to a simmer and keep warm.

In a high-speed blender or food processor, combine the carrot tops, spinach, parsley, ½ cup of the warm stock, and salt and pepper to taste. Puree and set aside.

In a risotto pot (see box, page 184) or other round-bottomed pan, heat the remaining 2 tablespoons oil (2 turns of the pan) over medium to medium-high heat. Add the onion and garlic and stir for 1 to 2 minutes to soften. Add the toasted barley and the thyme and season with salt and pepper. Ladle in a couple cups of the stock and stir. Keep adding stock occasionally and cook for 40 minutes. Stir in the green puree and keep cooking the risotto until tender, about 45 minutes total.

Stir in the butter and Parm, and squeeze in the lemon juice to finish. Serve the risotto in shallow bowls, topped with almonds and carrots.

BARLEY RISOTTO WITH BUTTERNUT SQUASH

SERVES 4

Roasted, pureed butternut squash is a delicious addition to any rice or grain made in the style of risotto. In this dish, the squash cooks directly with the barley in the pot—even easier.

7 cups vegetable or chicken stock, preferably homemade (pages 65 and 64)
2 tablespoons olive oil
1 onion, finely chopped
2 large cloves garlic, finely chopped
1¼ cups pearl barley (orzo perlato)
2 tablespoons thinly sliced fresh sage leaves
Salt and pepper
1 cup dry white wine
1 small butternut squash, peeled, seeded, and chopped into small bite-size pieces
3 tablespoons butter, cut into pieces

1 cup freshly grated Parmigiano-Reggiano cheese
Freshly grated nutmeg
Optional garnishes: chopped toasted hazelnuts, pine nuts, or sliced almonds; crispy fried sage leaves; shaved Parmigiano-Reggiano cheese; minced fresh chives

In a saucepan, bring the stock to a simmer and keep warm.

In a risotto pot (see box, page 184) or other round-bottomed pan, heat the oil (2 turns of the pan) over medium to medium-high heat. Add the onion and garlic and cook to soften, 5 to 6 minutes. Add the barley, sage, salt, and pepper and stir for 2 minutes to lightly toast the barley. Add the wine and stir until almost completely evaporated. Add half the warm stock and simmer, stirring occasionally, for 20 minutes.

Add the butternut squash and the remaining warm stock and cook, stirring occasionally, until the squash and barley are tender, 20 to 25 minutes. Add a little water if the pan gets too dry.

Stir in the butter and Parm to finish. Season with a little nutmeg and adjust the seasonings. Serve immediately with the garnishes of your choice.

ORZO SALAD WITH CHERRY TOMATOES

SERVES 4 TO 6

This salad is a common dish in Tuscany, and each time I prepare it, I think of one of my favorite restaurants in Florence (a meat lover's haven, ironically), Il Latini. People stand in line for hours in the street to sit at the tables of Il Latini, which is famous preparing for the simple meats of Tuscany grilled over olive wood and brushed with swags of rosemary. The owner, Torello, became my Godfather almost instantaneously (think movie, not religion) more than fifteen years ago. *Torello* means "bull," and he is, as his name dictates, a large, bullish man in appearance. He is intimidating, until he approaches you for the first time and smiles. His smile is infectious, his food is delicious, and he reminds me of another friend, Mario Batali, in one distinctive way: He knows how to eat life itself. He lives big.

My grandpa Emmanuel, a central figure in my life, was a man much like Torello. He believed that life is good and that the good life does not belong to the rich. Both Emmanuel and Torello were children who didn't go as far as they may have liked with their educations, so they educated themselves. My grandfather came to America when he was a boy, but he taught me to read. Torello's restaurant has many sprawling rooms filled with his collection of books (including more than one signed by a Nobel laureate).

Grandpa was, and Torello is, a proud, educated man. Both of them taught me not to dumb down life or your palate. We all have the gift of learning with every word and every bite.

Salt
1 cup pearl barley (orzo perlato)
1 small red onion, finely chopped
Grated zest and juice of 1 organic lemon
1 pint cherry tomatoes, halved or quartered (depending on your patience level)
1 cup finely chopped seeded cucumber or young zucchini
1 cup fresh flat-leaf parsley tops, chopped
1 large clove garlic (2 cloves, if you're me), grated or minced
¼ cup pignoli (pine nuts), toasted
¼ cup EVOO
Pepper

Bring a medium pot of water to a boil. Salt the water, add the barley, and cook the barley until tender, about 25 minutes. Drain and cold-shock under cold running water to stop the cooking process. Let sit in the strainer for a few minutes to drain well. Set aside.

In a large bowl, combine the onion, lemon zest, lemon juice, and a little salt. Let the onion bleed out into the acid for 10 minutes.

Add the barley, tomatoes, cucumber, parsley, garlic, pine nuts, and EVOO. Toss to combine and season with pepper.

> **VARIATION**
>
> ## Pearled Barley and Corn Salad
>
> Scrape the kernels off a couple of grilled or raw ears of corn (see Tip, page 163 for how to remove the kernels). Add to the salad.

FARRO WITH PEAS, FAVAS, AND MINT

SERVES 4 TO 6

I am a sucker for any dish with peas or favas and mint. I made up a salad using all three.

1 cup pearled farro
Salt
1 cup shelled fresh spring peas
1 cup peeled shelled fava beans (see Tip, page 76)
Grated zest of 1 organic lemon
Juice of 1½ lemons
1 small red onion, or 3 shallots, finely chopped
1 cup chopped mixed celery tops and fresh flat-leaf parsley
1 cup fresh mint leaves, torn or chopped
1 large clove garlic, grated or pasted
Pepper
5 to 6 tablespoons olive oil (enough to coat the salad lightly)

In a pot, combine the farro with water to cover by a couple of inches. Cover, bring to a boil, and season with salt. Cook the farro until tender, 25 to 30 minutes. Drain.

Set up a bowl of ice and water. In a deep skillet or shallow pan, bring a few inches of water to a boil. Salt the water, add the peas and fava beans, and cook for 2 minutes. Drain and add to the ice water to cold-shock. Drain.

In a large bowl, combine the lemon zest, lemon juice, onion, celery tops, and a little salt. Let stand for 10 minutes.

Add the farro, peas and favas, mint, garlic, pepper to taste, and oil and toss. Adjust the seasonings.

FARRO WITH HAZELNUTS AND GREENS

SERVES 4 TO 6

This is a really easy side, but so tasty. It is terrific with roasted turkey breast.

1 cup pearled farro
Salt
3 tablespoons olive oil
¼ pound pancetta or guanciale, chopped
4 shallots, or 1 small onion, chopped
4 cloves garlic, chopped
1 bunch lacinato kale (also called black, Tuscan, or dinosaur kale), stemmed and chopped, or 1 head escarole, chopped
Freshly grated nutmeg
Pepper
½ cup chicken stock
Juice of ½ lemon
⅓ cup chopped hazelnuts, toasted

In a small pot, combine the farro with water to cover by a couple of inches. Cover, bring to a boil, and season with salt. Cook the farro to al dente, 23 to 25 minutes. Drain.

Meanwhile, in a skillet, heat the oil (3 turns of the pan) over medium to medium-high heat. Add the pancetta and cook until lightly browned. Add the shallots and stir for 3 to 4 minutes, adding the garlic for the last minute or so.

Wilt in the kale and season with the nutmeg and pepper. Add the stock and reduce the heat.

To serve, toss together the farro and the greens mixture. Stir in the lemon juice and nuts. Adjust the salt, pepper, and nutmeg.

FARRO

Farro has the nuttiest flavor and the heartiest chew of my go-to grains. I especially love it in salads, as it never bloats or clumps like pasta salad. I often pair it with sweet ingredients like fruit or peas to balance the earthy flavor of the grain. I also like pasta made from farro. Check out Farro Spaghetti with Shallots, Kale, and Hazelnuts (page 149) and Farro Spaghetti with Chickpeas and Roasted Cauliflower (page 150).

CHEESY FARRO AND ROASTED CAULIFLOWER

SERVES 8

This is a nice holiday side that's a break from potatoes and a nutty alternative to mac and cheese. With a dark green salad, it can be as comforting as risotto for a meal as well.

1 head garlic, roasted (see box, page 312)
1 head cauliflower, cut into florets
Olive oil, for drizzling
Leaves from a few sprigs fresh thyme
Leaves from a few sprigs fresh rosemary
Salt and pepper
4 cups chicken stock, preferably homemade (page 64)
1½ cups pearled farro
5 tablespoons butter
¼ cup flour
2½ cups milk, warmed
Freshly grated nutmeg
1½ cups freshly grated Parmigiano-Reggiano or Grana Padano cheese
1½ cups shredded Fontina Val d'Aosta or Gruyère cheese
½ cup homemade bread crumbs or panko bread crumbs
Finely chopped fresh chives and parsley, for serving

Preheat the oven to 425°F.

Roast the garlic. When cool enough to handle, squeeze the garlic from the skins into a bowl and mash to a paste.

On a rimmed baking sheet, toss the cauliflower with a drizzle of oil (enough to coat lightly), the thyme, rosemary, salt, and pepper. Roast until tender and browned at the edges, 30 to 35 minutes. Remove from the oven; reduce the oven temperature to 375°F.

Meanwhile, in a pot, combine the stock and 2 cups water and bring to a boil. Add the farro and cook at a low rolling boil until tender, about 25 minutes. Drain off any excess liquid.

In a saucepan, melt the butter over medium heat. Whisk in the flour and cook for 1 minute. Whisk in the milk and season with salt and pepper and a little nutmeg. Cook the sauce until thick enough to coat the back of a spoon. Stir in the garlic paste. Add half the Parm and melt it into the sauce. Stir in the Fontina.

In a 9 x 13-inch baking dish, combine the farro, cauliflower, and cheese sauce. Top with the bread crumbs and the remaining Parm.

Bake until golden, crispy on top, and bubbling, about 20 minutes. Serve sprinkled with chives and parsley.

FARRO, BEANS, AND BACON

SERVES 6

Add bacon to anything, and I am in! This, to me, is an Italian-influenced alternative to baked beans. Serve with grilled pork chops, ribs, chicken, and on and on.

1 cup dried borlotti beans
2 onions: 1 halved, 1 finely chopped
2 bay leaves
2 sprigs fresh rosemary
Salt
1 cup pearled farro
2 tablespoons olive oil
⅓ pound smoky bacon, cut crosswise into 1-inch pieces
2 small ribs celery, finely chopped
3 or 4 cloves garlic (to taste), sliced
3 tablespoons tomato paste
1 cup chicken stock, preferably homemade (page 64)
2 tablespoons balsamic vinegar
1 tablespoon Worcestershire sauce
2 tablespoons light brown sugar
Pepper
¼ cup fresh flat-leaf parsley tops, chopped

Soak the beans in a bowl with water to cover overnight. (Alternatively, quick-soak the beans: Place them in a heatproof bowl and cover with boiling water by 3 inches. Let stand for 1 hour.)

Rinse the soaked beans and transfer to a pot. Add fresh water to cover the beans by 3 to 4 inches, add the halved onion, bay leaves, and rosemary and bring to a boil. Salt the beans and cook until tender, about 40 minutes. Drain, fish out and discard the onion, bay leaves, and rosemary, and set aside.

In a small pot, combine the farro with water to cover by a couple of inches. Cover, bring to a boil, and season with salt. Cook the farro to al dente, 23 to 25 minutes. Drain and set aside.

In a Dutch oven, heat the oil (2 turns of the pan) over medium-high heat. Add the bacon and render until almost crisp. Add the chopped onion, celery, and garlic and stir for 5 minutes to soften the onion. Add the tomato paste and stir to loosen it. Add the stock, vinegar, Worcestershire sauce, brown sugar, and salt and pepper to taste. Add the beans, farro, and parsley and season with salt and pepper. Add stock if the beans and farro seem dry. Serve warm.

FARRO SALAD WITH CHERRIES

Once, many years back now, my mom and I made a special trip to Martha's Vineyard, just the two of us. We stayed at a place called the Tuscany Inn, which was run by a true Italian lady, a hostess of the first order. It was so memorable, and is vivid to this day. She served simple, divine breakfasts including a cherry focaccia with rosemary and sea salt. Ever since that trip, I have been hooked on that flavor combination. Divine. The added charms of nutty farro may be a rival to that warm bread. Make both (see Cherry Focaccia, page 102).

I should mention that my mother's second favorite ingredient after lemons is cherries; even though she broke a tooth once on a cherry pit, she continues to be faithful to them. That's love.

1 cup pearled farro
Salt
½ pound black or red cherries, pitted
1 small red onion, finely chopped
¼ cup pignoli (pine nuts), toasted
¼ cup sliced almonds, toasted
½ cup chopped fresh mint
½ cup chopped fresh flat-leaf parsley
3 tablespoons fresh rosemary leaves, chopped
Juice of 1 lemon
Juice of ½ orange
2 tablespoons white wine vinegar or white balsamic vinegar
3 tablespoons acacia honey
⅓ cup EVOO
Pepper
1 cup crumbled ricotta salata cheese

In a small pot, combine the farro with water to cover by a couple of inches. Cover, bring to a boil, and season with salt. Cook the farro to al dente, 23 to 25 minutes. Drain and spread out on a baking sheet to cool.

In a large bowl, combine the cooled farro, cherries, onion, pine nuts, almonds, mint, parsley, and rosemary.

In a small bowl, whisk the lemon juice, orange juice, vinegar, honey, EVOO, salt, and pepper. Pour the dressing over the salad, add the crumbled ricotta salata, and toss.

QUINOA WITH ROASTED SNAP PEAS AND HEN-OF-THE-WOODS MUSHROOMS

The homemade mushroom stock makes all the difference in this quinoa dish. Oven-roasting makes the sweet snap peas smoky and the mushrooms crispy, fragrant, and nutty.

1 pound sugar snap peas
2 large shallots, peeled and cut into 8 thin wedges each, root end intact
2 tablespoons olive oil, plus more for drizzling
Salt and pepper
¾ pound hen-of-the-woods mushrooms (maitake), root cut away and mushrooms separated
Leaves from a few sprigs fresh thyme
1¾ cups mushroom stock (page 65)
1 cup quinoa

Preheat the oven to 450°F.

Arrange the snap peas and shallots on a baking sheet. Toss with 2 tablespoons oil and season liberally with salt and pepper. Arrange the mushrooms on a second baking sheet and drizzle with oil. Add the thyme, season with salt and pepper, and toss. Roast both baking sheets of vegetables until the mushrooms are crispy and the snap peas are browned at the edges, about 25 minutes.

In a saucepan, bring the stock to a boil. Add the quinoa and salt and pepper, cover, reduce to a simmer, and cook until the liquids have been absorbed and the grain looks translucent, 18 to 20 minutes. Fluff with a fork.

Toss the quinoa with half the peas and shallots and the mushrooms and serve in shallow dishes topped with the remaining peas and mushrooms.

QUINOA AND VEGETABLE STUFFED PEPPERS

SERVES 6

This makes a colorful starter or side on a buffet table and a terrific vegetarian entrée option at dinner parties.

1 cup white or red quinoa

1¾ cups vegetable stock, preferably homemade (page 65)

6 small bell peppers, mixed colors, halved lengthwise (to make little boats)

3 tablespoons olive oil, plus more for drizzling

Salt and pepper

1 small to medium zucchini, seeded and chopped

1 red onion, chopped

1 small eggplant, half the skin peeled (in stripes), chopped

4 cloves garlic, thinly sliced

1 fresh red chile (such as Fresno), thinly sliced, or 1 teaspoon crushed red pepper flakes

2 plum tomatoes, chopped

½ cup fresh flat-leaf parsley tops, chopped

1 cup crumbled ricotta salata cheese

¼ cup fresh mint leaves, chopped

Preheat the oven to 450°F.

In a saucepan, combine the quinoa and stock and bring to a boil. Cover, reduce to a simmer, and cook until the liquids have been absorbed and the grain looks translucent, 18 to 20 minutes. Fluff with a fork. You will have about 4 cups cooked quinoa.

Drizzle the pepper halves with oil and season both sides with salt and black pepper. Place them cut side down on a baking sheet and roast until the skins begin to char and the peppers are just tender, about 20 minutes. Leave the oven on but reduce the temperature to 375°F. Let the peppers cool to room temp, then arrange in a baking dish, cut side up.

Meanwhile, in a large skillet, heat the oil (3 turns of the pan) over medium-high heat. Add the zucchini, onion, eggplant, garlic, chile, salt, and black pepper. Partially cover and cook until tender, 10 to 12 minutes. Add the tomatoes and half the parsley. Combine the vegetable mixture with the quinoa.

Fill the pepper halves with the quinoa-and-vegetable stuffing. Roast until the peppers are hot through. Serve the pepper halves topped with lots of crumbled ricotta salata and scatter with the mint and remaining parsley.

QUINOA

Quin-what? Okay, this grain is somewhat new to me, and I have never seen it on an Italian menu in my life. It is very tasty and fun to eat, too. I include a stuffed pepper because when (insert name drop here) President Clinton was persuaded by Chelsea to go meat-free, he came to our show shortly thereafter and his team requested quinoa-stuffed peppers as a favorite of his for the greenroom. We even discussed the recipe on air.

Quo vadis? No, I said "Quinoa."

Clockwise from upper left:
Linguine con Vongole (page 151); Celery, Portobello, and Parsley Salad (page 23); and Grilled or Roasted Whole Branzino (page 210).

CHAPTER 7

SEAFOOD

For a girl with Sicilian roots, I have to say we don't eat as much seafood as we should, or as much as I would like to. My husband and I love seafood, but some members of both our families do not eat seafood at all, or are very picky about the seafood they do eat. This collection of seafood recipes has broad appeal, and I think many of the dishes will convert any seafood skeptic.

Sustainable seafood is available everywhere, including Target and Walmart, so ask before you buy, including canned tuna. Seafood is the key to sustainable food for the planet and it's good for us, so we should all GO FISH!

CHECK THIS OUT

There are other seafood recipes scattered throughout the book.

- Barley Risotto with Crab and Pink Peppercorns (page 190)
- Fat Spaghetti with Frutti di Mare (page 155)
- Linguine con Vongole (page 151)
- Linguine with Cherry Tomato-Red Clam Sauce (page 152)
- Linguine with Crab (page 153)
- Linguine with Hot Sausage and Clam Sauce (page 152)
- Linguine with Shrimp Fra Diavolo (page 154)
- Linguine with White Clam Sauce from the Cupboard (page 153)
- Pasta con Sarde (page 156)
- Regina Pizza (page 98)
- Swordfish Polpette (page 49)
- Tuna Polpette (page 52)
- White Clam Pizza (page 93)
- White Zuppa di Pesce (page 83)

TILAPIA PICCATA

SERVES 4

I love piccata because it's so easy and quick to prepare. Making it with fish eliminates the extra step of pounding out the chicken breasts. This is a great go-to on busy days and also makes a lovely, simple meal to entertain with for lunch or light supper.

4 pieces tilapia fillet or other sustainable firm white fish
Salt and pepper
Flour, for dredging
4 tablespoons olive oil
4 tablespoons (½ stick) butter
2 lemons: 1 juiced, 1 sliced
1 large shallot, finely chopped
2 large cloves garlic, finely chopped
½ cup dry vermouth or dry white wine
2 tablespoons capers, drained
A handful of fresh flat-leaf parsley tops, finely chopped

Set the oven to its lowest setting. Put dinner plates or a platter in the oven to warm up.

Pat the fish dry. Season with salt and pepper and dredge lightly in flour.

In a large skillet, heat 2 tablespoons of the oil (2 turns of the pan) over medium-high heat. When the oil smokes, add 1 tablespoon of the butter and cook 2 pieces of fish for 2 to 3 minutes on each side. Transfer to warmed plates or a platter. Wipe the skillet clean and repeat with more oil, butter, and the remaining pieces of fish.

Add 1 tablespoon of the butter to the skillet and lightly brown the lemon slices on each side. Top the fish with the browned lemon slices.

Add the shallot and garlic to the pan and stir for 1 minute. Add the vermouth, capers, parsley, and lemon juice. Swirl in the remaining 1 tablespoon butter and cook for a minute to thicken.

Spoon the sauce evenly over the fish and serve.

COD SALTIMBOCCA

Skinned black cod or any sustainable white fish will work for this dish. White fish, like veal and white meat chicken, are innocuous and make a perfect backdrop for the sage and prosciutto used in saltimbocca, which literally means "jumps in your mouth." This dish will also serve 8 as a first course.

Juice of 1½ lemons
4 tablespoons EVOO
8 (4- to 5-ounce) thick center-cut pieces cod
½ teaspoon granulated garlic
Salt and pepper
16 small fresh sage leaves
8 thin slices prosciutto di Parma (thin but not shaved)
½ cup dry vermouth
2 tablespoons butter

In a bowl, combine two-thirds of the lemon juice and 3 tablespoons of the EVOO. Add the fish and turn to coat in the lemon oil. Remove the fish and season with the garlic and salt and pepper. Top each piece of fish with 2 small sage leaves and wrap evenly in a layer of prosciutto. Refrigerate the fish for at least 1 hour or up to overnight to allow the sage to perfume the fish.

In a large nonstick skillet, heat the remaining 1 tablespoon EVOO (1 turn of the pan) over medium to medium-high heat. Add the fish and cook to brown and crisp the ham on both sides. Add the vermouth and partially cover the pan or tent with foil and reduce the heat a bit. Cook until the fish is opaque (look at the exposed ends) and cooked through, about 4 minutes. Transfer the fish to plates.

Add the butter to the skillet and melt. When it foams, add the remaining lemon juice and swirl it in. Drizzle the sauce over the fish.

SNAPPER LIVORNESE

This is one of my favorite easy suppers. If the snapper doesn't look good, substitute branzino.

4 tablespoons olive oil
1 onion, finely chopped
2 or 3 cloves garlic (to taste), thinly sliced or chopped
Salt and pepper
1 cup dry vermouth or dry white wine
3 tablespoons capers, drained
1 cup green Cerignola olives, pitted and chopped
1 (28- to 32-ounce) can San Marzano tomatoes (look for DOP on the label)
4 to 6 (6-ounce) pieces red snapper fillet
Wondra (quick-mixing flour), for dredging
¼ cup chopped fresh flat-leaf parsley leaves

In a large skillet, heat 2 tablespoons of the oil (2 turns of the pan) over medium-high heat. Add the onion and garlic and season with salt and pepper. Stir for a few minutes to soften. Add the vermouth and cook until reduced by half, about 2 minutes. Add the capers and olives. Hand-crush the tomatoes as you add them to the skillet, then add the juices from the can. Simmer for 15 to 20 minutes.

In a large nonstick skillet, heat the remaining 2 tablespoons oil (2 turns of the pan) over medium-high heat. Score the snapper skins in a 1-inch crosshatch pattern with a sharp knife. Season both sides with salt and pepper and dredge lightly in Wondra to coat. Add the fish to the skillet, skin side down, and cook until the skin is crisp, 2 to 3 minutes. Flip the fillets and cook on the second side until the flesh is firm and opaque, about 3 minutes.

Transfer the fillets to a warm, shallow serving dish and top with the sauce and parsley.

SWORDFISH CUTLETS

For each cutlet, I use a very thin slice of swordfish that I pound between two sheets of parchment paper until it's paper-thin, so you can almost read the newspaper through it. To bread them, you don't need flour and egg; the breading is fine bread crumbs (they're Italian bread crumbs that look like dust; I get them from Buon Italia in Chelsea Market in Manhattan) mixed with an equal quantity of panko. Or instead of panko, you can use homemade bread crumbs and make them nice and coarse.

8 thin (about ½ inch thick) swordfish steaks, cut from one side of the bloodline

2 cups fine dry bread crumbs

2 cups panko bread crumbs

Grated zest of 2 organic lemons

½ cup fresh flat-leaf parsley leaves, finely chopped

2 or 3 cloves garlic (to taste), chopped

1 flat anchovy fillet, very finely chopped (optional)

Sea salt and pepper

EVOO, for frying and serving

1 lemon, cut into wedges, for serving

Fresh Tomato Relish (optional; see box)

Preheat the oven to 275°F. Set a cooling rack over a rimmed baking sheet (see Tip).

Trim the skin from the edges of the fish. Place the fish between two pieces of parchment paper and pound gently to a ¼-inch thickness.

In a shallow dish, combine the fine bread crumbs and panko. Stir in the lemon zest, parsley, garlic, and anchovy (if using). Work the ingredients through the bread crumbs with your fingers.

Season the swordfish cutlets on both sides with salt and pepper. Press the cutlets firmly into the bread crumb mixture so that they are evenly coated on both sides.

In a large skillet, heat a layer of EVOO (about ⅛ inch) over medium to medium-high heat. Working in batches, add the swordfish cutlets and cook until they're deep golden brown, about 2 minutes per side. Keep them warm in the oven until you're ready to serve. Serve with lemon wedges for squeezing. Top with tomato relish, if desired.

SETTING A RACK over a baking sheet allows the heat to circulate all the way around the cutlets so they'll stay nice and crispy on both sides. If you put them directly on a baking sheet, they'll tend to get a little sweaty on the bottom and stay crisp only on top.

FRESH TOMATO RELISH

I like to top swordfish cutlets with a fresh tomato relish, sort of a tomato raw sauce: Gently seed plum or vine tomatoes, then chop them into small cubes (about ¼ inch). Mix that with minced or finely chopped red onion and some combination of chopped fresh basil leaves and fresh flat-leaf parsley leaves. Toss that together lightly, using your fingertips. Season it with sea salt.

FISH IN CRAZY WATER WITH FENNEL

SERVES 4

This is a twist on a family favorite, a Marcella Hazan recipe. In Marcella's original recipe, the "crazy" water is just tomatoes, water with garlic, and oil. But ours has shaved fennel and onions as well as a flavor combination we use with fish often, if not always.

1 (28- to 32-ounce) can San Marzano tomatoes (look for DOP on the label), or 1½ to 2 pounds in-season tomatoes, chopped

3 tablespoons EVOO, plus more for drizzling

5 cloves garlic: 4 thinly sliced, 1 halved

1 small bulb fennel, trimmed, quartered lengthwise, and very thinly sliced (about 1 cup)

1 leek, halved lengthwise, cut crosswise into half-moons, and washed well

1 small onion, quartered and very thinly sliced

1 teaspoon crushed red pepper flakes, or 1 small red Fresno chile, seeded and minced

A handful of fresh flat-leaf parsley tops, finely chopped

Sea salt and black pepper

4 (6- to 8-ounce) pieces red snapper or black cod fillet

A few fresh basil leaves, torn, or 1 or 2 sprigs fresh tarragon, coarsely chopped

4 slices peasant-style white bread

Flaky sea salt

In a wide pot with a tight-fitting lid, combine the tomatoes and EVOO (3 turns of the pan). Scatter the sliced garlic, fennel, leek, and onion around the pan in a thin layer. Add the red pepper flakes, parsley, sea salt, black pepper, and 3 cups water. Bring to a boil, then reduce to a rolling simmer and cover. Simmer for 45 minutes. Uncover and cook until the liquid has reduced by half, 10 to 15 minutes.

Add the fish, skin side up, and cook for 2 to 3 minutes. Flip, season the fish with sea salt and black pepper, and cook until firm and opaque, 5 minutes more. Finish with a few torn basil leaves.

Meanwhile, char or broil the bread. Rub with the cut garlic, drizzle with EVOO, and season with flaky sea salt.

Place the bread in shallow bowls. Top with a piece of fish and some sauce.

PAN-FRIED FISH AGRODOLCE (OR PEPERONATA)

SERVES 6 TO 8

Mild fish is perfectly complemented by the assertive flavors of either agrodolce or peperonata sauce. You can use any other sustainable mild fish instead of the branzino.

6 to 8 pieces branzino (European sea bass) fillet

Kosher or fine sea salt and pepper

Wondra (quick-mixing flour), for dredging

3 tablespoons EVOO or vegetable oil

4 tablespoons (½ stick) butter

1 lemon, halved

Agrodolce Sauce (page 207) or Peperonata (page 207)

Season the fish with salt and pepper and dredge the flesh side in Wondra. Fold the fillets gently in half with the skin facing in.

In a large nonstick skillet, heat 2 tablespoons of the EVOO (2 turns of the pan) over medium to medium-high heat. Melt 2 tablespoons of the butter into the oil.

When the foam subsides, add half the fillets (3 or 4) to the pan and cook until golden and crispy on the first side, 3 to 5 minutes. Flip and cook until the fish is golden and crispy on both sides and opaque, 3 to 4 minutes. Transfer to a warm platter and cover with foil. Add the remaining 1 tablespoon EVOO (1 turn of the pan) to the pan. Melt in the remaining 2 tablespoons butter. Repeat with the remaining fish.

When you remove the second batch of fish, add the lemon halves, cut side down, and increase the heat. Caramelize the cut lemon, 3 to 4 minutes. Squeeze the lemon juice over the fish.

Serve the fish topped with agrodolce or peperonata.

CHECK THIS OUT

If you're a fan of the delicious duo of fish and fennel, check these out:

- Cioppino (page 212)
- Fish in Cartoccio (page 209)
- White Zuppa di Pesce (page 83)

SAUCES FOR SEAFOOD

Both of these high-flavor sauces work beautifully with the mild flavors of white fish. But they are delicious on their own. I love the agrodolce with pecorino cheese or sheep's milk ricotta on charred bread. The peperonata, too, is delicious on charred bread as crostini or served cold on sandwiches.

Peperonata

SERVES 6

Serve this sauce with grilled halibut, sardines, or octopus.

2 large red field peppers (long, rectangular red peppers), or 5 red bell peppers
¼ cup olive oil
1 medium white onion, quartered and thinly sliced
1 medium red onion, quartered and thinly sliced
1 large mild frying pepper (such as cubanelle)
1 fresh red or green chile (such as Fresno or jalapeño), seeded and sliced
3 or 4 cloves garlic (to taste), thinly sliced
2 small sprigs fresh oregano
Salt and black pepper
2 tablespoons tomato paste
½ cup dry vermouth
1 tablespoon sugar
½ cup chicken stock or water
2 tablespoons white balsamic vinegar or white wine vinegar
3 tablespoons capers, drained
A handful of fresh flat-leaf parsley tops, chopped

Roast and peel the peppers (see box, page 334). Cut the peppers lengthwise into ¼-inch-wide strips, then halve them crosswise. Set aside.

In a large skillet, heat the oil (4 turns of the pan) over medium heat. When the oil ripples, add the onions, frying pepper, chile, garlic, oregano, salt, and black pepper. Partially cover and sweat the vegetables for 4 to 5 minutes to soften. Add the tomato paste and stir for 1 minute. Add the vermouth and stir to deglaze the pan. Stir in the roasted peppers, sugar, stock, vinegar, and capers. Reduce the heat to low to keep warm if serving right away, or let cool and refrigerate.

If made ahead, reheat the sauce over medium heat before serving, adding an extra splash of stock or water to loosen it up.

Agrodolce Sauce

SERVES 6

This sauce is an intense sweet-and-sour shallot-based condiment for fish and seafood. I like it with smoky grilled halibut as well as with mild sea bass or branzino. Agrodolce is fabulous on its own merits, but I love to garnish it with toasted almonds or pine nuts and lots of chopped parsley and celery tops or fennel fronds—making the overall sauce more delicious and very particular.

12 to 15 large shallots, 3 small to medium red torpedo onions, or 3 small to medium yellow onions
¼ cup olive oil
8 to 10 cloves garlic, thinly sliced
1 cup white balsamic vinegar
1 cup dry vermouth or dry white wine
⅓ cup sugar
3 tablespoons golden raisins
1 large fresh bay leaf
2 teaspoons kosher or sea salt
1 teaspoon coarsely ground pepper
Chopped fresh flat-leaf parsley, celery tops, and/or fennel fronds
Toasted sliced almonds or pignoli (pine nuts), for garnish

Halve the shallots lengthwise. Peel and cut lengthwise into ¼-inch-thick slices.

In a large skillet with a lid, heat the oil (4 turns of the pan) over medium heat. When the oil ripples and just begins to smoke, add the shallots and garlic. Partially cover and cook, stirring occasionally, to soften, 7 to 8 minutes.

Add the vinegar, vermouth, and 1 cup water and bring to a boil. Add the sugar, raisins, bay leaf, salt, and pepper. Reduce the heat to keep at a low rolling boil and cook until thickened but still liquid enough to make it pourable and balanced, 30 to 40 minutes. Reduce the heat to low to keep warm if serving right away, or let cool and refrigerate. Discard the bay leaf.

If made ahead, reheat the sauce over medium heat before serving, adding a splash of stock or water to loosen it up.

When serving, garnish the sauce with the herb or herbs of your choice and toasted nuts.

FISH IN CARTOCCIO

Fish *en papillote* (in a parchment paper pouch) is *in cartoccio* in Italian—or "fish in a sack," as our family calls it. I love serving fish or chicken in paper when entertaining. (This is a good thing, as my mother often requests it for her birthday celebrations.) Each person gets a pouch or packet, so starting dinner is like opening up a present. Plus, cooking in parchment has the virtue of being a very healthful preparation.

1 bulb fennel, trimmed and very thinly sliced on a mandoline or the slicer blade on a box grater

2 small yellow onions, very thinly sliced

4 small white or Yukon Gold potatoes (about 1 pound), very thinly sliced

4 cloves garlic, thinly sliced

Salt and pepper

EVOO, for drizzling

½ cup dry vermouth or dry white wine

4 pieces cod fillet or other sustainable firm white fish

4 teaspoons fresh lemon juice

4 thin pats of butter

Chopped fresh flat-leaf parsley

Preheat the oven to 400°F. Cut four 12 x 16-inch pieces of parchment paper (see Tip).

In a bowl, combine the fennel, onions, potatoes, garlic, salt, and pepper. Drizzle with just enough EVOO to lightly coat.

Divide the fennel mixture evenly among the pieces of parchment, placing it in the center of each. Drizzle each packet with 2 tablespoons vermouth. Top with a piece of fish and season with salt and pepper. Top each piece of fish with 1 teaspoon lemon juice, 1 pat of butter, and a little parsley. Bring the short ends of the parchment up to meet in the middle and fold over 1 inch, then fold down a few more turns (leave a little headroom for the steam). Fold in the ends to make half-moon-shaped packets (pouches).

Place the pouches on a baking sheet and roast the fish for 20 to 25 minutes.

Serve each person a pouch and make sure they are mindful that the pouches will release hot steam. Have them slide the contents away from the paper in a swift motion, like pulling out a tablecloth in a magic act. Place a bowl on the table to collect the papers.

TIP

Buy packaged precut half-sheets of parchment paper from any restaurant supply store.

GRILLED OR ROASTED WHOLE BRANZINO

SERVES 4

If I am entertaining, I order my branzino (European sea bass) with the heads and tails removed. Personally, I don't mind them, but some people find the eyes distracting while they're eating. These delicate fish are actually great on the grill and hold up well, but if the weather isn't cooperating for outdoor grilling, they also roast up nicely. Serve with rice or grain salads in the summer and rice pilaf in the winter.

4 whole branzino (1 pound each), gutted and scaled
⅓ cup olive oil, plus more for coating
Salt and pepper
4 lemons: 2 sliced, 2 halved
1 medium onion, very thinly sliced
4 cloves garlic, very thinly sliced
8 bay leaves
8 sprigs fresh thyme
¼ cup white wine vinegar or dry white wine

Heat an outdoor grill to medium-high or preheat the oven to 450°F (with the rack at the center).

Liberally coat the fish in oil and season with salt and pepper inside and out. Dividing evenly, fill the fish cavities with the sliced lemons, onion, garlic, bay leaves, and thyme. Grill, covered, until the fish is opaque, about 15 minutes, turning once. Or roast until firm and opaque, 18 to 20 minutes.

Meanwhile, coat the cut sides of the halved lemons with oil and season with salt and pepper. Grill or char in a hot skillet, cut side down, for 4 to 5 minutes. Squeeze the juice from the charred lemon into a bowl and whisk with the vinegar and the ⅓ cup olive oil.

Pour the lemon sauce over the fish and serve.

GRILLED FISH WITH ARUGULA-HERB PESTO

SERVES 4

Serve a halved whole fish or a large fillet per person.

PESTO:
½ cup sliced almonds or pignoli (pine nuts), toasted
1 cup packed fresh flat-leaf parsley tops
1 cup wild or baby arugula
3 tablespoons fresh thyme leaves
½ cup fresh tarragon leaves
3 tablespoons capers, drained
1 cup freshly grated Parmigiano-Reggiano cheese (optional)
2 or 3 cloves garlic (to taste), smashed
Grated zest and juice of 1 organic lemon
½ cup EVOO or olive oil
Salt and pepper

FISH:
4 pieces snapper, grouper, or other sustainable firm, mild fish
Salt and pepper
Grill planks, soaked in cold water for 30 minutes
1 lemon, halved

Make the pesto: In a food processor, combine the toasted nuts, parsley, arugula, thyme, tarragon, capers, Parm (if using), garlic, lemon zest, lemon juice, oil, salt, and pepper. Pulse to form a thick sauce.

Make the fish: Heat a grill to medium-high heat. When the grill is ready, season the fish with salt and pepper on both sides. Arrange on the soaked grill planks and slather the fish evenly with the pesto. Grill, covered, until the fish is opaque and the pesto is lightly browned at the edges, 15 to 18 minutes. Grill the halved lemons, cut side down, to caramelize.

When ready to serve, squeeze the lemon juice over the fish.

GRILLED FISH WITH ORANGE RELISH

SERVES 4

The orange relish is just a Sicilian salad chopped a bit finer.

4 (6- to 8-ounce) tuna, halibut, or swordfish steaks (1 inch thick)
Salt and black pepper
3 tablespoons olive oil, plus more for drizzling
1 teaspoon crushed red pepper flakes
1 teaspoon fennel seeds
1 tablespoon grated lemon zest (from an organic lemon)
1 tablespoon finely chopped fresh rosemary
2 cloves garlic, chopped
3 oranges, supremed (see box, page 221) and chopped
½ red onion, finely chopped
1 tablespoon fresh oregano leaves, finely chopped
1 cup loosely packed fresh flat-leaf parsley tops, chopped
3 tablespoons capers, drained
½ lemon

Skin the fish and remove any bloodline. Season with salt and black pepper.

In a shallow dish, combine the oil with the red pepper flakes, fennel seeds, lemon zest, rosemary, and garlic. Add the fish and turn to coat.

In a bowl, combine the oranges, onion, oregano, parsley, and capers. Drizzle with a little oil and season with salt and pepper.

Heat a grill or grill pan to medium-high heat. Grill the fish for 6 minutes for pink-center tuna or 8 minutes for opaque halibut or swordfish. Squeeze the lemon half over the fish. Serve topped with the orange relish.

SARDINES

Grilled or roasted sardines served with Agrodolce Sauce (page 207) or Peperonata (page 207) can make a great light supper or a delicious starter. Leftover grilled sardines with either of those sauces make a wonderful "san-gu-ich" the next day on some crusty bread. And if you really love sardines, check out my Pasta con Sarde (page 156). It's in my top five recipes of this entire book. YUM!

CIOPPINO

Not everyone in my family eats all the seafood that usually goes into this classic Italian American stew. So when we have this on Christmas Eve, I make the soup base in one main pot and then serve it in individualized versions. Serve this with plenty of crusty bread for mopping.

SOUP BASE:

3 tablespoons olive oil
1 small bulb fennel, trimmed, quartered lengthwise, and thinly sliced (save a handful of the fronds for garnish)
1 carrot, chopped
1 onion, chopped
2 ribs celery with leafy tops, chopped
3 or 4 cloves garlic (to taste), chopped
1 leek, halved lengthwise, cut crosswise into ½-inch half-moons, and washed well
Salt and pepper
Herb bundle: a few sprigs of fresh thyme, a handful of flat-leaf parsley, and 2 large fresh bay leaves, tied together with kitchen twine
2 tablespoons tomato paste
½ cup Pernod
1 cup dry vermouth or dry white wine
5 to 6 cups chicken or seafood stock
1 (28- to 32-ounce) can San Marzano tomatoes (look for DOP on the label)

SHELLFISH:

12 to 16 large shrimp, shell-on or peeled (tails left on) and deveined
¾ pound lump crabmeat, or 12 crab legs in cut shells
12 to 16 Manila clams, cleaned (see Tip, page 155), and/or 12 to 16 mussels, debearded and scrubbed

FISH AND SCALLOPS:

½ cup Wondra (quick-mixing flour)
1 tablespoon Old Bay seasoning (see Tip)
2 pounds cod, black cod, or halibut, cut into 2-ounce pieces
16 large scallops, trimmed and patted dry
Salt and pepper
2 tablespoons extra-light olive or vegetable oil
2 tablespoons butter

FOR SERVING:
EVOO
Crushed red pepper flakes
Crusty bread

Make the soup base: In a large braising pot or wide, deep skillet with a lid, heat the oil (3 turns of the pan) over medium-high heat. Add the fennel, carrot, onion, celery, garlic, leek, salt, and pepper. Add the herb bundle, cover, and cook, stirring occasionally, for 10 minutes.

Add the tomato paste and stir for 1 minute. Add the Pernod and let it almost evaporate. Add the vermouth and cook until reduced by half. Add the stock. Hand-crush the tomatoes as you add them to the pot, then add the juices from the can. Bring to a boil, then reduce to a simmer.

Make the shellfish: When you are almost ready to serve, increase the heat a bit under the soup base to keep it at a low rolling boil. Add the shrimp, crab, clams and/or mussels. Cover the pot and cook until the clam and/or mussel shells open and the shrimp are opaque, 6 to 8 minutes. Discard any clams and/or mussels that do not open.

Make the fish and scallops: In a shallow bowl, stir the Wondra and Old Bay. Season the fish and scallops with salt and pepper and dredge them in the flour mixture. In a large skillet, heat 1 tablespoon of the oil (1 turn of the pan) over medium-high heat. Melt in 1 tablespoon of the butter. When the foam subsides, add half the fish and scallops and cook for a few minutes on each side until golden and crispy. Transfer to a warm plate. Heat the remaining 1 tablespoon oil, melt in the remaining 1 tablespoon butter, and cook the remaining fish and scallops.

Warm shallow bowls to serve in. Remove the herb bundle. Ladle the stew into the bowls and set chunks of fish and scallops on top. Garnish with fennel fronds. Place EVOO and red pepper flakes at the table for topping. Serve with plenty of crusty bread.

TIP

Use your favorite seafood seasoning or try my Rachael Ray Seafood Seasoning, which comes in a spice grinder and is available in some larger markets and online.

TUNA STEAKS WITH RAW PUTTANESCA SAUCE

I love spaghetti puttanesca. I could easily eat half a pound of it. But eating half a pound of pasta at one sitting is not the most figure-friendly decision one can make. So this meal is a high-protein solution that provides tons of flavor without tons of calories, especially in the hot summer months when we have very little clothing with which to hide our spaghetti.

1 teaspoon anchovy paste, or 4 flat anchovy fillets, minced

1 teaspoon crushed red pepper flakes

1 large clove garlic, grated or minced

4 tablespoons olive oil

1½ pints cherry tomatoes, halved

½ small red onion, finely chopped

2 tablespoons capers, drained and chopped

½ cup oil-cured olives, pitted and chopped

A fat handful of fresh flat-leaf parsley tops, chopped

4 (6-ounce) tuna steaks

Salt and black pepper

A few leaves fresh basil, torn or shredded

In a bowl, whisk the anchovy paste, red pepper flakes, garlic, and about 3 tablespoons of the oil (pour slowly to a count of 3). Stir in the tomatoes, onion, capers, olives, and parsley and let stand for 30 minutes.

Heat a griddle or cast-iron skillet over medium heat. Drizzle the fish with the remaining 1 tablespoon oil and season with salt and black pepper. Cook the tuna for 2 to 2½ minutes on each side for rare, or up to 4 minutes on each side for fish that is opaque in the center.

Slice the tuna, arrange on plates, and top with lots of raw sauce and basil.

SLICED TUNA STEAK WITH KALE, TOMATO, AND BEAN SALAD

When I wander through strange villages in Italy, I will stop for a light lunch at any piazza café. I always pick menu items that are universally the same no matter the village or recipe; the dishes that I consider "safe" and not a question of the skills being practiced in the kitchen. One great salad that I order often is tomato, onion, and white beans with canned tuna. This is a fancier version of the classic combination, and one I proudly serve to guests as a light brunch or supper.

1 large clove garlic, pasted

Juice of 1 lemon

2 tablespoons white balsamic or white wine vinegar

2 teaspoons Dijon mustard

2 tablespoons fresh thyme leaves, chopped

⅓ cup EVOO, plus more for drizzling

4 plum or vine tomatoes, lightly seeded and chopped

1 small white onion, chopped

1 (15-ounce) can cannellini beans, rinsed and drained

3 small ribs celery from the heart with leafy tops, chopped

½ cup fresh flat-leaf parsley tops, chopped

4 fat handfuls of baby kale

Salt and pepper

4 (1- to 1½-inch-thick) tuna steaks

In a large bowl, combine the garlic, lemon juice, vinegar, mustard, and thyme. Slowly whisk in the ⅓ cup EVOO to emulsify the dressing. Add the tomatoes, onion, beans, celery, parsley, and kale. Season with salt and pepper and toss the salad to combine.

Heat a griddle or grill pan to medium-high heat. Drizzle the tuna with EVOO and season with salt and pepper.

Cook the tuna for 2 to 3 minutes on each side for rare to medium-rare.

To serve, divide the salad among 4 plates or shallow bowls. Slice the tuna and arrange over the salads.

CRISPY FISH STICKS WITH PARM AND PARSLEY-CAPER SAUCE

SERVES 4

Serve this with salt-and-vinegar potato chips and Roasted Broccoli or Broccolini (page 313) or grilled or roasted asparagus. As with most things that I coat with bread crumbs, I like to add grated cheese to the coating mixture; it makes the crust crispier, nuttier, and certainly tastier.

PARSLEY-CAPER SAUCE:
1½ cups packed fresh flat-leaf parsley tops
2 small cloves garlic, peeled
Grated zest and juice of 1 organic lemon
3 tablespoons capers, drained
Salt and pepper
3 to 4 tablespoons olive oil

FISH STICKS:
1½ pounds halibut, black cod, or other sustainable white fish, cut into 8 fat sticks
Salt and pepper
Flour, for dredging
2 large free-range organic eggs
½ cup fine dry bread crumbs
½ cup panko bread crumbs or large-flake fresh bread crumbs
½ cup freshly grated Parmigiano-Reggiano cheese
3 to 4 tablespoons olive oil
Lemon wedges, for serving

Make the parsley-caper sauce: In a food processor or blender, combine the parsley, garlic, lemon zest, lemon juice, capers, salt, and pepper and pulse-chop. Add the oil and puree into a sauce.

Make the fish sticks: Season the fish with salt and pepper.

Set up a breading station: Line up 3 shallow bowls on the counter. Spread the flour out in one, beat the eggs in the second, and mix the fine bread crumbs, panko, and Parm in the third.

In a large skillet, heat a shallow layer of oil (3 to 4 tablespoons) over medium to medium-high heat. Coat the fish in the flour, then in the egg, and finally in the bread crumb mix, pressing to make sure the coating sticks. Shallow-fry the fish for 2 to 3 minutes on each side. Drain on paper towels.

Serve the fish warm, with parsley sauce and lemon wedges.

MOM'S SHRIMP WITH SAGE AND PANCETTA

SERVES 4

I made this for a Food Network demo and the pilot for *30 Minute Meals*. I had to make it so many times that I got a bit tired of it. But it's been more than a dozen years now, and I'm into it all over again.

12 jumbo (16/18 count) shrimp or prawns, peeled (tails left on) and deveined
1 lemon, halved
1 tablespoon EVOO, plus more for liberal drizzling
Sea salt and pepper
12 large fresh sage leaves
12 slices pancetta or thinly sliced prosciutto
¼ cup dry vermouth

Rinse and dry the shrimp. Dress the shrimp with the juice of one lemon half. Cut the remaining lemon half into small wedges. Drizzle the shrimp liberally with EVOO and season with a little salt and some pepper. Place a sage leaf down the back of each shrimp where it has been deveined and then wrap the shrimp carefully and snugly with pancetta.

In a large skillet, heat the EVOO (1 turn of the pan) over medium to medium-high heat. Add the shrimp and cook, turning occasionally, until the pancetta is crisp and the shrimp are pink and firm, 6 to 8 minutes. Douse the pan with the vermouth and swirl. Serve with the lemon wedges alongside.

GRILLED SHRIMP WITH GAZPACHO

There's nothing better than gazpacho served in chilled mugs with hot grilled shrimp alongside to peel, dunk, and eat. Dress shell-on (but deveined) shrimp with EVOO and season with Old Bay (or try my seafood seasoning, which comes in a grinder). Grill until firm and opaque. Grill cut lemons alongside the shrimp and douse the cooked shrimp with the juice of the charred lemon. Serve the peel 'n' eat shrimp with chilled Italian-Style Gazpacho (page 68) or White Gazpacho (page 68).

VENETIAN SHRIMP

SERVES 4 TO 6

Venice was a spice port. Among the many wonders of the city are the unique flavors in the sauces and stews—a hint of saffron here or a pinch of cinnamon there, so unusual and sexy. You can add any seafood to this, the way you do with Cioppino (page 212). In Venice, they might add sliced cuttlefish. I like it with large, sweet prawns or shrimp and lots of warm bread for mopping.

A fat pinch of saffron
2 cups chicken or seafood stock
3 tablespoons olive oil
1 bulb fennel, trimmed, quartered lengthwise, cored, and thinly sliced
1 onion, quartered lengthwise and thinly sliced
2 ribs celery, chopped
3 cloves garlic, sliced
½ teaspoon crushed red pepper flakes
1 large fresh bay leaf
Salt and black pepper
1 (28- to 32-ounce) can San Marzano tomatoes (look for DOP on the label)
2 pounds jumbo (16/20 count) shrimp or prawns
2 lemons: 1 halved, 1 sliced
½ cup dry vermouth
2 tablespoons butter
A handful of fresh basil leaves, torn
Crusty bread, for mopping

In a small saucepan, combine the saffron and stock and warm over low heat.

In a braising pot or deep skillet with a lid, heat 2 tablespoons of the oil (2 turns of the pan) over medium to medium-high heat. Add the fennel, onion, celery, garlic, red pepper flakes, bay leaf, salt, and black pepper. Partially cover and cook to soften, 8 to 10 minutes. Add the saffron stock. Hand-crush the tomatoes and add them with the juices from the can. Simmer the sauce for 15 minutes at a low bubble to the combine the flavors and thicken a bit. Fish out and discard the bay leaf.

Meanwhile, peel the shrimp, leaving the tails intact. With a sharp knife, cut into the back of the shrimp, following the vein, and cut almost but not all the way through to the other side.

In a large skillet, heat the remaining 1 tablespoon oil (1 turn of the pan) over medium-high to high heat until it smokes. Add the lemon halves, cut side down, and char. Remove and set aside. Add the shrimp and lemon slices to the pan and season liberally with salt and black pepper. Toss to cook the shrimp quickly until pink, light brown at the edges, and opaque, 2 to 3 minutes. Douse the pan with the vermouth, then melt in the butter, swirling the pan.

Combine the shrimp, pan juices, and lemon slices with the red sauce. Squeeze the charred lemon halves over the shrimp and top with basil. Serve the shrimp in warm bowls with bread for mopping.

SHRIMP SCAMPI

SERVES 6 TO 8

I line a platter with charred or toasted bread before I serve the shrimp and sauce. The sauce seeps into the bread, and it's like a sweet dessert when you are done devouring the shrimp. This also makes a terrific appetizer and will serve 12 to 16 people.

¼ cup olive oil

2 pounds large shrimp, peeled (tails left on), deveined, and butterflied

Salt and black pepper

2 lemons: 1 thinly sliced, 1 halved

5 or 6 cloves garlic (to taste), chopped

1 teaspoon crushed red pepper flakes

Leaves from 2 small sprigs fresh oregano, finely chopped

1 cup dry vermouth

3 tablespoons butter, cut into small pieces

A generous handful of fresh flat-leaf parsley tops, finely chopped

6 to 8 slices ciabatta or crusty Italian bread, charred or toasted

In a large skillet, heat the oil (4 turns of the pan) over medium-high heat. Add the shrimp and season with salt and black pepper. Add the lemon slices and toss until they begin to firm up and start to brown at the edges, 3 to 4 minutes. Add the garlic, red pepper flakes, and oregano, and toss for 2 minutes more. Add the vermouth and cook until reduced by half. Melt in the butter, stir in the parsley, and squeeze in the lemon juice from the halved lemon.

Arrange the toasted bread on a platter and top with the shrimp. Pour the sauce over the top and serve.

LEMON CREAM SCAMPI

SERVES 4 TO 6

This is based on a dish I had once upon a time in Amalfi, so it's all about the lemon. Serve with warm crusty bread, or toss with thin linguine or thin spaghetti and some starchy cooking water. If you serve with pasta, you can offer grated Parm for topping, but in my family, most dishes with seafood are not eaten with cheese.

3 to 4 tablespoons olive oil

1 small onion, finely chopped

4 cloves garlic, finely chopped

1½ to 2 pounds large shrimp, peeled (tails left on) and deveined

Salt and pepper

1 tablespoon grated lemon zest (from an organic lemon)

½ cup vodka or dry vermouth

⅓ cup crème fraîche or mascarpone cheese

2 tablespoons finely chopped fresh flat-leaf parsley

A small handful of fresh basil leaves, torn

Juice of ½ lemon

Crusty bread, for mopping

In a large skillet, heat about ⅛ inch of oil (3 to 4 turns of the pan) over medium-high heat. When the oil ripples, add the onion and garlic and stir for 4 to 5 minutes to soften. Add the shrimp, season with salt and pepper, add the lemon zest, and toss until opaque, 2 to 3 minutes. Add the vodka and toss for 1 minute. Melt in the crème fraîche. Remove from the heat and stir in the parsley and basil.

Divide the shrimp among shallow bowls and drizzle each with a few drops of lemon juice. Serve crusty bread alongside.

SCAMPI WITH CHERRY TOMATOES

Serve this beautiful dish with lots of warm, charred or grilled ciabatta bread for mopping.

2 pounds 10/12 count ("colossal") shrimp
¼ cup olive oil
2 large shallots, finely chopped
4 large cloves garlic, thinly sliced
1 teaspoon crushed red pepper flakes
½ teaspoon fennel seeds
¼ cup brandy or sherry
¾ cup dry white wine or dry vermouth
½ cup chicken or seafood stock
1½ pints cherry or grape tomatoes, halved
A fat handful of fresh flat-leaf parsley, finely chopped
1 tablespoon fresh lemon juice
Ciabatta bread, grilled or broiled, for mopping

Peel the shrimp, leaving the tails intact. With a sharp knife, cut into the back of the shrimp, following the vein, and cut almost but not all the way through to the other side.

In a large skillet with a tight-fitting lid, heat the oil (4 turns of the pan) over medium-high heat. Add the shallots, garlic, red pepper flakes, and fennel seeds and stir for 2 to 3 minutes. If using brandy, add it and ignite it with a long match. If using sherry, stir it in. Add the wine and cook until reduced by half. Add the stock and tomatoes and heat through.

Add the shrimp, cover, and cook, shaking the pan occasionally, for 7 to 8 minutes. Add the parsley and lemon juice and toss.

Serve in shallow bowls, with bread alongside for mopping.

GRILLED MUSSELS WITH GARLICKY TOMATO RAW SAUCE

Grilling mussels in the shell is a simple trick that works for clams or oysters, too, but I find the smoky flavor of grilling best complements mussels. Grilling the lemons as well gives them a concentrated sweet-smoky flavor. Serve the mussels with grilled bread, rubbed with garlic, drizzled with oil, and sprinkled with flaky sea salt.

½ red onion, finely chopped
6 cloves garlic, finely chopped
3 lemons, halved
Salt
3 tablespoons fresh thyme leaves, chopped
½ cup fresh flat-leaf parsley tops, chopped
1 small fresh red chile, halved
6 plum tomatoes, chopped
48 mussels, debearded and scrubbed
Olive oil, for drizzling
Pepper

In a medium bowl, combine the onion and garlic. Squeeze in the juice from 2 lemon halves. Season with salt and let stand for 10 minutes. Add the thyme, parsley, chile, and tomatoes. Let the raw sauce stand while you prepare the grill.

Heat a charcoal grill or a gas grill to high.

Scatter the mussels over the grill, close the lid, and grill until they open, 4 to 7 minutes. Drizzle the cut sides of the remaining lemon halves with oil and season with salt and pepper. Grill the lemons, cut side down, for 4 minutes.

Discard any mussels that do not open. Carefully transfer the mussels with a spider or large spatula to a shallow platter and douse with the juice of the grilled lemons. Then toss the mussels with the raw sauce.

GRILLED OCTOPUS
WITH GREENS AND GRAPEFRUIT

SERVES 4

I will only prepare octopus if we are grilling outdoors and I can start partially cooking the octopus a day ahead. Much like when I poach chicken, I like to let it cool in its own cooking juices completely before refrigerating and to let it sit overnight. Then I grill it over a natural charcoal fire or a Tuscan grill and hardwood flame.

I marinate the octopus in the same parsley-caper sauce I use for my grilled calamari (see page 223). After grilling, I douse the octopus with juice from a grilled grapefruit and finish with sea salt, then serve it on an arugula and grapefruit salad. The smoky, charred grilled octopus is also delicious served with greens and topped with Agrodolce Sauce (page 207) or even Peperonata (page 207), as both have a sweet-and-sour profile that stands up to the char.

OCTOPUS:
3 pounds cleaned octopus
1½ cups crisp, dry white wine
2 bay leaves
A few black peppercorns
1 or 2 wine corks (traditional; some say it makes the octopus more tender, so why not?)
1 lemon, sliced
1 or 2 large cloves garlic, smashed
Salt

SAUCE:
Parsley-Caper Sauce (from Crispy Fish Sticks, page 215)
¼ cup olive oil
1 or 2 cloves garlic, peeled
½ teaspoon crushed red pepper flakes
1 grapefruit, halved
Flaky sea salt

SALAD:
5 to 6 cups baby or wild arugula
2 or 3 ribs celery, very thinly sliced on an angle
1 cup fresh flat-leaf parsley tops, coarsely chopped
1 medium grapefruit, supremed (see box)
½ cup sliced almonds, toasted and chopped

Make the octopus: A day before grilling, place the octopus in a pot with the wine, bay leaves, peppercorns, wine corks, lemon slices, garlic, and water to cover by 1 to 2 inches. Bring to a boil, season with salt, reduce the heat a bit, and cook at a low rolling boil for 1 hour. Remove from the heat and let the octopus cool completely in its cooking liquid. Remove, pat dry, wrap well, and refrigerate.

Prepare a charcoal grill.

Make the parsley-caper sauce, adding the oil, garlic, and red pepper flakes. Pour half the sauce over the octopus and marinate for 30 minutes. Set the rest of the sauce aside for serving.

Remove the octopus from the marinade, shake off the excess, and grill, turning occasionally, until crispy at the edges but still tender, 8 to 10 minutes. Grill the halved grapefruit, cut side down, alongside. When the octopus is done, squeeze the juice from the grilled grapefruit over it and sprinkle with sea salt.

Slice the tentacles on an angle into 1- to 2-inch pieces.

Make the salad: On a large platter, arrange the arugula, celery, parsley, and grapefruit segments. Top with the almonds and sliced octopus. Drizzle the remaining parsley sauce over the salad and serve.

MAKING CITRUS SUPREMES

To "supreme" citrus fruit is to cut the sections away from the membranes. To do this, slice off the peel at the top and bottom of the fruit so it will sit flat. With a sharp knife, follow the curve of the fruit to remove the peel and the membrane just underneath it (exposing the fruit). Working over a bowl, use the knife to release the segments from between the membranes.

CALAMARI FRITTI

Even people who claim not to care much for seafood love properly cooked calamari rings because they do not taste like "seafood." They are tender, sweet, and crispy, and make a perfect palette for spicy red tomato dipping sauce. I feel the key to success here is to use small calamari and make sure the oil is very hot for each batch you fry. Also, as we did in the restaurants I worked in as a kid, be sure to shake off excess flour in a sieve or strainer basket so the rings do not get gummy.

DIPPING SAUCE:

3 tablespoons EVOO
3 cloves garlic, finely chopped
    or grated
1 small sprig fresh oregano
1 (28- to 32-ounce) can San
    Marzano tomatoes (look
    for DOP on the label)
2 or 3 fresh basil leaves, torn
1 teaspoon sea salt or kosher salt

CALAMARI AND HERBS:

Canola, vegetable, or sunflower
    oil, for deep-frying
3 pounds smallish calamari,
    cleaned
2 cups flour
1 teaspoon granulated garlic
1 teaspoon kosher salt
1 cup mixed fresh herb sprigs:
    flat-leaf parsley, tarragon,
    rosemary, oregano, thyme,
    and/or basil
2 organic lemons: 1 very thinly
    sliced, 1 halved
A couple of fresh or dried chiles
Flaky sea salt, for serving

Make the dipping sauce: In a saucepan, heat the EVOO (3 turns of the pan) over medium-low heat. Add the garlic and oregano and stir for 1 or 2 minutes. Hand-crush the tomatoes as you add them to the pot, then add the juices from the can. Stir in the basil and salt. Partially cover and bring to a bubble, then reduce the heat and let simmer for 20 minutes.

Make the calamari and herbs: Fill a countertop fryer with oil or pour a few inches of oil into a large Dutch oven. Heat the oil to 365° to 375°F (on a deep-fry thermometer if using a Dutch oven).

Trim the calamari of their tips (which may hold grit) and any fin/scrap left. Cut the body sacs crosswise into ¼-inch rings and cut the tentacles into 1½- to 2-inch pieces if they're longer than bite-size.

In a bowl, season the flour with the granulated garlic and salt. Working in batches, toss a handful of rings in the seasoned flour and shake off the excess in a sieve. Fry in the hot oil until golden and crisp, about 2 minutes. Drain on a cooling rack set over paper towels. Let the oil come back up to temp before dredging and frying the next batch.

After the last batch of calamari is cooked, add the herbs, lemon slices, and chiles to the fryer and flash-fry for 30 seconds to 1 minute. Drain, lightly crush, and toss with the calamari.

Sprinkle everything with flaky sea salt and squeeze lemon juice over them. Serve immediately with dipping sauce alongside.

GRILLED CALAMARI WITH ARUGULA

SERVES 4 TO 6

Here I use the sauce that goes with the Crispy Fish Sticks (page 215) as both the marinade and the topping for calamari, which works out well. I upped the amount of EVOO and garlic because the sauce does double duty as marinade and topping, and I added some pepper flakes to stand up to the grilling, adding heat to smoke. I finish with juice from a grilled lemon and spicy greens as a bed for smoky squid.

2 to 3 pounds small calamari (about 3-inch-long sacs), cleaned

Parsley-Caper Sauce (from Crispy Fish Sticks, page 215)

¼ cup olive oil

1 or 2 cloves garlic, peeled

½ teaspoon crushed red pepper flakes

1 lemon, halved

6 cups wild or baby arugula

Trim the calamari of their tips, which may hold grit.

Make the parsley-caper sauce, adding the oil, garlic, and red pepper flakes. Toss half the sauce with all the calamari and thread 2 or 3 calamari on thin metal skewers.

Heat a grill or grill pan to just under high heat.

Grill the skewered calamari and the halved lemon, cut side down, for 3 to 4 minutes, turning the skewers once.

Douse the squid with juice from the grilled lemon and serve whole or sliced on a bed of arugula. Serve the rest of the parsley-caper sauce alongside.

Clockwise from upper left: The 3 B's: Berries, Balsamic, and Basil (page 28); Slow-Roasted Bone-in Leg of Lamb (page 242); Mom's Fresh Mint Sauce (page 243); Zucchini with Mint and Almonds (page 347); Rachael's Polenta (page 179); and Herbed Fennel Slaw (page 329).

CHAPTER 8

PORK
AND
LAMB

PORK

My husband loves pork so much that every Valentine's Day, I give him a bouquet of twelve different flavors and types of cured sausages and salamis. For his birthday meal the year I met him, I offered to make him anything in the world for dinner and his answer was immediate: carbonara, which is bacon and egg spaghetti. If he were placed on a desert island and offered three items he would take a pork product, Scotch (Johnnie Walker Double Black), and the dog. I am not convinced I would make the short list. That being said, he might need me to prepare the pork, so he would argue the exception and attach me to the pork. This chapter represents John's favorite pork recipes—first and foremost, Porchetta (see right), a four-day labor of love.

PORCHETTA

This is a great weekend meal for a crowd, but it needs four days' lead time so plan ahead. Serve the meat as sandwiches on warm, crusty ciabatta rolls, with lots of lemon wedges (or lemon halves caramelized in a hot skillet or on the grill) to squeeze over the meat. Layer the sandwiches with some bitter greens, like wild arugula or baby kale.

12 to 14 pounds skin-on pork belly (2 inches thick)
Grated zest of 2 organic lemons (3 to 4 tablespoons)
3 tablespoons fennel seeds
12 large cloves garlic, chopped
5 to 6 tablespoons fresh rosemary leaves, coarsely chopped
¼ cup kosher salt
2 tablespoons coarsely ground pepper
5 pounds boneless pork loin roast
2 teaspoons baking soda

Trim the pork belly to the length of the loin and trim the edges to make a rectangle. With a long side of the belly facing you, trim the fat down to ¾ inch for 1 to 2 inches in from the edge; this will form an even flap once the loin is rolled and the pork belly overlaps. Score the fat layer inside the belly in a 1-inch crosshatch pattern. Evenly scatter the lemon zest, fennel seeds, garlic, rosemary, salt, and pepper over the fat.

Place the loin at the untrimmed edge of the belly and roll toward the trimmed edge. Tie the belly in place every 2 inches with kitchen twine. Rub the skin with the baking soda. Wrap the porchetta in plastic, then double-wrap in foil. Refrigerate for 3 full days. On the fourth day, remove the meat from the refrigerator and let sit at room temperature (wrapped) for 2 full hours before cooking.

Position a rack in the center of the oven and preheat the oven to 325°F. Place a cooling rack on a large rimmed baking sheet.

Place the roast on the rack and roast for 3 hours. Remove the roast from the oven and unwrap it. Increase the oven temperature to 450°F and return the pork to the oven to crisp the skin, 12 to 15 minutes.

Transfer the meat to a large carving board and let stand for 20 minutes. Carve into ¾-inch slices.

CITRUS AND GARLIC BONE-IN PORK LOIN ROAST

This is an easy roast for any holiday or occasion. Serve with Roasted Broccoli or Broccolini (page 313) or green beans and tomatoes, and mashed or roasted potatoes.

5 pounds bone-in pork loin roast, frenched by your butcher and tied
1 organic orange
2 organic lemons
Kosher salt and pepper
6 cloves garlic, finely chopped
3 tablespoons fresh rosemary leaves, chopped
2 tablespoons fresh thyme leaves, chopped
2 tablespoons fennel seeds
2 tablespoons Dijon mustard
3 tablespoons olive oil, plus more for drizzling

Position a rack in the center of the oven and preheat the oven to 400°F. Bring the roast to room temp.

Grate the zest from the orange and lemons into a bowl. Halve the orange and lemons and set aside.

Score the fat on the roast and place fat side up in a roasting pan. Season the meat liberally all over with salt and pepper. To the bowl with the citrus zest, add the garlic, rosemary, thyme, fennel seeds, mustard, and oil and stir to combine. Slather the mixture all over the roast. Drizzle the orange and lemon halves with some oil and place in the pan, cut side down, alongside the roast.

Roast the pork until it reaches 145°F on a meat thermometer, 1¼ hours to 1½ hours. Let stand for 20 minutes, then douse with the juice from the roasted citrus and carve.

PORK LOIN COOKED IN MILK

This recipe is from Emilia-Romagna and is probably as well-loved as a good Bolognese. The milk curd serves as a golden, nutty sauce over pork so tender it can be pulled with a fork. This meal makes your kitchen smell amazing—the scent of butter and cream in the air hangs thick and makes your mouth water well in advance of dinner. Serve with a simple salad of greens dressed with lemon, EVOO, and sea salt; roasted or boiled potatoes; and warm, crusty bread for mopping.

2½ pounds boneless center-cut pork loin roast, with a thin layer of fat
2½ cups milk
1 strip of lemon zest
2 fresh bay leaves
4 fresh sage leaves
½ teaspoon freshly grated nutmeg
Kosher salt and coarsely ground pepper
2 tablespoons olive oil
2 tablespoons butter

Bring the roast to room temp.

In a small saucepan, combine the milk, lemon zest, bay leaves, sage, and nutmeg and warm over medium-low heat.

Season the roast liberally with salt and pepper. In a Dutch oven, heat the oil (2 turns of the pan) over medium-high heat. Melt in the butter. When the foam subsides, add the meat and brown the meat well all over, developing its sugars and color. Add the warm milk and herbs and bring to a bubble. Partially cover the pan (leave a small crack for steam to escape), reduce the heat to low, and cook until the pork is very tender, about 2 hours. Discard the bay leaves.

Transfer the roast to a platter and slice. Add ½ cup hot water to the Dutch oven and loosen all the milk curds and drippings from the bottom of the pan. Simmer for a few minutes to reduce. Serve this as a sauce to spoon over the sliced pork.

PORK LOIN WITH ORANGE-PIGNOLI SAUCE

SERVES 6

A boneless pork loin roast is easily prepared within an hour, and leftovers make wonderful sandwich meat. This simple and lovely pork dinner can feed 6 adults, but I make it when cooking for as few as 2 people, because I love to have thin slices of this pork with lettuce, very thinly sliced red onion, and orange marmalade mixed with Dijon mustard slathered on charred bread.

2½ pounds boneless pork loin roast

2 tablespoons EVOO, plus more for drizzling

1 tablespoon fennel seeds

2 teaspoons granulated garlic

Grated zest and juice of 2 organic oranges

3 tablespoons fresh thyme leaves, finely chopped

2 teaspoons dried marjoram or oregano

Kosher salt and pepper

1 head garlic, top cut off to expose the cloves

1 cup Marsala

1½ cups chicken stock

¼ cup chopped golden raisins

¼ cup pignoli (pine nuts), toasted and chopped

¼ cup finely chopped fresh flat-leaf parsley

Place the pork in a shallow baking dish and rub the 2 tablespoons EVOO all over. Rub with the fennel seeds, garlic, orange zest, thyme, marjoram, and lots of salt and pepper. Cover the dish and refrigerate overnight.

Preheat the oven to 400°F. Let the pork come to room temperature before roasting.

Drizzle the garlic with some EVOO and season with salt and pepper. Wrap in foil and roast until tender and caramel in color, about 40 minutes. Set it aside to cool slightly.

Meanwhile, get the pork ready to go into the oven. It will go into the oven while the garlic is still roasting. In a large heavy skillet or small roasting pan, brown the pork loin over medium-high heat. Add the Marsala to the pan and cook until reduced by half. Add the stock, orange juice, and raisins. Transfer the pork to the oven and roast until the pork reaches 145°F on a meat thermometer, 35 to 40 minutes.

Transfer the meat to a cutting board and let rest while you make the sauce. Squeeze the roasted garlic from the skins into a bowl and mash into a smooth paste. Mix the paste into the juices in the roasting pan. Stir the pine nuts and parsley into the sauce.

Slice the pork ⅛ inch thick and spoon the sauce on top.

THE ULTIMATE PULLED PORK SANDWICHES

SERVES 8

Chili? Wings? Philly cheesesteaks? Next Super Bowl Sunday or big game-day gathering, make these instead. You may never make another pot of chili. Everyone is Italian on Sunday. Everyone is a football (or soccer) fan to some degree. Everyone loves these sandwiches.

13 long red chiles

6 sweet peppers: cubanelles (frying peppers), red bell peppers, or a mix

5 to 6 pounds boneless pork shoulder (pork butt)

Juice of 1 lemon

¼ cup EVOO, plus more for drizzling

1 head garlic, cloves separated and peeled

6 fresh bay leaves

Leaves from 4 sprigs fresh rosemary

2 tablespoons fresh thyme leaves

¼ cup fresh flat-leaf parsley tops

Salt and black pepper

1 large onion, very thinly sliced

1 cup dry white wine

2 cups chicken stock

1 (28- to 32-ounce) can San Marzano tomatoes (look for DOP on the label)

2 bunches broccoli rabe, tough ends trimmed

8 large Italian sub-style rolls or ciabatta breads cut for 8 sub-size sandwiches

4 cups shredded sharp provolone cheese, or 24 slices deli-cut provolone

Giardiniera, homemade (page 31) or store-bought, pulse-chopped into relish

Preheat the broiler to high.

Arrange 12 of the chiles and all of the sweet peppers on a baking sheet and broil until charred evenly all over; keep the oven door slightly ajar to allow steam to escape while the peppers char. Place the charred peppers in a bowl and cover with plastic wrap to cool. When cool enough to handle, peel, seed, and slice the peppers.

Leave the oven on but reduce the temperature to 325°F.

Take a very sharp knife and butterfly the pork: Slice the shoulder lengthwise going almost through to the other side, and open the meat like a book. Flatten out the meat.

Coarsely chop the reserved unroasted chile and put in a food processor. Add the lemon juice, ¼ cup EVOO, garlic cloves, bay leaves, rosemary, thyme, and parsley and pulse-chop into a thick, pestolike sauce.

Season the meat with salt and black pepper and slather the meat with the sauce. Roll the meat up and tightly secure with kitchen twine. Drizzle the meat roll with EVOO to coat and season liberally with salt and black pepper.

Heat a large Dutch oven over medium-high heat. Add the meat and brown evenly. Set the meat aside. Add the onion and wine to the pan and stir to deglaze. Add the stock and return the meat to the pan. Hand-crush the tomatoes as you add them to the pan, arranging them over the meat, then add the juices from the can. Cover and roast until very tender, 2½ to 3 hours.

Meanwhile, fill a bowl with ice and water. In a deep skillet, bring a few inches of water to a simmer. Salt the water and cook the broccoli rabe for 3 to 4 minutes. Cold-shock in the ice water. Drain.

When the pork is cool enough to handle, pull the meat apart with a fork and place in a large serving bowl. Strain the pan juices over the meat (or pass the onions and juices through a food mill). If not serving right away, rewarm the pork when ready to serve.

When ready to make sandwiches, preheat the broiler. Split the rolls, cover with cheese, and broil to melt.

Top each roll with broccoli rabe and sliced peppers, then cover that with hot, juicy pork. Garnish with giardiniera relish.

PULLED PORK WITH ARUGULA, MEYER LEMON, AND PASTA

SERVES 6

New York restaurateur Danny Meyer has a restaurant named Maialino, which means "little piggy." They make roast suckling pig, and with the leftovers they prepare a dish of pulled pork with maltagliati (irregular-shaped torn pasta), broth, lemon, arugula, and cheese. When I am in the Adirondacks, we make our own home version. This is our recipe for this bright, delicious dish.

2½ pounds boneless pork shoulder (pork butt), at room temperature
1 teaspoon fennel seeds
Salt and pepper
Olive oil, for sautéing
1 head garlic, cloves separated and smashed
1 onion, chopped
2 or 3 ribs celery with leafy tops, coarsely chopped
2 medium carrots, coarsely chopped
Herb bundle: a few sprigs of fresh flat-leaf parsley, thyme, and rosemary, tied together with kitchen twine
1 cup dry vermouth or white wine
2 Meyer lemons or organic lemons: 1 sliced, 1 juiced
2 cups chicken stock
1 teaspoon mild honey or agave
1 pound maltagliati, pappardelle, or egg tagliatelle
6 cups baby arugula
Parmigiano-Reggiano cheese, shaved into large curls with a vegetable peeler

Preheat the oven to 325°F.

Pat the pork dry. Coat with the fennel seeds and season with salt and pepper.

In a Dutch oven, heat just enough oil to coat the bottom over medium to medium-high heat. When the oil smokes, add the pork and brown on all sides. Transfer to a plate.

Add the garlic, onion, celery, carrots, and herb bundle to the pan and season with salt and pepper. Cook to soften the vegetables a bit, about 5 minutes. Add the vermouth and stir to deglaze the pan. Add the lemon slices and stock and return the pork to the pot. Cover and bake for 3 hours.

Transfer the pork to a platter. Strain the sauce and return it to the Dutch oven. Bring to a simmer and cook until reduced by half. Stir in the lemon juice and honey. Pull the pork into shreds with a fork and return it to the sauce.

Bring a large pot of water to a boil for the pasta. Salt the water and cook the pasta to al dente. Before draining, ladle out about a cup of the starchy pasta cooking water and add it to the sauce. Drain the pasta and add it to the sauce along with the arugula. Toss with tongs for 1 to 2 minutes for the flavors to be absorbed.

Serve on a warm platter or in shallow bowls, topped with shaved Parm.

PORK CHOPS IN THE STYLE OF PORCHETTA

SERVES 4

"In the style of porchetta" means with fennel, rosemary, garlic, and, for me, lemon. Many Italian recipes refer to this manner of flavoring, including recipes for roast chicken (see page 286), rabbit, pork chops, and roasts. If you crave porchetta but don't have four days to plan your meal, these chops are a great idea for dinner.

1 organic lemon
4 thick-cut, bone-in pork chops (about 1½ inches thick)
4 tablespoons olive oil
6 cloves garlic: 2 chopped, 4 smashed
1 tablespoon fennel seeds
2 tablespoons fresh rosemary leaves, finely chopped
Coarsely ground pepper
Kosher salt
2 bulbs fennel, trimmed and cut into 8 wedges each
8 large shallots, quartered lengthwise
4 medium potatoes, cut into wedges
½ cup dry white wine or chicken stock

Preheat the oven to 400°F.

Grate the zest from the lemon. Halve the lemon and set aside.

Place the chops in a shallow dish with 2 tablespoons of the oil, the chopped garlic, fennel seeds, rosemary, lemon zest, and about 1½ teaspoons pepper. Season the chops liberally with salt and slather the porchetta seasoning evenly all over the chops, turning to coat both sides. Let stand for 30 minutes.

Meanwhile, in a large bowl, combine the fresh fennel, shallots, potatoes, smashed garlic, remaining 2 tablespoons oil, and salt and pepper to taste. Toss to coat, then arrange on baking sheets. Place the lemon halves cut side down on the baking sheet. Roast until the potatoes are crispy and the fennel and shallots are caramelized at the edges, about 35 minutes.

Heat a cast-iron skillet over medium-high heat. Add the chops to the hot pan and brown for 3 to 4 minutes on each side. Transfer to the oven and roast for about 8 minutes. Remove from the oven and douse the skillet with the wine. Squeeze the juice from the roasted lemon halves over the top.

Serve the chops with the roasted vegetables alongside.

PORK CHOPS WITH BALSAMIC BROWN BUTTER

SERVES 4

Serve these rich pork chops with Applesauce with Thyme (page 310) and Mashed Celery Root and Potatoes (page 322).

4 thick-cut, bone-in pork chops (about 1½ inches thick)
Kosher salt and pepper
1 tablespoon olive or canola oil
4 tablespoons (½ stick) butter
1 large clove garlic, smashed
1½ tablespoons aged balsamic vinegar

Preheat the oven to 400°F.

Bring the pork chops to room temp and season with salt and pepper.

In a large cast-iron skillet, heat the oil (1 turn of the pan) over medium-high heat. Add the chops and brown on both sides and the edges, 7 to 8 minutes total. Place the pan in the oven and roast to finish cooking through, 8 to 10 minutes.

Meanwhile, in a small skillet, melt the butter over medium heat. Add the garlic and cook until the butter is nutty and fragrant. Remove from the heat and stir in the balsamic vinegar.

Spoon the brown butter over the chops to serve.

PORK CHOPS
WITH PLUM RAW SAUCE

The strong flavors and acid level in this marinade mean you don't have to let the meat sit; you can just coat it and throw it right on the grill. The plum sauce is so simple, and simply delicious. You can marinate the chops ahead if you want, but if you do, do not let them sit for more than a few hours.

4 to 6 bone-in pork chops (about 1 inch thick)
Salt and pepper
3 tablespoons aged balsamic vinegar
1 tablespoon Worcestershire sauce
2 large cloves garlic, chopped
2 tablespoons fresh rosemary leaves, chopped
¼ cup plus 2 tablespoons EVOO
6 plums, or 10 to 12 Italian plums (small, black-skinned plums), finely chopped
½ to ⅔ cup finely chopped red onion (½ small)
¼ cup fresh mint leaves, chopped
12 to 15 fresh basil leaves, torn or shredded
1 teaspoon sugar

Heat a grill or grill pan to medium-high heat.

Season the chops with salt and pepper on both sides.

In a shallow dish, combine 2 tablespoons of the vinegar, the Worcestershire sauce, garlic, rosemary, and ¼ cup of the EVOO. Add the chops and turn to coat evenly.

Grill the pork chops for 10 to 12 minutes, turning occasionally. Let the chops rest while you make the raw sauce.

In a small bowl, combine the plums, red onion, mint, basil, sugar, and remaining 1 tablespoon vinegar and 2 tablespoons EVOO. Season with salt and pepper.

Serve the pork chops topped with the plum raw sauce.

PORK TENDERLOIN WITH
PARSLEY-CITRUS SAUCE

Pork tenderloins really *are* the other white meat, lean and like a blank sheet of paper. They need flavor. This parsley-citrus sauce does the trick. The pork is paired with the tart flavors of a simple arugula and orange salad.

2 (1-pound) pork tenderloins, trimmed of silverskin
2 tablespoons plus ⅓ cup olive oil
Salt and black pepper
1 organic orange
1 organic lemon
3 to 4 tablespoons fresh thyme leaves
1 cup fresh flat-leaf parsley tops
2 or 3 flat anchovy fillets
½ teaspoon crushed red pepper flakes
3 tablespoons capers, drained
Orange and Arugula Salad (page 26)

Heat a grill. (Or preheat the oven to 350°F and heat a cast-iron skillet to medium-high heat.)

Coat the pork with 2 tablespoons of the oil and season with salt and black pepper.

Grill, covered, turning occasionally, until the pork reaches 145°F on a meat thermometer, about 20 minutes. (Or brown in the hot skillet for 5 to 6 minutes, then finish in the oven for 15 minutes.) Let stand for 5 minutes before carving.

Meanwhile, grate the zest from the orange and the lemon into a food processor. Halve the orange and the lemon and squeeze the juice from half of each into the food processor. Add the thyme, parsley, anchovies, red pepper flakes, capers, and remaining ⅓ cup oil and process into a sauce. Season with black pepper and adjust the salt.

Slice the tenderloins on an angle into medallions. Serve topped with the sauce, with the salad alongside.

PORK MEDALLIONS WITH GREEN PEPPERCORNS ON TOAST POINTS

Serving anything on toast points reminds me of my childhood. It's nostalgic. (My favorite toast-point dinner was not Italian at all; it was Welsh rarebit—beer and cheese on toast topped with bacon bits and tomatoes. YUM.) This dish is Italian pub-style fare suitable for watching a big game. It's spicy and flavorful and should be served with icy cold Peroni beer.

1½ pounds pork tenderloin, trimmed of silverskin
Salt and pepper
2 tablespoons flour, plus more for dredging
3 to 4 tablespoons olive oil
2 tablespoons butter
2 large cloves garlic, chopped
½ cup dry vermouth
2 tablespoons Worcestershire sauce
2 tablespoons grainy Dijon or smooth Dijon mustard
1 cup chicken stock
2 tablespoons green peppercorns
¼ cup heavy cream
6 slices white bread, lightly toasted, crusts trimmed, halved on an angle
Chopped fresh flat-leaf parsley tops, for garnish

Cut the pork crosswise on an angle into ½-inch slices and pound to ⅛ inch thick. Season the medallions with salt and pepper and dredge in flour.

In a large nonstick skillet, heat 2 tablespoons of the oil (2 turns of the pan) over medium to medium-high heat. Working in batches, cook half the pork for 2 minutes on each side. Transfer the pork to a warm platter and cover with foil to keep warm. Add more oil as needed to cook the second batch of pork.

In a saucepan, melt the butter over medium heat. Stir in the garlic. Whisk in the 2 tablespoons flour and cook for 1 minute. Add the vermouth and cook until reduced by half. Add the Worcestershire sauce, mustard, and stock and cook to thicken, about 1 minute. Stir in the peppercorns and cream, reduce the heat to low, and stir for a minute more.

Arrange 3 toast points on each dinner plate and top with pork medallions. Spoon the sauce over the top and garnish with parsley.

BALSAMIC AND HONEY PORK MEDALLION SALAD

This is a marriage of my strawberry salad and balsamic-honey pork. It's a fabulous meal for a summer brunch when baby berries are abundant.

7 to 8 cups mixed wild arugula and baby kale
1 small red onion, quartered and very thinly sliced
½ cup fresh tarragon leaves
1 pint small field strawberries, left whole if very tiny, halved if an inch or more in size
1½ pounds pork tenderloin, trimmed of silverskin
Salt and pepper
3 to 4 tablespoons olive oil
⅔ cup good-quality aged balsamic vinegar
¼ cup honey
2 tablespoons Worcestershire sauce
2 tablespoons Dijon mustard
Juice of ½ lemon

Arrange the greens, onion, tarragon, and berries on a large platter.

Cut the tenderloin crosswise on an angle into ½-inch slices. Pound the slices to ⅛ inch thick to make medallions. Season the meat with salt and pepper.

In a large nonstick skillet, heat 2 tablespoons of the oil (2 turns of the pan) over medium to medium-high heat. Working in batches, cook half the pork for 2 to 3 minutes on each side. Transfer the pork to a warm plate and cover with foil to keep warm. Add more oil as needed to cook the second batch of pork.

Arrange the medallions down the center of the platter on top of the greens.

Add the vinegar and honey to the skillet and cook until reduced to ¼ to ⅓ cup. Stir in the Worcestershire sauce, mustard, and lemon juice and remove from the heat. Liberally drizzle the warm glaze over the pork and greens and serve.

PORK MARSALA
WITH PAPPARDELLE

SERVES 4

When I make this pork and pasta dish, I serve a first course of fresh berries tossed with balsamic syrup and fresh basil (see page 28) on a bed of wild arugula as the first course. It is a knockout menu for a date night or for weeknight entertaining.

1½ pounds pork tenderloin, trimmed of silverskin

Salt and pepper

2 tablespoons flour, plus more for dredging

3 to 4 tablespoons olive oil

4 tablespoons (½ stick) butter

1 pound cremini mushrooms, thinly sliced

2 tablespoons fresh thyme leaves, chopped

2 shallots, finely chopped

3 or 4 cloves garlic (to taste), finely chopped

¾ to 1 pound pappardelle or tagliatelle

1 cup Marsala

1 cup chicken stock

A handful of fresh flat-leaf parsley tops, chopped, plus more for garnish

Juice of ½ lemon

Cut the tenderloin crosswise on an angle into ½-inch slices. Pound the slices to ⅛ inch thick to make medallions. Season the medallions with salt and pepper and dredge lightly in flour.

In a large nonstick skillet, heat 2 tablespoons of the oil (2 turns of the pan) over medium to medium-high heat. Working in batches, cook half the pork for 2 to 3 minutes on each side. Transfer the pork to a warm platter and cover with foil to keep warm. Add more oil as needed to cook the second batch of pork.

When the pork is finished cooking, add 2 tablespoons of the butter to the skillet. When the foam subsides, add the mushrooms and brown. Add the thyme, shallots, garlic, and salt and pepper to taste and stir for 2 minutes more.

Bring a large pot of water to a boil for the pasta. Salt the water and cook the pasta to al dente. Before draining, ladle out about ½ cup of the starchy pasta cooking water.

Meanwhile, sprinkle the mushrooms with the flour. Then add the Marsala to the mushrooms and cook until reduced by half. Add the chicken stock and bring the sauce up to a bubble. Stir in half the parsley, remove from the heat, and stir in the lemon juice and remaining 2 tablespoons butter, swirling to melt the butter.

Drain the pasta and return it to the pot. Add half of the sauce and the starchy water, tossing with tongs for 1 to 2 minutes for the flavors to be absorbed.

Spoon the remaining mushroom sauce over the pork on the platter and garnish with the remaining parsley. Serve the pasta alongside the pork.

HOMEMADE SAUSAGE

The basic technique for making homemade sausage is shared by all three of the styles here. The only things that switch up are the seasonings. The recipe makes 1 pound of whichever sausage you choose, but if you only need ½ pound for a recipe, just divide all the ingredients in half. On the other hand, you could make the whole recipe and form the portion you don't need into patties that you can freeze.

Sausage Base
MAKES 1 POUND

1½ teaspoons kosher salt
¼ teaspoon baking soda
1 tablespoon very hot water
1 pound ground pork
Seasonings from sweet Italian, hot Italian, or Norcia sausage (below)

In a small bowl, combine the salt, baking soda, and hot water, stirring to dissolve the salt and baking soda.

In a medium bowl, using a spatula, combine the pork and the salt mixture. Add the seasonings for the type of sausage you're making. Let stand for at least 30 minutes at room temperature or overnight in the refrigerator before using to allow the flavors to combine.

Hot Italian Sausage
MAKES 1 POUND

Sausage Base (at left)
3 tablespoons dry red wine
3 large cloves garlic, finely chopped or grated
2 teaspoons sweet paprika
1½ teaspoons crushed red pepper flakes, ground pepperoncini, or other ground red pepper
1½ teaspoons granulated onion
1 teaspoon ground coriander
½ teaspoon black pepper

Follow the directions for the sausage base, adding the seasonings where directed.

Sweet Italian Sausage with Fennel
MAKES 1 POUND

Sausage Base (above)
3 tablespoons dry white wine or red wine
2 large cloves garlic, finely chopped or grated
1½ teaspoons ground sage, or 1 tablespoon finely chopped fresh sage leaves (6 to 7 leaves)
1 teaspoon pepper
1 teaspoon ground coriander
1 teaspoon fennel seeds
1 teaspoon granulated onion

Follow the directions for the sausage base, adding the seasonings where directed.

Norcia-Style Sausage
MAKES 1 POUND

Sausage Base (at left)
3 tablespoons dry red wine
2 tablespoons fresh rosemary leaves, very finely chopped
1 teaspoon pepper
1 teaspoon fennel seeds
2 large cloves garlic, finely chopped or grated

Follow the directions for the sausage base, adding the seasonings where directed.

NORCIA SAUSAGE PATTIES WITH GRAPES

SERVES 4

1 tablespoon EVOO
1 pound Norcia-Style Sausage (page 237), formed into four 6-inch patties
2 cups mixed black and red grapes
Balsamic reduction (see box, page 28), for serving

In a large skillet, heat the EVOO (1 turn of the pan) over medium to medium-high heat. Add the sausage patties and cook for 3 to 4 minutes on each side. Transfer to a warm platter.

Add the grapes to the skillet and cook in the drippings over medium-high heat for a few minutes, stirring and shaking the pan often, until the skins begin to burst.

Scatter the grapes over the sausages and drizzle with a little balsamic reduction.

ITALIAN SAUSAGE BURGERS WITH PROVOLONE AND BROCCOLI RABE

What makes these burgers really crazy good are the details: The homemade beef and pork sausage patties, the giardiniera relish, the surprise of crunchy potato chips on the burger. These patties are *pazzo!* CRAZY!

Salt

1 bunch broccoli rabe, tough ends trimmed, cut into 1½-inch pieces

3 tablespoons EVOO, plus more for drizzling

3 large cloves garlic, chopped

1 scant teaspoon crushed red pepper flakes

1 pound Hot Italian Sausage, homemade (page 237) or store-bought, casings removed

1 pound ground beef (80% lean)

2 tablespoons Worcestershire sauce

2 to 3 tablespoons grated onion (to taste)

Black pepper

4 thick-cut deli slices provolone cheese

1 cup drained giardiniera, homemade (page 31) or store-bought, pulse-chopped into relish

4 (5-inch) squares focaccia or ciabatta rolls, split horizontally and toasted

Garlic and/or herb or salt-and-vinegar potato chips

In a deep large skillet, bring a few inches of water to a boil. Salt the water, add the broccoli rabe, and cook for 3 minutes. Drain.

Return the skillet to medium heat and add the EVOO (3 turns of the pan). Add the garlic and red pepper flakes and stir for 1 minute. Add the broccoli rabe and toss for 2 to 3 minutes more. Adjust the salt.

In a bowl, combine the sausage, beef, Worcestershire sauce, grated onion, and salt and black pepper to taste. Gently but thoroughly combine. Form the meat mixture into 4 patties slightly thinner at the center than at the edges for even cooking and to ensure a flat surface (burgers plump as they cook).

Heat a cast-iron skillet or griddle pan over medium-high to high heat. Drizzle the burgers with EVOO and cook, turning occasionally, for 10 minutes. Top the burgers with the provolone for the last minute of cooking, tenting the pan with foil, if you like, to help melt the cheese.

To serve, place the giardiniera relish on the focaccia/roll bottoms. Top with the burgers, broccoli rabe, and potato chips. Set the focaccia/roll tops in place.

SAUSAGES WITH ROASTED POTATO CAKE AND GREENS

⅓ cup EVOO, plus more for drizzling

2 large cloves garlic, smashed

1 fresh red Fresno chile, halved

2½ pounds Yukon Gold potatoes, cut into ⅛-inch-thick slices

Kosher or fine sea salt

3 tablespoons fresh rosemary leaves, chopped

2 teaspoons fennel seeds

½ cup freshly grated Parmigiano-Reggiano cheese

2 pounds sweet Italian sausage links

½ cup chicken stock

8 cups lacinato kale (also called black, Tuscan, or dinosaur kale), Swiss chard, or spinach, stemmed and coarsely chopped

Pepper

Freshly grated nutmeg

Preheat the oven to 425°F.

In a small saucepan, combine the EVOO, garlic, and chile and heat over medium heat for 2 to 3 minutes to infuse the oil. Set aside to cool slightly, then fish out and discard the garlic and chile.

Place the potatoes in a bowl and season liberally with salt.

Add the garlic-chile oil, rosemary, fennel seeds, and Parm. Toss to coat evenly.

In a 10-inch ovenproof skillet, arrange an overlapping layer of potatoes, beginning at the center of the skillet and moving outward and up the sides to form a shell. Gently pile in the remaining potatoes and press them down.

Cook over medium-high heat for 7 to 8 minutes to get the bottom layer of potatoes and the pan itself nice and hot. Cover the potatoes with parchment paper and set a pie plate on top. Fill the plate with beans or pie weights, transfer the skillet to the oven, and bake for 20 minutes. Remove the pie plate, weights, and parchment and return the skillet to the oven.

Bake until the potatoes are deep golden on top, 10 to 15 minutes more. Remove from the oven and let cool to room temp.

In a large skillet, combine the sausages with ¼ inch water and a fat drizzle of EVOO. Bring to a boil, then reduce the heat a bit. The sausages will cook through as the water evaporates, then the oil will brown and crisp the casings. Transfer the sausages to a plate.

Add the stock to the skillet and bring to a boil. Wilt in the greens and season with salt, pepper, and nutmeg.

Place a plate over the potato cake, flip, and unmold onto the plate. Cut the potato cake into wedges and serve alongside the sausages and greens.

VARIATION

Sausages with Roasted Potato Cake and Crispy Kale

Use kale for the greens. Instead of wilting it in the skillet, coat it with EVOO spray and season it with salt and pepper. Spread the kale on a baking sheet in a single layer (use multiple baking sheets or work in batches if necessary) and put it in the oven when you bake the potato cake. Bake to brown the edges and crisp the leaves.

ROASTED SAUSAGES WITH BLACK GRAPES AND BALSAMIC

Serve this with crusty bread for mopping.

2 pounds Italian sausage links, a combination of hot and sweet
EVOO, for liberal drizzling
2 shallots, cut into very thin wedges
8 large cloves garlic, peeled
4 cups seedless black grapes
Leaves from a few small sprigs fresh rosemary
Salt and pepper
½ cup good-quality balsamic vinegar
2 tablespoons butter

Preheat the oven to 400°F.

In a large ovenproof skillet, combine the sausages with ¼ inch water and a fat drizzle of EVOO. Bring to a boil, then reduce the heat a bit. The sausages will cook through as the water evaporates, then the oil will brown and crisp the casings. When the water has evaporated, add the shallots, garlic, grapes, rosemary, salt, and pepper. Drizzle with EVOO. Transfer to the oven and roast for 20 minutes.

Transfer the sausages, grapes, and garlic to a platter and return the pan to the stove over medium heat. Add the vinegar, stir to deglaze the pan, and cook until reduced by half. Swirl in the butter.

Pour the sauce over the sausages and grapes.

COTECHINO WITH SPICY LENTILS

Cotechino is a sausage that Italian markets carry, especially around New Year's Day. It is traditional to eat it with lentils, which bring good luck for the coming year because they resemble small coins and represent prosperity.

Spicy Lentils (page 331)
1½ to 2 pounds fresh or precooked cotechino (see Tip)
1 small onion, halved
2 fresh bay leaves

Make the Spicy Lentils.

Meanwhile, poke a few holes with the tines of a fork in the sausage casings. Place in a pan, cover with water, and add the halved onion and the bay leaves. Bring to a simmer and cook for 30 to 40 minutes for fresh sausage, 15 to 20 minutes for precooked. Transfer to a carving board.

Slice the sausages and remove the casings. Serve on a bed of lentils.

TIP

IF YOU CAN'T find cotechino, you can make this with regular sweet Italian sausage links. Poke a few holes with the tines of a fork in the sausage casings. Simmer the sausages in a skillet in ½ inch of water plus 1 tablespoon oil. When the water evaporates, continue cooking to crisp up the casings in the drippings and oil. Leave the sausage links whole to serve.

LAMB

I love lamb—lamb burgers, roast lamb, lamb ragu—but I have to say that I pretty much don't think of it most of the year. I think of it in early spring and at Easter, and then I seem to make so much of it that by late May we are tired of it and it pops off our dinner radar until the following year. But in compiling this section, I have renewed my love of lamb—for all four seasons.

SLOW-ROASTED BONE-IN LEG OF LAMB

SERVES 8

Serve this with Mom's Fresh Mint Sauce (page 243), Herbed Fennel Slaw (page 329), and Green Beans with Shallots (page 317).

1 (7- to 8-pound) bone-in leg of lamb, at room temperature
Kosher salt and pepper
Olive oil, for liberal drizzling
1 (750ml) bottle dry, crisp white wine
4 cups chicken stock
Large herb bundle: a few sprigs of fresh thyme, rosemary, flat-leaf parsley, and bay leaves, tied together with kitchen twine
3 heads garlic, tops cut off to expose the cloves
4 tablespoons (½ stick) butter
¼ cup flour

Preheat the oven to 300°F.

Season the lamb all over with salt and pepper. Coat a large roasting pan with oil and heat over high heat. Add the lamb and brown all over. Add the wine, stock, and herb bundle and bring to a low boil.

Transfer to the oven and roast for 2 hours, basting occasionally.

Cover and roast until the meat is super-tender and pulling away from the bone, 3 to 4 hours more. Two hours before the lamb is done, wrap the garlic heads in a foil packet and add to the pan.

Transfer the meat to a warm platter. Cut into slices or chunks to serve. Strain the pan drippings into a bowl. Squeeze the roasted garlic out of the skins into a bowl and mash the garlic to a paste.

In a small saucepan, melt the butter. Whisk in the garlic paste. Whisk in the flour and stir for 1 to 2 minutes. Whisk in the strained drippings and cook to thicken into a gravy. Season with salt and pepper.

Spoon some gravy over the lamb and pass extra gravy at the table.

CHECK THIS OUT

Be sure to check out the lamb ragus in the pasta chapter:

- Spicy Lamb Ragu (page 132)

- Tagliatelle with Lamb Ragu with Meyer Lemon and Olives (page 134)
- Pappardelle with Lamb Ragu (page 133)

ROAST BONELESS LEG OF LAMB

Leg of lamb is a must for every Easter Sunday, but I think the leftovers are the best part. Cold roast lamb makes a tasty sandwich. Also, try crisping finely chopped lamb and adding finely chopped potatoes, onion, garlic, thyme, and a splash of sherry and stock. Top with poached or over-easy eggs for a delicious hash!

1 (4- to 5-pound) boneless leg of lamb, at room temperature
Olive oil, for drizzling
Kosher salt and pepper
2 or 3 large bay leaves
1 bunch fresh mint
1 bunch fresh rosemary
1 head garlic, separated into cloves and peeled
1 cup white wine
Mom's Fresh Mint Sauce (see box)

Position a rack in the center of the oven and preheat the oven to 425°F.

Pat the lamb dry and rub oil all over the outside and inside. Season the inside cavity heavily with salt and pepper. Place the bay leaves and mint at the center, then roll the leg of lamb into the shape of a roast. Cut several shallow slits into the lamb and stuff with sprigs of rosemary and cloves of garlic until the roast is studded evenly all over. Rub the fatty side of the lamb with lots of salt and pepper and tie with kitchen twine.

Arrange the lamb on a roasting rack in a roasting pan or set a cooling rack over a rimmed baking sheet. Roast the lamb for 20 to 25 minutes.

Add the wine to the pan and reduce the oven temperature to 325°F. Roast until the lamb reaches 135° to 140°F on a meat thermometer, about 12 minutes per pound. Let the meat rest before slicing and serving with the mint sauce.

MOM'S FRESH MINT SAUCE

MAKES 2½ CUPS

This is my mom Elsa's recipe. *Everyone* loves this mint sauce. It is so easy and fresh—way better than jelly.

1 cup white balsamic vinegar
½ cup sugar
2 tablespoons kosher salt
6 large shallots, coarsely chopped
1½ cups packed fresh mint leaves
1½ cups packed fresh flat-leaf parsley tops

In a small saucepan, combine the vinegar, ½ cup water, and the sugar. Bring to a boil over medium heat. Add the salt and stir until the sugar and salt have dissolved. Reduce the heat to low.

In a food processor, combine the shallots, mint, and parsley and pulse to finely chop. Transfer the mixture to a heatproof bowl or container. Pour the hot brine over the shallot mixture. Cover and refrigerate or let stand at room temperature until ready to serve.

LAMB STEAKS WITH MASHED PEAS AND MASCARPONE

I love lamb steaks. This dish, basted in butter and topped with creamy mashed sweet peas, is so good that I actually prefer it to our Easter leg of lamb. The mascarpone peas are also delicious on pork chops or ham steaks. The rosemary-scented potato chips are a fast dodge for potato wedges roasted with rosemary, which I make if I have potatoes on hand and time to spare.

4 (1¼-inch-thick) lamb leg steaks
2 teaspoons fennel seeds
Kosher salt and pepper
2 tablespoons olive oil
2 cloves garlic, smashed
5 tablespoons butter
2 tablespoons fresh thyme leaves, chopped
2 large shallots, or 1 small onion, finely chopped
3 cups shelled fresh peas
½ cup chicken stock
¼ cup fresh tarragon leaves, chopped
¼ cup fresh mint leaves, chopped
⅓ to ½ cup mascarpone cheese (to taste)
Good-quality rosemary or herb potato chips, for serving

Rub the lamb with the fennel seeds and salt and pepper.

Heat a cast-iron skillet over high heat. Add 1 tablespoon of the oil (1 turn of the pan), then add the lamb and brown well on each side. Reduce the heat to medium and add the garlic, 4 tablespoons of the butter, and the thyme. Cook the lamb for about 10 minutes, turning once and basting occasionally with butter. Let rest for 5 to 10 minutes before serving.

Meanwhile, in a second skillet, heat the remaining 1 tablespoon oil (1 turn of the pan) over medium to medium-high heat. Melt in the remaining 1 tablespoon butter. When it foams, add the shallots and stir for 1 to 2 minutes. Add the peas and stock and simmer for 4 to 5 minutes. Season with salt and pepper. Mash the peas with a potato masher. Remove from the heat. Mash in the tarragon, mint, and mascarpone. Adjust the seasonings.

Pour the basting butter over the sliced lamb steaks. Garnish plates with a small pile of potato chips. Serve the lamb either topped with the creamy peas or alongside.

EASTER MEATLOAF

This meatloaf looks very pretty on the platter or plate, as each slice has the bright concentric rings of hard-boiled eggs running down the center of the loaf. We make it at some point during Easter week, but it is a delicious spring staple, and the leftovers make wonderful sandwiches.

10 extra-large free-range organic eggs

3 cups coarsely chopped or torn stale peasant-style white or Italian bread

1 cup milk

2 tablespoons EVOO, plus more for drizzling

1 onion, finely chopped

1 large shallot, finely chopped

4 cloves garlic, finely chopped

½ cup dry white wine

2 pounds ground lamb

1 tablespoon chopped fresh oregano, or 1 teaspoon dried

1 tablespoon grated lemon zest (from an organic lemon)

Kosher or sea salt and coarsely ground pepper

1 (10-ounce) box frozen chopped spinach, thawed and wrung dry in a kitchen towel

¼ teaspoon freshly grated nutmeg

½ cup finely crumbled feta cheese

½ cup fresh mint leaves, finely chopped, plus more for garnish

½ cup fresh flat-leaf parsley tops, finely chopped, plus more for garnish

Lemon wedges, for serving

In a medium pot, combine 8 of the eggs with cold water to cover. Bring to a full boil, turn off the heat, cover, and let stand for 10 minutes. Crack the shells and run under cold water to cool quickly. Peel the eggs and trim ½ inch off the top and bottom of each egg (the eggs will sit in the center of the meatloaf as it cooks, and when you slice it, each person will get some yolk and white, if the whites have been trimmed a bit).

Preheat the oven to 400°F.

In a medium bowl, soak the bread in the milk for 5 minutes.

In a large skillet, heat the EVOO (2 turns of the pan) over medium to medium-high heat. Add the onion, shallot, and garlic and cook until tender, 3 to 4 minutes. Add the wine and stir to deglaze the pan. Remove from the heat and set aside to cool.

Place the lamb in a large bowl.

Wring out the bread crumbs and crumble them into the bowl with your fingertips. Add the oregano, lemon zest, and salt and pepper to taste. Pull the spinach into shreds as you add it to the bowl. Season with the nutmeg. Lightly beat the remaining 2 eggs and add to the bowl. Add the cooled onion mixture, the feta, mint, and parsley. Mix well to combine.

On a baking sheet, form a 2-inch-thick and 10-inch-long layer of meatloaf. Arrange the hard-boiled eggs in a line running down the center. Use the remaining meatloaf mixture to encase the eggs in the center of the loaf. Drizzle the loaf with EVOO and roast for 1 hour. Switch on the broiler to crisp up the top. Let stand for 10 minutes before slicing and serving.

Serve garnished with chopped mint and parsley, with lemon wedges alongside.

SPEZZATINO
(SICILIAN BRAISED LAMB CHOPS)

This is a beautiful, fragrant family meal, especially perfect for springtime through early autumn. It is foolproof in that it is braised, which is code for "always tender, cannot fail with flavor." Some years we have a real crowd at Easter, and we do a whole leg of lamb, but some years we have a small gathering, making individual lamb chops a great option. Serve the lamb with Lemon and Olive Oil Potatoes (page 337); they're great with the sauce over them.

A fat pinch of saffron threads

3 cups chicken or lamb stock

4 pounds lamb shoulder chops
  (1½ to 2 inches thick), at room
  temperature

Kosher salt and black pepper

1½ tablespoons neutral oil (such
  as canola)

2 medium red onions, chopped

4 large cloves garlic, very thinly
  sliced

1 teaspoon crushed red pepper
  flakes or pepperoncini

2 teaspoons grated orange or
  lemon zest (from organic
  citrus)

2 tablespoons fresh thyme leaves,
  chopped

Leaves from 1 sprig fresh
  rosemary

1 large fresh bay leaf

3 tablespoons tomato paste

1½ cups dry white wine

1 cup loosely packed fresh mint
  leaves, chopped

½ cup loosely packed fresh flat-
  leaf parsley tops, chopped

In a small saucepan, combine the saffron and stock and bring to a low simmer. Reduce the heat to keep the stock warm and infuse the stock with saffron.

Season the lamb liberally with salt and black pepper.

In a deep large skillet with a lid, heat the oil (1½ turns of the pan) over medium-high to high heat. Add the chops and brown on both sides and the edges. Transfer to a plate. Add the onions, garlic, red pepper flakes, citrus zest, thyme, rosemary, and bay leaf to the skillet. Reduce the heat a bit and cook to soften the onions, 7 to 8 minutes. Stir in the tomato paste until fragrant. Add the wine, increase the heat, and cook until reduced by half.

Add the saffron stock to the skillet and bring to a bubble. Return the chops to the pan, cover, and braise at a low simmer for 30 minutes. Uncover and simmer to thicken the sauce, about 15 minutes more. Transfer the meat to a warm platter. Whisk the sauce a bit and keep cooking if you wish to reduce and thicken it a bit more. Discard the bay leaf.

Stir the mint and parsley into the lamb sauce. Serve the chops doused in sauce. Pass more sauce at the table.

LAMB BURGERS
WITH RICOTTA SALATA SAUCE

Serve these burgers with Giardiniera (page 31) alongside oven fries with balsamic ketchup (see box, page 271) for dipping.

SAUCE:
1 cup crumbled ricotta salata or
    smoked ricotta salata cheese
⅓ to ½ cup milk
¼ cup walnuts, toasted

BURGERS:
1 shallot, coarsely chopped
2 cloves garlic, smashed
1 cup fresh flat-leaf parsley tops
¼ cup fresh mint leaves
Grated zest of 1 organic lemon
Leaves from 2 sprigs fresh
    oregano
1 teaspoon crushed red pepper
    flakes
1 tablespoon sherry vinegar
2 tablespoons olive oil, plus more
    for cooking the burgers

1½ to 2 pounds ground lamb
Salt and black pepper
4 ciabatta rolls or large squares
    cut from a ciabatta loaf, split
    and toasted
Lettuce, tomato, and red onion

Make the sauce: In a food processor, combine the ricotta salata, ⅓ cup milk, and the walnuts. Process into a creamy sauce, adding more milk if needed.

Make the burgers: In a food processor, combine the shallot, garlic, parsley, mint, lemon zest, oregano, red pepper flakes, vinegar, and oil and pulse into a fine mixture.

Place the lamb in a bowl, season with salt and black pepper, add the herb mixture, and mix gently but thoroughly. Score the mixture into 4 equal portions and form them into patties slightly thinner at the center than at the edges, for even cooking and to ensure a flat surface (burgers plump as they cook).

Heat a cast-iron skillet or griddle pan over medium-high heat. Drizzle with a little oil. Add the burgers and cook to your desired doneness, 6 to 7 minutes for a pink center.

Serve on toasted rolls with lettuce, tomato, onion, and the ricotta sauce.

LAMB RAGU WITH POTATOES

You can also toss this ragu with pasta (pappardelle or egg tagliatelle). Or, on the flip side, you can take the Spicy Lamb Ragu (page 132) from the pasta chapter and serve it over these potatoes.

2 cups chicken stock
A fat pinch of saffron threads
2 tablespoons olive oil
1½ pounds ground lamb
Salt and pepper
4 cloves garlic, chopped
1 onion, finely chopped
1 carrot, finely chopped
2 large shallots, finely chopped
2 tablespoons fresh rosemary
    leaves, chopped
1 large strip of lemon zest, plus
    1 tablespoon grated zest
    (from an organic lemon)
3 tablespoons tomato paste
1 cup dry white wine
2 pounds russet (baking)
    potatoes, cut into wedges
½ cup fresh flat-leaf parsley tops
Leaves from a few sprigs fresh
    mint

In a small saucepan, combine the stock and saffron and heat to infuse the stock.

In a Dutch oven or deep large skillet, heat the oil (2 turns of the pan) over medium to medium-high heat. Add the lamb and cook, breaking it up into crumbles as it browns. Season with salt and pepper. Add the garlic, onion, carrot, shallots, rosemary, and lemon zest strip and stir for 2 to 3 minutes. Add the tomato paste and stir for 1 minute. Add the wine and cook until reduced by half. Add the saffron stock, reduce the heat, and simmer while you cook the potatoes.

Bring a large saucepan of water to a boil. Salt the water and cook the potatoes until fork-tender. Before draining, scoop out ½ cup of the cooking water and add it to the lamb ragu.

On a cutting board, finely chop together the grated lemon zest, parsley, and mint to make a gremolata.

Serve the potatoes in shallow bowls topped with the sauce. Garnish with the gremolata.

LAMB CHOPS OREGANO

Serve with Cherry Tomato and Red Onion Salad (page 24) or Roasted Green Beans and Tomatoes (page 317).

4 (1-inch-thick) lamb shoulder
    chops or leg chops
2 tablespoons olive oil
2 large cloves garlic, sliced
Leaves from 2 sprigs fresh
    oregano, finely chopped
1 teaspoon crushed red pepper
    flakes
Salt and black pepper
1 lemon, halved

In a shallow container, combine the lamb with the oil, garlic, oregano, red pepper flakes, and salt and black pepper to taste. Turn to coat and let stand for 20 minutes.

Heat a grill or grill pan to medium-high heat. Add the chops and cook for 2 to 3 minutes per side for medium-rare or to your desired doneness. Grill the lemon halves, cut side down, until caramelized, 3 to 4 minutes

To serve, squeeze the lemon halves over the chops.

LAMB CHOPS WITH MIXED HERB PESTO AND ROASTED EGGPLANT PASTA

SERVES 4

The lamb and the pasta in this dish share a gremolata-style herb mixture, and both could be served as stand-alone dishes. Pair either one with a simple tomato salad.

1 medium eggplant

¼ cup olive oil, plus more for drizzling

Salt and pepper

3 cloves garlic, finely chopped or grated

1 cup packed fresh flat-leaf parsley tops

Leaves from 1 or 2 sprigs fresh rosemary, finely chopped

Leaves from 1 or 2 sprigs fresh thyme, finely chopped

Grated zest and juice of 1 organic lemon

1 pound capricci pasta curls or other short-cut pasta

1 cup freshly grated pecorino cheese

8 frenched lamb rib chops

1 cup diced cherry or grape tomatoes

Preheat the oven to 400°F.

Halve the eggplant lengthwise. With a sharp paring knife, cut a crosshatch pattern into the flesh on an angle, ½ inch apart. Run the knife all around the edge of the eggplant, too. Drizzle a baking sheet with oil and season the eggplant with salt and pepper. Roast the eggplant cut side down until very tender, about 30 minutes.

Meanwhile, in a food processor, combine the garlic, parsley, rosemary, thyme, and lemon zest and process to finely chop. Place half the mixture in a large bowl. Place the other half in a small bowl and add the lemon juice and the ¼ cup oil. Season with salt and pepper.

Scoop the eggplant flesh into the large bowl with the herb mixture.

Bring a large pot of water to a boil for the pasta. Salt the water and cook the pasta to al dente. Before draining, ladle out about a cup of the starchy pasta cooking water. Drain the pasta and return it to the pot. Add the eggplant mixture, pecorino, and starchy water, tossing with tongs for 1 to 2 minutes for the flavors to be absorbed.

Position a rack in the top third of the oven and preheat the broiler.

Drizzle the chops with a bit of oil and season with salt and pepper. Broil the chops for 2 to 3 minutes on each side for medium-rare.

Serve the chops topped with the herb pesto. Garnish with the chopped tomatoes. Serve the pasta alongside.

Clockwise from upper left: Easy Rib Roast with Roasted Garlic and Herbs (page 255); Beet Carpaccio with Campari Vinaigrette (page 29); Green Beans with Shallots (page 317); Roasted Tomato Halves with Thyme and Garlic (page 346); Mashed Potatoes with Soft Cheese and Herbs (page 339); and Mom's Horseradish Sauce (page 255).

CHAPTER 9

BEEF AND VEAL

BEEF

In my family, we grew up on a largely Mediterranean diet that included primarily vegetables, pastas, and grains. The go-to protein was chicken, and beef made only rare appearances. So when we had beef for dinner, it always seemed "special" in some way—even if it was just a burger. Mom would make these big, beefy burgers with Worcestershire sauce, garlic, and grated onion mixed into ground sirloin, and she served them on buttered toast, open-face with a light gravy spooned over the top. She called them "knife and fork burgers" and served them with a fork and steak knife. So even burger night felt special.

The beef recipes in this chapter are all special to me. I cannot play favorites with my own recipes, but all the people I cook for can and do. These are their favorites. All these dinners have earned me lots of kisses and hugs, lots of "mmmmmm" moans and big smiles around the dinner table. From quick, crispy Beef Milanese (page 264) to Short Ribs Nested in Pasta e Fagioli (page 259) to Porterhouse Steaks with Salsa Verde (page 262), these meals deliver.

ITALIAN POT ROAST (GRANDPA'S BEEF)

SERVES 8 TO 10

As a little girl, my mom remembers my grandfather carrying dishes like this in a large black pan from the oven to the table, where all the kids (she was the first of ten) gathered around to get the first chunk of bread into the bubbling juices. So be sure to serve this with warm ciabatta for mopping.

3 tablespoons olive oil
4 to 5 pounds beef chuck, cut as a slab about 3 inches thick, 8 to 10 inches long, and 6 to 8 inches wide
Kosher salt and pepper
2 cups dry white or red wine
1½ cups veal stock
EVOO, for liberal drizzling
3 medium onions, thinly sliced
4 to 5 large russet (baking) potatoes, thinly sliced
Leaves from 4 sprigs fresh rosemary, chopped
Cloves from 1 head garlic, thinly sliced
A couple handfuls of freshly grated Parmigiano-Reggiano cheese
1 (28- to 32-ounce) can San Marzano tomatoes (look for DOP on the label)
Leaves from a few sprigs fresh thyme
A handful of fresh basil leaves, torn

Preheat the oven to 325°F.

In a large Dutch oven, heat the oil (3 turns of the pan) over high heat. Season the meat with salt and pepper. Add to the pan and brown well on both sides and the edges, 12 to 15 minutes. Transfer the meat to a plate. Add the wine, stir to deglaze the pan, and cook to reduce the wine by half. Add the stock.

Remove the pan from the heat and return the beef to the pan. Across the beef, make thin and even layers in this order (drizzling with EVOO and seasoning with salt and pepper as you go): half the onions, half the potatoes, half the rosemary, half the garlic, half the Parm, half the tomatoes (hand-crush them as you add them), and half the thyme. Repeat the layers again, adding the juices from the tomato can.

Cover the pan and roast for 2½ hours. Remove from the oven and let stand, covered, for 30 to 45 minutes. Top with basil. Cut into large chunks and serve with pan juices.

EASY RIB ROAST WITH ROASTED GARLIC AND HERBS

This is a beautiful holiday or special occasion roast that is impressive but very simple to prepare. We keep the rest of the menu equally simple and easy to prepare: watercress or arugula salad dressed with lemon and EVOO, roasted halved tomatoes, green beans with shallots, mashed potatoes and parsnips. Though my mom's horseradish sauce is not a traditional Italian recipe, it is traditional in our family and she is an Italian, so it makes the cut. Serve this with popovers or a baguette warmed in the oven and then sliced.

2 heads garlic, tops cut off to expose the cloves
EVOO, for drizzling
Salt and pepper
4 ounces (1 stick) butter, softened
Leaves from 4 sprigs fresh rosemary, finely chopped
Leaves from a few sprigs fresh marjoram, finely chopped
2 tablespoons fresh thyme leaves, chopped
1 (10- to 12-pound) boneless beef rib roast, at room temperature
Mom's Horseradish Sauce (see box)

Position a rack in the center of the oven and preheat the oven to 400°F.

Drizzle the garlic with some EVOO and season with salt and pepper. Wrap in foil and roast until tender and caramel in color, about 40 minutes. When the garlic is done, leave the oven on, but reduce the temperature to 325°F.

When cool enough to handle, squeeze the roasted garlic into a bowl and mash the garlic to a paste. Add the butter, rosemary, marjoram, thyme, salt, and pepper. Coat the rib roast with the herb butter and stand it up in a roasting pan.

Cook the beef until it reaches 125° to 130°F on a meat thermometer (for medium-rare), about 2¾ hours. Remove and let rest, covered with foil and a kitchen towel, for 1 hour.

Carve and serve with the horseradish sauce.

MOM'S HORSERADISH SAUCE

MAKES ABOUT 3 CUPS

2 cups sour cream or crème fraîche
½ cup unsweetened applesauce, preferably organic
¼ cup fine dry bread crumbs
¼ cup minced fresh chives
¼ cup prepared horseradish, or 3 tablespoons grated peeled fresh horseradish root
Salt and pepper

In a bowl, combine all the ingredients and let stand to soften the bread crumbs. Adjust the seasonings.

BEEF TENDERLOIN WITH POTATO WEDGES AND HORSERADISH SAUCE

SERVES 6 TO 8

This is a leaner alternative to the Easy Rib Roast (page 255). Although this cooks quickly, the beef does sit with garlic and herbs for 1 to 2 days before roasting. Serve with a salad of your choice and popovers or a baguette warmed in the oven and split.

4 pounds beef tenderloin, trimmed of tail and chain and tied
Kosher salt and coarsely ground pepper
A few sprigs fresh rosemary
4 cloves garlic, smashed
6 tablespoons olive or canola oil
2 tablespoons dry sherry
2 tablespoons Worcestershire sauce
¼ cup Dijon mustard
2 tablespoons fresh thyme leaves
6 large russet (baking) potatoes, cut into 8 wedges each
Watercress or arugula, for serving
Mom's Horseradish Sauce (page 255)

Season the meat with salt and pepper and wrap it in parchment paper with the rosemary and garlic. Refrigerate for 1 to 2 days.

Preheat the oven to 450°F. Bring the meat to room temp.

Place a roasting pan on the stovetop over high heat with 3 tablespoons of the oil. When the oil smokes, add the beef and brown it all over, about 12 minutes. Remove the roasting pan from the heat. Brush the meat with the sherry and Worcestershire sauce, slather it with the mustard, and sprinkle with the thyme.

Meanwhile, toss the potatoes with the remaining 3 tablespoons oil and season liberally with salt and pepper. Spread the potatoes on a baking sheet. Put in the oven when you put in the meat and roast until golden and firm-tender, 30 to 40 minutes, turning once.

Transfer the meat to the oven and roast until the meat reaches 125° to 130°F on a meat thermometer, 20 to 25 minutes. Transfer to a carving board and let stand for 10 to 20 minutes before slicing.

Arrange on a bed of watercress. Serve with the potatoes and horseradish sauce.

PETITE FILET OF BEEF WELLINGTON WITH PROSCIUTTO

SERVES 4

Serve with broiled tomatoes and wilted spinach or sautéed dark greens such as kale or chard.

2 (10- to 12-ounce) petite filets (shoulder tenders of beef), at room temperature
Kosher salt and coarsely ground pepper
2 tablespoons EVOO or canola oil
4 tablespoons (½ stick) butter
1 pound cremini mushrooms, finely chopped
4 shallots, finely chopped
4 cloves garlic, finely chopped
2 tablespoons thinly sliced fresh sage leaves
2 tablespoons fresh thyme leaves, finely chopped
½ cup brandy, dry sherry, or Marsala
Flour, for dusting
1 sheet frozen all-butter puff pastry (I use Dufour), thawed but still cold
12 slices prosciutto di Parma
¼ cup grainy Dijon mustard
1 large free-range organic egg, lightly beaten with a splash of water

Preheat the oven to 375°F.

Season the meat liberally with salt and pepper. In a large heavy skillet, heat the oil (2 turns of the pan) over medium-high heat. Add the beef and brown it all over. Transfer to a plate and let cool.

Add the butter to the skillet and when it foams, add the mushrooms and brown, about 10 minutes. Add the shallots, garlic, sage, thyme, salt, and pepper and stir for 2 to 3 minutes more. Add the brandy and stir to deglaze the pan.

On a lightly floured surface, roll out the pastry to flatten it a bit. Cut the pastry in half crosswise. Cover both pieces of pastry with overlapping slices of prosciutto, leaving a 1-inch border. Divide the mushrooms between the pieces of pastry over the prosciutto.

Slather the beef with the mustard. Center one piece of beef on each piece of pastry and wrap and roll to encase the beef in the pastry. Arrange on a baking sheet and brush with the egg wash. Bake until deep golden and puffed, about 30 minutes.

BRAISED BRISKET WITH ALMOND GREMOLATA

SERVES 6 TO 8

The beef is brined and braised, which guarantees flavor and moisture. I like to serve this dish with my Potato-Vegetable Pancakes with Herbs (page 339).

4 to 5 pounds well-trimmed brisket

BRINE:
¼ cup Worcestershire sauce
1 organic orange, sliced
1 bunch fresh flat-leaf parsley, coarsely chopped
2 bay leaves
Pepper
½ cup kosher salt

BRAISE:
2 tablespoons olive oil
4 tablespoons (½ stick) butter or olive oil
4 large onions, sliced
3 tablespoons fresh thyme leaves
3 cups chicken stock
8 carrots, peeled but left whole

GREMOLATA:
Grated zest of 1 organic orange
1 cup fresh flat-leaf parsley tops
1 cup carrot tops
¼ cup almonds, toasted

Pat the meat dry and pierce it all over on both sides with a skewer or the tip of a small, sharp knife.

Make the brine: In a 2-gallon plastic bag, combine 3 quarts ice-cold water, the Worcestershire sauce, orange slices, parsley, bay leaves, and pepper.

In a small saucepan, bring 1 cup water to a boil and add the salt. Stir to dissolve. Add the water to the brine. Add the meat, remove all the air, and seal the bag. Place the bag on a tray and weight it down under a second tray. Refrigerate for 1 to 2 days.

When ready to braise, remove the meat from the brine and pat dry. Heat a Dutch oven over medium-high heat and add the oil (2 turns of the pan). Add the meat and brown on all sides. Transfer to a plate. Add the butter to the pot to melt. When it foams, add the onions, thyme, and stock. Bring to a bubble and return the meat to the pot. Cover, reduce the heat, and simmer for 2½ hours. For the last 45 minutes of cooking, add the carrots.

Make the gremolata: On a cutting board, finely chop the orange zest, parsley, carrot tops, and almonds.

Transfer the vegetables to a warm platter. Slice the meat and top it with the pan juices. Serve with the gremolata.

SLOW-ROASTED BEEF RIBS

SERVES 6

I present the ribs with lots of gremolata and toasted bread crumbs on top, and bitter greens dressed with lemon and tossed with shaved pecorino alongside. If you want to turn the meal into a feast, add Marsala Mushrooms (page 331) and Roasted Garlic Mashed Potatoes (page 338) to the menu.

6 (10-inch-long) English-cut beef ribs
4 tablespoons olive oil, plus more for drizzling
2 teaspoons granulated onion
2 teaspoons granulated garlic
Kosher salt and coarsely ground pepper
2 cups veal or beef stock
½ cup panko bread crumbs or homemade bread crumbs
½ cup packed fresh flat-leaf parsley tops, finely chopped
Leave from 1 or 2 sprigs fresh rosemary, finely chopped
¼ cup minced fresh chives
4 lemons: 2 zested, all halved
4 cloves garlic, finely chopped
¼ cup grated horseradish root
8 cups wild arugula or baby kale
Pecorino cheese, shaved with a vegetable peeler
A handful of cracked green Cerignola olives
½ cup walnut pieces, toasted

Drizzle the meat with a little oil and rub the ribs with the onion, garlic, salt, and pepper. Transfer to a platter and refrigerate, uncovered, overnight.

Preheat the oven to 325°F.

Arrange the ribs in a roasting pan, meat side up. Add the stock, cover the pan with foil, and roast for 3 hours. Increase the oven temperature to 425°F, uncover, and cook the ribs until crispy, 20 to 25 minutes.

In a skillet, heat 2 tablespoons of the oil (2 turns of the pan) over medium heat. Add the panko and toast until deeply golden.

In a bowl, combine the parsley, rosemary, chives, lemon zest, garlic, and horseradish to form a gremolata. Add the panko and toss to combine.

Place the greens in a bowl and squeeze 2 of the lemon halves over them. Add the remaining 2 tablespoons oil, season with salt and pepper, and toss. Toss in the pecorino, olives, and walnuts.

To serve, place a rib on each dinner plate, top with lots of gremolata, then squeeze a lemon half over it all. Serve some salad alongside.

HALF-AND-HALF SHORT RIBS WITH POLENTA

SERVES 6

These short ribs are cooked in half a bottle of ruby port and half a bottle of bold Barolo wine. Serve these short ribs on a bed of Basic Polenta (page 179). The leftovers are reason enough to make these wonderful ribs I use the leftovers to make what I call a "rollover meal" (see box). Two great nights of food—now that's a deal!

3 tablespoons olive or vegetable oil

6 (14-ounce) beef short ribs

1 large onion, chopped

4 cloves garlic, sliced

3 carrots, chopped

3 or 4 ribs celery, chopped

2 large bay leaves

Herb bundle: a few sprigs of fresh flat-leaf parsley, sage, and rosemary, tied together with kitchen twine

5 or 6 juniper berries (optional)

Kosher salt and pepper

2 tablespoons balsamic vinegar

2 cups ruby port

2 cups Barolo or other dry red wine

4 cups veal or beef stock

Basic Polenta (page 179), for serving

Pomegranate seeds, for garnish

Chopped toasted pistachios, for garnish

Preheat the oven to 325°F.

In a large Dutch oven, heat the oil (3 turns of the pan) over medium-high heat. When the oil smokes, add 3 ribs to the pan and brown deeply on all sides. Transfer to a plate and brown the remaining ribs.

When all the meat has been browned, add the onion, garlic, carrots, celery, bay leaves, herb bundle, and juniper berries (if using) to the pan. Season with salt and pepper. Partially cover and cook, stirring occasionally, to soften the vegetables, 8 to 10 minutes. Add the vinegar and stir to deglaze the pan. Add the port and wine and cook to reduce by half. Add the stock and settle the meat back into the pan, bone side up. Cover and roast until very tender, 2½ to 3 hours.

Cool the ribs, then remove the fat. (Making them a full day ahead is best.)

For extra-crispy ribs, remove the ribs from the braising liquids and roast them on a rimmed baking sheet in a preheated 400°F oven on a baking sheet for 10 to 15 minutes.

Meanwhile, make the polenta. Strain the defatted sauce, discarding the solids. Reheat gently over medium-low heat. Pour it over the meat when you serve. Serve on a bed of the polenta topped with pomegranate seeds and pistachios.

ROLLOVER MEAL: SHORT RIB DEBRIS WITH DRUNKEN PAPPARDELLE

Make a "debris sauce" by pulling or chopping the short rib meat. Reheat the sauce and thin with a little veal or beef stock, then return the pulled rib meat to the sauce and heat both through gently. Make Drunken Pasta (page 135) with pappardelle. Drain and toss with a drizzle of EVOO and salt and pepper to taste. Toss with the debris sauce and top with freshly grated pecorino cheese.

SHORT RIBS NESTED IN PASTA E FAGIOLI

SERVES 4 TO 6

This is a wonderful mash-up of a classic soup and a hearty, slow-cooked beef supper. This is a comfort-food dinner that will end with lots of long winter naps. It's truly amazing.

3 tablespoons olive oil

⅓ pound bacon or pancetta, diced

6 bone-in beef short ribs

Salt and pepper

2 carrots, chopped

2 ribs celery, chopped

1 onion, chopped

4 cloves garlic, sliced

1 teaspoon ground fennel or fennel pollen

1 large bay leaf

2 tablespoons tomato paste

Herb bundle: a few sprigs of fresh sage, flat-leaf parsley, rosemary, and thyme, tied together with kitchen twine

2 cups dry red wine

1 (10.5-ounce) can beef consommé, or 2 cups veal or beef stock

2 cups chicken stock

¾ pound ditalini or elbow macaroni

1 (15-ounce) can cannellini beans, rinsed and drained

1 cup freshly grated Parmigiano-Reggiano cheese

1 cup freshly grated Pecorino Romano cheese

Chopped fresh flat-leaf parsley, for garnish

Preheat the oven to 325°F.

In a Dutch oven, heat the oil (3 turns of the pan) over medium-high heat. Add the bacon and brown. Transfer to paper towels to drain.

Pat the short ribs dry and season liberally with salt and pepper. Add the meat to the pan and brown evenly. Transfer to a plate. Add the carrots, celery, onion, and garlic and stir for 5 minutes. Add the fennel, bay leaf, salt, and pepper. Add the tomato paste and stir for 1 minute. Add the herb bundle. Pour in the wine and stir to deglaze the pan. Add the consommé and chicken stock. Return the beef and bacon to the pan and cover. Roast until tender, about 2½ hours.

Meanwhile, bring a large pot of water to a boil for the pasta. Salt the water and cook the pasta for 5 minutes. Drain.

Remove the meat from the Dutch oven and cover to keep warm. Remove and discard the bay leaf and the herb bundle. Position a rack in the center of the oven and preheat the broiler.

Add the pasta and beans to the Dutch oven and stir in ½ cup each of the Parm and pecorino. Set the beef into the pasta-and-bean nest and cover with the remaining cheese. Brown under the broiler. Garnish with the parsley.

FLANK STEAK TAGLIATA
WITH BURST TOMATO PIZZAIOLA

Pizzaiola sauce is usually spooned over a strip, rib-eye, or sirloin steak. I prefer this lighter fresh tomato version of the sauce spooned over very thin slices (*tagliata* means "sliced") of flank steak. I serve it with a Spicy Baby Greens Salad with Shaved Pecorino (see box) on the side. My husband also likes this dish with a small side of spaghetti or linguine. So if you're like him, then cook some spaghetti and toss it with a little butter, some of the burst tomato sauce, and some grated pecorino or Parm.

3 or 4 sprigs fresh rosemary

6 cloves garlic: 2 smashed,
 4 sliced

2 pounds flank steak

2 tablespoons olive oil, plus more
 for drizzling

Kosher salt and cracked black
 pepper

1 teaspoon fennel seeds

2 pints cherry or grape tomatoes

1 tablespoon finely chopped fresh
 oregano, or 1 teaspoon dried

1 teaspoon crushed red pepper
 flakes

1 tablespoon aged balsamic
 vinegar

½ cup fresh flat-leaf parsley tops,
 chopped

Place the rosemary and smashed garlic on the steak and wrap in butcher paper or plastic wrap. Refrigerate overnight.

Bring the meat to room temperature. Discard the rosemary and garlic. Drizzle the steak with oil and season liberally with salt and cracked black pepper.

Heat a grill to high heat, or heat a grill pan or cast-iron skillet over high heat.

In a large skillet with a lid, heat the oil (2 turns of the pan) over medium-high heat. Add the fennel seeds and sliced garlic and stir for 15 to 30 seconds. Add the tomatoes, oregano, red pepper flakes, salt, and black pepper. Cover and cook, shaking the pan frequently without removing the lid, until all the tomatoes have burst, 15 to 20 minutes. Stir in the vinegar and parsley.

Grill the meat for 12 minutes for medium-rare, 2 minutes less for rare, and 3 to 5 minutes longer for medium-well. Let rest for 10 to 15 minutes. Thinly slice the meat against the grain.

Arrange the sliced steak on dinner plates and top with a generous amount of pizzaiola sauce.

SPICY BABY GREENS SALAD WITH SHAVED PECORINO

Dress 6 to 8 cups baby kale and/or arugula with the juice of 1 lemon, salt to taste, and EVOO to lightly coat. Shave young to mid-aged pecorino, *pepato* (pecorino with black pepper), or pecorino with red pepper flakes with a vegetable peeler. Add to the salad and toss.

PORTERHOUSE STEAKS WITH SALSA VERDE

I call this a true date-night meal. Remember, when you have date night at home, you can afford more of them. (And chances are you won't make it to dessert!) I love to serve these steaks with my Roasted Garlic Mashed Potatoes (page 338) and my Cherry Tomato and Red Onion Salad (page 24).

2 (1½-inch-thick) porterhouse steaks
A few sprigs fresh rosemary
4 cloves garlic, smashed
Classic Salsa Verde (see right)
Kosher salt and coarsely ground pepper
1 tablespoon canola or extra-light olive oil
4 tablespoons (½ stick) butter

Cover the steaks with the rosemary and garlic. Wrap in butcher paper or plastic wrap and refrigerate for several hours or overnight.

Make the Classic Salsa Verde. Preheat the oven to 325°F. Unwrap the steaks and let come to room temperature. Set the garlic and rosemary aside. Season the meat liberally with salt and pepper.

Heat a cast-iron skillet over medium-high heat until very hot. Add the oil (1 turn of the pan) to the skillet. Add the steaks and cook until deep brown with a good crust, 3 to 4 minutes per side. Reduce the heat to medium and add the butter. When the butter foams, add the reserved garlic and rosemary. Baste the steak with the garlic butter for 2 minutes. Transfer the pan to the oven and roast for 5 minutes for rare, 7 minutes for medium.

Remove the steaks from the pan and let the meat stand for 5 to 10 minutes. Cut the strip steak and filet from the bone, then slice against the grain into ¼- to ½-inch slices. Arrange some of the sirloin and filet pieces layered on each dinner plate and top with a generous strip of the salsa verde.

CLASSIC SALSA VERDE

This versatile sauce is not only great over steak, but you can also spoon it over fish, poultry, or grilled vegetables, or even toss it with pasta, gnocchi, or gnudi, using a little starchy cooking water to help the sauce adhere.

1 small slice stale peasant-style white bread
3 tablespoons sherry vinegar or red wine vinegar
Juice of ½ lemon
2 cups loosely packed fresh flat-leaf parsley
1 shallot, coarsely chopped
4 cloves garlic, peeled
4 flat anchovy fillets
2 hard-boiled egg yolks
3 tablespoons capers
½ teaspoon black pepper
½ teaspoon crushed red pepper flakes
⅓ cup olive oil

In a bowl, sprinkle the bread with the vinegar and 2 tablespoons water to moisten. Tear and transfer to a blender. Add the lemon juice, parsley, shallot, garlic, anchovies, egg yolks, capers, black pepper, red pepper flakes, and oil. Process until fairly smooth.

ROLLOVER MEAL: STEAK AND MUSHROOM SALAD

I make a main-course salad by dressing chopped romaine lettuce and baby spinach with leftover salsa verde. Top that with leftover thinly sliced cold steak and leftover Cherry Tomato and Red Onion Salad (page 24). Separately, bake bacon until crispy and crumble. Sauté cremini mushrooms until browned. Add the bacon and mushrooms to the salad and top with lots of crumbled blue cheese, dry Gorgonzola cheese, or smoked blue cheese.

BISTECCA FIORENTINA
WITH PARSLEY SAUCE

SERVES 4 TO 6

Tuscan steaks are Tuscan because the meat is basted with oil using rosemary sprigs. I warm EVOO with cracked garlic and rosemary to infuse the oil before basting the meat. Also, if you bring the steaks home a day early, wrap them in butcher paper with some rosemary and refrigerate overnight to intensify the scent in the meat even more. My friend, master meat chef Adam Perry Lang, taught me to attach the rosemary to a wooden spoon handle with twine or a rubber band to create a rosemary basting brush. Genius. I use a parsley sauce on the sliced steak, but truth be told, it's great just with a charred lemon half squeezed over the top. I love to serve this with Mom's Warm Potato Salad (page 340).

1 bunch fresh rosemary
½ cup good-quality olive oil, plus more for drizzling
2 large cloves garlic, smashed
2 (2-inch-thick) porterhouse steaks
Kosher or sea salt and coarsely ground pepper
2 lemons, halved
Parsley Sauce for Steak (see box)

Attach 4 or 5 rosemary sprigs to a wooden spoon handle with twine or a rubber band to form a basting brush.

In a small saucepan, combine the oil, garlic, and a few small pieces of rosemary and heat over low heat to infuse the oil.

Let the steaks come to room temperature and season liberally with salt and pepper.

Heat a grill to high heat. If making a charcoal or wood fire, bank your coals to one side to intensify the heat and also provide a cool side where you can rest the meat. (As an alternative to grilling, heat a large cast-iron skillet over high heat and preheat the oven to 325°F.)

Grill the steaks for 6 to 7 minutes per side, turning once and basting frequently with the garlic-rosemary oil, until the meat reaches 125°F on a meat thermometer. Pull off the heat and let rest for 10 minutes before slicing. (If cooking indoors, brown the steaks in the preheated skillet for 4 minutes on each side and the edges. Transfer the skillet to the oven and cook until the meat

reaches 125°F, 6 to 8 minutes more. Transfer the meat to a carving board and let rest for 10 minutes.)

Drizzle the cut lemons with EVOO and season with salt and pepper. Grill, cut side down, on the grill or in the skillet until caramelized, 4 to 5 minutes.

Carve the filet and sirloin off the bone and cut ½-inch-thick slices, working perpendicular to the bone, against the grain of the meat. Douse the meat with the juice from the charred lemon.

Arrange a few slices of steak on a plate and spoon a generous strip of parsley sauce across them.

PARSLEY SAUCE FOR STEAK

=== MAKES ABOUT 1 CUP ===

Like the title says, this is delicious served over steak.

1½ cups packed fresh flat-leaf parsley tops
Leaves from 2 sprigs fresh rosemary
2 cloves garlic, peeled
Grated zest and juice of 1 organic lemon
2 flat anchovy fillets
3 tablespoons Worcestershire sauce
⅓ cup good-quality olive oil
Salt and pepper

In a food processor or blender, combine the parsley, rosemary, garlic, lemon zest, lemon juice, anchovies, Worcestershire sauce, oil, and salt and pepper to taste. Puree into a sauce.

BEEF MILANESE

Veal Milanese may be more well known than beef Milanese, but beef cutlets are quick to prepare and I love the unique, nuttier flavor. The raw sauce is delicious, and I sometimes make it as an appetizer to serve with charred bread.

4 large, thin-cut slices beef top round
Kosher salt and pepper
1 cup flour
1 teaspoon ground sage
3 large free-range organic eggs
1 cup fine dry bread crumbs
½ cup panko bread crumbs
½ cup freshly grated pecorino cheese
Canola or other light oil, for shallow-frying
Tomato, Basil, and Bitter Greens Raw Sauce (page 299)
4 lemon wedges, for squeezing

Preheat the oven to 275°F. Place a cooling rack on a rimmed baking sheet and place it in the oven.

Pound the meat slices to a ⅛-inch thickness and season with salt and pepper.

Set up a breading station: Line up 3 shallow bowls on the counter. Combine the flour and sage in one, beat the eggs in the second, and mix the fine bread crumbs, panko, and pecorino in the third.

In a large skillet, heat about ⅛ inch of oil over medium to medium-high heat.

Turn 2 pieces of beef in flour, then the egg, then the bread crumb mixture, pressing to make sure the coating sticks. Add to the pan and fry until deep golden, 2 to 3 minutes on each side. Transfer to the baking sheet in the oven to keep warm. Repeat with the remaining cutlets, replenishing the oil as needed.

Serve the cutlets topped with the raw sauce, with lemon wedges alongside.

VARIATION

Beef Milanese with Corn, Tomato, and Tarragon Raw Sauce

In the summer, I make a raw sauce with corn kernels from raw corn on the cob when it is at its sweetest, or I grill corn and then scrape it down (a good use for leftovers). Then I combine the corn with quartered grape tomatoes, finely chopped red onion, and lots of fresh tarragon. If I have it, I add thinly sliced baby fennel. It gets lightly dressed with EVOO, salt, and pepper.

BRACIOLE WITH BACON AND ONION SAUCE

Who doesn't love this Italian American classic? Stuffed beef bundles simmered in another classic, *amatriciana* (bacon and onion sauce). This dish is a favorite because it turns any day I make it into my day: Sunday (my middle name, *Domenica*, means Sunday!). It's a day to share food, conversation, and naps with the ones you love.

BEEF:
3 large free-range organic eggs

2 cups crustless stale white or peasant-style bread cubes

Milk, for soaking the bread

3 tablespoons pignoli (pine nuts), toasted

3 tablespoons dried currants

½ cup fresh flat-leaf parsley tops, finely chopped

1 cup baby kale, spinach, or arugula, chopped

2 large cloves garlic, finely chopped

1 teaspoon crushed red pepper flakes

A handful of freshly grated Parmigiano-Reggiano cheese

12 large, thin-cut slices beef top round (about 2 pounds total)

Salt and black pepper

12 slices prosciutto di Parma

⅓ pound unsliced provolone or young pecorino cheese, cut into twelve sticks (2 to 3 inches long and ¼ inch thick)

Olive oil, for browning the meat

BACON AND ONION SAUCE:
⅓ pound pancetta, cut into ¼-inch cubes

2 onions, chopped

4 cloves garlic, sliced

2 fresh bay leaves

Black pepper

3 tablespoons tomato paste

1½ cups dry white or red wine

2 cups chicken or veal stock

1 (28- to 32-ounce) can San Marzano tomatoes (look for DOP on the label)

Pasta or garlic bread, for serving (see Tip)

Make the beef: Place the eggs in a small saucepan with water to cover. Bring to a rapid rolling boil. Cover the pan, remove from the heat, and let stand for 10 minutes. Drain. Crack the shells and let stand for 10 minutes in very cold water. Peel and chop the eggs and put them in a large bowl.

In a small bowl, soak the bread with milk to soften, then squeeze out the excess milk. Pull the bread apart into shreds as you add it to the bowl with the eggs. Add the pine nuts, currants, parsley, chopped greens, garlic, red pepper flakes, and Parm.

Pound the meat slices to a ⅛-inch thickness and season with salt and black pepper. Top each slice of beef with 1 slice prosciutto. Add a few spoonfuls of stuffing at one end of each slice of beef. Nest a stick of provolone in the stuffing. Tuck in the sides of the beef as you roll it into bundles. Secure the rolls with kitchen twine.

In a large Dutch oven, heat 2 tablespoons oil (2 turns of the pan) over medium-high heat. Working in 3 batches, add the beef and brown well all over. Add more oil to the pan as needed. Transfer the beef bundles to a plate.

Make the bacon and onion sauce: Add the pancetta to the Dutch oven and render for 2 to 3 minutes, stirring constantly. Add the onions, garlic, and bay leaves, and season with black pepper. Partially cover and cook to soften the onions, 7 to 8 minutes. Add the tomato paste and stir for 1 to 2 minutes. Add the wine, stir to deglaze the pan, and cook to reduce the wine by half. Add the stock. Hand-crush the tomatoes as you add them to the pan, then add the juices from the can.

Slide the meat rolls into the sauce and bring the sauce to a bubble. Simmer gently over low heat, covered, stirring occasionally, until very tender, 1½ to 2 hours. Discard the bay leaves.

Transfer the meat rolls to a warm platter and cut off the twine. Top with some of the sauce to keep the rolls moist. Serve with either pasta or charred bread (see Tip).

IF SERVING WITH pasta, cook the pasta in salted boiling water until al dente and reserve about 1 cup of the starchy cooking water before draining. Remove the beef rolls from the sauce, whisk the sauce, and stir in the starchy water before tossing the pasta with the sauce. Top with grated Parm.

If serving with bread, char split ciabatta or sliced rustic bread under a hot broiler on both sides. Rub the charred bread with halved cloves of garlic, drizzle the bread with EVOO, and sprinkle with flaky sea salt. Pass a bowl of sauce at the table with a ladle so everyone can mop it up with the charred bread.

BEEF STEW WITH BUTTERNUT SQUASH

SERVES 6

This is a beef stew made with sweet vermouth and butternut squash. It is affordable and yet unusual enough to entertain with. It celebrates the flavors of autumn. Warm crusty bread in the oven and pass with butter and flaky sea salt at the table.

3 pounds beef chuck

Olive or vegetable oil, for sautéing and drizzling

⅓ pound speck (smoky ham), cut into ¼-inch cubes, or 6 slices good-quality lean smoky bacon, cut into 1-inch pieces

Kosher salt and pepper

2 carrots, chopped

2 or 3 ribs celery, chopped

1 large onion, chopped

3 or 4 cloves garlic (to taste), sliced or chopped

1 tablespoon chopped fresh marjoram, or 1 teaspoon dried

3 tablespoons fresh thyme leaves, chopped

2 fresh bay leaves

2 tablespoons tomato paste

1 cup sweet vermouth

2 fat strips of organic orange zest

4 cups veal or beef stock

1 medium-large butternut squash, peeled and cut into 1½-inch chunks

Freshly grated nutmeg

2 tablespoons acacia honey

3 tablespoons grainy Dijon mustard

Toasted sliced almonds, for garnish

Bring the meat to room temp and pat dry. Cut into 2-inch chunks.

Preheat the oven to 325°F.

In a large Dutch oven, heat 2 tablespoons oil (2 turns of the pan) over medium-high heat. Add the speck and stir until crisp. Transfer to a plate. Season the beef with salt and pepper. Working in batches to avoid crowding the pan, brown the beef on all sides. Add more oil as needed. Transfer the beef to the plate with the speck.

Add the carrots, celery, onion, garlic, marjoram, thyme, bay leaves, salt, and pepper to the pan. Partially cover and cook, stirring occasionally, to soften the vegetables, 5 to 7 minutes. Stir in the tomato paste and cook for 1 minute. Add the vermouth and orange zest, stir to deglaze the pan, and cook to reduce the liquid by half. Add the stock and slide the meat and speck back into the pot. Bring to a bubble, cover, and transfer to the oven. Bake for 2½ hours. Remove the stew and let it stand, covered, while you roast the squash. Leave the oven on and increase the temperature to 425°F.

Drizzle the squash with oil, season with salt, pepper, and nutmeg, and toss to coat. Arrange the squash on a baking sheet and roast, turning once, until browned at the edges, 30 to 35 minutes.

Transfer the meat to a large shallow serving bowl and combine with the squash. Stir the honey and mustard into the sauce in the Dutch oven. Fish out and discard the bay leaves. Pour the sauce over the beef and squash. Garnish with the almonds.

BEEF WITH BAROLO OVER TALEGGIO MASHED POTATOES

Beef slowly simmered in a red wine tomato sauce with cheesy mashed potatoes is a wonderful comfort-food meal, especially in the late fall and winter. Taleggio is my husband's favorite cheese, and he has a point: It has a unique flavor and texture. It's tangy, creamy, buttery, and delicious.

2½ to 3 pounds beef stew meat, cut into 2-inch cubes
Kosher salt and pepper
Flour, for dredging
2 tablespoons EVOO
2 cups beef stock
1 (750ml) bottle Barolo or spicy dry red wine
5 or 6 cloves garlic (to taste), smashed
1 large bay leaf
2 tablespoons tomato paste
Taleggio Mashed Potatoes (see box)
Coarsely chopped fresh flat-leaf parsley, for garnish

Preheat the oven to 325°F if you want to make this in the oven. Otherwise, it can be made on the stovetop.

Bring the beef to room temp and pat dry. Sprinkle with salt and pepper, then dredge lightly in flour, shaking off the excess.

In a Dutch oven, heat 1 tablespoon of the EVOO (1 turn of the pan) over medium-high heat. Add half the beef and cook until browned. Transfer to a plate. Brown the remaining beef in the remaining 1 tablespoon EVOO. Return all the beef to the pot and add the stock and wine. Stir in the garlic, bay leaf, and tomato paste

and bring to a boil. Cover and transfer to the oven or continue simmering on the stovetop. Cook/bake until very tender, about 3 hours.

About 30 minutes before you're ready to serve the stew, make the mashed potatoes.

Transfer the beef to a serving platter and cook the sauce on the stovetop to reduce and thicken a bit. Fish out and discard the bay leaf. Pour the sauce over the beef.

Divide the beef and sauce among shallow bowls and sprinkle with parsley. Serve a mound of potatoes alongside to pull into the beef as you eat.

TALEGGIO MASHED POTATOES

4 russet (baking) potatoes, peeled and diced
Salt
8 ounces ripe Taleggio cheese (soft and with a little give to it)
About 1 cup milk or half-and-half
A few fresh sage leaves, torn
Pepper
Freshly grated nutmeg

In a large pot, combine the potatoes with water to cover. Bring the water to a boil, salt the water, and cook the potatoes until tender, 12 to 15 minutes.

Drain the potatoes and return to the hot pot. Cut the Taleggio into a few pieces and mash it into the potatoes with enough milk to reach the desired consistency. Stir in the sage and season with salt, pepper, and nutmeg.

MUSHROOM AND CHESTNUT MEATLOAF WITH GRAVY

SERVES 8

Meatloaf may not be the first dish that comes to mind for an Italian cookbook, but this meatloaf combines beef, pork, veal, and chestnuts. It is an American classic with Italian influences. Like me, it's a mix of two influences and two worlds. Serve the meatloaf with Duchess Potatoes (page 338), which you can have in the oven for the last 30 minutes of the meatloaf cooking time.

MEATLOAF:

6 tablespoons (¾ stick) butter

1 cup panko bread crumbs or homemade coarse bread crumbs

2 teaspoons celery salt

Salt and pepper

¼ cup finely chopped fresh flat-leaf parsley

Cloudy apple cider or milk, for moistening the bread crumbs

½ pound cremini mushrooms, finely chopped

1 teaspoon fennel seeds

4 shallots, or 1 small onion, finely chopped

2 or 3 small ribs celery with leafy tops, finely chopped

1 crisp apple (such as Honeycrisp), peeled and finely chopped

2 tablespoons fresh thyme leaves, finely chopped

2 tablespoons thinly sliced fresh sage leaves

1 cup roasted or jarred chestnuts, finely chopped

¼ cup Calvados, brandy, or dry sherry

2 pounds mixed ground beef, pork, and veal

1 cup shredded sharp white cheddar cheese

¼ cup freshly grated Parmigiano-Reggiano cheese

2 large free-range organic egg yolks

GRAVY:

4 tablespoons (½ stick) butter

1 teaspoon coarsely ground pepper

3 tablespoons flour

3 cups veal or beef stock

1 tablespoon Worcestershire sauce or balsamic reduction (see box, page 28)

Make the meatloaf: Position a rack in the center of the oven and preheat the oven to 375°F. Line a baking sheet with parchment paper.

In a small skillet, melt 2 tablespoons of the butter over medium heat. Add the bread crumbs, season with the celery salt and pepper to taste, and toast until golden. Remove from the heat and let cool. Toss the toasted bread crumbs with the parsley and moisten them with a little apple cider or milk. Set aside.

In a large skillet, melt the remaining 4 tablespoons (½ stick) butter over medium heat. Add the mushrooms and fennel seeds and cook to lightly brown. Season with salt and pepper. Add the shallots, celery, apple, thyme, sage, and chestnuts and cook to soften, 6 to 8 minutes. Add the Calvados and stir to deglaze the pan. Remove from the heat and let cool.

In a large bowl, season the meat with salt and pepper. Add the cooled mushroom mixture, the bread crumbs, cheddar, Parm, and egg yolks and mix to combine.

Form a loaf on the prepared baking sheet and bake for 1 hour. Let stand for about 10 minutes before slicing and serving.

Make the gravy: In a saucepan, combine the butter and pepper and melt over medium heat. Whisk in the flour and bring to a bubble. Whisk in the stock and simmer to thicken. Stir in the Worcestershire sauce or balsamic reduction.

Slice the meatloaf and serve topped with the gravy.

ROLLOVER MEAL: MEATLOAF SANDWICHES

What's even better than this meal? My meatloaf sandwiches, that's what. Heat a skillet or griddle and slice the cold meatloaf about ¾ inch thick. Grill or griddle the meatloaf until crispy and browned on both sides. Toast sliced white Italian bread and layer with grainy mustard, baby kale, thinly sliced red onion or shallots, sliced grilled or sautéed apples, sliced cornichons, and the meatloaf. Masterpiece.

BOLOGNESE SHEPHERD'S PIE
WITH ROASTED GARLIC POTATOES

A meat sauce casserole topped with potatoes? Um, yes, I did. You can, too.

2 heads garlic, roasted
(see box, page 312)

FILLING:
2 tablespoons EVOO, plus more
for drizzling
1 (¼-pound) chunk guanciale
or pancetta, cut into ¼-inch
cubes
1½ pounds coarse-ground sirloin
Salt and pepper
2 carrots, chopped
2 ribs celery from the heart,
chopped
1 onion, chopped
1 bay leaf
Herb bundle: a few sprigs of fresh
flat-leaf parsley, sage, and
rosemary, tied together with
kitchen twine
2 tablespoons tomato paste
Rind from a small wedge of
Parmigiano-Reggiano cheese
(optional)
1½ cups dry red or white wine
2 cups beef or veal stock
1 cup milk

POTATO TOPPING:
2½ pounds russet (baking)
potatoes (5 large), peeled
and diced
Salt
1 cup milk
1½ cups freshly grated
Parmigiano-Reggiano cheese
Pepper
Freshly grated nutmeg
2 large free-range organic egg
yolks

Roast the garlic and set aside to cool.

Make the filling: In a Dutch oven or heavy pot, heat the EVOO (2 turns of the pan) over medium-high heat. Add the guanciale and lightly brown, about 2 minutes. Add the sirloin, breaking it up into crumbles as it browns. Season with salt and pepper and add the carrots, celery, and onion. Squeeze the garlic from 1 of the heads into the pan and stir well to incorporate. Add the bay leaf and herb bundle, partially cover, and cook over medium heat to soften the vegetables, stirring occasionally, 10 to 12 minutes. Add the tomato paste and stir until fragrant, 1 to 2 minutes. Add the Parm rind (if using), wine, stock, and milk and bring to a bubble. Reduce the heat and simmer.

Meanwhile, make the potato topping: In a saucepan, combine the potatoes with water to cover and bring to a rolling boil. Salt the water and cook the potatoes until tender. In a small saucepan, warm the milk. Drain the potatoes and pass them through a ricer into a bowl. Add ½ cup of the warm milk, the remaining garlic, 1 cup of the Parm, salt, pepper, and nutmeg to taste. Add more of the milk if the potato mixture is too tight to be piped. Adjust the seasonings, then mix in the egg yolks.

Position a rack in the center of the oven and preheat the broiler.

Discard the bay leaf, herb bundle, and cheese rind. Transfer the beef filling to a casserole or individual bowls. Spread or pipe (in a pastry bag or a zip-top bag with a small corner cut off) the potatoes over the top, and sprinkle with the remaining ½ cup Parm. Broil to brown and serve.

CHIANTI BURGERS

Red wine burgers are delicious with a few cheese choices: young pecorino, blue cheese, or Fontina Val d'Aosta. They're a sophisticated version of an American classic, and I think they're fun to entertain with, especially on a weekend afternoon.

2 tablespoons EVOO, plus more for drizzling

2 large onions, sliced

Salt and pepper

½ cup veal or beef stock

2 pounds ground beef (80% lean)

½ cup Chianti or dry red wine

2 large cloves garlic, grated or finely chopped

2 tablespoons fresh rosemary leaves, finely chopped

2 tablespoons thinly sliced fresh sage leaves

½ pound Fontina Val d'Aosta cheese, sliced

4 (5-inch) squares focaccia, split horizontally

Baby arugula or baby kale

Balsamic ketchup (see box)

In a large skillet, heat the EVOO (2 turns of the pan) over medium-low heat. Add the onions, season with salt and pepper, and cook, stirring occasionally, until caramelized and very sweet, 25 to 30 minutes. Add the stock to the pan to keep the onions moist.

Heat a cast-iron skillet or griddle pan over medium-high heat.

In a bowl, combine the beef, wine, garlic, rosemary, sage, and salt and pepper to taste. Score the mixture into 4 equal portions and form them into patties slightly thinner at the center than at the edges, for even cooking and to ensure a flat surface (burgers plump as they cook). Drizzle the patties with EVOO, transfer to the skillet, and cook for 8 minutes, turning once. Top the burgers with the cheese for the last minute of cooking, tenting the pan with foil, if you like, to help melt the cheese.

Make a bed of greens on the focaccia bottoms and top with the burgers, caramelized onions, and a little balsamic ketchup. Set the focaccia tops in place.

BALSAMIC KETCHUP

Stir 2 tablespoons balsamic reduction (store-bought or homemade, page 28) into 1 cup good-quality organic ketchup.

VEAL

Veal is like cilantro. (Hear me out.) People tend to react to the mere mention of it—they either love it or hate it.

Ever since I was a child, I've found it important to know and understand where my food comes from. I was not born with this curiosity about food—I was taught it by my grandfather, who showed and explained to me why and how plants grew, why the fish resting at the water's edge had to die, and why the ducks who lived in the Mallard Duck Lying-In Hospital (anchored in the bay across from my childhood home) had babies every spring.

My mom was one of ten children, the first-born. As the eldest, she was the one who had to understand, come winter, what had happened to the family's rabbits and livestock (which she might have given names to). If I had to stand in my grandfather's, or any farmer's, shoes, I just might be a vegetarian. However, I know that the livestock and animal protein I source for my family today and the meat that my grandfather raised and provided to his kids was responsibly farmed and, as much as is possible by definition, killed responsibly and humanely.

To eat meat or not to eat meat is a question unto itself. But if you are a meat eater, when it comes to veal, if you have a good local butcher and farmer you can rely on, these are very tempting veal dishes. I have included the classics from Milanese to osso buco. Enjoy.

BRAISED WHOLE VEAL SHANK

This is one of our special holiday meals. When white truffle is available, we add it to the gravy even though the gravy is very delicious without it. We start this meal with Risotto with Porcini and Celery (page 188). Then for sides, we have Cauliflower with Rosemary au Gratin (page 321) and Sautéed Lady Apples (page 310). Note that the veal shank has to be brined the day before you plan on cooking.

2 cups cloudy apple cider
¼ cup kosher salt
¼ cup superfine sugar
1 (3½- to 4-pound) veal shank (hind shank)
Salt and pepper
2 tablespoons olive oil
2 bay leaves
Herb bundle: a few sprigs of fresh rosemary, sage, flat-leaf parsley, and carrot tops, tied together with kitchen twine
A few juniper berries (optional)
1 celery root, peeled and chopped, or 3 large ribs celery with leafy tops, chopped
2 large carrots, chopped
1 large onion, chopped
2 or 3 cloves garlic (to taste), smashed
1 cup dry white wine
3 cups veal stock, plus more for the gravy
3 tablespoons butter
Shaved fresh white truffle, at your discretion (optional)
3 tablespoons flour

In a 2-gallon brine bag, combine 6 cups water, the cider, kosher salt, and superfine sugar. Whisk to dissolve the salt and sugar. Add the veal and refrigerate overnight.

Preheat the oven to 350°F. Pat the veal dry and bring to room temperature.

Season the veal with salt and pepper. In a large Dutch oven, heat the oil (2 turns of the pan) over high heat. Add the veal and brown evenly all over. Transfer the shank to a platter. Reduce the heat under the pan a bit and add the bay leaves, herb bundle, juniper berries (if using), celery root, carrots, onion, and garlic. Season with salt and pepper, partially cover, and cook to soften the vegetables, stirring occasionally, 8 to 10 minutes. Add

the wine and stir to deglaze the pan. Add the stock and settle the meat back into the pan. Cover and transfer to the oven. Roast for 2½ hours, then transfer the veal to a warm platter and cover with foil to keep warm.

Strain the pan juices into a bowl. Fish out and discard the bay leaves, herb bundle, and juniper berries. Pass the vegetables through a food mill into the bowl with the pan juices to make a sauce.

In a skillet, melt the butter over medium heat. Add the shaved truffle (if using). Whisk in the flour and cook for 1 minute. Whisk in the sauce. Add extra stock, if needed, to stretch the gravy.

Spoon the sauce over the shank and serve family-style, pulling off pieces of the tender meat.

OSSO BUCO WITH SAFFRON AND PISTACHIO GREMOLATA

This is a recipe for osso buco with a Sicilian edge that comes from a fat pinch of *zafferano* (saffron) and a mixed citrus gremolata made with toasted pistachio nuts. I love the complexity and balance of the finished dish. Instead of serving over polenta, you could keep this simple and serve with warm, crusty bread for mopping.

2 cups chicken stock

1 fat pinch of saffron threads

4 to 6 center-cut pieces veal shank, about ½ pound each, tied with kitchen twine to keep together while cooking

3 tablespoons olive oil

Salt and black pepper

1 teaspoon fennel seeds

1 large carrot, chopped

2 or 3 small ribs celery with leafy tops, chopped

1 onion, chopped

1 organic orange

1 organic lemon

4 or 5 cloves garlic (to taste), finely chopped

2 large fresh bay leaves

2 tablespoons fresh thyme leaves, chopped

2 tablespoons fresh rosemary leaves, finely chopped

2 tablespoons tomato paste

2 tablespoons flour

1 cup dry white wine

1 teaspoon crushed red pepper flakes

1 (28- to 32-ounce) can San Marzano tomatoes (look for DOP on the label)

Basic Polenta (page 179)

½ cup fresh flat-leaf parsley leaves

⅓ cup pistachios or pignoli (pine nuts), toasted and finely chopped

In a small pot, combine the stock and saffron and heat over low heat to infuse the stock.

Preheat the oven to 325°F. Bring the meat to room temperature.

In a large Dutch oven, heat 2 tablespoons of the oil (2 turns of the pan) over high heat. Season the shanks with salt and black pepper, add to the hot pan, and brown all over, turning occasionally, about 12 minutes. Transfer to a large plate.

Reduce the heat to medium. Add the remaining 1 tablespoon oil (1 turn of the pan) and the fennel seeds and stir for a minute.

Add the carrot, celery, and onion. Season with salt and black pepper and stir for 5 minutes.

Meanwhile, grate the zest from the orange and lemon and set aside. Halve the orange and cut the lemon into fat wedges.

Add 3 or 4 garlic cloves, the bay leaves, thyme, rosemary, tomato paste, and salt and pepper to taste to the pan and stir for a minute more. Sprinkle the flour over the vegetables and stir for a minute more. Add the wine and stir to deglaze the pan. Stir in the saffron stock and red pepper flakes. Hand-crush the tomatoes as you add them to the pan, then add the juices from the can. Squeeze the juice from the halved orange into the sauce. Scrape the ingredients down and settle the meat in the pot. Cover and transfer to the oven. Roast for 2 hours, turning the meat once about halfway through.

Meanwhile, make the polenta. When the meat is about ready to come out of the oven, combine the orange and lemon zests, remaining 1 garlic clove, the parsley, and pistachios and finely chop to combine and form a gremolata.

Remove the veal from the oven. Place a serving platter and shallow bowls (if they're oven safe) in the oven to warm. Transfer the veal to the warm platter and cut off the strings.

Place the Dutch oven over medium heat, fish out and discard the bay leaves, and cook the sauce, whisking to combine and thicken, 4 to 5 minutes. Turn off the heat and add the juice of 1 fat wedge of lemon.

Serve the shanks in the warm bowls on a bed of polenta with chunky sauce and some of the gremolata.

LEMON OSSO BUCO

This is a simple, no-nonsense recipe for osso buco, and we serve it simply as well, with bread for mopping and some wilted greens (escarole, chard, or kale). Bread can be swapped out for steamed or boiled potato wedges.

6 center-cut pieces veal shank, about ½ pound each, tied with kitchen twine to keep together while cooking
Salt and pepper
3 tablespoons olive oil
5 or 6 flat anchovy fillets, chopped
4 cloves garlic, smashed
½ cup dry vermouth
2 lemons: 1 sliced, 1 juiced
1 cup veal stock
Herb bundle: a few sprigs of fresh flat-leaf parsley and thyme, tied together with kitchen twine
2 tablespoons butter
¼ cup chopped fresh flat-leaf parsley

Bring the veal to room temperature. Season with salt and pepper.

In a large deep pan with a lid or a Dutch oven, heat the oil (3 turns of the pan) over medium-high heat. Add the anchovies, cover the pan with a splatter screen or lid, and shake until the anchovies begin to break up. Reduce the heat a bit, uncover, and stir until the anchovies melt into the oil. Add the veal and brown well all over. Add the garlic, vermouth, lemon slices, stock, and herb bundle. Cover and cook, stirring occasionally, for 2 hours.

Transfer the meat to a warm platter. Cut off the strings. Fish out and discard the herb bundle and lemon slices and swirl the butter, chopped parsley, and lemon juice into the sauce. Spoon the sauce over the meat.

VEAL FRANCESE

Serve this classic with Duchess Potatoes (page 338) and Garlicky Wilted Spinach (page 342) or Tricolor Salad (page 304).

8 (3- to 4-ounce) thinly sliced veal leg cutlets or scaloppine
Salt and pepper
1 cup flour
½ teaspoon ground sage
½ teaspoon granulated garlic
3 tablespoons butter, cut into 1-tablespoon slices
3 large free-range organic eggs
½ cup freshly grated Parmigiano-Reggiano cheese
Juice of ½ lemon, plus 1 lemon, thinly sliced
3 tablespoons olive oil
½ cup dry white wine
½ cup veal or chicken stock
A handful of fresh flat-leaf parsley, chopped

Preheat the oven to 175°F and place a platter in the oven to warm.

If the veal is thicker than ⅛ inch, pound it lightly to make it thinner. Season with salt and pepper on both sides.

In a shallow bowl, combine the flour, sage, and garlic. Roll the butter slices in the seasoned flour and set aside.

In another shallow bowl, beat the eggs with the Parm and the lemon juice.

In a large skillet, heat the oil (3 turns of the pan) over medium to medium-high heat. Working in two batches, dredge the veal in the seasoned flour, then coat in the egg-Parm mixture, shaking off the excess. Add to the pan and sauté to deep golden, 2 to 3 minutes on each side. Transfer the veal to the warm platter and cover loosely with foil. Repeat for the second batch.

Add the lemon slices to the pan and caramelize on one side. Flip, add the wine to the pan, and cook until it has reduced to a few tablespoons. Pour in the stock and bring to a bubble. Add the flour-coated butter and swirl the pan to form a sauce. Cook to reduce and thicken a bit.

Pour the hot sauce over the veal and garnish with the parsley. Serve with the lemon slices.

VEAL MILANESE

I use coarse homemade bread crumbs combined with fine bread crumbs and grated cheese for extra-crispy coating. The fun part is trying to pound the bone-in chops as thin as possible. If you are patient, you can get the veal so thin that light can pass through it. If the meat tears on you, overlap it and tap it back together. There are several toppings for Milanese (see box, page 299), but my favorite is the arugula salad called for here.

4 (1½-inch-thick) bone-in veal chops (see Tip)
Kosher salt and pepper
Flour, for dredging
4 large free-range organic eggs
1 cup fine dry bread crumbs
½ cup panko bread crumbs or homemade coarse bread crumbs
½ cup finely grated Parmigiano-Reggiano cheese
A little freshly grated nutmeg
Olive oil, for shallow-frying
2 lemons, halved and caramelized (see Tip), or cut into wedges
Arugula Salad with Sage and White Balsamic Vinaigrette (page 25)

VARIATION

Veal Milanese with Celery, Portobello, and Parsley Salad

Switch the arugula salad for the Celery, Portobello, and Parsley Salad on page 23.

Set a chop upright on a cutting board with the meaty side facing up. Using a thin sharp knife, cut into the meat and cut through the center, toward the bone. Stop short of the bone, then open up the meat like a book. Do not remove the meat from the bone; the bone itself will be at the center of the butterflied chop. Place the meat between sheets of parchment or plastic with a dab of water and gently and evenly pound the meat out with a meat mallet, flipping the meat a couple of times, until it's ¼ to ⅛ inch thick. Season with salt and pepper.

Set up a dredging station: Line up 3 shallow bowls on the counter. Spread flour in one, beat the eggs in the second, and mix the fine bread crumbs, panko, Parm, nutmeg, and salt and pepper to taste in the third.

Preheat the oven to 250°F. Place a cooling rack over a rimmed baking sheet and set in the oven.

In large cast-iron skillet, heat about ¼ inch of oil over medium-high heat.

Coat the veal in flour and shake off the excess. Turn a chop in the egg, shaking off the excess, then press into the bread crumb mixture. Fry the chops, one at a time, until deep golden, about 3 minutes on each side. Keep the cutlets warm on the prepared baking sheet in the oven.

Serve the veal with lemon for squeezing. Place the salad under or on top of each cutlet.

ASK FOR END chops; they are cheaper than the rib chops, the first cuts of the rib.

AN OPTIONAL EXTRA STEP TO give the lemon juice more flavor is to caramelize the cut lemons in a hot pan. This also gets their juices to flow. Do this in a small skillet.

GRILLED STUFFED VEAL CHOPS WITH ESCAROLE AND FONTINA

The Val d'Aosta region of Italy made chops stuffed with Fontina famous. I like these chops best grilled and topped with charred smoky lemon juice, but you can also make the chops indoors (see Tip).

4 (1½-inch-thick) bone-in veal chops
Salt and pepper
1 tablespoon olive oil, plus more for coating
2 large cloves garlic, smashed
½ pound escarole, chopped (about 4 cups)
Freshly grated nutmeg
⅓ pound Fontina Val d'Aosta cheese, shredded or sliced
8 fresh sage leaves
2 lemons, halved

Set a chop upright on a cutting board with the meaty side facing up. Using a thin sharp knife, cut into the meat and cut through the center, toward the bone. Stop short of the bone, then open up the meat like a book. Do not remove the meat from the bone. Place the meat between sheets of parchment or plastic wrap with a dab of water and gently and evenly pound the meat out with a meat mallet, flipping the meat a couple of times, until it's ¼ to ⅛ inch thick. Season with salt and pepper.

In a medium skillet, heat the oil (1 turn of the pan) over medium heat. Add the garlic and stir for 1 minute. Wilt in the greens and season with salt, pepper, and a bit of nutmeg. Let the greens cool, then drain well.

Heat a grill to medium-high to high heat.

Top each chop with some greens, Fontina, and 2 sage leaves. Close the chops and seal with a couple of toothpicks each.

Coat the chops with oil. Brush the cut sides of the lemon halves with oil. Grill the chops, covered, for about 3 minutes on each side. Grill the lemons, cut side down, for 3 to 4 minutes. Douse the chops with the juice from the charred lemons and serve.

TIP

To make these on the stovetop, dredge the chops in flour, brown them in canola oil in a cast-iron skillet, then finish them in a preheated 325°F oven. Drizzle the chops with fruity olive oil to serve.

CAST-IRON VEAL CHOPS WITH SAGE AND GORGONZOLA TOASTS

Serve with a wilted spinach or arugula salad. Ideally, I like the chops to be ¾ to 1 inch thick.

4 (¾- to 1-inch-thick) veal rib chops (about 12 ounces each)
Kosher salt and pepper
10 to 12 fresh sage leaves, thinly sliced, torn, or coarsely chopped
Flour, for dredging
2 tablespoons olive oil
1 large clove garlic, smashed
½ cup dry vermouth or dry white wine
2 tablespoons butter
4 pieces peasant-style white or ciabatta bread, toasted
6 to 8 ounces Gorgonzola dolce cheese, melted in the microwave or in a small skillet over low heat
Light honey (such as acacia), for drizzling

Preheat the oven to 175°F and set a platter or some dinner plates in the oven to warm them. Let the veal come to room temperature.

Rub the veal with salt and pepper and press the sage into the chops. Lightly dredge in a little flour.

Heat a cast-iron skillet over medium-high heat. Add the oil (2 turns of the pan). Add the garlic, stir for 1 minute or so, then remove the garlic. Add the chops and cook until well browned (including the bone), turning occasionally, 8 to 10 minutes. Transfer the chops to the warm platter. Add the vermouth to the pan, swirl, and melt in the butter.

Spoon the sauce over the chops. Slather the charred bread with the warm cheese and add a drizzle of honey. Serve a piece of toast with each chop.

TUSCAN GRILLED VEAL CHOPS WITH CHARRED LEMON

It doesn't get easier than this recipe, and it really symbolizes what is so perfect about Tuscan cooking: the fire and flavor of grilling and the simplicity of preparation.

4 veal rib chops
¼ cup olive oil, plus more for drizzling
Kosher salt and pepper
2 lemons, halved
2 large cloves garlic, very thinly sliced
Leaves from 2 sprigs fresh rosemary, chopped
8 to 10 fresh sage leaves, thinly sliced or torn

Bring the veal to room temp.

Heat a grill to high (or heat a charcoal grill to white coals).

Drizzle the veal chops with some oil and rub them all over. Season liberally with salt and pepper. Grill, uncovered, for about 6 minutes, turning once. Add the lemons to the grill, cut side down, for the last 2 to 3 minutes to caramelize them.

Meanwhile, on a platter, combine the ¼ cup oil, garlic, rosemary, and sage.

Transfer the hot chops to the platter and turn to coat them evenly. Douse with juice from the grilled lemons and serve.

SCALOPPINE ALLA MARSALA
(VEAL MARSALA)

Many Italian American families and Italian American restaurants make veal or chicken Marsala with lots of mushrooms, and they serve it with pasta. In researching Marsala itself and the making of this unique Sicilian fortified wine, I read many, many recipes (almost all identical) for the preparation of veal Marsala, and not one of them had mushrooms in it. And also it seems that for decades, my family has been using far too little Marsala in our Marsala sauce. We hope this recipe redeems us. Serve with potatoes tossed with lemon and parsley and Garlicky Wilted Spinach (page 342). You can easily convert this dish to Chicken Marsala (see Variation).

8 (3- to 4-ounce) thinly sliced veal leg cutlets or scaloppine
1 cup flour
1 teaspoon ground sage
Salt and pepper
3 tablespoons olive oil
1 lemon, halved
1½ cups Marsala
3 tablespoons butter
¼ cup chopped fresh flat-leaf parsley

Preheat the oven to 175°F and place a platter in the oven to warm.

If the veal is thicker than ⅛ inch, pound it lightly to make it thinner. Place the flour in a shallow dish and season with the sage and salt and pepper.

In a large skillet, heat the oil (3 turns of the pan) over medium to medium-high heat.

Season the veal with salt and pepper on both sides. Working in two batches, dredge the veal in the seasoned flour, add to the pan, and cook until golden on each side, about 4 minutes total, turning once. Transfer the veal to the warm platter and cover loosely with foil. Repeat for the second batch.

Add the lemon halves, cut side down, to the drippings in the pan. Increase the heat and sear the lemon for 2 to 3 minutes to caramelize. Remove the lemon halves and set aside. Add the Marsala to the pan and cook at a rolling boil until reduced to ½ cup.

Squeeze the juice from the caramelized lemon over the veal. Swirl the butter into the sauce and remove from the heat. Pour the sauce over the veal and garnish with the parsley.

VARIATION

Chicken Marsala

Substitute 1½ pounds chicken breast medallions (breasts cut on an angle into thin circles or ovals) for the veal. The rest of the recipe is the same.

VEAL SALTIMBOCCA WITH MARSALA AND ASPARAGUS

SERVES 4

Saltimbocca means "jump in your mouth!" The dish is a salty marriage of ham and sage leaves. I always pair the meal with asparagus and add a light mushroom-Marsala sauce so it is a marriage of two classics, Saltimbocca and Veal alla Marsala. This dish is equally delicious made with chicken medallions if you prefer chicken to veal.

8 (3- to 4-ounce) veal leg cutlets or scaloppine
Salt and pepper
16 fresh sage leaves
8 slices prosciutto di Parma
Flour, for dredging
4 to 5 tablespoons olive oil
½ pound mixed mushrooms, sliced or chopped
1 large shallot, finely chopped
2 cloves garlic, finely chopped
1 cup Marsala
½ cup veal stock
3 tablespoons butter
1 pound asparagus
A handful of fresh flat-leaf parsley tops, chopped

Preheat the oven to 175°F and place a platter in the oven to warm.

If the veal is thicker than ⅛ inch, pound it lightly to make it thinner. Season with salt and pepper on both sides. Arrange 2 leaves of sage on each cutlet and wrap with prosciutto. Dredge the cutlets in flour and shake off the excess.

In a large skillet, heat 2 tablespoons of the oil (2 turns of the pan) over medium heat. Working in batches, add the cutlets and cook for 2 to 3 minutes on each side. Transfer the cooked cutlets to the warm platter and repeat with the remaining cutlets, adding another tablespoon of oil to the pan if necessary.

Add the remaining 2 tablespoons oil to the pan and brown the mushrooms, 7 to 8 minutes. Add the shallot and garlic and stir for a minute. Add the Marsala, stir to deglaze the pan, and cook until reduced by half. Add the stock and swirl the butter into it to thicken the sauce a bit.

Meanwhile, in a separate pan, bring a few inches of water to a boil. Salt the water, add the asparagus, and cook for 3 minutes. Drain.

Arrange one-quarter of the asparagus on each of four warm plates. Top each with 2 veal cutlets, then spoon the mushroom and Marsala sauce evenly over the veal and asparagus. Garnish with parsley.

VEAL AND PORCINI STEW

I love entertaining with stew because "the longer it sets, the better it gets," so I am motivated to make the meal ahead of time. This stew is easy yet elegant in flavor.

3 pounds veal shoulder

Salt and pepper

4 cups veal or chicken stock

1 cup loosely packed dried porcini mushrooms

Olive oil, for sautéing and coating

¼ pound pancetta, diced

3 large carrots: 1 chopped, 2 cut on an angle into 1- to 1½-inch pieces

2 ribs celery, chopped

1 large onion, chopped

8 cloves garlic: 4 sliced or chopped, 4 cracked and left in skins

4 tablespoons fresh rosemary leaves, chopped

2 fresh bay leaves

2 tablespoons tomato paste

1 cup dry vermouth

2 or 3 fat strips of lemon zest (from an organic lemon)

1 medium celery root, peeled and cut into 1- to 1½-inch pieces

2½ pounds potatoes, peeled and cut into 1- to 1½-inch chunks or wedges

Juice of 1 lemon

Fennel-Apple Slaw (page 328; optional)

Bring the meat to room temp and pat dry. Cut into 2-inch pieces. Just before cooking, season with salt and pepper.

Preheat the oven to 325°F.

In a small saucepan, heat 1 cup of water and 1 cup of the stock along with the mushrooms to soften, 10 to 15 minutes. Scoop out the mushrooms, reserving the soaking liquid in the pan.

In a large Dutch oven, heat 2 tablespoons of oil (2 turns of the pan) over medium-high heat. Add the pancetta and stir until crisp. Transfer to a plate. Working in batches of a few pieces at a time, add the meat to the hot oil and brown on all sides. Transfer to a plate. Add more oil between batches, if necessary.

Add the chopped carrot, celery, onion, sliced garlic, 2 tablespoons of the rosemary, and the bay leaves. Season with salt and pepper. Partially cover and cook, stirring occasionally, for 5 to 7 minutes. Add the tomato paste and stir for 1 minute. Stir in the vermouth and strips of lemon zest, stir to deglaze the pan, and cook to reduce the vermouth by half.

Add the reconstituted porcini and carefully pour in the mushroom soaking liquid, leaving the last few spoonfuls in the pan as grit may have settled there.

Return the meat and pancetta to the pot and add the remaining 3 cups stock. Bring to a bubble, cover, and transfer to the oven. Bake for 30 minutes. Add the celery root and carrots and bake for 1½ hours more. Remove the stew and increase the oven temperature to 450°F. Let the stew stand, covered, while you roast the potatoes.

Arrange the potatoes and whole garlic cloves on a rimmed baking sheet. Coat with olive oil and toss with the remaining 2 tablespoons rosemary and salt and pepper to taste. Roast until crispy, turning once, 30 to 35 minutes.

Stir the lemon juice into the stew. Fish out and discard the lemon zest strips and bay leaves. Serve the stew in shallow bowls topped with crispy potatoes and some Fennel-Apple Slaw, if desired.

Baked Devil's Chicken (page 289);
Aglio e Olio pasta (page 139);
and Roasted Broccoli (page 313).

CHAPTER 10

CHICKEN

Chicken is everyone's "go-to." No matter how many dozens, hundreds, or perhaps thousands of chicken recipes I have shared, taught, televised, etc., these remain the most frequent questions I'm asked: "What's your go-to chicken dish?" and "What's your favorite chicken dish?"

I was very discriminating with this section, including only favorites and familiar recipes for chicken that everyone associates with Italian food. There are a few surprises—inspired roast chickens especially.

My favorite? I won't tell . . . until you eat your way through the choices, too, and then we can compare.

ROAST CHICKEN IN THE STYLE OF PORCHETTA WITH ROAST LEMON, FENNEL, AND POTATOES

SERVES 4

"In the style of porchetta" means to prepare as porchetta, which is pork loin wrapped in pork belly with rosemary. Here, I finely chop prosciutto and pancetta and combine it with garlic, rosemary, and lemon zest to add a layer of flavor between the skin and meat of a whole chicken. I have my butcher spatchcock the chicken (remove the backbone), but for instructions on doing this yourself see the Basics box, below. Roasting a chicken that is spatchcocked cuts down on roasting time and makes it easier to carve.

3 organic lemons

½ pound prosciutto cotto (cooked ham), coarsely chopped

⅓ pound pancetta, finely diced

3 to 4 tablespoons fresh rosemary leaves, coarsely chopped, plus a few sprigs for roasting

4 large cloves garlic, grated, finely chopped, or very thinly sliced

2 teaspoons fennel seeds, or 1 teaspoon fennel seeds plus 1 teaspoon fennel pollen

1 whole chicken (4 to 5 pounds), spatchcocked (see box)

Olive oil, for liberal drizzling

Kosher salt and pepper

1 large bulb fennel, cut into 1½-inch wedges

4 medium-large potatoes, peeled and cut into wedges

1 large onion, cut into wedges

½ cup dry white wine or chicken stock

Position a rack in the center of the oven and preheat the oven to 350°F.

Grate 2 teaspoons zest from one of the lemons. Cut all the lemons in half and set aside.

In a food processor, combine the prosciutto, pancetta, rosemary leaves, and garlic and pulse into a fine chop. Pulse in the lemon zest and fennel seeds.

Loosen the skin of the chicken all over the breasts and legs. Spread the garlic-pork mixture in an even layer between the meat and skin. Drizzle the chicken liberally on both sides with oil and season on both sides with salt and pepper.

Brush a roasting pan with oil. Arrange the lemon halves, cut side down in the pan. In a bowl, toss the fennel, potatoes, and onion with oil and season with salt and pepper. Add to the roasting pan along with a few rosemary sprigs. Arrange the chicken on a rack over the vegetables or directly on top of the vegetables and roast for 30 minutes. Remove the chicken from the oven and increase the oven temperature to 450°F.

Add the wine to the roasting pan. Turn the vegetables, return the chicken to the oven, and roast for 30 minutes more. Remove from the oven and let rest for 10 to 15 minutes. Transfer the chicken to a cutting board and cut into 8 serving pieces. Squeeze the juice from the roasted lemons over the chicken. Serve with the roasted vegetables alongside.

BASICS

HOW TO SPATCHCOCK (OR BUTTERFLY) A CHICKEN

Spatchcocked or butterflied birds cook more quickly and evenly in the oven or on a grill or in a smoker. You can preorder a spatchcocked chicken from your butcher, but you can also do it yourself. First, remove the neck and giblets from the bird. Rinse the chicken and pat dry. Turn the chicken breast side down. With sharp kitchen shears, cut along each side of the backbone as close as you can to it. Pull out the backbone and reserve it for stock. Flip the chicken over, breast side up, and press down firmly on each side of the breastbone until you hear it crack. Snip the wing tips and save them for the stockpot.

ROAST CHICKEN
WITH CITRUS AND HERB BUTTER

This is my poultry option for Easter buffets for those who do not care for lamb. Its bright citrus flavor is a real crowd-pleaser, and any leftovers make a delicious chicken salad.

1 organic orange

1 organic lemon

4 ounces (1 stick) butter, softened

2 tablespoons Dijon mustard

4 cloves garlic, pasted or chopped

¼ cup chopped mixed fresh herbs: tarragon, rosemary, and thyme

Salt and pepper

1 whole chicken (4 to 5 pounds), spatchcocked (see box, page 286)

Olive oil

1 bulb fennel, trimmed and cut into wedges

4 russet (baking) potatoes, peeled and cut into wedges

1 onion, cut into wedges

3 sprigs fresh rosemary

½ cup dry white wine

Preheat the oven to 350°F.

Grate the zest from the orange and lemon into a bowl. (Set the fruit aside.) Add the butter, mustard, garlic, herbs, and salt and pepper to taste.

Loosen the skin of the chicken all over the breasts and legs. Spread the citrus-herb butter in an even layer between the meat and skin. Drizzle the chicken liberally with oil on both sides and season liberally with salt and pepper on both sides.

Brush a roasting pan with oil, halve the orange and the lemon, and arrange them cut side down in the pan. In a bowl, toss the fennel, potatoes, and onion with oil and season with salt and pepper. Add to the pan along with the rosemary sprigs. Arrange the chicken on a rack over the vegetables or directly on top of the vegetables and roast for 30 minutes. Remove the chicken from the oven and increase the oven temperature to 450°F.

Add the wine to the roasting pan. Turn the vegetables, return the chicken to the oven, and roast for 30 minutes more. Remove from the oven and let rest for 10 to 15 minutes. Transfer the chicken to a cutting board and cut into 8 serving pieces. Squeeze the juice from the roasted lemon and orange halves over the chicken. Serve with the roasted vegetables alongside.

RIDICULOUSLY EASY CHICKEN

1 whole chicken (4 to 5 pounds)
Kosher salt
Olive oil, for liberal drizzling
Pepper
2 heads garlic, tops cut off to expose the cloves
2 small onions, quartered
2 pounds baby potatoes
Fresh bay leaves
A few sprigs fresh rosemary
4 cups chicken stock
3 tablespoons butter
3 tablespoons flour

Salt the chicken liberally and refrigerate, uncovered, overnight.

Preheat the oven to 500°F.

Slather the chicken with oil and season with pepper. Oil a roasting pan and arrange the garlic, onions, potatoes, bay leaves, and rosemary in the pan. Drizzle with oil and season with salt and pepper. Add 1 cup of the stock to the pan.

Roast the chicken for 20 minutes. Turn off the oven but do not open the door. Let the chicken rest in the hot oven for 30 minutes.

Transfer the chicken to a cutting board and carve into 8 serving pieces. Arrange on a platter with the potatoes and onions. Scatter roasted rosemary leaves over the potatoes.

Squeeze the garlic from the skins and paste with your knife.

In a saucepan, melt the butter over medium heat. Season with some pepper. Whisk in the flour and cook for 1 minute. Whisk in the remaining 3 cups stock and cook a bit to form a loose gravy. Whisk in the pasted garlic.

Pass the garlic gravy at the table with the chicken and potatoes.

BAKED DEVIL'S CHICKEN

This is a crispy, spicy chicken that can be served hot, but much like traditional fried chicken, I think it's best at room temperature or cold the next day. This chicken is addictive and wonderful for picnics and potlucks. Serve it with a fresh Citrus Slaw (page 329).

1 cup Dijon mustard
2 tablespoons olive oil
2 large cloves garlic, grated, finely chopped, or pasted
1 tablespoon fresh thyme leaves, chopped
1 tablespoon fresh rosemary leaves, finely chopped
1½ cups fine dry bread crumbs
½ cup panko bread crumbs or homemade coarse bread crumbs
½ cup freshly grated Pecorino Romano cheese
2 teaspoons ground pepperoncini or crushed red pepper flakes
1 tablespoon paprika
½ teaspoon freshly grated nutmeg
4 tablespoons (½ stick) butter, melted
6 to 8 bone-in, skin-on chicken quarters (from 1½ or 2 small 2- to 3-pound chickens)
Salt and black pepper

Preheat the oven to 350°F. Place a cooling rack on a large rimmed baking sheet.

In a small bowl, stir the mustard, oil, garlic, thyme, and rosemary. In another small bowl, combine the fine bread crumbs, panko, pecorino, pepperoncini, paprika, nutmeg, and melted butter.

Season the chicken with salt and black pepper on both sides. Slather the chicken with the mustard mixture. Coat the chicken liberally with the bread crumb mixture, pressing the coating to adhere. Arrange the chicken on the rack in the baking sheet and bake until deeply crispy and golden and cooked through, about 2 hours.

LEMON AND BLACK PEPPER GRILLED CHICKEN WITH ROSEMARY

SERVES 4

This recipe is super easy and is based on a Roman dish of grilled chicken *alla diavola* (devil-style). The dish is "devilish" because of the amount of pepper used. I salt the chicken 1 to 2 days before I marinate and grill it, leaving it uncovered in the fridge on the lowest shelf. Salting it ensures a crispy skin and tender meat. Chicken that is spatchcocked (backbone removed) cooks in just 30 to 40 minutes on the grill.

1 whole chicken (3 to 4 pounds), spatchcocked (see box, page 286)

1 tablespoon fine sea salt or kosher salt

3 to 4 tablespoons fresh rosemary leaves

2 tablespoons black peppercorns, finely crushed (see Tip)

3 to 4 tablespoons good-quality olive oil

2½ organic lemons

2 cloves garlic, finely chopped

1 cup fresh flat-leaf parsley tops, chopped

Rub the chicken all over with the salt. Loosen the skin of the chicken all over the breasts and legs. Scatter the rosemary between the meat and skin. Place the chicken in an open container and refrigerate, uncovered, for 1 to 2 days.

Cover both sides of the chicken with the crushed peppercorns. Add the oil and juice of ½ lemon and coat evenly. Return the chicken to the fridge to marinate for 3 hours.

Grate the zest from 2 of the lemons. (Halve the lemons and set aside.) On a cutting board, combine the lemon zest, garlic, and parsley and chop everything together. Set the gremolata aside.

Heat a grill (preferably charcoal or wood fire) to medium-high heat.

Let the chicken come to room temperature.

Grill the chicken, turning occasionally, until the thickest part of the chicken reaches 160°F on a meat thermometer, 30 to 40 minutes. Grill the lemon halves, cut side down, for 4 minutes to caramelize.

Squeeze the juice from the charred lemons over the chicken. Cut the chicken into quarters with a cleaver and sprinkle with the gremolata.

TIP

Grind the peppercorns using a mortar and pestle or put them in a sturdy plastic bag and crush them with a mallet or a small heavy pan.

RED WINE ROAST CHICKEN THIGHS ON BREAD

This rustic meal is filling and simple, and can be made with rabbit as well.

8 bone-in, skinless chicken thighs
2 or 3 cloves garlic, smashed
A few sprigs fresh sage
A few sprigs fresh rosemary, plus
    2 tablespoons chopped fresh
    rosemary leaves
A few juniper berries (optional)
1 carrot, coarsely chopped
1 rib celery, coarsely chopped
1 onion, coarsely chopped
2 bay leaves
2 cups dry red wine
Salt and coarsely ground pepper
4 tablespoons olive oil
2 tablespoons butter
4 slices crusty peasant-style white
    bread
1 pound spinach or Swiss chard,
    stemmed and coarsely
    chopped
Freshly grated nutmeg

Place the chicken, garlic, sage, rosemary sprigs, juniper berries (if using), carrot, celery, onion, bay leaves, and wine in a shallow dish or zip-top bag. Cover or seal and marinate overnight in the refrigerator.

Preheat the oven to 400°F.

Pat the chicken dry. Strain the marinade into a bowl (discard the solids in the strainer).

Season the chicken with the chopped rosemary and salt and coarsely ground pepper. In a large, heavy ovenproof skillet, heat 1 tablespoon of the oil (1 turn of the pan) over medium-high heat. Add the chicken and brown for 3 to 4 minutes per side. Transfer to a plate.

Add 2 tablespoons of the oil (2 turns of the pan) to the skillet and melt in the butter. Brush the bread on both sides with the oil-butter mixture, add the bread to the pan, and brown the bread on one side. Flip the bread and top with the chicken, 2 thighs per slice of bread. Pour the strained marinade evenly over the chicken and bread. Place in the oven and roast for 20 minutes.

Meanwhile, in a second skillet, heat the remaining 1 tablespoon oil (1 turn of the pan) over medium-high heat. Wilt in the spinach and season with salt, pepper, and nutmeg.

Serve the chicken and bread with the wilted greens alongside.

CACCIATORE
(HUNTER-STYLE CHICKEN)

Regionally, this braised dish can be prepared with or without chile pepper. It can be made with rabbit or dark-meat chicken, and the add-in vegetables can vary. My favorite basic recipe is Marcella Hazan's from her *Essentials of Classic Italian Cooking*: chicken, onion, garlic, wine, tomatoes, salt, and pepper. Basic. Delicious.

Though I cannot improve on Marcella's, I do love this recipe, too. I use earthy mushrooms (meaty cremini or portobello) plus reconstituted porcini and their rich broth. As with many Italian American versions of the classic, the dish includes sweet bell peppers, but I roast them first for a smoky flavor. Serve with charred bread (toasted, rubbed with garlic, drizzled with olive oil, and sprinkled with flaky sea salt) to mop up the sauce. Or serve with pasta alongside or as a first course (see Tip).

2 cups chicken stock

A fat handful of dried porcini mushroom slices

12 bone-in, skin-on chicken thighs

Salt and black pepper

Flour, for dredging

2 tablespoons olive oil

½ pound cremini or portobello mushrooms, trimmed and sliced

1 large onion, chopped

3 or 4 large cloves garlic (to taste), sliced or chopped

1 teaspoon crushed red pepper flakes

1 cup dry white wine

2 (28- to 32-ounce) cans San Marzano tomatoes (look for DOP on the label)

1 large red bell pepper, roasted (see box, page 334) and chopped (optional)

A few fresh basil leaves, torn

A handful of fresh flat-leaf parsley tops, finely chopped

In a small saucepan, heat the stock along with the porcini to soften, 10 to 15 minutes. Scoop out the mushrooms and chop them, reserving the soaking liquid in the pan.

Season the chicken with salt and black pepper on both sides and dredge lightly in flour.

In a large Dutch oven, heat the oil (2 turns of the pan) over medium-high heat. Working in two batches, add the chicken and brown until crispy on both sides. Transfer the chicken to a plate.

To the pan drippings, add the cremini and cook until browned. Add the onion, garlic, and red pepper flakes and stir to soften, 5 to 6 minutes. Add the wine, stir to deglaze the pan, and cook to reduce by half. Hand-crush the tomatoes as you add them to the pan, then add the juices from the cans. Add the roasted pepper (if using), basil, and chopped reconstituted porcini. Carefully pour in the mushroom soaking liquid, leaving the last few spoonfuls in the pan as grit may have settled there. Cook the sauce at a gentle bubble for 20 to 30 minutes to thicken a bit.

Return the chicken to the pan and simmer until the chicken is cooked through, 20 to 30 minutes. Transfer the chicken to a warm serving platter and cover with half the sauce. Garnish with the parsley. Pass extra sauce at the table.

I LIKE TO SERVE cacciatore with hearty whole wheat or farro spaghetti. Cook 1 pound pasta in boiling salted water and reserve 1 cup of the starchy cooking water before you drain it. Then toss the drained pasta with 2 tablespoons butter, half the cacciatore sauce, lots of grated pecorino cheese, and the starchy water. To serve the pasta as a first course, just cover the chicken with foil and keep it warm in a low oven.

CRISPY-SKIN CHICKEN BREASTS WITH ESCAROLE AND WHITE BEANS

SERVES 4

This chicken has the crispiest skin—like a potato chip. It is the most delicious chicken breast you can make in 20 minutes' time. This method of cooking, by weighting the chicken, is called "chicken under a brick," but a skillet with weights in it is easier to manage than bricks. Serve with crusty bread, for mopping.

Scratch Beans (page 75) made with cannellini (see Tip)

4 large cloves garlic, thinly sliced

2 tablespoons fresh rosemary leaves, chopped

2 tablespoons fresh thyme leaves, chopped

4 pieces boneless, skin-on chicken breast

Salt and black pepper

2 tablespoons olive oil

½ cup dry white wine

1 onion, chopped

½ teaspoon crushed red pepper flakes

1 large head escarole, cored and coarsely chopped

Freshly grated nutmeg

½ cup chicken stock

1 lemon, halved

Cook the beans, then drain and discard the rosemary, onion, and bay leaf.

Preheat the oven to 175°F and place a platter in the oven to warm.

In a small bowl, combine half the garlic and all the rosemary and thyme. Loosen the skin of the chicken and rub the mixture in an even layer between the meat and skin. Pull the skin back into place. Season with salt and black pepper.

Place 1 tablespoon of the oil (1 turn of the pan) in a large cast-iron skillet (not on the heat). Place the chicken, skin side down, in the cold pan and place another heavy skillet or a skillet with something heavy in it on top of the chicken. Turn the heat under the skillet to medium-high and cook for 12 minutes. Flip the chicken, replace the weight, and cook for 6 minutes more.

Transfer the chicken to the warmed platter. Add the wine to the pan and stir to deglaze the pan, and pour the pan juices onto the platter.

Add the remaining 1 table-spoon oil (1 turn of the pan) to the skillet, reduce the heat a bit, and add the onion and remaining garlic. Stir to soften, 7 to 8 minutes. Stir in the red pepper flakes. Wilt in the escarole and season with salt, black pepper, and nutmeg. Add the stock and beans and simmer for a few minutes, then squeeze the lemon halves over the mixture.

Serve the beans and greens in shallow bowls and top with the crispy chicken.

TIP

For a quick supper, use a 15-ounce can of cannellini beans, rinsed and drained.

CHICKEN IN CARTOCCIO WITH GREEN BEANS AND CHERRY TOMATOES

SERVES 4

Chicken *in cartoccio* in Italian means in parchment, or "chicken in a sack," as our family calls it. I love serving chicken or fish in cartoccio when entertaining (a good thing, as my mother often requests it for her birthday celebrations).

4 boneless, skinless chicken breasts
Salt and pepper
1 pint cherry or grape tomatoes, halved
¾ pound haricots verts
3 large shallots, thinly sliced
3 cloves garlic, thinly sliced
3 tablespoons olive oil
3 tablespoons fresh tarragon leaves
½ cup dry white wine
4 slices lemon
4 tablespoons (½ stick) butter
2 tablespoons chopped fresh flat-leaf parsley

Preheat the oven to 400°F.

Lightly pound the chicken breasts and season both sides with salt and pepper.

In a bowl, toss together the tomatoes, haricots verts, shallots, garlic, oil, tarragon, and salt and pepper to taste.

Cut four 12 x 16-inch pieces of parchment paper (see Tip, page 209). Arrange one-quarter of the bean mixture in the center of each piece of parchment. Add 2 tablespoons of the wine to each. Top with a chicken breast, lemon slice, 1 tablespoon butter, and some parsley. Bring the short ends of the parchment up to meet in the middle and fold over 1 inch, then fold down a few more turns (leave a little headroom for the steam). Fold in the ends to make half-moon-shaped packets (pouches).

Place the packets on a baking sheet and roast for 25 to 30 minutes.

Serve each person a pouch and make sure they are mindful that the pouches will release hot steam. Have them slide the contents away from the paper in a swift motion, like pulling out a tablecloth in a magic act. Place a bowl on the table to collect the papers.

CHICKEN IN CARTOCCIO WITH FENNEL, POTATO, AND ASPARAGUS

SERVES 4

The variations for chicken in a paper packet are endless. Here is a popular variation of my Chicken in Cartoccio with Green Beans and Cherry Tomatoes (page 295).

4 boneless, skinless chicken breasts
Salt and pepper
3 to 4 bulbs baby fennel, very thinly sliced on an angle, plus a handful of fronds, chopped
12 baby white or yellow potatoes, very thinly sliced
½ pint cherry tomatoes, halved
3 large shallots, thinly sliced
3 cloves garlic, thinly sliced
3 tablespoons EVOO
3 tablespoons fresh tarragon leaves
½ cup dry white wine
4 slices lemon
4 tablespoons (½ stick) butter
2 tablespoons chopped fresh flat-leaf parsley

Preheat the oven to 400°F.

Lightly pound the chicken breasts and season both sides with salt and pepper.

In a bowl, toss together the fennel, potatoes, tomatoes, shallots, garlic, EVOO, fennel fronds, tarragon, and salt and pepper to taste.

Cut four 12 x 16-inch pieces of parchment paper (see Tip, page 209). Arrange one-quarter of the fennel-potato mixture in the center of each piece of parchment. Add 2 tablespoons of the wine to each. Top with a chicken breast, lemon slice, 1 tablespoon of the butter, and some parsley. Bring the short ends of the parchment up to meet in the middle and fold over 1 inch, then fold down a few more turns (leave a little headroom for the steam). Fold in the ends to make half-moon-shaped packets (pouches).

Place the packets on a baking sheet and roast for 25 to 30 minutes.

Serve each person a pouch and make sure they are mindful that the pouches will release hot steam. Have them slide the contents away from the paper in a swift motion, like pulling out a tablecloth in a magic act. Place a bowl on the table to collect the papers.

BASICS

MAKING CHICKEN CUTLETS AND MEDALLIONS

■ **Cutlets:** To make cutlets, start with a 6- to 8-ounce piece of boneless, skinless chicken breast. If the breast came with the finger-size portion of rib meat attached, remove it and save it for stock. Place the chicken breast bone side down vertically on a cutting board. Have the rounded thicker side of the breast facing your knife blade (on the right if right-handed, left if left-handed). Cut horizontally into the breast meat and head toward the opposite side, but do not go all the way through. Open the chicken up like a book. Place the meat between sheets of plastic wrap and gently pound the meat with a meat pounder or mallet to a ⅛- to ¼-inch thickness. If you're going to store the cutlet for future use, simply pound the meat right in a zip-top plastic freezer bag. This will help prevent tears in the meat. Store the cutlets individually in the bags, pressing all of the air out. Freezing them individually allows for quick thawing time and portion control.

■ **Medallions:** Chicken medallions are typically used in chicken piccata, Francese, or Marsala. To make medallions, cut boneless, skinless chicken breasts on an angle, starting at the fuller top of the breast, into ½- to ¾-inch-thick slices. Carefully pound the pieces with a meat pounder or mallet into 3- to 4-inch rounds.

CHICKEN PAILLARD, PIZZETTE-STYLE

This is a high-protein, gluten-free alternative to pizza, best served as a light lunch, brunch, or early supper. It's delicious, nutritious, and may be even better than a Margherita pizza. I love this dish.

4 boneless, skinless chicken breasts (6 to 8 ounces each)
1 tablespoon olive oil, plus more for drizzling
Salt and black pepper
1 teaspoon granulated garlic
1 teaspoon granulated onion
1 teaspoon fennel seeds
½ teaspoon crushed red pepper flakes
2 tablespoons fresh thyme leaves, chopped
2 cloves garlic, thinly sliced
1½ pints grape or cherry tomatoes, halved
A fat handful of fresh basil leaves
1 pound fresh mozzarella cheese, very thinly sliced or shredded on the large holes of a box grater
Arugula or baby kale, for garnish

Butterfly and pound the chicken breasts into cutlets (see box, page 296).

In a shallow dish, drizzle the chicken with oil and season with salt, black pepper, granulated garlic, onion, fennel seeds, red pepper flakes, and thyme. Let marinate while you make the sauce.

In a large skillet with a lid, heat the oil (1 turn of the pan) over medium-high heat. Add the sliced garlic and stir for a minute. Add the tomatoes, season with salt, cover, and cook to soften the tomatoes, shaking the pan occasionally, 8 to 10 minutes. Wilt in the basil.

Preheat the broiler. Heat a large griddle pan or grill pan over medium-high heat.

Cook the chicken on the griddle pan for a few minutes on each side, then transfer to baking sheets. Treating the chicken like a small pizza crust, spread with sauce and top with mozzarella. Broil to brown and melt the cheese.

Serve topped with arugula or baby kale.

CHICKEN PARMIGIANA

Need I say more? This dish is simply a universal favorite. If you'd like, serve with pasta as a first course or as a side dish (see Tip).

4 boneless, skinless chicken breasts (6 to 8 ounces each)
Salt and pepper
Flour, for dredging
2 large free-range organic eggs
½ cup fine dry bread crumbs
1 cup panko bread crumbs
½ cup freshly grated Parmigiano-Reggiano cheese, plus more for serving
1 tablespoon finely chopped fresh flat-leaf parsley
Leaves from 1 sprig fresh rosemary, finely chopped
1 tablespoon minced fresh thyme
1 teaspoon granulated onion
1 teaspoon granulated garlic
2 teaspoons grated lemon zest (from an organic lemon)
Olive or canola oil, for frying
2 cups Pomodoro Sauce (page 121)
4 fresh basil leaves

Butterfly and pound the chicken breasts into cutlets (see box, page 296). Season the cutlets with salt and pepper on each side.

Preheat the oven to 200°F. Place a cooling rack on a baking sheet to keep the cutlets warm while preparing them in batches.

Set up a breading station: Line up 3 shallow bowls on the counter. Spread the flour in one, beat the eggs in the second, and mix the bread crumbs, panko, Parm, parsley, rosemary, thyme, onion, garlic, and lemon zest in the third.

In a large skillet, heat ⅛ to ¼ inch of oil over medium to medium-high heat. Coat the chicken in the flour and shake off the excess, then coat in the egg and drain the excess, and finally coat evenly in the crumb mixture. Working in batches, shallow-fry the cutlets on each side until deep golden. Keep warm in the oven while you fry the remaining cutlets.

In a small saucepan, heat the pomodoro sauce.

To serve, place a cutlet on a plate and top with a ladle of sauce. Grate a little Parm over the top and garnish with a basil leaf.

IF SERVING WITH pasta, make the full recipe of Pomodoro Sauce so you have enough to toss with the pasta. Cook 1 pound thin linguine. Drain and toss with half the red sauce. Serve topped with more sauce and some Parm.

CHICKEN MILANESE

SERVES 4

This crispy, breaded piece of meat is the most basic of dishes, and so incredibly satisfying. Serve simply with a wedge of lemon or choose the more traditional raw sauce (see box, page 299). I also enjoy a crispy shaved fennel slaw with warm Milanese for a balance of texture. I use coarse homemade bread crumbs combined with fine bread crumbs and grated cheese for an extra crispy coating.

4 boneless, skinless chicken breasts (6 to 8 ounces each)
Salt and pepper
Flour, for dredging
3 large free-range organic eggs, beaten
1 cup fine dry bread crumbs
½ cup panko bread crumbs or homemade coarse bread crumbs
½ cup finely grated Parmigiano-Reggiano cheese
Freshly grated nutmeg
Olive or canola oil, for shallow-frying
2 lemons or Meyer lemons, halved and caramelized (see Tip) or cut into wedges
Toppings (page 299)

Butterfly and pound the chicken breasts into cutlets (see box, page 296). Season the cutlets with salt and pepper on each side.

Preheat the oven to 250°F. Place a cooling rack on a baking sheet to keep the cutlets warm while preparing them in batches.

Set up a breading station: Line up 3 shallow bowls on the counter. Spread the flour out in one, beat the eggs in the second and season with salt and pepper. In the third, mix the fine bread crumbs, panko, Parm, and a few grates of nutmeg.

In a large skillet, heat ⅛ to ¼ inch of oil over medium to medium-high heat. Coat the chicken in the flour and shake off the excess, then coat in the egg and drain the excess, and finally coat evenly in the crumb mixture. Working in batches of 1 or 2 at a time, shallow-fry the cutlets on each side until deep golden. Keep warm in the oven while you fry the remaining cutlets.

Serve the chicken with caramelized lemon or lemon wedges for squeezing and topping of choice.

TIP

Brown the halved lemons, cut side down, in a small skillet to caramelize their sugars and get the juices to flow.

TOPPINGS FOR MILANESE

You can, of course, serve a Milanese with nothing more than a squeeze of lemon, but the contrast of a fresh, crisp salad or raw sauce with the hot crispy-coated cutlet (beef, chicken, or veal) of a Milanese can't be beat. In addition to the topping recipes below, check these out to top your Milanese: Arugula Salad with Sage and White Balsamic Vinaigrette (page 25); Orange and Arugula Salad (page 26); Corn, Tomato, and Tarragon Raw Sauce (page 264); Fennel-Apple Slaw (page 328).

Tomato-Parsley Raw Sauce
SERVES 4

3 plum or vine tomatoes,
   seeded and chopped
½ cup fresh flat-leaf parsley
   tops, finely chopped
½ small red or white onion,
   finely chopped
1 clove garlic, pasted

1 tablespoon EVOO
Salt and pepper

In a bowl, combine all the ingredients and let stand for 10 minutes. Stir again and serve.

Tomato, Basil, and Bitter Greens Raw Sauce
SERVES 4

2 cups wild or baby arugula or
   baby kale leaves
½ cup fresh basil leaves
2 small cloves garlic, grated or
   pasted
Juice of 1 lemon
Salt and pepper
⅓ cup EVOO
3 cups chopped seeded vine
   tomatoes (4 or 5 tomatoes)
½ medium red onion, finely
   chopped

In a food processor, combine the arugula, basil, garlic, lemon juice, salt, and pepper. Pulse-chop, then, with the machine running, stream in the EVOO to form a pestolike sauce.
   In a bowl, toss together the tomatoes, onion, and sauce.

Greens and Cherry Tomato Raw Sauce
SERVES 4

1 pint cherry tomatoes,
   quartered
3 cups baby arugula or baby
   kale leaves
Juice of ½ lemon
2 tablespoons EVOO

Salt
¼ to ½ cup shaved Parmigiano-
   Reggiano cheese

In a bowl, toss together the tomatoes and greens. Dress with the lemon juice, EVOO, and a sprinkle of salt. Toss in the Parm.

Pecorino and Lacinato
SERVES 4

Juice of 1 lemon
1 clove garlic, pasted
1 small bunch lacinato kale
   (also called black, Tuscan, or
   dinosaur kale), stemmed and
   shredded
¼ red onion, very thinly sliced
Salt and pepper
Freshly grated nutmeg
2 tablespoons olive oil
¼ to ½ cup shaved pecorino
   cheese

In a bowl, whisk the lemon juice and garlic. Add the kale and onion and season with salt, pepper, and a little nutmeg. Dress with the oil. Add the shaved cheese and serve.

NUTTY CHICKEN CUTLETS WITH ORANGE AND ARUGULA SALAD

This is a twist on Chicken Milanese (page 298). I always make this dish with whole wheat bread crumbs, as their nutty flavor blends better with the actual toasted nuts in the coating and because they offer a bit more nutritional value. I also love surprising friends who are gluten-free with this dish by coating the cutlets with rice flour and homemade gluten-free panko. Regardless, I always make this when blood oranges are in season, as it is the salad with its peppery, sweet, citrus surprise that makes the meal so memorable.

4 boneless, skinless chicken breasts (6 to 8 ounces each)
Salt and pepper
½ cup skinned hazelnuts, almonds, Marcona almonds, or pignoli (pine nuts), toasted
Flour, for dredging
2 large free-range organic eggs
½ cup fine dry bread crumbs
1 cup panko bread crumbs or homemade coarse whole wheat bread crumbs
A handful of fresh flat-leaf parsley tops, finely chopped
2 tablespoons finely chopped fresh thyme leaves
1 tablespoon grated lemon zest (from an organic lemon)
1 tablespoon grated orange zest (from an organic orange)

A handful of freshly grated Parmigiano-Reggiano cheese
Olive or canola oil, for shallow-frying
4 lemon wedges, for squeezing
Orange and Arugula Salad (page 26), made with blood oranges

Butterfly and pound the chicken breasts into cutlets (see box, page 296). Season the cutlets with salt and pepper on each side.

Preheat the oven to 250°F. Place a cooling rack on a baking sheet to keep the cutlets warm while preparing them in batches.

Pulse the toasted nuts in a food processor until finely ground but not oily.

Set up a breading station: Line up 3 shallow bowls on the counter. Spread the flour out in one, beat the eggs in the second. In the third, mix the nuts, fine bread crumbs, panko, parsley, thyme, lemon zest, orange zest, and Parm.

In a large skillet, heat ⅛ to ¼ inch of oil over medium to medium-high heat. Coat the chicken in the flour and shake off the excess, then coat in the egg and drain the excess, and finally coat evenly in the bread crumb mixture. Working in batches of 1 or 2 at a time, shallow-fry the cutlets on each side until deep golden. Keep warm in the oven while you fry the remaining cutlets.

Serve the cutlets with lemon wedges and the salad.

GRILLED LEMON-ORANGE CHICKEN

SERVES 4

The effect of letting quick-grilled meat stand with lots of acid on it is that of quick-pickling it. The result is tender, tangy, and unique. Here, the juice of grilled lemons and a blood orange permeates the medallions of white-meat chicken. Served on a bed of roasted garlic–rosemary rice, it's delicious hot, room temp, or cold.

½ recipe Rosemary and Roasted Garlic Wild Rice Blend (page 183)

1½ pounds boneless, skinless chicken breasts

2 tablespoons olive oil, plus more for drizzling

Seasoning blend of choice (see Tip)

Salt and pepper

2 lemons, halved

1 blood orange or navel orange, halved

1 small red onion, cut into 6 slices

6 (4- to 6-inch) skewers, soaked in water

A few handfuls of baby kale or baby arugula, for garnish

Make the rice and keep warm.

Heat a grill or grill pan to medium-high heat.

Slice and pound the chicken into medallions (see box, page 296). Dress the medallions with the 2 tablespoons oil and season with the seasoning blend of your choice.

Grill the chicken for about 2 minutes on each side and transfer to a platter. Grill the citrus, cut side down, until charred and well marked, about 4 minutes. Douse the chicken with the juices from the grilled citrus and let stand for at least 15 minutes and up to 1 hour.

Drizzle oil over the onions and season with salt and pepper. Run the skewers horizontally through the onion slices to hold all the rings in place. Grill the onions until marked and tender, 7 to 8 minutes.

Make a bed of the rice in shallow bowls. Top with grilled onion rings and chicken medallions and a few leaves of arugula or baby kale.

I USE MY OWN Italian seasoning (Rachael Ray Buon Appetito! Seasoning) or my everyday seasoning (Rachael Ray 24/7 Seasoning), but you can use a combo of ½ teaspoon crushed red pepper flakes and salt and black pepper to taste. Or swap in your favorite seasoning blend.

GRILLED ROSEMARY CHICKEN MELTS

SERVES 4

This is a tasty sammy for lunch or brunch. We usually make these with store-bought focaccia for a quick meal. John grills the chicken outside and I press the sandwiches in a panini press. It's like a no-cook, no-heat-in-the-kitchen meal, perfect for summertime.

4 boneless, skinless chicken breasts

1 large clove garlic, grated

Leaves from 2 sprigs fresh rosemary, finely chopped

1 teaspoon fennel seeds

½ teaspoon crushed red pepper flakes

3 tablespoons EVOO, plus more for drizzling

Salt and black pepper

2 lemons, halved

4 handfuls of baby kale or arugula

1 small bulb fennel, very thinly sliced on a mandoline, a box grater, or with a sharp knife

1 small red onion, very thinly sliced

4 (5-inch) squares focaccia or ciabatta, halved horizontally

8 thickish slices provolone cheese

Butterfly and pound the chicken breasts into cutlets (see box, page 296).

In a shallow dish, combine the garlic, rosemary, fennel seeds, red pepper flakes, and 3 tablespoons EVOO. Season with salt and black pepper. Add the chicken and turn to coat.

Heat a grill or grill pan to medium-high heat. Heat a sandwich/panini press to high (see Tip).

Grill the chicken until cooked through, turning occasionally, 7 to 8 minutes. Grill the lemons, cut side down, until caramelized.

In a bowl, combine the kale, sliced fennel, and onion. Squeeze in the lemon juice and dress with EVOO (about 1 tablespoon). Season with salt and black pepper.

Build sandwiches: bread bottom, a slice of cheese, salad, chicken, salad, another slice of cheese, bread top. Press or grill the sandwiches to mark and crisp the bread and melt the cheese. Cut corner to corner to serve.

IF YOU DO NOT have an electric sandwich press, wrap a brick or heavy pan in foil and use it to weight and press the sandwiches on the grill.

CHICKEN PICCATA WITH PROSCIUTTO-WRAPPED ASPARAGUS

SERVES 4

1½ pounds boneless, skinless chicken breasts

Salt and pepper

Flour, for dredging

2 tablespoons butter, cut into 1-tablespoon slices

4 tablespoons olive oil

2 organic lemons: 1 sliced, 1 juiced

3 cloves garlic, finely chopped

¼ cup capers, drained

½ cup dry white wine

½ cup chicken stock

¼ cup fresh flat-leaf parsley tops, finely chopped

Prosciutto-Wrapped Asparagus Bundles (see box)

Preheat the oven to 175°F and place a platter in the oven to get warm.

Slice and pound the chicken into medallions (see box, page 296). Season the medallions on both sides with salt and pepper.

Place the flour in a shallow bowl. Dredge the butter in the flour and set the butter aside.

In a large nonstick skillet, heat 2 tablespoons of the oil (2 turns of the pan) over medium to medium-high heat. Dredge half the chicken lightly in the flour. Add the chicken to the pan and cook to light golden, 2 to 3 minutes on each side. Transfer to the warm platter while you cook the second batch. Repeat with the remaining chicken and oil.

Add the sliced lemon to the pan and cook to caramelize. Add the garlic and capers and stir for 1 minute. Add the wine and cook until reduced by half. Add the stock and flour-coated butter and swirl to combine and thicken. Add the lemon juice and parsley.

Arrange the medallions and 1 asparagus bundle on each dinner plate and spoon the sauce and lemons over the chicken.

PROSCIUTTO-WRAPPED ASPARAGUS BUNDLES

SERVES 4

Salt

1 bunch asparagus

EVOO, for drizzling

2 tablespoons chopped fresh tarragon

1 tablespoon grated lemon zest (from an organic lemon)

Pepper

8 slices prosciutto di Parma

In a shallow pan, bring 1 inch of water to a simmer. Salt the water, add the asparagus, and blanch for 3 minutes. Drain. Drizzle the spears lightly with EVOO and toss with the tarragon, lemon zest, and pepper to taste.

Divide the asparagus into 4 bundles. Wrap each bundle with 2 slices of overlapped prosciutto, exposing the tips and ends a bit.

Drizzle some EVOO into a large nonstick skillet and heat over medium-high heat. Add the asparagus bundles and brown and crisp the prosciutto evenly all over.

CHICKEN FRANCESE
WITH TRICOLOR SALAD

1½ pounds boneless, skinless
    chicken breasts
Salt and pepper
1 cup flour
1 teaspoon granulated garlic
3 tablespoons butter, cut into
    1-tablespoon slices
3 large free-range organic eggs
½ cup freshly grated Parmigiano-
    Reggiano cheese
Juice of ½ lemon
4 tablespoons olive oil
1 lemon, thinly sliced
½ cup dry white wine
½ cup chicken stock
Tri-Color Salad (see box)

Preheat the oven to 175°F and place a platter in the oven to get warm.

Slice and pound the chicken into medallions (see box, page 296). Season the chicken with salt and pepper on both sides.

In a shallow bowl, combine the flour with the garlic. Roll the butter slices in the flour and set aside.

In a second shallow bowl, beat the eggs with the Parm and lemon juice.

In a large nonstick skillet, heat 2 tablespoons of the oil (2 turns of the pan) over medium to medium-high heat. Dredge half the medallions in the flour, then coat in the egg mixture. Add to the hot pan and sauté until deep golden, 2 to 3 minutes on each side. Transfer the browned chicken to the warm platter while you cook the second batch. Repeat with the remaining medallions and oil.

Add the lemon slices to the pan and cook to caramelize on one side, then flip and add the wine to the pan and cook until reduced to a few tablespoons. Pour in the stock and bring to a bubble. Add the flour-coated butter and swirl in the pan to form a sauce, then cook to reduce and thicken a bit.

Pour the hot sauce over the chicken and serve with the salad.

TRICOLOR SALAD

2 tablespoons grated shallot
Salt and pepper
2 teaspoons Dijon mustard
Juice of ½ lemon
1 tablespoon white balsamic or white wine vinegar
3 tablespoons olive oil
½ cup fresh flat-leaf parsley tops, chopped
¼ cup fresh tarragon leaves
5 to 6 cups tricolor salad mix: baby romaine or baby arugula,
    shredded endive, and radicchio

In a large bowl, season the shallot with salt and pepper and let stand to bleed out for a few minutes. Stir in the mustard, lemon juice, and vinegar. Whisk in the oil and adjust the seasonings. Add the parsley, tarragon, and tricolor salad mix to the bowl with the dressing and toss to combine.

CHICKEN FRANCESE WITH GRAPEFRUIT AND TARRAGON

SERVES 4

This is a sweet and tangy take on chicken Francese. I love grapefruit, and this is a different way to enjoy it.

4 boneless, skinless chicken breasts (6 to 8 ounces each)
Salt and pepper
½ cup flour
3 large free-range organic eggs
1 tablespoon fresh lemon juice
4 tablespoons olive oil
¼ cup chicken stock
½ cup fruity white wine
2 tablespoons butter
2 tablespoons chopped fresh tarragon
2 tablespoons finely chopped fresh chives
2 ruby red grapefruits, supremed (see box, page 221)

Preheat the oven to 175°F and place a platter in the oven to get warm.

Cut the chicken into medallions or butterfly and pound into cutlets (see box, page 296). Season the chicken with salt and pepper on both sides.

Place the flour in a shallow dish. Whisk the eggs with the lemon juice in a second shallow bowl.

In a large nonstick skillet, heat 2 tablespoons of the oil (2 turns of the pan) over medium to medium-high heat. Dredge half the chicken in the flour, then turn in the egg. Sauté until golden, puffed, and cooked through, about 3 minutes on each side. Transfer to the warm platter while you cook the second batch. Repeat with the remaining chicken and oil.

Add the stock to the skillet and heat through for a minute. Add the wine and reduce for a minute. Melt in the butter and remove from the heat. Stir in the tarragon, chives, and grapefruit. Pour the sauce over the chicken and serve.

SPINACH-RICOTTA STUFFED CHICKEN TIED IN SPECK

SERVES 6

Stuffed anything is so exciting. Stuffed chicken breasts are especially enticing since chicken breasts on their own can be bland and dry. This meal is good for weeknight entertaining. Make the stuffing a day ahead, if you like. Serve rice or potatoes alongside.

6 boneless, skinless chicken breasts (6 to 8 ounces each)
Salt and pepper
1 (10-ounce) box frozen chopped spinach, thawed and wrung dry in a kitchen towel
1 cup fresh cow or sheep's milk ricotta cheese, homemade (see box, page 40) or store-bought
1 large free-range organic egg yolk, beaten
3 to 4 tablespoons walnuts, toasted, cooled, and chopped
¾ cup freshly grated Parmigiano-Reggiano cheese
Freshly grated nutmeg
2 tablespoons olive oil, plus more for drizzling
12 slices speck (smoky ham)
Lemon wedges, for serving

Preheat the oven to 350°F.

Butterfly and pound the chicken breasts into cutlets (see box, page 296). Season the inside of the meat with salt and pepper.

Separate the spinach with your fingertips as you drop it into a bowl. Add the ricotta, egg yolk, walnuts, Parm, and salt, pepper, and nutmeg to taste and stir to combine.

Cover one half of each cutlet with a few tablespoons of the ricotta mixture. Flip the breast over, drizzle with a little oil, and season lightly with salt and pepper. Wrap each piece of stuffed chicken with 2 slices of speck.

In a large skillet, heat the oil (2 turns of the pan) over medium-high heat. Add the chicken and brown for 3 to 4 minutes on each side. (If necessary, work in batches, using more oil for each batch.) Transfer the chicken to a baking sheet and bake for 15 minutes to finish cooking through.

Slice the stuffed chicken on an angle and fan it out on warm dinner plates. Serve with lemon wedges.

PULLED CHICKEN PILAF WITH ZAFFERANO (SAFFRON)

===== SERVES 6 =====

Chicken and rice are basic staples, the go-to dinner. Start by poaching a whole chicken. That way you'll have the benefit of the stock as well as plenty of meat to work with (though you can also use any leftover chicken or rotisserie chicken). Try this saffron-scented pilaf with golden raisins.

5 cups chicken stock, homemade (page 64) or store-bought
A fat pinch of saffron threads
4 tablespoons (½ stick) butter
¼ pound thin linguine, broken into 2-inch pieces
2 tablespoons olive oil
1 small onion, finely chopped
4 cloves garlic, finely chopped
1½ cups long-grain white rice
2 tablespoons fresh thyme leaves, finely chopped
3 tablespoons golden raisins or currants
Salt and pepper
4 cups pulled cooked chicken, from chicken stock (page 64) or store-bought rotisserie chicken
1 cup shelled fresh peas
½ cup sliced almonds or pignoli (pine nuts), toasted
1 tablespoon grated lemon or orange zest (from organic citrus)
¼ cup fresh flat-leaf parsley tops, chopped

In a medium saucepan, heat the stock with the saffron to infuse the stock.

In a deep large skillet with a lid, melt the butter over medium heat. When it foams, add the pasta and stir to toast until deep golden. Transfer to a plate.

Add the oil (2 turns of the pan) to the skillet, then add the onion and garlic and stir to soften, 3 to 5 minutes. Add the rice and stir for 1 minute. Add the thyme, raisins, and salt and pepper to taste. Add the remaining 4½ cups stock and return the pasta to the pan. Bring to a boil, reduce the heat to low, cover, and simmer for 15 minutes.

Stir in the chicken and peas, cover, and cook for 3 minutes more. Turn off the heat and let stand, covered, for 5 minutes. Add the almonds, citrus zest, and parsley and fluff with a fork.

PULLED CHICKEN PILAF WITH SPINACH AND GARLIC

===== SERVES 6 =====

This is ideally made with home-poached chicken, which also yields the stock you need. If you are crunched for time, use rotisserie chicken and store-bought stock in a box.

5 cups chicken stock, homemade (page 64) or store-bought
A fat pinch of saffron threads
2 cups packed baby spinach
1 cup packed fresh flat-leaf parsley
Grated zest and juice of 1 organic lemon
Salt and pepper
4 tablespoons (½ stick) butter
¼ pound thin linguine, broken into 2-inch pieces
2 tablespoons EVOO
3 large shallots, finely chopped
4 cloves garlic, finely chopped
1½ cups long-grain white rice
4 cups pulled cooked chicken from chicken stock (page 64) or store-bought rotisserie chicken
Freshly grated nutmeg
½ cup sliced almonds or pignoli (pine nuts), toasted

In a medium saucepan, heat the stock with the saffron to infuse the stock.

In a food processor, combine ½ cup of the stock, the spinach, parsley, lemon zest, lemon juice, and salt and pepper to taste and puree. Set the spinach puree aside.

In a deep large skillet with a lid, melt the butter over medium heat. When it foams, add the pasta and stir to toast until deep golden. Transfer to a plate.

Add the EVOO (2 turns of the pan) to the skillet, then add the shallots and garlic and stir to soften, 3 to 5 minutes. Add the rice and stir for 1 minute. Season with salt and pepper. Add the remaining 4½ cups saffron stock and return the pasta to the pan. Bring to a boil, reduce the heat to low, cover, and simmer for 15 minutes.

Stir in the chicken, spinach puree, and a little nutmeg. Cover and cook for 3 minutes more. Turn off the heat and let stand, covered, for 5 minutes. Add the almonds and fluff with a fork.

CHICKEN STEW

This is a complex dish that is very layered and totally unusual. My sister, Maria, loves to use chicken wings to deepen the flavor of many dishes. The flavor combination has the components used in recipes that are umami, or that hit every flavor sense on the palate, creating a new sense overall. Anchovies and sun-dried tomato paste anchor the unusual background notes.

2 tablespoons olive oil

⅓ pound guanciale, pancetta, or uncured bacon, cut into ½-inch pieces

6 chicken wings

3 or 4 small ribs celery with leafy tops, chopped

2 medium onions, chopped

4 cloves garlic, thinly sliced

3 or 4 flat anchovy fillets, chopped

¼ cup fresh rosemary leaves, chopped

2 tablespoons fresh thyme leaves, chopped

2 large fresh bay leaves

2 tablespoons sun-dried tomato paste or tomato paste

2 tablespoons Worcestershire sauce

1 tablespoon tamari

1 cup dry white wine

3 tablespoons butter

¼ cup flour

6 cups chicken stock

1½ to 2 pounds small white-skinned potatoes, quartered

2½ pounds boneless, skinless chicken thighs, halved

Juice of ½ organic lemon

½ cup fresh flat-leaf parsley tops, chopped

Preheat the oven to 325°F.

Heat a large Dutch oven over medium-high heat. Add the oil (2 turns of the pan) and guanciale and cook to render out the fat, then use a slotted spoon to transfer the cooked guanciale to a plate. Add the chicken wings to the Dutch oven and brown on each side. Transfer to the plate with the guanciale.

Add the celery, onions, garlic, anchovies, rosemary, thyme, and bay leaves to the pan and cook until the onions are tender. Add the tomato paste and stir for 1 minute. Add the Worcestershire sauce, tamari, and wine and cook, stirring, until almost evaporated. Melt in the butter. Add the flour and stir for 1 minute. Stir in the stock.

Return the wings and guanciale to the pan. Add the potatoes and chicken thighs and bring the stew to a simmer. Cover, transfer to the oven, and bake until the potatoes are tender and the chicken is cooked through, about 30 minutes. Fish out and discard the bay leaves and chicken wings. Stir the lemon juice and parsley into the stew before serving.

Roasted Whole Cauliflower with Ricotta Cream and Thyme Coating (page 320) and Sicilian Vegetable-Stuffed Eggplant (page 324).

CHAPTER 11

VEGETABLES

My grandfather had a huge garden to help feed the many mouths at the dinner table. He did a lot of canning and pickling to preserve vegetables for his children so they could eat a proper diet with plenty of vegetables all winter long. (And winters were always very, very long in Ticonderoga, New York.)

Mom remembers some winter afternoons when she'd run home from school hoping to beat all of her brothers and sisters by just enough time to sneak to the cellar and steal a jar of my grandfather's canned eggplant and eat it all by herself.

Today we have a large garden of our own, and my mom doesn't need to steal the eggplant. We grow enough to go around and then some. I cook so many vegetables that after cooking enough soups and sauces to fill the fridge and freezer of everyone in our immediate family, I still have plenty to bring to work or to gift to neighbors.

We love vegetables, and many nights eat a vegetable-based diet. I could easily be a vegetarian. I don't know about the vegan thing, though. An Italian girl like me might get really cranky without her cheese.

SAUTÉED LADY APPLES

I know this is a fruit and not a vegetable, but it makes an excellent side for veal, pork, or lamb. I also serve it with Cauliflower with Rosemary au Gratin (page 321).

5 tablespoons butter
6 shallots, halved and sliced lengthwise into thin wedges
12 to 16 lady apples, quartered
Salt and pepper
2 tablespoons fresh thyme leaves
½ cup Calvados or other apple brandy
Juice of ½ lemon

In a large skillet, heat the butter over medium to medium-high heat. Add the shallots and cook until tender-crisp, 2 to 3 minutes. Add the apples and season with salt and pepper. Add the thyme and sauté for 6 to 8 minutes to lightly brown the apples. Add the Calvados, stir to deglaze the pan, and cook to reduce to 2 to 3 tablespoons. Remove from the heat and stir in the lemon juice.

APPLESAUCE WITH THYME

5 Honeycrisp or Gala apples, peeled and coarsely chopped
1½ cups cloudy apple cider, plus more as needed
1 tablespoon fresh lemon juice
2 tablespoons chopped fresh thyme
⅛ teaspoon freshly grated nutmeg
A pinch of salt

In a pot, combine the apples, cider, lemon juice, thyme, nutmeg, and salt. Cook over medium-high heat until the apples break down into a sauce, about 20 minutes. Add more cider as needed if the apples get too dry.

GRILLED OR ROASTED ARTICHOKES

SERVES 6 TO 8

Roasted or grilled artichokes are easy to prepare and the smoky flavor can be a nice added touch. They're great with just charred lemons squeezed over the top, but you could also serve them with Bagna Cauda (page 37) or Garlic Butter with Parsley and Mint (see box) for dipping, or topped with Cherry Tomato and Red Onion Salad (page 24).

½ lemon
6 firm artichokes with tight leaves and green stems

GRILLED ARTICHOKES:
EVOO, for brushing
Salt and pepper
3 lemons, halved

ROASTED ARTICHOKES:
½ cup EVOO
2 large cloves garlic, smashed
6 flat anchovy fillets
3 lemons, halved
Salt and pepper

Fill a bowl with water and squeeze the juice from the lemon half into the water; add the juiced shell. Trim the stems of the artichokes and peel them to the tender centers, leaving as much of the stem intact as possible for grilling. Pull off the dark outer leaves until you reach the pale leaves. With scissors, trim the spiny tops. Halve the artichokes lengthwise and scrape out the fibrous choke (this job is a great double-duty use for a serrated-tip grapefruit spoon). As you finish trimming each artichoke, transfer it to the lemon water to keep it from browning.

Grilled artichokes: Preheat an outdoor grill. Steam or boil the artichokes to just tender but not overcooked at the heart, 15 to 20 minutes depending on the size of the artichokes. Brush the artichokes with EVOO and season liberally with salt and pepper. Brush the cut sides of the lemons with EVOO. Grill the artichokes and lemon halves until marked and smoky. Squeeze the juice from the charred lemons over the artichokes. Set out bowls for the discarded leaves.

Roasted artichokes: Position a rack in the lower third of the oven and preheat the oven to 450°F.

In a small saucepan, heat the EVOO and garlic over medium-low heat. Add the anchovies, cover the pan with a splatter screen or lid, and shake until the anchovies begin to break up. Reduce the heat a bit, uncover, and stir until the anchovies melt into the oil. Cool the oil to infuse with the garlic flavor; fish out and discard the garlic. Brush the lemon halves with some of the oil and season the cut sides with salt and pepper.

Drain the trimmed artichokes and toss with the garlic-anchovy oil. Season with salt and pepper. Arrange the artichokes and halved lemons cut side down in a roasting pan and cover with heavy-duty or doubled foil. Roast until the hearts are tender and the leaves can be pulled away easily, 30 to 40 minutes, depending on the size of the artichokes. Serve cut side up on a platter and douse with the juice of the roasted lemons. Set out bowls for the discarded leaves.

GARLIC BUTTER WITH PARSLEY AND MINT

MAKES ABOUT 1½ CUPS

Serve this as a dip for steamed or roasted artichokes in small ramekins (I warm small ramekins in the oven and it keeps the butter hot). This is also a tasty dip for sweet lobster or even poured over hot toasted bread.

6 ounces (1½ sticks) butter
1 head garlic (8 to 10 cloves), finely chopped
½ cup dry white wine
1 teaspoon crushed red pepper flakes
½ cup fresh flat-leaf parsley tops, finely chopped
½ cup fresh mint leaves, finely chopped
Juice of 1 lemon

In a medium skillet, melt the butter over medium heat. When it begins to foam, add the garlic and stir for 2 to 3 minutes. Add the wine and cook to reduce by half. Add the red pepper flakes and remove from the heat. Stir in the herbs and lemon juice and serve.

ROASTED BEETS WITH RICOTTA SALATA, WALNUTS, AND BALSAMIC DRESSING

This side dish is delicious warm, or cold with lunches or dinners. You can roast the garlic ahead, or at the same time as you have the beets and onion in the oven.

1 head garlic, roasted (see box)
6 to 8 medium-large beets
1 medium red onion, peeled and halved
Olive oil, for drizzling
Salt and pepper
2 teaspoons Dijon mustard
2 tablespoons aged balsamic vinegar
1 tablespoon acacia honey
⅓ cup EVOO
1 cup coarsely chopped fresh flat-leaf parsley tops
1 cup walnut halves, chopped
1 cup crumbled ricotta salata cheese

Preheat the oven to 400°F.

Make the roasted garlic and let cool.

Cut off the beet greens; wash, chop, and set them aside (you should have 2 to 3 cups). Trim the beets and place in a baking dish with the onion halves. Drizzle everything lightly with oil and season with salt and pepper. Cover with foil and roast until very tender, 40 to 50 minutes. Let cool. When cool enough to handle, wipe off the beet skins with paper towels and thinly slice the beets. Chop the onion.

Squeeze the garlic from the skins into a bowl. Mash the garlic to a paste and whisk in the mustard, vinegar, and honey. Whisk in the EVOO to form a dressing. Season with salt and pepper.

Arrange the beets and onion on a platter with the beet tops, parsley, and walnuts. Drizzle liberally with the dressing and top with ricotta salata.

BASICS

ROASTING GARLIC

You can roast just 1 head of garlic, but while you're at it, why not roast several? It's a nice ingredient to have on hand. I use it in lots of things, from pasta sauces to salad dressings and aioli to mashed potatoes and gravy. Depending on how I'm using the roasted garlic, I often throw in a sprig of a fresh herb. Preheat the oven to 400°F. Cut off the top of a head of garlic to expose the cloves. Drizzle the garlic with some olive oil and season with salt and pepper. Wrap in foil and roast until tender and caramel in color, about 40 minutes.

ROASTED BROCCOLI OR BROCCOLINI

SERVES 6

This may be my favorite roasted vegetable because I love nuts. Roasting crisps the edges of the florets of broccoli or broccolini, giving them an especially nutty flavor.

1 large bunch broccoli, or
  2 bunches broccolini,
  trimmed of tough ends
4 large cloves garlic, smashed
Olive oil, for drizzling
1 teaspoon crushed red pepper
  flakes (optional)
Salt and black pepper
1 lemon, halved

Preheat the oven to 425°F.

Cut the broccoli lengthwise into spears (with the florets still on) and use a vegetable peeler to trim the leaves and woody portion of the stems.

Drizzle the broccoli spears and garlic with oil, just enough to coat lightly, and toss. Spread on a baking sheet. Sprinkle with red pepper flakes (if using) and season with salt and black pepper. Place the lemon halves cut side down on the baking sheet.

Roast until the florets are crispy, about 25 minutes. Douse the broccoli with the juice of the roasted lemon and serve.

ROASTED ROMANESCO (ROMAN BROCCOLI)

SERVES 6

The pointy, light green, cauliflower-like heads look like they arrived at the produce department or farmers' market via Mars, but they are Roman-style broccoli. They taste much the same, but they sure are cute. As with my broccoli, I love roasting it up to develop a nutty flavor, and in this case, I garnish with nuts as well.

½ cup EVOO
6 to 8 flat anchovy fillets
4 large shallots, or 1 small red
  onion, finely chopped
5 or 6 cloves garlic (to taste),
  sliced
3 or 4 fresh red Fresno chiles,
  small hot red cherry peppers,
  or finger peppers, sliced (and
  seeded and deribbed to tame
  the heat, if you like)
½ cup dry vermouth
2 heads Romanesco (2½ to 3
  pounds total), cut into florets
1 lemon, halved
½ cup sliced almonds, toasted
½ cup chopped mixed fresh mint
  and flat-leaf parsley

Position a rack in the center of the oven and preheat the oven to 450°F.

In a medium saucepan, heat the EVOO over medium heat. Add the anchovies, cover the pan with a splatter screen or lid, and shake until the anchovies begin to break up. Reduce the heat a bit, uncover, and stir until the anchovies melt into the oil. Add the shallots, garlic, and chiles and stir for 2 to 3 minutes. Add the vermouth and remove from the heat.

Toss the Romanesco with the anchovy oil and arrange on a large baking sheet. Roast for 15 minutes, flip the Romanesco, and add the lemon halves, cut side down. Continue roasting until the Romanesco is tender-crisp, 10 to 15 minutes more.

Douse the roasted Romanesco with the roasted lemon juices. Serve topped with the almonds and herbs.

BROCCOLI RABE (RAPINI) WITH RICOTTA SALATA

On any holiday buffet, this recipe gets a lot of attention and rarely results in leftovers, but a clever use-up? Sandwiches. Layer rabe and cheese (provolone or mozzarella) on split focaccia and press in a panini press. Or, for a meatier sandwich, layer on ciabatta with cooked chicken, deli-sliced roast pork, or prosciutto cotto with rosemary and heat in a panini press.

Salt
2 bunches broccoli rabe, trimmed and cut into 3-inch pieces
¼ cup EVOO
5 or 6 flat anchovy fillets
4 large cloves garlic, chopped
1 teaspoon crushed red pepper flakes
1 cup chicken stock
1½ cups crumbled or grated ricotta salata

In a deep skillet or large saucepan, bring 3 inches of water to a boil. Salt the water, add the broccoli rabe, and cook for 3 to 4 minutes. Drain well.

In a large skillet, heat the EVOO (4 turns of the pan) over medium heat. Add the anchovies, cover the pan with a splatter screen or lid, and shake until the anchovies begin to break up. Reduce the heat a bit, uncover, and stir until the anchovies melt into the oil. Add the garlic and red pepper flakes and stir for 1 minute. Add the chicken stock and heat through. When ready to serve, add the broccoli rabe and heat through.

Transfer to a serving platter and top with the ricotta salata.

VARIATION

Pasta with Broccoli Rabe and Ricotta Salata

Toss with a little pasta and broccoli rabe becomes one of our favorite pasta nights. Prepare the broccoli rabe as directed. Meanwhile, cook 1 pound short-cut pasta in salted boiling water. Drain, reserving 1 cup of the starchy cooking water. Toss the drained pasta with the broccoli rabe, the ricotta salata, and the starchy water.

SALT AND PEPPER BRUSSELS SPROUTS

SERVES 6

These are addictive. They remind me of oven fries—crispy and hard to stop eating once you start. Adding a splash of vinegar or lemon juice while the sprouts are still hot gives them a tangy, acidic finish.

1½ pounds Brussels sprouts, trimmed and quartered
¼ cup olive oil
1 teaspoon kosher salt
1 teaspoon coarsely ground pepper
½ teaspoon freshly grated nutmeg
A splash of lemon juice, malt vinegar, or aged balsamic vinegar

Preheat the oven to 400°F.

Toss the Brussels sprouts with the oil. Arrange on a rimmed baking sheet and sprinkle with the salt, pepper, and nutmeg. Roast until crispy and golden brown, 40 to 45 minutes.

Finish with a little lemon juice, toss, and transfer to a serving dish.

BRUSSELS SPROUTS WITH BACON, BAY, AND ONIONS

SERVES 6

Bay and onions are so great together that the only thing I can think of to make them better is what makes everything smell and taste better: bacon.

1 tablespoon olive oil
⅓ pound bacon or pancetta, chopped
1 large onion, chopped
2 cloves garlic, sliced
2 small fresh bay leaves
1 large russet (baking) potato, peeled and cut into ¼-inch cubes
1½ pounds Brussels sprouts, trimmed and halved
1½ cups chicken stock
Salt and pepper

In a large skillet, heat the oil (1 turn of the pan) over medium-high heat. Add the bacon and cook until lightly brown. Transfer to a plate.

Stir in the onion, garlic, bay leaves, and potato. Partially cover and cook to soften the onion, a few minutes, stirring occasionally. Add the sprouts and return the bacon to the pan. Stir, add the stock, and simmer to just cook the Brussels sprouts through to tender-crisp, 7 to 8 minutes. Discard the bay leaves. Season with salt and pepper.

ROASTED GREEN BEANS AND TOMATOES

Green beans and tomatoes are often served stewed. I prefer them roasted, as it makes the beans a little nutty and intensifies the sweetness of the tomatoes, turning them a little tangy.

1½ pounds green beans or haricots verts
4 shallots, peeled and sliced into thin wedges, root end intact
1 pint cherry tomatoes
6 cloves garlic, smashed
1 cup pitted black olives
¼ cup EVOO
Salt and pepper
1 cup crumbled ricotta salata cheese
Torn small fresh basil leaves, for garnish

Position a rack in the center of the oven and preheat the oven to 500°F.

In a bowl, toss together the green beans, shallots, tomatoes, garlic, olives, EVOO, salt, and pepper. Arrange on a rimmed baking sheet and roast until the beans are tender and the tomatoes burst, about 25 minutes

To serve, top with the ricotta salata and garnish with basil.

GREEN BEANS WITH SHALLOTS

I was a customer of the Montcalm restaurant in the Lake George region of New York from the time I was a little girl until the restaurant closed, when I was forty-five. I always ordered the same meal: roast chicken with no potatoes and extra green beans. They were the most delicious green beans ever in the history of green bean preparation. Dino, the owner, told me it was about the slow-cooking of shallots or onions in lots of butter. Now I am famous for the green beans, too. We make these for every single holiday.

6 tablespoons (¾ stick) butter
6 large shallots, chopped
2 cups chicken stock
Salt
1½ pounds haricots verts

In a large skillet, melt the butter over medium heat. Add the shallots, partially cover, and cook, stirring occasionally, until very soft and sweet but not browned, about 20 minutes. If the shallots start to brown, reduce the heat.

Add the stock and turn off the heat.

Fill a bowl with ice and water. In a deep skillet, bring 3 inches of water to a boil. Salt the water, add the green beans, and cook for 3 to 4 minutes. Drain the beans and cold-shock them in the ice water. Drain them well.

Add the green beans to the shallots and cover until ready to serve. Reheat over medium heat until just hot through.

ORANGE-ROSEMARY BRAISED CARROTS

SERVES 6

My mom always placed carrots in a pot with chicken stock, a pat of butter, and a drizzle of honey. It's a perfect dish and a great base—sometimes she'd add a little curry powder and ginger, sometimes citrus and herbs. I love orange and rosemary with mine.

4 tablespoons (½ stick) butter
3 large shallots, chopped
3 tablespoons fresh rosemary leaves, coarsely chopped
2 large strips of orange zest (from an organic orange)
1½ pounds carrots, thinly sliced crosswise on an angle
Salt and pepper
½ cups chicken or vegetable stock

In a large saucepan, heat the butter over medium heat. Add the shallots, rosemary, and orange zest. Cover and cook to soften, about 5 minutes.

Stir in the carrots and season with salt and pepper. Add the stock, bring to a boil, reduce to a simmer, cover, and cook until tender, 15 to 20 minutes.

ROASTED CARROTS

SERVES 6

Roasting any vegetable—asparagus, green beans, broccoli, or cauliflower—really develops its flavor in a unique way. The vegetables get nutty and smoky, and the flavors become more intense. Carrots get sweet and caramelized at the edges. Yum.

1½ pounds baby carrots or regular carrots
¼ cup olive oil
3 large shallots, peeled and sliced into thin wedges, root end intact
3 tablespoons fresh thyme leaves
Salt and pepper
1 lemon, halved
½ cup finely chopped carrot tops (if they're nice and leafy green), for garnish

Position a rack in the center of the oven and preheat the oven to 450°F.

In a bowl, toss the carrots with the oil, shallots, thyme, salt, and pepper. Arrange the carrots on a rimmed baking sheet with the lemon halves, cut side down. Roast until the carrots are caramelized at the edges, 20 to 25 minutes.

Douse the carrots with the juice from the roasted lemon, toss, and transfer to a serving dish. Garnish with carrot tops.

Roasted Whole Cauliflower

==== SERVES 6 TO 8 ====

This is the basic recipe for roasting a head of cauliflower, plus four different coating ideas. But try your own versions and inspirations with this dish.

1 large head cauliflower, leaves trimmed and core cut away
1 cup chicken or vegetable stock
Salt and pepper
Coating of choice (recipes follow)
2 lemons, halved
Olive oil, for brushing

Position a rack in the center of the oven and preheat the oven to 375°F.

Place the whole cauliflower in a shallow baking dish and add the stock. Season with salt and pepper. Cover the dish with foil and roast for 1 hour.

Remove the cauliflower from the oven and increase the oven temperature to 450°F. Remove the foil from the cauliflower and spread with the coating of choice. Return it to the oven to brown, 10 to 15 minutes.

Meanwhile, brush the cut side of the lemon with oil. In a small skillet, cook the lemon cut side down over medium-high heat until caramelized, 4 to 5 minutes.

Douse the cauliflower with the juice from the lemon to serve.

Roasted Garlic-Parm Coating

1 head garlic, roasted (see box, page 312) with 1 sprig fresh rosemary included in the packet
1 medium free-range organic egg yolk
1 tablespoon fresh lemon juice
1 teaspoon Dijon mustard
½ cup grapeseed oil
Fine sea salt
½ cup freshly grated Parmigiano-Reggiano cheese

Squeeze the roasted garlic from the skins into a bowl and mash to a paste.

In a bowl, whisk the egg yolk, lemon juice, and mustard. While whisking, stream in the oil to emulsify. Season with sea salt. Stir in the garlic paste and ¼ cup of the Parm.

When the basic cauliflower recipe directs you to do so, spread on the coating. Sprinkle the cauliflower with the remaining ¼ cup Parm and continue as directed.

Anchovy-Rosemary-Pecorino Coating

This cauliflower coating tastes like Caesar salad dressing. Yum!

1 medium free-range organic egg yolk
1 tablespoon fresh lemon juice
1 teaspoon Dijon mustard
½ cup grapeseed oil
Fine sea salt
3 or 4 flat anchovy fillets, minced and mashed
2 large cloves garlic, grated or pasted
1 teaspoon Worcestershire sauce
2 tablespoons fresh rosemary leaves, chopped
Coarsely ground pepper
½ cup freshly grated Pecorino Romano cheese

In a bowl, whisk the egg yolk, lemon juice, and mustard. While whisking, stream in the oil to emulsify. Season with sea salt. Stir in the anchovies, garlic, Worcestershire sauce, rosemary, pepper, and ¼ cup of the pecorino.

When the basic cauliflower recipe directs you to do so, spread on the coating. Sprinkle the cauliflower with the remaining ¼ cup pecorino and continue as directed.

Ricotta Cream and Thyme Coating

1 cup fresh cow's or sheep's milk ricotta cheese, home-made (see box, page 40) or store-bought, drained
2 to 3 tablespoons heavy cream
2 tablespoons EVOO
3 tablespoons chopped fresh thyme
Kosher or sea salt and coarsely ground pepper
½ cup grated Parmigiano-Reggiano cheese

In a small bowl, stir the ricotta with a little cream to make it more spreadable. Stir in the EVOO and thyme and season with salt and pepper. Stir in ¼ cup of the Parm.

When the basic cauliflower recipe directs you to do so, spread on the coating. Sprinkle the cauliflower with the remaining ¼ cup Parm and continue as directed.

Variation
Goat Cheese and Thyme Coating: Sub in 1 cup soft, fresh goat cheese for the ricotta.

CAULIFLOWER WITH ROSEMARY AU GRATIN

At the holidays I serve this side dish with roast veal shank, but it is popular at any special dinner. I pair it with roast chicken or red meats, and vegetarians love it as a hearty main. You can add macaroni or farro penne to the dish as well for a great potluck casserole.

Salt
1 large or 2 medium heads cauliflower, cut into florets
4 tablespoons (½ stick) butter
2 cloves garlic, finely chopped
2 tablespoons fresh rosemary leaves, finely chopped
3 tablespoons flour
½ cup dry white wine or vegetable or chicken stock
2½ cups milk, warmed
Pepper
Freshly grated nutmeg
1 large free-range organic egg yolk
1½ cups freshly grated Parmigiano-Reggiano cheese

Preheat the oven to 375°F.

Fill a bowl with ice and water. In a large pot, bring about 4 inches of water to a rolling boil. Salt the water. Add the cauliflower and cook until tender-crisp, 3 to 4 minutes. Drain and cold-shock in the ice water. Drain very well.

In a saucepan, melt the butter over medium to medium-high heat. When it foams, add the garlic and rosemary. Whisk in the flour and when the flour bubbles, add the wine and cook until reduced to a few tablespoons. Whisk in the warm milk and season with salt, pepper, and nutmeg. Beat the egg yolk in a small bowl and add a ladle of sauce to temper it, then pour the tempered yolk into the sauce. Stir in ¾ cup of the Parm to melt.

Pour half the sauce into a 9 x 13-inch baking dish and add all of the cauliflower. Top with the remaining sauce and the remaining ¾ cup Parm. (This dish may be made ahead to this point and refrigerated. Just bring it back to room temperature before baking.)

Bake until browned and bubbling on top and hot through, 15 to 20 minutes.

BRAISED CELERY

Marcella Hazan has a wonderful recipe for braised celery that is a family favorite of ours: basically pancetta, onions, and tomatoes. It's lovely, but I have to say that celery is at its best, from your own garden or from a local market, when it has a lot of leafy greens and firm but very green stalks. At this point I prefer to braise the celery in homemade chicken stock with or without the pancetta, but always with mild onion and lots of parsley to finish. This side dish is clean-tasting, light, and easy. Wonderful with chicken or a simple sliced steak and boiled potato wedges both dressed with lemon juice, EVOO, and flaky sea salt.

3 tablespoons olive oil
¼ to ⅓ pound thinly sliced pancetta, chopped
1 large sweet onion, chopped
1 large bunch celery (about 2 pounds)
2 fresh bay leaves
1½ cups chicken stock
Salt and pepper
½ lemon
A handful of fresh flat-leaf parsley tops, chopped

In a deep skillet with a lid, heat the oil (3 turns of the pan) over medium to medium-high heat. Add the pancetta and stir to render its fat, 2 to 3 minutes. Stir in the onion, partially cover the pan, and sweat for 6 to 7 minutes.

Trim the celery bunch and separate the ribs. Use a vegetable peeler to peel away the very fibrous lower portions of the celery ribs, then cut them on an angle into 3-inch pieces. Add the celery to the skillet and stir to coat in the drippings and oil. Add the bay leaves and chicken stock and season with salt and pepper. Reduce the heat to medium-low, cover, and cook until tender-crisp, 15 to 20 minutes. Discard the bay leaves.

Just before serving, squeeze in the lemon juice and add the parsley.

MASHED CELERY ROOT AND POTATOES

SERVES 4

1 pound celery root, trimmed and cut into 2-inch cubes

2 pounds starchy potatoes (such as russets), peeled and cut into 2-inch cubes

Salt

1 (5.4-ounce) round Boursin cheese, or 5 to 6 ounces goat cheese with herbs

½ to ¾ cup milk

Pepper

In a large pot, combine the celery root and potatoes with cold water to cover. Bring to a boil, salt the water, and cook until the vegetables are tender, 15 to 18 minutes. Drain and return to the hot pot to dry them a bit. Add the cheese and milk and mash to the desired consistency. Season with salt and pepper.

BACON, CORN, AND MASCARPONE WITH FRESH HERBS

SERVES 6 TO 8

I love corn so much that there is a picture of me as a teething child asleep in a high chair sucking on a corncob like a bottle. My mother couldn't get it away from me, and I fell asleep with it in my hand. My birthday is in late August, so corn is always at its best and sweetest come my special day. I also use this fantastic combination of flavors as a pasta dish (see page 163).

2 tablespoons EVOO

⅓ pound thick-sliced lean center-cut bacon or pancetta, cut into ¼-inch cubes

1 medium onion, chopped

2 ribs celery, chopped

4 cloves garlic, finely chopped

1 small fresh or dried chile, seeded and finely chopped

2 tablespoons fresh thyme leaves, chopped

6 ears sweet corn, kernels scraped (see Tip, page 163)

Salt and pepper

1 cup chicken stock

½ cup mascarpone cheese

1 cup loosely packed chopped mixed fresh herbs: flat-leaf parsley, tarragon or basil, and chives

½ pint cherry tomatoes, quartered

In a large skillet, heat the EVOO (2 turns of the pan) over medium-high heat. Add the bacon and cook until crisp. Transfer to a plate. Add the onion, celery, garlic, chile, thyme, and corn and cook until the corn just begins to lightly brown. Season lightly with salt and pepper. Add the stock and bring to a bubble. Cook for a minute or so to reduce. Stir in the mascarpone.

Just before serving, stir in the crispy bacon and herbs. Taste and adjust the seasonings. Transfer to a serving platter or dish and top with the tomatoes.

MAKING EGGPLANT SHELLS FOR STUFFING

My grandfather was a great gardener. I am not. The real reason our garden grows well is because of my mom, Elsa, and my husband. But I will say that I love being a part of a garden, and watching our food grow. Also, I like to think I do my part by preparing what comes out of the garden. A few years ago, my husband and my dog gave me garden seeds from Italy for Mother's Day. The eggplant *loves* to grow in our backyard, so we make a lot of eggplant dishes. One of my favorite ways to use eggplant is to take advantage of its shape, using the eggplant shells to make beautiful, self-contained casseroles.

Here's a simple method of making eggplant shells. The recipes that follow will give you some ideas for what you can stuff the eggplants with.

Medium eggplant(s)
Salt and pepper
Olive oil, for drizzling

Preheat the oven to 425°F.

Halve the eggplant lengthwise. With a small paring knife, score the flesh in a diamond pattern at about ½-inch intervals, cutting all the way through the flesh but taking care not to pierce the skin. Take the knife and cut around the edges of the eggplant ¼ inch in from the sides; again, go as deep as you can without piercing the skin.

With a spoon, carefully scoop out the flesh, leaving ¼ inch of eggplant flesh (so that the shell has some stability) to make eggplant shells or boats for stuffing.

In each of the stuffing recipes in this book, I use the eggplant flesh as part of the stuffing. To prep the flesh for use, chop it and season with some salt. Drain on a kitchen towel or paper towels.

Dress the eggplant shells with a drizzle of oil to coat the fleshy insides and season with a little salt and pepper. Arrange the eggplant shells cut side down on a baking sheet and roast for 15 minutes. (Meanwhile, make whatever stuffing you're using.)

Remove the eggplant shells from the oven and turn them cut side up. Reduce the oven temperature to 375°F. At this point, you are ready to stuff and bake the eggplant shells. Follow the stuffing and baking directions in the individual recipe.

SICILIAN VEGETABLE-STUFFED EGGPLANT

SERVES 8 AS A SIDE DISH OR STARTER, OR 4 AS A MAIN

This eggplant recipe is hearty enough for a vegetarian entrée, but it's a colorful addition to any buffet as a side dish as well.

2 medium eggplants
¼ cup EVOO
1 medium onion, chopped
4 cloves garlic, finely chopped
2 ribs celery with leafy tops, chopped
1 cubanelle (frying pepper), seeded and chopped
1 red bell pepper, roasted (see box, page 334), peeled, and chopped
Black pepper
¼ cup pignoli (pine nuts), lightly toasted
3 tablespoons capers, drained
A handful of green Sicilian olives, coarsely chopped
Salt
1 (28- to 32-ounce) can San Marzano tomatoes (look for DOP on the label)
1 cup fresh basil leaves (about 20), torn or chopped
1 pound fresh or smoked mozzarella cheese, sliced

Preheat the oven to 425°F.

Make the eggplant shells (see box). Reduce the oven temperature to 375°F.

Meanwhile, make the stuffing. In a skillet, heat the EVOO (4 turns of the pan) over medium-high heat. Add the reserved chopped eggplant flesh, the onion, garlic, celery, and cubanelle and cook to soften the vegetables. Add the roasted red pepper and season everything with black pepper. Cook for 5 minutes, then add the pignoli, capers, and olives. Taste and add salt if needed.

Hand-crush the tomatoes as you add them to the pan. Add only a few spoonfuls of the can juices, just to moisten the veggies. Wilt the basil into the vegetables.

Fill the roasted eggplant shells with the veggie stuffing. Top with the mozzarella. Bake for 10 minutes to melt the cheese and set the filling.

Cut into quarters to serve as a side or starter. Leave whole if serving as a main.

MEAT-STUFFED EGGPLANT

This is as fulfilling as a lasagna Bolognese, but it takes less time to prepare and it feels a little lighter than the pasta an hour after you eat it.

2 medium eggplants

STUFFING:
2 tablespoons EVOO
1 pound ground beef or mixed ground beef, pork, and veal
1 small onion, finely chopped
3 or 4 cloves garlic (to taste), finely chopped
1 small fresh chile, seeded and finely chopped, or 1 teaspoon crushed red pepper flakes
Salt and black pepper
2 tablespoons tomato paste
1 cup veal or chicken stock
1 (28- to 32-ounce) can San Marzano tomatoes (look for DOP on the label), or 8 to 10 Roasted Tomato Halves with Thyme and Garlic (page 346)
A few fresh basil leaves, torn

BESCIAMELLA:
4 tablespoons (½ stick) butter
3 tablespoons flour
2 cups milk, warmed
Salt and pepper
Freshly grated nutmeg

½ cup freshly grated Parmigiano-Reggiano cheese, for topping

Preheat the oven to 425°F.

Make the eggplant shells (see box, page 324). Reduce the oven temperature to 375°F.

Meanwhile, make the stuffing: In a skillet, heat the EVOO (2 turns of the pan) over medium-high heat. Add the meat, breaking it up into crumbles as it browns. Add the reserved chopped eggplant flesh, the onion, garlic, chile, salt, and black pepper. Cook to soften the onion and eggplant, 7 to 8 minutes. Stir in the tomato paste. Stir in the stock. Hand-crush the tomatoes as you add them to the pan (add the can juices, too, if using canned tomatoes). Add the basil. Reduce the heat a bit and simmer to thicken.

Make the besciamella: In a saucepan, melt the butter over medium heat. Whisk in the flour and cook for 1 minute. Whisk in the milk, season with salt, pepper, and a little nutmeg. Cook the besciamella sauce until thick enough to coat the back of a spoon.

Arrange the roasted eggplant shells in a baking dish. Fill with the stuffing mixture. Pour some besciamella over each stuffed eggplant half and top with a little Parm. Bake until browned and bubbling on top, 15 to 20 minutes.

Cut into quarters to serve as a side or starter. Leave whole if serving as a main.

EGGPLANT, MUSHROOM, AND CHESTNUT–STUFFED EGGPLANT

SERVES 8 AS A SIDE DISH
OR STARTER, OR 4 AS A MAIN

I served this recipe as a vegetarian main for a friend of mine on the same night I prepared Mushroom and Chestnut Meatloaf with Gravy (page 269) for the meat eaters. I love this entrée and I joined my friend and enjoyed this rather than the meat. (However, that choice didn't keep me from enjoying my special meatloaf sandwiches the next day!)

2 medium eggplants

STUFFING:
1 tablespoon butter
1 cup panko bread crumbs or homemade coarse bread crumbs
About ¼ cup cloudy apple cider
2 tablespoons EVOO
¾ pound cremini mushrooms, chopped
Pepper
3 or 4 shallots, chopped
3 or 4 cloves garlic, finely chopped
2 ribs celery with leafy tops, finely chopped
2 tablespoons fresh thyme leaves, chopped
¼ cup Calvados or brandy
1 cup jarred or freshly roasted chestnuts, chopped
½ cup freshly grated Parmigiano-Reggiano cheese
½ cup freshly grated sharp cheddar cheese

BESCIAMELLA:
4 tablespoons (½ stick) butter
3 tablespoons flour
2 cups milk, warmed
Salt and pepper
Freshly grated nutmeg

Preheat the oven to 425°F.

Make the eggplant shells (see box, page 324). Reduce the oven temperature to 375°F.

Meanwhile, make the stuffing: In a medium skillet, melt the butter over medium heat. Add the panko and stir to coat. Cook until browned and toasty. Remove the skillet from the heat and toss the bread crumbs with the apple cider to moisten them. In a large skillet, heat the EVOO (2 turns of the pan) over medium-high heat. Add the mushrooms and cook to brown. Add the reserved chopped eggplant flesh and season with pepper. Add the shallots, garlic, celery, and thyme and cook to soften. Add the Calvados and stir to deglaze the pan. Add the chestnuts, half the toasted bread crumbs, and a small handful each of the Parm and cheddar.

Make the besciamella: In a saucepan, melt the butter over medium heat. Whisk in the flour and cook for 1 minute. Whisk in the milk and season with salt and pepper and a little nutmeg. Cook the besciamella sauce until thick enough to coat the back of a spoon.

Arrange the roasted eggplant shells in a baking dish. Fill with the stuffing mixture. Pour some besciamella over each eggplant half and sprinkle with the remaining bread crumbs and cheeses. Bake until browned and bubbling on top, 15 to 20 minutes.

Cut into quarters to serve as a side or starter. Leave whole if serving as a main.

WHOLE ROASTED EGGPLANT PARMIGIANA

SERVES 4 TO 8

These hasselback-style eggplants are really attractive on a platter and are easily divided for serving.

4 small to medium eggplants
Salt
¼ cup olive oil
4 tablespoons (½ stick) butter
4 cloves garlic, thinly sliced
1 cup panko bread crumbs
1 onion, halved
1 bay leaf
2 (28- to 32-ounce) cans San Marzano tomatoes (look for DOP on the label)
A couple sprigs fresh thyme
1 cup chicken or vegetable stock
A few fresh basil leaves, torn
1 teaspoon sugar (optional)
Pepper
1½ pounds fresh or smoked mozzarella cheese, cut into ½-inch-thick slices
1½ cups freshly grated Parmigiano-Reggiano cheese
½ cup fresh flat-leaf parsley tops, chopped
¼ cup fresh mint leaves, chopped

Make crosswise slits ⅛ inch apart down the length of the eggplants, being careful not to cut all the way through. The eggplant will look like an armadillo. Salt the flesh of the eggplant in the slits and let stand for 30 minutes. Pat the moisture away with paper towels.

Meanwhile, in a medium saucepan, heat the oil (4 turns of the pan). Melt in the butter. Add the garlic and swirl for 2 minutes. Spoon off a few tablespoons of the butter-oil mixture and use to moisten the panko.

Add the halved onion and bay leaf to the pan. Hand-crush the tomatoes as you add them to the pan, then add the can juices. Add the thyme, stock, basil, and sugar (if using). Simmer for 20 to 30 minutes. Fish out and discard the thyme stems, bay leaf, and onion halves. Season the sauce with salt and pepper.

Preheat the oven to 400°F.

Fill the accordion folds of the eggplants with slices of mozzarella. Choose two baking dishes that leave some room around the eggplants. Divide the sauce between the dishes, arranging 2 eggplants in each. Cover with foil and bake for 25 minutes. Remove the foil and bake until the eggplant is crispy at the edges, 20 to 30 minutes more.

Toss the garlic-butter panko with the Parm. Once the eggplant is crispy at the edges, top with the cheesy bread crumbs and return to the oven to brown, 10 minutes more.

Leave whole or cut in half, depending on how many people you are serving. Serve the eggplant scattered with the parsley and mint.

DEEP-DISH EGGPLANT PARMIGIANA

**SERVES 12 AS A SIDE DISH
OR 6 TO 8 AS A MAIN**

This is a traditional dish made very simply with sautéed eggplant, sweet red sauce, and cheese. It is gluten-free and makes a hearty vegetarian entrée or a side dish to feed an army.

3 medium eggplants
Salt
Olive oil, for shallow-frying
Pomodoro Sauce (page 121)
1½ pounds fresh mozzarella
    cheese, cut into small cubes
1½ cups freshly grated
    Parmigiano-Reggiano cheese
A handful of fresh basil leaves
A handful of fresh flat-leaf parsley
    tops, finely chopped

Trim off the bulges on two opposite sides of the eggplant to make them more rectangular. Then cut the eggplant lengthwise into ¼- to ½-inch-wide planks. Salt the eggplant and layer between kitchen towels. Weight and drain the eggplant for 1 hour.

In a large skillet, heat a ⅛-inch layer of oil over medium to medium-high heat. Working in batches, cook the eggplant for 2 minutes on each side until light golden. Drain on paper towels. Replenish the oil as needed between batches.

Preheat the oven to 375°F.

Assemble the dish: In a 9 x 13-inch baking dish, spread a layer of the pomodoro sauce. Top with one-third of the eggplant slices, a few spoonfuls of sauce, one-third each of the mozzarella and the Parm, and a few torn basil leaves. Repeat the layering two more times.

Bake until the top is browned and bubbling, 35 to 40 minutes. Serve topped with the parsley.

FENNEL-APPLE SLAW

SERVES 4

I use this to top Chicken Milanese (page 298) or Veal Milanese (page 277) or even a bowl of stew, such as Veal and Porcini Stew (page 283).

1 shallot
Salt
Juice of 1 lemon
1 teaspoon superfine sugar, or
    2 teaspoons acacia honey
1 teaspoon fennel seeds, toasted
Pepper
¼ cup olive oil
1 bulb fennel, trimmed and very
    thinly sliced on a mandoline
    or the slicing blade in a food
    processor
2 ribs celery with leafy tops, very
    thinly sliced on an angle
1 small Honeycrisp apple, or
    2 lady apples, peeled and
    very thinly sliced
¼ cup fresh flat-leaf parsley tops,
    chopped

Grate the shallot into a large bowl and season with salt. Add the lemon juice, sugar, and fennel seeds and let stand for 10 minutes. Season with pepper and whisk in the oil.

Add the sliced fennel, celery, apple, and parsley and toss to combine.

HERBED FENNEL SLAW

MAKES ABOUT 4 CUPS

Serve this with roast lamb or roast chicken.

Juice of 3 Meyer lemons, or juice of ½ orange plus 1 lemon

2 large bulbs fennel, trimmed and very thinly sliced or shredded on a mandoline, plus ½ cup fronds, chopped

1 large red onion, halved and very thinly sliced

1 cup fresh flat-leaf parsley tops, coarsely chopped

¼ cup fresh tarragon leaves, chopped

¼ cup EVOO

Kosher salt and pepper

In a bowl, combine the lemon juice, fennel and fennel fronds, onion, parsley, tarragon, and EVOO. Season with salt and pepper and toss to combine. Let stand for 30 minutes to wilt.

CITRUS SLAW

SERVES 6 TO 8

Juice of 1½ lemons

3 tablespoons acacia honey

⅓ cup EVOO

Salt and pepper

4 to 5 cups shredded green cabbage or savoy cabbage (about ½ head)

3 to 4 cups very thinly sliced or shaved fennel (about 2 bulbs)

1 bunch red radishes, cut into matchsticks

1 red onion, halved and thinly sliced or shaved on a mandoline

3 citrus fruits (such as blood oranges, Cara Cara oranges, or red grapefruit), supremed (see box, page 221)

In a bowl, whisk the lemon juice, honey, and EVOO. Season with salt and pepper.

Add the cabbage, fennel, radishes, onion, and citrus segments and toss to coat with the dressing.

NEW YEAR'S FANCY LENTILS

It is good luck in Italian culture to eat lentils often at or around the New Year. The lentils represent little coins, so those who eat them will have good fortune for the year to come. I decided to prepare lentils for a potluck we were invited to around New Year's Day, but how would I dress them up for a party? Porcini and white truffle, that's how. These are some fancy-pants lentils, and they were the hit of the potluck.

3 cups veal or chicken stock

1 ounce good-quality (large, thin slices) dried porcini mushrooms

1 pound Norcia lentils (see box, page 38)

2 onions: 1 quartered, 1 finely chopped

2 fresh bay leaves

Salt

¼ cup olive oil

3 or 4 small ribs celery with leafy tops, chopped

3 or 4 cloves garlic, chopped

2 tablespoons fresh thyme leaves

1 cup jarred or fresh roasted chestnuts, chopped

Pepper

A handful of fresh flat-leaf parsley tops, finely chopped

Freshly shaved white truffle or a drizzle of natural truffle oil (optional)

In a medium saucepan, heat the stock with the mushrooms over medium heat to soften them, 10 to 15 minutes. Scoop out the mushrooms and chop them; set aside the soaking liquid in the pan.

In a large saucepan, combine the lentils with water to cover (a couple of quarts). Add the quartered onion and bay leaves and bring the water to a boil. Salt the water and cook the lentils at a low rolling boil until tender, 35 to 40 minutes. Drain; fish out and discard the onion and bay leaves.

In a large skillet, heat the oil (4 turns of the pan) over medium to medium-high heat. Add the chopped onion, celery, garlic, thyme, chestnuts, and salt and pepper and stir for 5 minutes to soften the onion and celery. Add the drained lentils and chopped porcini. Carefully pour in the reserved mushroom soaking liquid, leaving the last few spoonfuls in the pan as grit may have settled there.

Stir in the parsley and serve. If desired, garnish with shaved truffle or stir in truffle oil.

CHECK THIS OUT

It's good luck to eat lentils, especially on New Year's Day, but they're delicious year-round. In addition to the side dishes in this chapter, I use lentils as a starter, in soups, and in pasta dishes.

- Cotechino with Spicy Lentils (page 241)
- Deviled Lentils (page 38)
- Lentil Soup with Sausage and Kale (page 82)
- 'Nduja and Lentil Soup (page 82)
- Penne with Lentils and Sausage (page 167)

SPICY LENTILS

These lentils make a great bed for sausages. Check out Cotechino with Spicy Lentils (page 231). You can find Norcia lentils online, or you can substitute brown lentils.

1 pound Norcia lentils (see box, page 38)

2 medium onions: 1 quartered, 1 finely chopped

2 fresh bay leaves

Salt

2 tablespoons olive oil

¼ pound 'nduja (see box, page 123)

2 carrots, chopped

2 or 3 ribs celery with leafy tops, chopped

3 or 4 cloves garlic, chopped

2 tablespoons fresh thyme leaves

2 tablespoons fresh rosemary leaves, chopped

2 tablespoons tomato paste

1 cup chicken stock

1 cup loosely packed fresh flat-leaf parsley tops, chopped

In a large saucepan, combine the lentils with water to cover (a couple of quarts). Add the quartered onion and bay leaves and bring the water to a boil. Salt the water and cook the lentils at a low rolling boil until tender, 35 to 40 minutes. Drain; fish out and discard the onion and bay leaves.

Heat a deep large skillet over medium to medium-high heat. Add the oil (2 turns of the pan) and melt in the 'nduja. Add the chopped onion, carrots, celery, garlic, thyme, and rosemary and stir for 3 to 5 minutes to soften. Add the tomato paste and stir for 1 minute. Add the drained lentils and stock and simmer for a few minutes for the flavors to combine and to let the liquid almost evaporate.

Stir in the parsley and serve the lentils warm.

MARSALA MUSHROOMS

This is a must-serve side dish for our family whenever I prepare roast beef dishes of any kind. The mushrooms are a favorite snack or starter on buffets or at potlucks as well, and they make a great pizza topping (Capricciosa Pizza, page 92).

¼ cup olive oil

1½ pounds cremini mushrooms or a mix of your favorite fresh mushrooms

Salt and pepper

4 cloves garlic, smashed

3 tablespoons fresh thyme leaves, chopped

1 cup Marsala

3 tablespoons butter

A fat handful of fresh flat-leaf parsley tops, chopped

Heat a large cast-iron or other heavy-bottomed skillet over medium-high heat. Add the oil (4 turns of the pan) and when it ripples, add the mushrooms. Cook, turning frequently, until browned, about 10 minutes. Season with salt and pepper. Add the garlic and thyme and toss for 1 to 2 minutes more. Add the Marsala and cook until it has reduced to about ⅓ cup. Swirl the butter into the pan and toss in the parsley. Transfer to a serving dish.

VARIATION

Sherry Mushrooms

Substitute dry sherry for the Marsala.

BUTTER-BASTED HEN-OF-THE-WOODS MUSHROOMS WITH ROSEMARY AND THYME

I would be happy eating these mushrooms with just a hunk of crusty bread for lunch or dinner.

3 tablespoons EVOO
1½ pounds hen-of-the-woods mushrooms (maitake), root cut away and mushrooms separated
Salt and pepper
3 tablespoons fresh rosemary leaves, coarsely chopped
2 tablespoons fresh thyme leaves, chopped
2 large cloves garlic, chopped
3 tablespoons butter
A splash of Worcestershire sauce
A splash of dry sherry or brandy

Heat a large cast-iron skillet over high heat. Add the EVOO (3 turns of the pan). Add the mushrooms and brown for 3 minutes. Stir and reduce the heat. Season with salt and pepper; add the rosemary, thyme, and garlic; and toss for 2 to 3 minutes. Add the butter to one side of the pan to melt. Tilt the skillet to pool the butter and baste the mushrooms with the melted butter for 1 to 2 minutes more. Add the Worcestershire sauce and sherry. Remove from the heat and serve.

STUFFED ONIONS

Stuffed onions can be served as a light entrée with a side salad; or for large holiday meals or buffets, they make a hearty side dish that pairs well with roasts and stews.

3 large red or yellow onions, halved from root to stem
1 cup chicken stock
Salt and pepper
2 tablespoons olive oil
1½ pounds Sweet Italian Sausage with Fennel, homemade (page 237) or store-bought, casings removed
1½ cups panko bread crumbs or lightly toasted fresh bread crumbs
1½ cups freshly grated Parmigiano-Reggiano cheese
½ cup fresh flat-leaf parsley tops, chopped

Preheat the oven to 375°F.

Place the onion halves and stock in a baking dish and season the onions with salt and pepper.

Cover the dish with foil and bake for 45 minutes. Remove from the oven and let cool. When cool enough to handle, remove the centers of each onion, leaving 2 or 3 layers as the shell. Chop the roasted onion centers.

In a large skillet, heat the oil (2 turns of the pan) over medium-high heat. Add the sausage, breaking it up into crumbles as it browns. Add the chopped roasted onions, the panko, 1 cup of the Parm, and half the parsley. Remove from the heat.

Fill the onions with the sausage stuffing and top with the remaining parsley and remaining ½ cup Parm. Bake until golden, about 20 minutes.

PEAS WITH MASCARPONE

SERVES 6

This is a creamy, sweet vegetable side dish. These peas also make a delicious filling for ravioli and a nice sauce for any short-cut pasta.

1 tablespoon olive oil
2 tablespoons butter
2 cloves garlic, smashed
2 large shallots, or 1 small onion, finely chopped
3 cups shelled fresh peas
½ cup chicken stock
Salt and pepper
¼ cup fresh tarragon leaves, chopped
¼ cup fresh mint leaves, chopped
⅓ to ½ cup mascarpone cheese (to taste)

In a skillet, heat the oil (1 turn of the pan) over medium to medium-high heat. Melt in the butter. When the butter foams, add the garlic and shallots and stir for 1 to 2 minutes. Add the peas and stock, cover, and simmer for 4 to 5 minutes. Season with salt and pepper.

Mash the peas a bit with a potato masher. Stir in the herbs and mascarpone to combine. Adjust the seasonings.

PEAS WITH PROSCIUTTO

SERVES 8

Many people would associate this combination of ham and peas with a tomato-basil sauce served with pasta. I love the combination of ham and sweet peas, but I prefer to keep it that way. Go heavy on the amount of ham you buy—you will steal more than a few bits from the pan, I am sure!

3 tablespoons EVOO
½ pound prosciutto (ask for the "ends," see Tip, page 157), finely chopped or pulse-ground in a food processor
1 large fresh bay leaf
1 onion, finely chopped
2 cups chicken stock
4 to 5 cups shelled fresh peas
Salt and pepper
½ cup chopped fresh flat-leaf parsley

In a large skillet, heat the EVOO (3 turns of the pan) over medium heat. Add the prosciutto and cook until lightly browned, 3 to 4 minutes. Add the bay leaf and onion, cover, and cook, stirring occasionally, to soften the onion, about 5 minutes. Add the stock and bring to a boil. Reduce to a simmer, add the peas, and simmer for 5 minutes. Season with salt and pepper. Fish out and discard the bay leaf. Just before serving, toss in the parsley.

TRICOLOR ROASTED PEPPERS WITH GARLIC AND PIGNOLI

SERVES 6 TO 8

6 to 8 large sweet peppers, a mix of green, red, and yellow

8 cloves garlic, cracked but unpeeled

Olive oil, for liberal drizzling

Salt and black pepper

3 or 4 flat anchovy fillets, minced and pasted, or 1 rounded teaspoon anchovy paste

2 tablespoons aged balsamic vinegar or balsamic reduction (see box, page 28)

2 tablespoons fresh thyme leaves, chopped

¼ cup sliced almonds or pignoli (pine nuts), toasted

A handful of fresh basil leaves, shredded

A handful of fresh flat-leaf parsley tops, chopped

Preheat the oven to 425°F.

On a large rimmed baking sheet, drizzle the whole peppers and garlic with oil and toss to coat. Season with salt and black pepper. Roast, turning once, until the skins are charred, 35 to 40 minutes. Reserve the pan juices. Let cool. When cool enough to handle, peel, seed, and slice the peppers. Peel and chop the garlic.

Transfer the pan juices to a serving dish and add the anchovies, vinegar, thyme, and garlic. Use a fork to mash and mix. Add the peppers and toss to coat with tongs.

Serve the peppers topped with the nuts, basil, and parsley.

BASICS

ROASTING PEPPERS

Roasted peppers are great as an appetizer, a pizza topper, a sandwich ingredient, and in pasta sauces. Use field peppers (the long rectangular peppers), frying peppers, or large bell peppers. Char the skin of the peppers on the stovetop over a gas flame or under the broiler with the oven door ajar to let steam escape. Place the peppers in a bowl and cover tightly so the peppers will steam. When cool, rub off the charred skins with a paper towel, then halve and seed the pepper. Cut up according to whatever recipe you're using.

STUFFED PEPPERS

MAKES 12 STUFFED PEPPER HALVES; SERVES 6

These peppers are versatile because once baked, they are delicious served hot, room temperature, or cold.

6 red frying peppers or red bell peppers

2½ cups (¼-inch) cubes stale ciabatta or peasant bread

2 or 3 flat anchovy fillets, finely chopped

2 or 3 large cloves garlic, finely chopped or grated

1 pound fresh mozzarella cheese, cut into ½-inch cubes

1 cup cherry or grape tomatoes, quartered

¾ cup green and/or black olives, pitted and chopped

3 tablespoons capers, drained

2 small ribs celery with leafy tops, finely chopped

¼ cup fresh flat-leaf parsley tops, chopped

A handful of fresh basil leaves, torn

4 tablespoons EVOO

1 medium free-range organic egg

Salt and black pepper

1 cup panko bread crumbs or homemade coarse bread crumbs

¾ cup freshly grated Parmigiano-Reggiano or Pecorino Romano cheese

Preheat the oven to 400°F.

Char the peppers and place them in a bowl, covered, according to the instructions (see box). When cool enough to handle, lay the peppers on their sides on a work surface. Cut about one-quarter of the pepper lengthwise off the top to make roasted pepper boats. Chop the trimmed pieces and set aside.

In a small bowl, soak the bread cubes in water to soften, then wring out the excess water. Pull the bread into shreds and drop into a large bowl. Add the chopped peppers, anchovies, garlic, mozzarella, tomatoes, olives, capers, celery, parsley, basil, 2 tablespoons of the EVOO, the egg, and salt and black pepper.

Fill the pepper boats with the stuffing. In a small bowl, combine the remaining 2 tablespoons EVOO with the panko and cheese. Top the peppers with the cheesy bread crumbs. Bake until golden, about 30 minutes.

RATATOUILLE AND RICOTTA–STUFFED PEPPERS

SERVES 4

4 frying peppers or bell peppers, halved lengthwise and seeded

Olive oil, for drizzling

Salt and black pepper

3 cups fresh ricotta cheese, homemade (see box, page 40) or store-bought

1 large free-range organic egg yolk

1 (10-ounce) box frozen chopped spinach, thawed and wrung dry in a kitchen towel

4 cups Ratatouille (page 345)

1½ cups grated Fontina or young Asiago cheese

½ cup freshly grated Parmigiano-Reggiano cheese

Preheat the oven to 425°F.

Drizzle the peppers with oil and season with salt and black pepper. Spread on a baking sheet and roast until tender, 15 to 20 minutes. Leave the oven on.

Meanwhile, in a bowl, combine the ricotta and egg yolk. Pull the spinach into shreds with your fingers as you add it to the bowl. Season with salt and pepper and mix well.

Divide the ricotta stuffing among the peppers. Top with the ratatouille. Sprinkle the Fontina and Parm over the top. Bake until browned and bubbling, about 15 minutes.

TWICE-BAKED POTATOES WITH CARAMELIZED ONION AND CHEESE

SERVES 8 AS A STARTER
OR 4 AS A MAIN

This is a rich side dish to be shared or a wonderful meat-free, hearty entrée for chilly days. If serving as an entrée, top the potatoes with Roasted Broccoli or Broccolini (page 313).

4 large russet (baking) potatoes, scrubbed and dried

Olive oil, for drizzling

Salt and pepper

3 tablespoons butter

3 onions, thinly sliced

¼ cup crème fraîche or heavy cream

1 cup shredded Fontina Val d'Aosta or Gruyère cheese

½ cup freshly grated Parmigiano-Reggiano cheese

Preheat the oven to 400°F.

Rub the potato skins with a little oil. Season with salt and pepper and prick the skins in several places with a fork. Roast until firm-tender, about 1 hour. When cool enough to handle, halve the potatoes lengthwise.

In a large skillet with a lid, melt the butter over medium heat. When it foams, add the onions and season with salt. Cover and cook, stirring occasionally, for 10 minutes. Uncover and cook, stirring occasionally, for 20 minutes more.

Scoop the flesh of the potatoes into a bowl, leaving enough flesh in the skins to make shells. Add the onions, crème fraîche, Fontina, and salt and pepper to the bowl with the potato flesh and mash together.

Fill the potato skins with the mashed potatoes, arrange on a baking sheet, and top with the Parm. Roast the potatoes until the mashed potato filling is browned, about 15 minutes.

ROASTED GARLIC POTATOES STUFFED WITH RATATOUILLE

SERVES 4

1 head garlic, roasted (see box, page 312) with a sprig of fresh rosemary in the packet
4 large russet (baking) potatoes, scrubbed and dried
Olive oil, for drizzling
Salt and pepper
¼ to ⅓ cup milk
Freshly grated nutmeg
1 cup grated Gruyère cheese
4 cups Ratatouille (page 345), warmed
1 cup shredded Parmigiano-Reggiano cheese

Preheat the oven to 400°F.

Roast the garlic. At the same time, rub the potatoes with oil and season with salt and pepper. Roast the potatoes for 1 hour. Leave the oven on.

When the roasted garlic is cool enough to handle, squeeze the garlic from the skins into a large bowl and mash to a paste.

When the potatoes are just cool enough to handle, halve them lengthwise and scoop the flesh into the bowl with the garlic, leaving enough flesh in the skin to make sturdy shells. Arrange the potato shells on a baking sheet.

Add the milk, a few grates of nutmeg, the Gruyère, salt, and pepper to the bowl with the potato flesh and mash together.

Fill the potato shells with the mashed potatoes and top with the warm ratatouille. Sprinkle with the Parm and bake for a few minutes to brown the cheese a bit. Serve 2 stuffed skins per person.

ROASTED POTATOES WITH ROSEMARY

SERVES 8 TO 10

A classic and all-around favorite, these chunky wedges can be served with balsamic ketchup (see box, page 271) for an American Italian twist. Or, my favorite, douse the roasted potatoes with a little hot pickled Italian cherry pepper juice.

6 to 8 medium russet (baking) potatoes, scrubbed and cut into 8 to 10 wedges each
Olive oil, for liberal drizzling
Salt
Black pepper and/or crushed red pepper flakes
8 cloves garlic, smashed
¼ cup fresh rosemary leaves
3 to 4 tablespoons brine from a jar of pickled hot peppers (optional)

Preheat the oven to 425°F.

Place the potatoes on large rimmed baking sheet and coat with a liberal drizzle of oil. Season with salt and black pepper and/or red pepper flakes. Add the garlic and rosemary and toss everything to coat. Roast until very crispy and browned at the edges, 40 to 45 minutes, turning once. If desired, douse the hot potatoes with pickled hot pepper juice.

ROASTED POTATOES WITH FENNEL AND ONION

This is another basic that everyone loves. I roast the three main ingredients separately, then combine them so the potatoes are crispy and the fennel and onions are tender and sweet.

4 large russet (baking) potatoes, scrubbed and cut into 8 to 10 wedges each
Olive oil, for liberal drizzling
Salt and pepper
1 teaspoon granulated garlic
1 teaspoon granulated onion
2 medium bulbs fennel, trimmed and cut into 1-inch wedges
2 medium-large sweet onions, cut into 1-inch wedges
8 cloves garlic, smashed
1 cup dry white wine and/or chicken stock

Preheat the oven to 425°F.

Place the potatoes on a large rimmed baking sheet and coat with a liberal drizzle of oil. Season with salt and pepper. Sprinkle with the granulated garlic and granulated onion and toss everything to coat. Roast until crisp, 40 to 45 minutes, turning once.

At the same time, place the fennel, sweet onions, and garlic on a separate rimmed baking sheet or in a shallow baking dish. Drizzle with oil, season with salt and pepper, add the wine, and toss to coat. Roast for 40 to 45 minutes.

Combine the potatoes with fennel and onions in a large serving dish.

LEMON AND OLIVE OIL POTATOES

My family, Mom especially, loves these, and I think this is the easiest recipe in this book.

6 medium russet (baking) potatoes, peeled and cut into 6 wedges each
Salt
Juice of 1½ lemons
¼ cup EVOO
Flaky sea salt

In a large pot, combine the potatoes with cold water to cover. Bring to a boil, salt the water, and cook until the potatoes are tender but not falling apart, 12 to 15 minutes. Drain the potatoes and return them to the hot pot. Add the lemon juice and let it be absorbed into the hot potatoes. Drizzle in the EVOO (count to 4 while adding the oil in a slow, steady stream around the pot), carefully toss to coat, and season with flaky sea salt.

ROASTED GARLIC MASHED POTATOES

SERVES 6

Everyone is Italian on Sunday, and everyone loves mashed potatoes, every day. I must admit, spaghetti comes first in my list of favorite things, but these potatoes make my Top 10 for sure.

6 large russet (baking) potatoes, peeled and diced
Salt
1 large head garlic, roasted (see box, page 312) with a sprig of rosemary added to the packet
1 cup milk, warmed
3 tablespoons butter, cut into small pieces
1 cup freshly grated Parmigiano-Reggiano cheese
Pepper
Freshly grated nutmeg

In a large pot, combine the potatoes with cold water to cover. Bring to a boil, salt the water, and cook to tender, 12 to 15 minutes. Drain the potatoes and return to the hot pot to dry them a bit.

Squeeze the garlic from the skins into a bowl and mash the garlic to a paste. Add the paste to the pot with the potatoes and add the rosemary leaves from the garlic packet. Mash the potatoes to the desired consistency with the warm milk. Mash in the butter and Parm and season with salt, pepper, and nutmeg.

VARIATION

Duchess Potatoes

This a fancy way to serve mashed potatoes. Reduce the amount of Parm in the mixture to ½ cup and add 2 egg yolks when you mash everything together. Fit a pastry bag with a ¾-inch star tip. Line a baking sheet with parchment paper and pipe out cones of mashed potato about 3 inches wide and a couple of inches high. Bake the potatoes in a preheated 375°F oven until browned and crisp, 25 to 30 minutes.

MASHED POTATOES WITH RICOTTA AND HONEY

SERVES 6

I'd rather eat these potatoes than a bowl of ice cream. Really.

2½ to 3 pounds starchy potatoes (such as russets), peeled and cut into chunks
Salt and pepper
½ to ¾ cup milk, warmed
1½ cups fresh cow or sheep's milk ricotta cheese, homemade (see box, page 40) or store-bought, drained
3 tablespoons fresh thyme leaves, chopped
3 to 4 tablespoons good-quality olive oil
3 tablespoons acacia honey
Freshly grated nutmeg

In a large pot, combine the potatoes with cold water to cover. Bring to a boil, salt the water, and cook until the potatoes are tender, 12 to 15 minutes. Drain the potatoes and return them to the hot pot to dry them a bit.

Season with salt and pepper. Mash the potatoes to the desired consistency with the warm milk, ricotta, thyme, oil, honey, and nutmeg. Adjust the seasonings.

MAKE-AHEAD MASHED

When it comes to getting everything on the table hot, at least mashed potatoes don't have to stress you out. You can make mashed potatoes ahead and keep them hot for hours. Here's how: Heat a large pot with about 1 inch of water to a low boil, then reduce the heat to a simmer. Place the mashed potatoes in a covered saucepan that can fit into the larger pot and will be deep enough to reach the simmering water. Set the pan right into the water bath (bain-marie). This makeshift bain-marie will hold your potatoes at the right consistency and keep them nice and hot for hours. Add a little more water to the larger pan if it gets too low to touch the potato pot.

MASHED POTATOES WITH SOFT CHEESE AND HERBS

SERVES 8

These are the crowd-pleasing favorite and a must on our Thanksgiving table every year.

8 medium starchy potatoes (such as russets), peeled and diced
Salt
5 to 6 ounces Boursin garlic and herb cheese or soft goat cheese with herbs
1 cup milk, warmed
1 cup chicken stock
¼ cup minced mixed fresh herbs: flat-leaf parsley, chives, and thyme
Grated zest of 1 organic lemon
2 cloves garlic, grated or pasted (optional)
Pepper

In a large pot, combine the potatoes with cold water to cover. Bring to a boil, salt the water, and cook the potatoes until tender, 12 to 15 minutes. Drain the potatoes and return them to the hot pot to dry them a bit.

Mash the potatoes with the soft cheese of your choice, the warm milk, stock, herbs, lemon zest, garlic (if using), salt, and pepper.

POTATO-VEGETABLE PANCAKES WITH HERBS

MAKES 6 CAKES

This is not a latke recipe. These pancakes should be nice and thick, about 1 inch thick.

Salt
4 large russet (baking) potatoes
Fresh horseradish root, peeled
1 medium onion, peeled
1 large carrot, peeled
2 large cloves garlic, peeled
2 tablespoons fresh rosemary leaves, finely chopped
2 tablespoons fresh thyme leaves, finely chopped
Pepper
Canola oil, for shallow-frying
1 large free-range organic egg
3 tablespoons flour
1½ cups crème fraîche
A handful of fresh flat-leaf parsley and/or chives, finely chopped
Juice of ½ lemon
Unsweetened applesauce, homemade (see page 310) or store-bought

Fill a large bowl with cold, salted water. Peel the potatoes and grate them on the large holes of a box grater or with the grating blade in a food processor, putting them in the bowl of salted water as you work. Once they're all grated, drain the potatoes and place them in a sieve set in the sink. Press on the potatoes to squeeze out more liquid.

Transfer the drained, grated potatoes to a bowl. Finely grate enough horseradish to get 3 tablespoons and add to the potatoes. Grate the onion, carrot, and garlic into the bowl with the potatoes. Add the rosemary and thyme and season with salt and pepper.

Preheat the oven to 275°F. Place a cooling rack on a rimmed baking sheet.

In a large skillet, heat ½ inch of canola oil over medium to medium-high heat.

Beat the egg and add it to the potatoes and vegetables. Sprinkle in the flour and stir to combine. Pile the potato-and-vegetable mixture into 3-inch-round mounds about 1 inch thick.

Working in batches, transfer the potato mounds to the skillet and cook for 3 minutes on each side to deep golden brown. Transfer to the prepared baking sheet and place in the oven to keep warm.

In a small bowl, mix the crème fraîche, parsley/chives, and lemon juice.

Serve the pancakes with the crème fraîche mixture and applesauce at the table.

MOM'S WARM POTATO SALAD

This potato salad is my mom's brilliant idea. She always doused potatoes with beef consommé while they were still warm, then she would dress the salad with oil and vinegar. This is the side dish that I love to serve with Bistecca Fiorentina with Parsley Sauce (page 263).

3 pounds medium russet (baking) potatoes, peeled and cut into 6 wedges each
Salt
1 cup veal or beef stock or beef consommé
Juice of 1½ lemons, or 3 tablespoons white balsamic or white wine vinegar
⅓ to ½ cup good-quality olive oil
Pepper
4 ribs celery with leafy tops, finely chopped
1 medium red onion, finely chopped
1 cup fresh flat-leaf parsley tops, chopped

In a large pot, combine the potatoes with cold water to cover. Bring to a boil, salt the water, and cook until the potatoes are tender, 12 to 15 minutes. Drain the potatoes and return them to the hot pot to dry them a bit.

Add the stock, lemon juice, oil, salt, and pepper. Cover the pot to keep warm until ready to serve. Just before serving, toss in the celery, onion, and parsley.

CARBONARA-STYLE POTATO, BACON, AND EGG SALAD

This recipe takes the Lemon and Olive Oil Potatoes (page 337) and turns them into a potato salad with bacon and eggs.

6 large free-range organic eggs
½ pound bacon
6 large russet (baking) potatoes, peeled and cut lengthwise into 8 wedges each, then halved crosswise
Salt
Juice of 2 lemons
2 or 3 cloves garlic, chopped
½ cup EVOO, plus more as needed
1 tablespoon coarsely ground pepper
½ cup freshly shaved or grated Romano cheese
½ cup freshly shaved or grated Parmigiano-Reggiano cheese
½ cup chopped fresh flat-leaf parsley
½ cup chopped celery tops
Flaky sea salt

Place the eggs in a medium saucepan with water to cover. Bring to a rapid rolling boil. Cover the pan, remove from the heat, and let stand for 10 minutes. Drain. Crack the shells and let stand for 10 minutes in very cold water, then peel and chop.

Preheat the oven to 375°F.

Arrange the bacon on a slotted broiler pan or on a cooling rack set over a rimmed baking sheet and bake until crisp, 15 to 17 minutes. Transfer the bacon to a cutting board and chop into ½-inch pieces.

In a large pot, combine the potatoes with cold water to cover. Bring to a boil, salt the water, and cook the potatoes until tender, 12 to 15 minutes. Drain the potatoes and return them to the hot pot to dry them a bit.

Add the lemon juice, garlic, and EVOO and toss the potatoes to coat. Add the pepper, Romano, and Parm. Taste and adjust the seasonings. Add more oil if the potatoes seem dry.

Add the eggs and bacon and stir to combine. Transfer to a serving dish and top with the parsley and celery tops and a little flaky sea salt.

CREAMED SPINACH

Steakhouse-style spinach is best made with frozen chopped spinach, which is a real bargain—and the prep work has been done for you. I add a little soft cheese (cream cheese, Boursin, or goat cheese) in addition to heavy cream. Some steakhouses finish their creamed spinach with truffle oil—not bad. Occasionally we add a drizzle at home as well. Even better, we add shaved fresh truffles when we are lucky enough to have them.

When I make this dish, I usually sneak downstairs late at night and eat the leftovers before anyone else can get to them. If you can stand the wait, however, the leftovers do make an amazing filling for rolled omelets.

3 tablespoons butter
2 large shallots, finely chopped
6 cloves garlic, finely chopped
½ cup heavy cream
½ cup chicken stock, plus more as needed
5 to 6 ounces soft cheese (such as cream cheese, Boursin, or fresh goat cheese)
2 (16-ounce) bags frozen chopped spinach, thawed and wrung dry in a kitchen towel
Salt and pepper
Freshly grated nutmeg
½ to ¾ cup freshly grated Parmigiano-Reggiano cheese
Natural truffle oil, for drizzling (optional)

In a large skillet, melt the butter over medium heat. When it foams, add the shallots and garlic and stir for 2 to 3 minutes. Add the cream and stock and heat to a bubble. Melt the soft cheese into the sauce. Add the spinach, separating it with your fingertips as you add it to the pan. Season the spinach with salt, pepper, and a little nutmeg. Heat through and stir in Parm to taste. Keep warm over low heat until ready to serve, adding a bit more stock if it gets too dry. If desired, add a drizzle of truffle oil to finish.

GARLICKY WILTED SPINACH

This may be our family's favorite side dish and the easiest to make. Keep it simple: oil, garlic, salt, pepper, nutmeg, and a splash of lemon. I figure 1 pound of spinach for every 4 diners.

¼ cup olive oil
4 large cloves garlic, chopped
1 pound fresh spinach, stemmed and coarsely chopped
Salt and pepper
Freshly grated nutmeg
Juice of ½ lemon

In a large skillet, heat the oil (4 turns of the pan) over medium heat. Add the garlic and swirl for 1 to 2 minutes to infuse the oil. Wilt the spinach into the garlic oil. Season the spinach with salt, pepper, and nutmeg. Remove from the heat and add the lemon juice. Transfer to a serving dish.

FOUR-CHEESE STUFFED BUTTERNUT SQUASH

SERVES 8 AS A SIDE DISH
OR 4 AS A MAIN

This is a great meat-free entrée—serve half a squash per person. For buffets, place a serving spoon in front of a platter of stuffed squash so guests can scoop servings of the filling from the squash shells.

1 head garlic, roasted (see box, page 312)
2 butternut squash, halved lengthwise and seeded
Olive oil, for brushing
Salt and pepper
Freshly grated nutmeg
1½ cups fresh ricotta cheese
3 tablespoons fresh thyme leaves
1 tablespoon grated lemon or orange zest (from organic citrus)
1 cup grated sharp white cheddar cheese
1 cup freshly grated pecorino cheese
1 cup freshly grated Parmigiano-Reggiano cheese

Preheat the oven to 400°F.

Roast the garlic. When cool enough to handle, squeeze the garlic from the skins into a bowl and mash to a paste. At the same time as the garlic is roasting, brush the squash with oil and season with salt, pepper, and nutmeg. Roast the squash until just tender, 35 to 40 minutes. Leave the oven on.

When the squash is cool enough to handle, carefully scrape out the flesh into a bowl, leaving just enough flesh to keep the shells intact. Add the garlic paste, ricotta, thyme, lemon zest, and ¾ cup each of the cheddar, pecorino, and Parm to the bowl with the squash flesh and mix well.

Fill the squash shells and top with the remaining cheeses. Bake until browned and bubbling, 15 to 20 minutes.

SWISS CHARD WITH BESCIAMELLA SAUCE

SERVES 6 TO 8

I prefer chard for this dish, but the deer in my neck of the Adirondack woods prefer chard, too. They leave the kale and spinach undisturbed, so we often make this casserole with a combination of the two instead. I use the stems, chopped, as well.

1 head garlic, roasted (see box, page 312)
2½ cups milk
2 bay leaves
1 strip of lemon zest (from an organic lemon)
Salt and pepper
Freshly grated nutmeg
2½ pounds Swiss or rainbow chard, stems included but trimmed of very tough ends
6 tablespoons (¾ stick) butter
¼ cup flour
1 large free-range organic egg yolk
2 cups freshly shredded Parmigiano-Reggiano cheese

Preheat the oven to 400°F.

Roast the garlic. When cool enough to handle, squeeze the garlic from the skins into a bowl and mash to a paste. Leave the oven on.

In a small saucepan, combine the milk, bay leaves, lemon zest, and salt, pepper, and nutmeg to taste. Heat to warm.

Bring a large pot of water to a boil. Salt the water. Working in two batches, drop the chard into the boiling water and cook for 4 to 5 minutes. Transfer to a colander and run under cool water, then drain well. Transfer the leaves to clean kitchen towels and wring out excess liquid. Chop the greens and stems into small bite-size pieces.

In a saucepan, melt the butter over medium heat. Whisk in the flour and cook for 1 minute. Fish out and discard the bay leaves and lemon zest from the milk, then whisk the milk into the butter-flour mixture. Cook the sauce until thick enough to coat the back of a spoon. Stir in the garlic paste. Adjust the seasonings. Beat the egg yolk in a small bowl. Ladle some hot sauce into the egg yolk to temper it, then stir the tempered egg yolk into the sauce.

In an 8 x 10-inch baking dish, layer half the chard. Top with half the sauce and half the Parm. Repeat the layering.

Bake until golden brown and bubbling, 15 to 20 minutes.

MEATBALL-STUFFED TOMATOES

Why should peppers have all the fun? These are a delicious light entrée or wonderful as a party offering or weekend potluck dish, served warm or at room temperature.

1½ cups bread cubes

Milk, for moistening the bread

4 large beefsteak tomatoes

3 tablespoons EVOO, plus more for drizzling

1 tablespoon fresh thyme leaves, chopped

Salt and pepper

1 teaspoon fennel seeds

¾ pound mixed ground beef, pork, and veal

Freshly grated nutmeg

¼ cup grated onion

2 or 3 large cloves garlic, finely chopped or grated

½ cup loosely packed fresh flat-leaf parsley tops, chopped

1 large free-range organic egg

½ cup freshly grated Parmigiano-Reggiano cheese

½ cup panko bread crumbs or homemade coarse bread crumbs

Preheat the oven to 350°F.

In a bowl, soak the bread in milk (about ½ cup) to soften.

Cut about ½ inch off the tops of the tomatoes. Scoop out the seeds and heart of the flesh (discard the pulp). Set the tomatoes cut side up in a baking dish and drizzle each cavity of the tomatoes with EVOO. Sprinkle the tomatoes with the thyme and season with salt and pepper.

In a small pan, heat 1 tablespoon of the EVOO (1 turn of the pan) over medium-high heat. Add the fennel seeds and stir. Add the meat, breaking it up into crumbles as it browns. Season with salt, pepper, and a few grates of nutmeg. Add the onion and garlic and stir for 2 minutes. Transfer to a large bowl to cool.

Squeeze the excess milk from the bread and pull the bread into crumbles with your fingers as you add it to the cooled meat mixture. Add the parsley, egg, and ¼ cup of the Parm and stir to combine.

Fill the tomatoes with the stuffing. Cover and bake for 20 minutes.

Meanwhile, in a bowl, toss the panko with the remaining 2 tablespoons EVOO and ¼ cup Parm.

Top the tomatoes evenly with the bread crumb mixture and bake until lightly golden brown on top, 12 to 15 minutes.

VARIATION

Stuffed Tomatoes with Caprese Topping

In a large bowl, combine 1 pint quartered grape or small cherry tomatoes, ½ pound finely diced fresh mozzarella cheese, 12 shredded fresh basil leaves, 1 tablespoon aged balsamic vinegar or balsamic reduction (see box, page 28), a drizzle of EVOO, and salt and pepper. When the stuffed tomatoes come out of the oven, serve them in shallow bowls topped with the caprese salad.

RATATOUILLE
(PRETEND IT'S ITALIAN, NOT FRENCH)

Ratatouille freezes really well and makes a great make-ahead base for all sorts of dishes:

- Serve it with toasted crusty bread for a starter.
- Serve with poached or fried eggs for brunch or an easy elegant meal.
- Serve it in a frittata (see Ratatouille Frittata, page 5).
- Top French bread with ratatouille and shredded mozzarella or Gruyère cheese. Bake to melt the cheese to make bread pizzas.
- Use it to stuff twice-baked potatoes (see Roasted Garlic Potatoes Stuffed with Ratatouille, page 337).
- Use it to stuff peppers (see Ratatouille and Ricotta–Stuffed Peppers, page 335).
- And of course you can serve it as a vegetable side.

Ratatouille
MAKES 3 QUARTS

2 eggplants, half the skin peeled (in stripes), then diced into bite-size pieces
Salt
¼ cup EVOO
1 rounded tablespoon herbes de Provence
2 large onions, chopped
4 large cloves garlic, sliced
2 fresh bay leaves
Black pepper
1 cup vegetable stock
2 pounds zucchini (about 3 medium), seeded and diced into bite-size pieces
2 sweet red peppers (bell or frying peppers), chopped
A few fresh basil leaves, torn
¼ cup fresh flat-leaf parsley tops, chopped
1 (28- to 32-ounce) can San Marzano tomatoes (look for DOP on the label)

Preheat the oven to 400°F.

Toss the diced eggplant with salt and drain on a kitchen towel for about 20 minutes. Pat dry.

In a large Dutch oven, heat the EVOO (4 turns of the pan) over medium-high heat. Add the herbes de Provence and stir. Add the onions, garlic, and bay leaves and season with a little salt and some black pepper. Partially cover and cook for 10 minutes to soften the onions. Add the stock, eggplant, zucchini, sweet peppers, basil, and parsley. Hand-crush the tomatoes as you add them to the pan, then add the juices from the can. Stir to combine.

Transfer the pan to the oven and roast, uncovered and stirring every 20 minutes or so, for 1 hour. Turn off the oven and let stand in the oven for 20 minutes more.

Serve or cool to store. Fish out and discard the bay leaves before serving.

ROASTED TOMATO HALVES WITH THYME AND GARLIC

SERVES 6

I make several pounds of this recipe each week in late summer. I use roasted tomatoes as a side dish, sure, but they make the best BLT sandwiches or Italian hoagies, too. I also puree them and use them as a pasta or pizza sauce. And if I add homemade stock to the pureed tomatoes, it turns into the best tomato soup ever. In addition, in the 8 or 9 months of the year when tomatoes are not so tasty, roasting them really gives them some life.

3 pounds plum or vine tomatoes, halved
¼ cup olive oil
Salt and pepper
5 or 6 sprigs fresh thyme
5 cloves garlic, smashed but unpeeled

Position a rack in the center of the oven and preheat the oven to 325°F.

Arrange the tomatoes cut side up on a rimmed baking sheet. Drizzle with the oil and season with salt and pepper. Scatter the thyme sprigs and garlic around the pan. Roast until the tomatoes are charred at the edges and slumped, but still juicy with some structure left to them (not like sun-dried tomatoes). This will take 1 hour to 1½ hours, depending on how large the tomatoes are.

Remove the garlic from the skins and strip the thyme leaves from the stems. Add both to the tomatoes. Serve or store.

STEWED ZUCCHINI

SERVES 6

Add a little extra stock and this becomes a quick, tasty soup as well as a classic side dish.

3 tablespoons olive oil
2 medium zucchini, halved lengthwise, seeded, and cut crosswise into half-moons
1 large onion, chopped
1 green bell pepper, chopped
2 or 3 ribs celery with leafy tops, chopped
4 cloves garlic, sliced
2 bay leaves
2 tablespoons chopped fresh thyme
Salt and black pepper
1 cup chicken or vegetable stock
1 (28- to 32-ounce) can San Marzano tomatoes (look for DOP on the label), or 2 or 3 pounds fresh tomatoes, peeled (see Tip, page 67), seeded, and chopped
A few fresh basil leaves, torn

In a saucepan, heat the oil (3 turns of the pan) over medium-high heat. Add the zucchini, onion, bell pepper, celery, garlic, bay leaves, and thyme. Season with salt and black pepper. Partially cover and cook, stirring occasionally, for 7 to 8 minutes. Add the stock. Hand-crush the canned tomatoes as you add them to the pan, then add the juices from the can. (Or just add the chopped fresh tomatoes.) Simmer over low heat for 20 minutes. Discard the bay leaves. Stir in the basil and serve.

ZUCCHINI WITH MINT AND ALMONDS

SERVES 6

This is a delicious side for lamb chops, grilled or broiled, with lemon. It's also terrific tossed with orzo or bow-tie pasta as a simple meal: Add a little extra lemon juice and EVOO, and top with grated cheese.

Salt
2 medium or 3 small zucchini, thinly sliced
¼ cup olive oil
Black pepper
4 cloves garlic, chopped
½ teaspoon crushed red pepper flakes
1 lemon, halved
½ cup fresh mint leaves, chopped
¼ cup sliced almonds, toasted

Salt the zucchini and sweat for 10 minutes on kitchen towels or paper towels. Pat dry.

In a large skillet, heat the oil (4 turns of the pan) over medium-high heat. When the oil ripples, add the zucchini, season with black pepper, and cook for 2 to 3 minutes on each side, until light golden. Add the garlic and red pepper flakes and stir for 1 minute. Squeeze the lemon juice over the zucchini. Toss with the mint. Serve topped with the almonds.

ZUCCHINI AND CORN FRITTERS

MAKES 10 TO 12 FRITTERS

These are fun to throw together the day after a summer cookout when you have leftover corn on the cob.

1 medium zucchini, shredded on the large holes of a box grater
Salt
1½ cups fresh corn kernels (see Tip, page 163)
⅔ cup flour
½ teaspoon baking powder
2 large free-range organic eggs
½ cup finely chopped scallions (white and light green parts only)
¼ pound sharp white cheddar or Parmigiano-Reggiano cheese, grated
Pepper
EVOO, vegetable, or canola oil, for shallow-frying

Preheat the oven to 250°F. Place a cooling rack over a rimmed baking sheet.

Place the shredded zucchini in a strainer, salt it liberally, and set it in the sink to drain for 15 to 20 minutes. Press out the excess liquid.

Transfer the zucchini to a food processor and add ¾ cup of the corn. Pulse to finely chop.

In a bowl, combine the flour, baking powder, eggs, scallions, and cheese. Season with salt and pepper. Add the chopped corn-zucchini mixture and the remaining whole corn kernels. Stir to combine.

In a large skillet, heat about ¼ inch of oil over medium to medium-high heat. Once the oil is hot and ripples, spoon in 2- to 3-inch mounds of the fritter batter. Fry until deeply golden, 2 to 3 minutes on each side. Transfer to the prepared baking sheet and keep warm in the oven while you make the rest of the fritters. Add more oil to the pan as needed.

Clockwise from upper left:
Coffee Cream (page 358);
individual servings of Polenta
Cake (page 361) with Cake
Cream (page 357); Espresso
Martini (page 375); Almond Fig
Biscotti (page 352); and Sponge
Cake (page 359) with coffee
cream and hazelnuts.

CHAPTER 12

DESSERTS

BY MARIA BETAR (MY SISTER)

The end of an Italian meal usually means a glass of sweet wine, accompanied by a biscotti, some fruit, and cheese. But on Sundays, holidays, and special occasions, Italians roll out their sweet tooth and end their meal with some of the world's best pastries, tarts, cakes, tortas, cookies, custards, and creams layered and flavored with nuts or fruit.

NUT COOKIES

MAKES 20 TO 24 COOKIES

This dough is supposed to feel a little dry and coarse, and will bake crisp and brittle.

1 cup flour, sifted
½ cup chopped pecans, finely ground
Scant ¼ cup sugar
4 ounces (1 stick) butter, softened
½ teaspoon vanilla extract

Preheat the oven to 350°F. Line a baking sheet with parchment paper.

In a bowl, combine the flour, ground pecans, sugar, butter, and vanilla. Work with your hands to form a dough. Using a melon baller, scoop out ½-inch balls and set 2 inches apart on the prepared baking sheet. Refrigerate for 10 minutes.

Flatten the dough balls to ¼ inch thick with the bottom of a drinking glass. Bake until lightly golden, about 20 minutes. Let cool on the pan for 1 to 2 minutes, then transfer to a rack to cool completely.

PIGNOLI COOKIES

MAKES ABOUT 24 COOKIES

These pine nut cookies originated in Sicily. They are basically an almond macaroon covered in pine nuts.

1 (7-ounce) tube almond paste
⅔ cup sugar
2 large free-range organic egg whites
⅓ cup sliced almonds, finely ground (see Tip, page 362)
10 ounces pignoli (pine nuts) (about 2 cups)

Position a rack in the center of the oven and preheat the oven to 350°F. Line a baking sheet with parchment paper.

Crumble the almond paste with your fingers into a bowl and mash with a fork into small crumbles. With an electric mixer on low speed, beat in the sugar and egg whites. When combined, increase the mixer speed to medium and beat until smooth. Reduce the mixer speed to low and mix in the ground almonds. The mixture will be gooey.

Spread the pine nuts in a shallow bowl. Using a melon baller, scoop up some dough and drop it into the pine nuts. Quickly roll the dough in the nuts and immediately transfer to the prepared baking sheet (the balls will droop and flatten on the sheet). Repeat with the remaining dough.

Bake until lightly golden brown (take care not to burn the nuts), 15 to 20 minutes. The cookies will feel a little spongy when lightly touched. Let cool on the pan for 1 to 2 minutes, then transfer to a rack to cool completely.

CANTUCCI (ALMOND-FIG BISCOTTI)

MAKES 32 TO 36 BISCOTTI

Tuscany's trademark cookies are biscotti, and the best-known biscotti are these little almond cookies that always accompany the Tuscan dessert wine, vin santo.

1 cup sliced almonds
2¼ cups flour, sifted
2 large free-range organic eggs
3 large free-range organic egg yolks
1¼ cups sugar
½ teaspoon vanilla extract
3 dried Mission figs, finely minced
1 tablespoon cream

In a food processor, very finely grind ½ cup of the sliced almonds. In a bowl, mix the ground almonds into the flour.

In a bowl, with an electric mixer, beat the whole eggs, 2 of the egg yolks, and the sugar until the sugar dissolves. Beat in the vanilla. By hand, mix in the flour-almond mixture until a dough forms. Mix in the figs and remaining ½ cup sliced almonds with your hands.

Divide the dough in half and shape each portion into a log 2 inches in diameter. Cover and refrigerate for 1 hour.

Preheat the oven to 400°F. Line two baking sheets with parchment paper.

In a small bowl, beat the remaining egg yolk with the cream. Cut the dough logs crosswise into ½-inch-thick slices. Place them standing up on the prepared baking sheet and brush the tops with the yolk-cream mixture.

Reduce the oven temperature to 375°F. Bake until golden brown on top, 10 to 15 minutes. Turn the oven off and prop the oven door open slightly. Leave the biscotti to cool in the oven. Store in an airtight container.

SESAME COOKIES

MAKES ABOUT 24 COOKIES

Sesame cookies are just as common as biscotti in Italy, and just as good with dessert wine.

1½ cups flour
1½ teaspoons baking powder
4 ounces (1 stick) butter, softened
½ cup sugar
2 large free-range organic eggs
1 teaspoon vanilla extract
¼ teaspoon anise extract
½ cup sesame seeds (about 3 ounces)

Position a rack in the center of the oven and preheat the oven to 425°F. Line a baking sheet with parchment paper.

In a small bowl, whisk the flour and baking powder.

In a bowl, with an electric mixer on medium speed, cream the butter and sugar. Reduce the mixer speed to low and beat in the eggs, vanilla, and anise. Add the flour in three additions and beat on low speed until combined.

Spread the sesame seeds in a shallow bowl. With your fingers, pinch off pieces of dough (the dough will be tacky) the size of small prunes and shape them into 2-inch logs. Roll the logs in the sesame seeds and place on the prepared baking sheet.

Bake until golden brown (be careful not to burn the bottoms), 15 to 20 minutes. Slide the cookies, still on the parchment, onto a rack to cool.

ZEPPOLE

This dessert of fried dough covered in sugar originates in southern Italy (where they're called *zeppoli*). They can be filled with custard or jelly and dusted with granulated sugar, or left plain and covered with powdered sugar.

1 envelope active dry yeast
½ cup warm water (105° to 115°F)
1½ cups flour
½ teaspoon ground cinnamon
Canola, vegetable, or sunflower
    oil, for deep-frying
Powdered sugar, for dusting

In a small bowl, sprinkle the yeast over the water and let sit 5 to 10 minutes to dissolve.

In a bowl, combine the flour, cinnamon, and yeast mixture and mix with your hands to form a dough. Turn the dough out onto a board and knead until smooth. Place the dough in bowl, cover with a kitchen towel, and let rise until doubled in size, 45 minutes to 1 hour.

Fill a countertop fryer with oil or pour a few inches of oil into a large Dutch oven. Heat the oil to 375°F (on a deep-fry thermometer if using a Dutch oven).

Working in batches, pinch off walnut-size pieces of the dough and fry until golden brown. Drain on paper towels, then dust with powdered sugar while still warm.

RICOTTA FRITTERS

Sweet fried doughs are found at all Italian festivals and street fairs. These ricotta-based fritters are sweet, fluffy little pillows.

2 large free-range organic eggs
1 tablespoon sugar, plus more for
    sprinkling
1 teaspoon vanilla extract
1 teaspoon grated orange zest
    (from an organic orange)
1 tablespoon fresh orange juice
1 cup fresh ricotta cheese,
    homemade (see box, page 40)
    or store-bought
¾ cup sifted flour
1½ teaspoons baking powder
½ teaspoon salt
Canola, vegetable, or sunflower
    oil, for deep-frying

In a bowl, whisk the eggs and sugar until creamy. Whisk in the vanilla, orange zest, and orange juice. Fold in the ricotta. Fold in the flour, baking powder, and salt.

Fill a countertop fryer with oil or pour a few inches of oil into a large Dutch oven. Heat the oil to 375°F (on a deep-fry thermometer if using a Dutch oven).

Drop the dough by level tablespoons into the hot oil and fry, turning the fritters as they cook, until medium brown, 3 to 4 minutes. Drain on paper towels and sprinkle with a little sugar while still warm.

CENCI

Cenci (rags) are fried pastries that appear in Italy at Carnevale time. They get their name from the raglike shapes the dough forms when fried.

2 cups flour, plus more for dusting
4 tablespoons (½ stick) butter, softened
2 large free-range organic eggs
1 tablespoon granulated sugar
1 tablespoon Grand Marnier
1 teaspoon grated orange zest (from an organic orange)
¼ teaspoon salt
Canola, vegetable, or sunflower oil, for deep-frying
Powdered sugar, for dusting

Place the flour in a large bowl. Make a well in the center of the flour. Place the butter, eggs, granulated sugar, Grand Marnier, orange zest, and salt in the well. With your fingers, mix everything to form a dough. Cover the bowl with a kitchen towel and let stand for 1 hour.

On a floured surface, roll the dough out to a ⅛-inch thickness. With a sharp knife, cut the dough into strips 1½ to 2 inches wide and 3 to 4 inches long.

Fill a countertop fryer with oil or pour a few inches of oil into a large Dutch oven. Heat the oil to 375°F (on a deep-fry thermometer if using a Dutch oven).

Working in batches, drop the dough strips into the oil. They will turn crisp and golden brown very quickly. Drain on paper towels, then dust while still warm with powdered sugar. Serve warm or cooled.

CANNOLI CREAM

This is the basic cannoli cream, but it can be customized (in fact, you can even customize individual cannolis) by adding personal favorites. For example, fold in mini chocolate chips, minced candied or dried fruit, citrus zest, or candied citrus peels. Buy empty cannoli shells, but do not fill them with this cream until ready to eat. Fill the shells using a pastry bag or a spoon.

½ cup heavy cream
2 cups fresh ricotta cheese
½ cup superfine sugar
1 tablespoon rum (a nice kicker, but optional)

In a bowl, with an electric mixer on high speed, beat the cream until soft peaks form.

In a separate bowl, with the electric mixer on medium speed, beat the ricotta, sugar, and rum (if using) until well mixed and smooth.

Fold the whipped cream into the ricotta mixture. Keep in the refrigerator, covered, until ready to fill cannoli.

DARK CHERRY PANNA COTTA

This recipe has a few steps, but they're not hard. Just leave yourself plenty of time because it requires a couple of hours of chill time. The panna cotta will be a little wobbly, but don't worry.

1 (15-ounce) can water-packed dark cherries
2½ cups heavy cream
2 tablespoons superfine sugar
1 vanilla bean
1 (¼-ounce) envelope unflavored gelatin
2 tablespoons light brown sugar

Set a sieve over a small saucepan. Dump the cherries and the juice from the can into the sieve. With your hands, gently squeeze most but not all of the juice from the cherries into the pan. Set the pan of juice aside. Transfer the cherries to a food processor and puree.

In another saucepan, combine the cream and superfine sugar. Split the vanilla bean lengthwise and scrape the seeds into the pan. Add the vanilla bean pod, too. Bring the cream almost to a boil over medium heat (take care not to boil or burn it). Remove from the heat and set aside. Fish out and discard the vanilla bean pod.

Choose a small bowl that can be set into a small pot to create a double boiler. Pour 2 inches of water into the pot and bring to a simmer.

Meanwhile, in the bowl, stir 7 tablespoons of the cherry puree and the gelatin. Let sit for a couple of minutes for the gelatin to swell, then place the bowl over the pot of simmering water. Stir in the brown sugar and whisk over the simmering water until the sugar has dissolved. Remove the bowl from the pot.

Measure out ½ cup of the cream mixture and stir it into the cherry gelatin mixture until well combined. Pour the cherry gelatin mixture back into the pot of cream, stirring the panna cotta mixture until well blended.

Divide the panna cotta mixture among six 6-ounce custard cups. Cover and chill until set, 2 to 3 hours.

Meanwhile, make the cherry sauce. Bring the saucepan of reserved cherry juice to a boil. Reduce the heat to a slow boil and cook for 10 minutes to reduce slightly. Add the remaining cherry puree and continue to slow boil for 10 minutes more. Let cool to room temp, then refrigerate

To serve, dip the bottom of a custard cup in a bowl of very hot water for 3 to 4 seconds and invert the panna cotta onto a plate. Pour a tablespoon or two of the cherry sauce over each panna cotta before serving.

ZABAGLIONE

This is a world-renowned, traditional Italian dessert. It's delicious over poached pears or peaches, or with a slice of Sponge Cake (page 359) and/or fresh fruit and dessert wine. This is a very rich dessert, so serve very small portions. A little goes a long way.

6 large free-range organic egg
  yolks
6 tablespoons sugar
½ cup Marsala
½ teaspoon ground cinnamon
Pinch of freshly grated nutmeg

Choose a bowl that can be set into a pot to create a double boiler. Pour about 2 inches of water into the pot and bring to a high simmer. Add the egg yolks and sugar to the bowl and place the bowl over the simmering water. Whisking constantly, stir the yolks and sugar until smooth. Whisking briskly, slowly add the Marsala. Whisk in the cinnamon and nutmeg, still stirring, until light gold in color and the consistency of pudding.

Remove the bowl from the pot and let cool to room temp. Serve it at room temp or refrigerate and serve chilled.

CAKE CREAM

Delicious with a bowl of berries, in a cream puff, or on top of a slice of cake.

2 cups milk
2 teaspoons vanilla extract
6 large free-range organic egg
  yolks
1 cup sugar
¼ cup flour
2 tablespoons cornstarch
1 tablespoon butter

In a saucepan, heat the milk over medium heat until just before boiling. Remove from the heat and stir in the vanilla. Set aside.

In a bowl, with an electric mixer on medium speed, beat the egg yolks and sugar until frothy and pale yellow. Whisk in the flour and cornstarch. Whisking briskly and constantly to keep the eggs from cooking, very slowly pour in the hot milk.

Return the mixture to the saucepan and cook, stirring constantly, until almost boiling, but do not allow to boil. Remove from the heat, stir in the butter, and let cool to room temp before refrigerating. The consistency when set should be similar to pudding.

COFFEE CREAM

A delicious topping for any cake. Serve with your favorite minced or roasted nuts on a slice of Sponge Cake (page 359).

2 cups milk
1½ teaspoons cornstarch
½ cup strong black coffee
2 large free-range organic eggs, separated
½ cup sugar
1 teaspoon vanilla extract

In a cup, mix a little of the milk into the cornstarch to make a thin paste.

In a small saucepan, bring the remaining milk and the coffee just to a boil over medium-high heat. Immediately reduce to a simmer and stir in the cornstarch paste. Cook, stirring constantly, for 5 minutes. Remove from the heat and let cool.

In a bowl, with an electric mixer on high speed, beat the egg whites until stiff peaks form. Set aside.

In a separate bowl, with an electric mixer on medium speed, beat the egg yolks and sugar until frothy and pale yellow. Whisking constantly and briskly, add ½ cup of the cooled coffee cream to the egg yolks, then add the yolks to the saucepan. Return the pan to medium-low heat and cook, stirring constantly, until thickened.

Remove from the heat, stir in the vanilla, and let cool to room temp. Fold in the egg whites and refrigerate to chill (see Tip) before using.

TIP
Cheat on the chilling time by setting the saucepan in a shallow dish (like a pie plate) filled with ice and water.

LEMON GRANITA

This is simple, but not a last-minute dessert: You need to have chilled sugar water ready before beginning, and then it takes about 2 hours of freezing time.

¾ cup sugar
2 teaspoons grated lemon zest (from an organic lemon)
½ cup fresh lemon juice, chilled

In a small saucepan, combine the sugar and 3 cups of water and bring to a boil. Reduce to a simmer and cook, stirring occasionally, for 5 minutes. Let cool to room temp, then refrigerate until well chilled.

Place a 7 x 11-inch or 8-inch square metal baking pan and a metal spoon in the freezer.

Stir the lemon zest and lemon juice into the chilled sugar water (the mixture should be very sweet because freezing will dull the sweetness). Pour the mixture into the chilled metal pan and return the pan to the freezer.

Check the granita every 15 to 20 minutes, and as ice crystals begin to form around the edges, use the chilled spoon to pull the ice from the edges into the center of the pan. Repeat until all the liquid has crystallized, about 2 hours.

RICOTTA CHEESECAKE

Italian cheesecakes are very creamy, so it is important not to cut into one until it has completely cooled and set.

SHORT PASTRY:

1 cup sifted flour, plus more
   for dusting
6 tablespoons (¾ stick) butter,
   softened, plus more for
   the pan
1 tablespoon sugar
1 tablespoon grated lemon zest
   (from an organic lemon)
¼ teaspoon salt
1 large free-range organic egg
   yolk
2 tablespoons ice water

FILLING:

2 cups fresh ricotta cheese,
   homemade (see box, page 40)
   or store-bought
3 large free-range organic eggs
½ cup sugar
2 teaspoons vanilla extract
2 tablespoons grated lemon zest
   (from an organic lemon)

Make the short pastry: In a bowl, combine the flour, butter, sugar, lemon zest, salt, and egg yolk, using your hands to mix everything until soft and crumbly. Add the water and form the mixture into a dough. Set aside.

Make the filling: In a bowl, beat the ricotta with a spoon until creamy. In a separate bowl, with an electric mixer on medium-high speed, beat the eggs until light yellow and frothy. Beat in the sugar, vanilla, and lemon zest. Beat in the ricotta until well combined.

Position a rack in the center of the oven and preheat the oven to 450°F. Grease and flour the bottom and sides of a 9-inch springform pan.

Roll the pastry dough out to a round large enough to cover the bottom and halfway up the sides of the prepared pan. Fit the dough into the pan, smoothing it into the corners and halfway up the sides.

Pour the filling into the dough. Push the dough on the sides of the pan down, bunching it up, until it touches the filling (making a lip).

Bake for 10 minutes. Reduce the oven temperature to 350°F and bake for 30 minutes more. Turn the oven off—DO NOT OPEN THE OVEN DOOR. Leave the cheesecake in the oven to cool completely, then refrigerate until well chilled.

SPONGE CAKE

This is the easiest and most versatile cake: frost it, fill it, drizzle it with liqueur, pile on fruit and cream, or eat it plain. Try it with fresh berries and Cake Cream (page 357) or chopped nuts and Coffee Cream (page 358).

Butter and flour, for the pan
1 cup flour
1 tablespoon baking powder
6 large free-range organic eggs,
   separated
1 cup sugar
2 teaspoons vanilla extract
1 teaspoon grated orange zest
   (from an organic orange)

Preheat the oven to 350°F. Grease and flour a Bundt pan or two 9-inch round cake pans.

Sift together the flour and baking powder into a bowl and set aside.

In a bowl, with an electric mixer on medium speed, beat the egg whites until very foamy, just before soft peaks form. Add the egg yolks one at a time, mixing well after each addition. With the mixer running, slowly stream in the sugar, beating until combined. Beat in the vanilla and orange zest. Add the flour mixture in three additions and mix well.

Scrape the batter into the prepared pan(s) and bake until the top springs back when touched and a wooden skewer inserted in the center comes out clean, 20 to 25 minutes for the 9-inch pans, 30 to 35 minutes for the Bundt pan. Let cool in pan(s), then turn out onto a cooling rack.

BLOOD ORANGE CAKE

SERVES 8 TO 12

An easy one-pan cake, moist and flavorful. If blood oranges are not available, substitute Seville oranges (the key flavor in orange marmalade), or large juicy navel oranges. Either will do the trick. My sister, Maria, leaves this on the counter and when people come over, she serves it as is, but you could also top it with berries and/or Cake Cream (page 357).

Butter and flour, for the pan
4 large free-range organic eggs, separated
2 cups flour, sifted
¼ cup sliced almonds, finely ground (see Tip, page 362)
2 tablespoons baking powder
¼ teaspoon salt
4 ounces (1 stick) butter, softened
1 cup sugar
Grated zest and juice of 2 large organic blood oranges
¼ cup whole milk

Position a rack in the center of the oven and preheat the oven to 375°F. Grease and flour a 9-inch round cake pan.

In a bowl, with an electric mixer on high speed, beat the egg whites until stiff peaks form. Set aside.

In a bowl, whisk together the flour, ground almonds, baking powder, and salt.

In a large bowl, with an electric mixer on high speed, beat the butter and sugar until fluffy. Beat in the egg yolks one at a time, beating well after each addition. Beat in the orange zest and juice. Add the flour mixture alternately with the milk and mix on low until combined. Fold in the egg whites.

Scrape the batter into the cake pan and bake until golden brown and a wooden skewer inserted in the center comes out clean, about 30 minutes. Let cool for 10 to 15 minutes in the pan before inverting onto a cooling rack.

OLIVE OIL CAKE

SERVES 8 TO 12

In this signature Italian dessert, olive oil replaces the usual butter. This cake is subtly sweet and citrusy. Serve as is or with fresh berries and some Cake Cream (page 357). A glass of *limoncello* would be a nice after-dinner treat to go with it.

Butter and flour, for the Bundt pan
4 large free-range organic eggs
¾ cup sugar
2 cups flour, sifted
1 cup cornmeal
1 tablespoon baking powder
1 pear (I use Anjou), peeled and grated
2 tablespoons limoncello
1 tablespoon grated lemon zest (from an organic lemon)
¾ cup extra-light olive oil
½ cup milk

Position a rack in the center of the oven and preheat the oven to 325°F. Grease and flour a Bundt pan.

In a bowl, with an electric mixer on medium speed, beat the eggs and sugar until creamy and light yellow. By hand, stir in the flour, cornmeal, baking powder, pear, limoncello, lemon zest, and olive oil just until combined. Add the milk and stir until combined.

Scrape the batter into the pan and bake until a wooden skewer inserted in the center comes out clean, about 50 minutes. Turn the oven off, open the oven door slightly, and leave the cake in the oven to cool.

POLENTA CAKE

Serve with your favorite cup of coffee or *limoncello*. You can also serve it topped with mixed fresh berries and a dollop of Cake Cream (page 357).

Butter and flour, for the Bundt pan
4 large free-range organic eggs, separated
Scant ¼ cup plus scant ½ cup sugar
¾ cup flour, sifted
¼ cup fine cornmeal
1 tablespoon grated orange zest (from an organic orange)
1 tablespoon grated lemon zest (from an organic lemon)
1 teaspoon vanilla extract

Position a rack in the center of the oven and preheat the oven to 350°F. Grease and flour a Bundt pan.

In a bowl, with an electric mixer on medium speed, beat the egg whites until very foamy, just before soft peaks form. With the mixer running, slowly add the scant ¼ cup sugar and beat until soft glossy peaks form. Set aside.

In a bowl, whisk the flour and cornmeal. Set aside.

In a bowl, with an electric mixer on medium speed, beat the egg yolks just until creamy. With the mixer running, slowly add the scant ½ cup sugar and beat until smooth and pale yellow. Beat in the orange zest, lemon zest, and vanilla. Gently fold in the egg whites, then fold in the flour mixture.

Scrape the batter into the prepared pan and bake until a wooden skewer inserted in the center comes out clean, 30 to 35 minutes. Let cool in the pan on a cooling rack.

PANETTONE

Panettone is a sweet brioche that has become a must-have for Christmas. This bread takes some time rising, so you might want to start it a day ahead. Leftover panettone makes delicious French toast for breakfast (see page 14).

¼ cup milk
6 tablespoons (¾ stick) butter, plus more for the pan(s)
1 envelope active dry yeast
2 cups sifted flour
3 large free-range organic egg yolks
¼ cup sugar
½ teaspoon salt
⅔ cup raisins
1 tablespoon grated lemon zest (from an organic lemon)
1 large free-range organic egg, beaten

In a small saucepan, heat the milk almost to boiling (but do not boil). Remove from the heat and stir in the butter until melted. Let cool to lukewarm (about 110°F). Add the yeast and stir until dissolved and smooth. Let stand for 20 minutes.

In a large bowl, mix 1 cup of the flour, the egg yolks, sugar, and salt. Beat thoroughly. Add the remaining 1 cup flour, the milk-yeast mixture, the raisins, and lemon zest. Mix with your hands into a firm dough. Knead the dough constantly for 5 minutes. Cover with a kitchen towel and let rest for 2 hours.

Butter a large panettone or two smaller ones.

Place the dough in the pan(s) and let stand until doubled in size, about 1 hour.

Position a rack in the center of the oven and preheat the oven to 400°F.

Brush the top of the dough with the beaten egg. Bake for 10 minutes. Reduce the oven temperature to 350°F and bake until a wooden skewer inserted in the center comes out clean, about 20 minutes more.

Remove from the pan(s) and let cool on a rack.

LEMON-ALMOND TART

For this dessert, it is important that the almonds be very finely ground.

CRUST:

1 cup sifted flour
6 tablespoons (¾ stick) butter, softened
1 tablespoon sugar
1 tablespoon grated lemon zest (from an organic lemon)
¼ teaspoon salt
1 large free-range organic egg yolk
2 tablespoons ice water

FILLING:

4 large free-range organic eggs
⅔ cup sugar
3 tablespoons grated lemon zest (from organic lemons)
⅓ cup fresh lemon juice
4 ounces (1 stick) butter, melted
⅔ cup finely ground almonds (see Tip)

Make the crust: In a bowl, mix the flour, butter, sugar, lemon zest, salt, and egg yolk with your hands until crumbly. Add the water and work in to form a dough. Set the dough aside to rest while you preheat the oven.

Position a rack in the center of the oven and preheat the oven to 375°F.

Roll out the dough to cover the bottom and sides of a 10-inch tart pan. Fit the dough into the pan and trim the dough off level with the rim of the pan. Prick the dough on the bottom and sides with a fork. Bake for 10 minutes to set the crust. Remove from the oven but leave the oven on.

Make the filling: In a bowl, whisk the eggs, sugar, lemon zest, and lemon juice. Stir in the melted butter and the ground almonds.

Pour the filling into the crust. Bake until golden brown on top, about 30 minutes. Let cool completely before cutting.

TO FINELY GRIND the almonds without making them too oily, take a couple tablespoons of the sugar from the filling and grind it along with the almonds. The sugar will absorb any oil and help keep the almonds dry, not pasty.

APPLE TORTE

This Tuscan torte is unusually flat, so don't think you made a mistake.

Butter and flour, for the pan
⅔ cup sifted flour
¼ cup finely ground almonds
2 teaspoons baking powder
¼ teaspoon salt
⅛ teaspoon freshly grated nutmeg
2 large free-range organic eggs
1 cup granulated sugar
1 teaspoon vanilla extract
4 tablespoons (½ stick) butter, softened
½ cup milk
1 cup grated apple (see Tip)
Powdered sugar, for dusting (optional)

Preheat the oven to 350°F. Grease and flour a 9-inch springform pan.

In a bowl, whisk the flour, ground almonds, baking powder, salt, and nutmeg.

In a bowl, with an electric mixer on medium-high speed, beat the eggs, granulated sugar, and vanilla until light and creamy. With the mixer on medium speed, beat in the butter until combined. Fold in the flour mixture by hand. Stir in the milk, then the apple.

Scrape the batter into the pan and bake until golden brown, about 50 minutes. Let cool completely in the pan, then remove the sides of the pan. Dust with a little powdered sugar before serving, if desired, for a sweeter taste.

USE AN APPLE with soft flesh, like McIntosh or Honeycrisp (I love Honeycrisp), that breaks down quickly in the oven. Grate the apple on the largest holes of a box grater, the size used for grating mozzarella cheese for pizza.

CHAPTER 13

COCKTAILS

BY JOHN CUSIMANO

In my experience, Italy is not really a hotbed of cocktail culture (with a few famous exceptions such as the Negroni and Bellini). Italians love wine, and produce some of the best on the planet. So what reason do they have for mixology?

That being said, Italians also produce some wonderful, unique, and flavorful spirits—such as Campari, *amaro*, *limoncello*, and grappa—many of which are enjoyed unmixed as an aperitif or an after-dinner digestif. I relied on some of these to create the cocktails in this book, which I hope evoke the flavors and spirit of a country that—I am 100 percent Italian American—is close to my heart.

Italians wear their hearts on their sleeves. Family dinners can be Shakespearean affairs—after a couple of glasses of wine, family and friends will loudly air old grievances and yell at each other over plates of pasta. Inevitably, by the time the meal is over, all is forgiven, and embraces are exchanged. This is the Italian way—big emotions and big flavors. And at the end of the night, no one goes to bed angry or hungry. Or thirsty.

RUBINO

Rachael's sister, Maria, loves champagne. She also loves raspberries. While she was visiting the stunning and striking Amalfi Coast of Italy, a bartender made a version of this for her, and it's become her favorite.

1 ounce fresh raspberry puree
½ ounce Lillet Blanc
4 ounces chilled prosecco
Fresh raspberries, for garnish

Combine the raspberry puree, Lillet Blanc, and prosecco in an ice-filled wine goblet. Stir gently, garnish with a couple of raspberries, and serve.

TESTAROSSA

Averna is an *amaro* (Italian for "bitter") liqueur produced in Sicily. Amaro can be slightly sweet and syrupy, and has flavors of herbs and bark. Depending on the brand, the flavors can be pretty intense. It is often drunk as an after-dinner digestif (our friend Mario Batali occasionally partakes in this custom).

Averna is a popular brand of amaro, and since both Rachael and I are part Sicilian, I chose to use it in this cocktail; but any amaro would work. This drink incorporates egg white, which gives it a frothy foam "head." With a finishing dash of red Peychaud's Bitters, the drink is named after the famous Ferrari model called Testarossa (Italian for "redhead").

2 ounces rye
1 ounce fresh blood orange juice
½ ounce Averna
½ ounce Campari
½ ounce simple syrup
1 organic egg white
Peychaud's Bitters, for garnish

Fill a cocktail glass with ice and water and set aside to chill. Shake the rye, orange juice, Averna, Campari, simple syrup, and egg white in an ice-filled cocktail shaker. Strain into the chilled glass. Garnish with a dash of Peychaud's Bitters.

BROOKLYN TOWNSHIP

I created this cocktail with my friend Mike Dirnt. He plays bass in a band called Green Day, and is an Oakland, California, native. I learned a great cocktail tip from him: Absinthe, which tastes of anise, pairs nicely with orange.

Rachael and I spent a few days with Mike and his lovely family in their hometown and were delighted to discover a thriving, exciting community bursting with artisanal shops and restaurants serving locally sourced produce, and all of it just a short trip across the bridge from San Francisco. Mike named this drink after what used to be an area of Oakland. It may sound like it is named for a borough across a bridge from where I live in downtown NYC, but it isn't.

The cocktail is garnished with a flamed orange peel—the technique is described below—and an amarena cherry. Amarena cherries are dark bitter cherries from Italy bottled in syrup. They are delicious not only in cocktails, but on a variety of desserts. Try them on gelato.

1½ ounces bourbon
½ ounce sweet vermouth
2 or 3 dashes of absinthe, for rinsing the glass
Amarena cherry, for garnish
Flamed orange peel, for garnish (see Tip)

Fill a coupe or cocktail glass with ice and water and set aside to chill. Shake the bourbon and vermouth in an ice-filled cocktail shaker. Pour the ice and water out of the coupe. Pour in the absinthe and swirl to coat the inside of the glass. Discard the excess. Strain the cocktail into the coupe. Garnish with the cherry and flamed orange peel.

 TO FLAME AN orange peel, light a match and hold it in one hand just above the cocktail. Between the thumb and forefinger of your other hand, hold a round, quarter-size piece of orange peel skin side down, just above the match, and squeeze it into the cocktail. The citrus oils will flame the match, caramelize, and then land in your drink. Add the peel to the drink. Feel free to experiment with this technique with any citrus and different drinks—you will impress your friends and have a yummy cocktail.

THE BACK ROOM

This is a boozy concoction that reminds me of a Manhattan. I use Carpano Antica—an Italian red (sweet) vermouth that happens to be exceptional—but any sweet vermouth will work. The cocktail is mellowed somewhat by the addition of egg white, which makes it creamy and frothy. I could imagine enjoying this in a private smoky back room next to the kitchen of an old-school Italian restaurant somewhere in Little Italy, just before diving into a bowl of pasta with meat sauce.

1½ ounces rye
½ ounce Carpano Antica
½ ounce simple syrup
5 dashes of Meyer lemon bitters
1 organic egg white
2 or 3 dashes of absinthe, for rinsing the glass

Fill a coupe or cocktail glass with ice and water and set aside to chill. Shake the rye, Carpano Antica, simple syrup, bitters, and egg white in an ice-filled cocktail shaker. Pour the ice and water out of the coupe. Pour in the absinthe and swirl to coat the inside of the glass. Discard the excess. Strain the cocktail into the coupe.

BLOOD ORANGE 75

French 75 is a classic cocktail comprising either gin or cognac (this is hotly contested), fresh lemon juice, simple syrup, and champagne. It has a kick that some used to say is like taking a shell from the powerful French 75mm gun. I made this version on Rachael's daytime show using blood orange juice. Rachael recommended cognac over gin to pair with blood orange.

1 ounce cognac
1 ounce fresh blood orange juice
Dash of orange bitters
Chilled champagne, to top
Blood orange twist, for garnish

Shake the cognac, blood orange juice, and bitters in an ice-filled cocktail shaker and strain into a champagne flute. Top with chilled champagne. Garnish with a blood orange twist.

AMARETTO NOG

An almond-flavored Italian liqueur, amaretto is delicious in zabaglione, on ice cream, or, if you like your drinks sweet, simply on the rocks. This cocktail tastes like an almond milk shake or eggnog.

2 ounces amaretto
1 organic egg white
3 ounces heavy cream
Freshly grated nutmeg, for
    garnish

Fill a cocktail glass with ice and water and set aside to chill. Shake the amaretto, egg white, and heavy cream in an ice-filled cocktail shaker and strain into the chilled glass. Garnish with nutmeg.

GRAPEFRUIT MARTINI

Rachael loves grapefruit. Grapefruit pairs perfectly with gin, as both are similarly refreshing, bracing, and bitter. If you can find grapefruit bitters, they will add an extra depth of flavor to this cocktail, and will also be handy for future cocktail experimentation. Bitters = the spices of your cocktail program!

2 ounces gin
2 ounces fresh grapefruit juice
½ ounce simple syrup
2 dashes of grapefruit bitters
2 dashes of sweet vermouth
Grapefruit twist, for garnish

Fill a cocktail glass with ice and water and set aside to chill. Shake the gin, grapefruit juice, simple syrup, bitters, and vermouth in an ice-filled cocktail shaker and strain into the chilled glass. Garnish with a grapefruit twist.

AMALFI-TINI

Lemons speckle the cliffs of Italy's beautiful Amalfi Coast. With all those lemons, *limoncello* is abundant. Rachael's mom loves limoncello so much that I nicknamed her "Mamacello."

4 ounces limoncello
2 dashes of dry vermouth
2 dashes of orange bitters
Lemon twist and orange twist, for garnish

Fill a cocktail glass with ice and water and set aside to chill. Shake the limoncello, vermouth, and bitters in an ice-filled cocktail shaker and strain into the chilled glass. Garnish with a lemon twist and an orange twist.

THE BITTER SPRITZ

Amaro is typically served as a digestif in Italy. It carries much more of a wallop than Aperol, which is normally used in a spritz. This drink turns a digestif into an apertif.

1 ounce amaro
2 ounces club soda
Juice of 1 lime
Lime wedge, for garnish

Combine the amaro, club soda, and lime juice in an ice-filled rocks glass and stir gently. Garnish with a lime wedge.

THE SPRITZ

If it's a hot summer afternoon and you crave a refreshing, light, and low-alcohol beverage, the classic Italian spritz is a perfect and friendly choice. This one features Aperol, which is similar to Campari but less bitter and with a lower alcohol content.

3 ounces prosecco
1½ ounces Aperol
Club soda, to top
Orange wheel and lemon wheel, for garnish

Combine the prosecco and Aperol in a tall, ice-filled glass. Top with club soda and stir gently. Garnish with an orange wheel and a lemon wheel and serve with a straw.

LITTLE ITALY

This is similar to a Negroni, but with scotch instead of gin. It is an easy cocktail to whip up, as it is built right in the serving glass, and it features that Italian classic, Campari.

2 ounces blended scotch
Juice of ¼ orange
1 ounce Campari
2 dashes of sweet vermouth
2 dashes of Angostura bitters
Seltzer, to top
Lemon twist, for garnish

Combine the scotch, orange juice, Campari, vermouth, and bitters in an ice-filled rocks glass. Top with seltzer and stir gently. Garnish with a lemon twist.

GRAPPA SMASH

Grappa—a brandy made from the skin, pulp, seeds, and stems from pressed grapes left over from winemaking—tends to be misunderstood in this country. While its flavor profile can be a bit intense at first, there are many different styles made from a variety of grapes and in different regions in Italy, and a good grappa can be a well-balanced and relaxing finish to a hearty meal.

4 or 5 red grapes, plus more
    for garnish
1½ ounces grappa
3 ounces prosecco

Muddle the grapes at the bottom of a cocktail shaker. Add the grappa and ice, shake well, and strain into an ice-filled rocks glass. Top with the prosecco and stir gently. Garnish with a few additional grapes.

THE ITALIAN FLAG

Make a pitcher of this Italian Bloody Mary mix ahead of time, and you can add the vodka by the glass when you serve.

8 fresh basil leaves
1 (1-quart) bottle tomato or spicy
    vegetable juice
Grated zest and juice of 1 organic
    lemon
1 teaspoon crushed red pepper
    flakes, or to taste
2 ounces balsamic vinegar
½ cup carrot juice
1 teaspoon celery salt
Vodka
Fresh basil sprigs, for garnish
Bocconcini (small mozzarella
    balls), for garnish

Muddle the basil at the bottom of a sealable pitcher or container. Add the tomato juice, lemon zest and juice, red pepper flakes, vinegar, carrot juice, and celery salt, shake well, and strain into a pitcher to serve.

For each drink, pour 1½ ounces vodka into an ice-filled rocks glass. Top with the Bloody Mary mix and stir gently. Garnish with a fresh basil sprig and a mozzarella ball stuck on a cocktail spear.

SALTY SOUR

A garnish of pepperoncini (hot Italian pepper flakes) adds a tingly finish to this bright, herbal twist on a classic cocktail.

1 sprig fresh thyme, plus a sprig
   for garnish
2 ounces bourbon
1 ounce fresh lemon juice
1 ounce simple syrup
Pinch of sea salt
Pinch of pepperoncini or crushed
   red pepper flakes, for garnish
Lemon wedges, for garnish

Muddle a sprig of thyme at the bottom of a cocktail shaker. Add the bourbon, lemon juice, simple syrup, salt, and ice. Shake well and strain into an ice-filled rocks glass. Garnish with red pepper flakes, a sprig of thyme, and a lemon wedge.

THE VESPA

In Rome, it appears that there are more scooters on the road than cars. This "spin" on the classic Italian cocktail, the Bicicletta (bicycle) substitutes refreshing and floral Lillet Rouge for dry white wine.

2 ounces Campari
2 ounces Lillet Rouge
Club soda, to top
Orange or blood orange slice,
   for garnish

Pour the Campari and Lillet Rouge into an ice-filled Collins glass. Top with club soda and stir gently. Garnish with an orange slice and serve with a straw.

ROMAN SOUR

Romans live *la dolce vita* (the sweet life). This twist on the classic New York Sour cocktail replaces a fruity red wine "topper" with a bold Italian red wine syrup—made by stirring equal parts red wine (a Chianti could work well) and sugar over low heat until combined. If you have extra red wine syrup, try serving it over vanilla ice cream or pound cake for dessert.

2 ounces rye
1 ounce fresh lemon juice
½ ounce simple syrup
½ ounce red wine syrup

Shake the rye, lemon juice, and simple syrup in an ice-filled cocktail shaker and strain into an ice-filled rocks glass. Gently pour the wine syrup over the back of a spoon held just over the glass so the syrup floats on top of the drink.

THE WORLD CUP

Outside of the United States, and for sure in Italy, soccer is a national obsession. Roto, the guitarist in my band, spent his formative years in Rome, and Johnny, the bass player, is Portuguese, and they are both huge soccer fans. This version of a Pimm's Cup (the proper English drink for watching a polo match) is designed to be consumed while watching the "other" football.

4 slices peeled seedless cucumber, plus unpeeled slices for garnish

1½ ounces Pimm's No. 1

Limonata or other Italian lemon soda, to top

Mint sprig, for garnish

Muddle the cucumber at the bottom of a cocktail shaker. Add the Pimm's and ice and shake well. Strain into an ice-filled Collins glass. Top with lemon soda and stir gently. Garnish with unpeeled cucumber slices and a sprig of mint and serve with a straw.

LA CONCA DEL SOGNO

La Conca del Sogno (The Bay of Dreams) is a magical little restaurant (and inn) just outside of Sorrento, Italy, at the northern edge of the lemon tree–lined Amalfi Coast. (It's also home to the family of Grandma Rose on my mother's side.) It is primarily accessible by boat, and is a perfect place to sit on a cliff overlooking a quiet little bay just across from Capri, and enjoy some of the freshest seafood pasta you've ever tasted. The beauty of the place inspired the creation of this lemony drink.

2 ounces limoncello

1 ounce lemon sorbet

Prosecco, to top

Mint sprig, for garnish

Stir the limoncello and lemon sorbet together in a cocktail glass until blended. Top with prosecco. Garnish with a sprig of mint.

CORRECTED COFFEE

In Italy, if you order *caffè corretto*, you get a small pour of liquor (usually grappa or sambuca) added to your espresso shot. A simple but effective recipe.

1 shot freshly brewed espresso

1 or 2 dashes of grappa or sambuca (or brandy, for that matter)

Combine the espresso and grappa in an espresso cup. Consume while hot.

MILANO MULE

Limoncello is the de rigueur after-dinner drink in Italy. This version of a Moscow Mule uses it in place of vodka.

2 or 3 fresh mint leaves
3 ounces limoncello
1 ounce ginger beer
Mint sprig, for garnish

Muddle the mint at the bottom of a cocktail shaker. Add the limoncello and ice, shake well, and strain into an ice-filled rocks glass (or a copper mug, if you have one). Top with the ginger beer and stir gently. Garnish with a sprig of mint.

ESPRESSO MARTINI

This drink is made with a lemon twist garnish—to balance out some of the bitterness of the strong coffee.

1½ ounces vodka
1 shot espresso, at room temperature
½ ounce simple syrup
Lemon twist, for garnish

Fill a cocktail glass with ice and water and set aside to chill. Shake the vodka, espresso, and simple syrup in an ice-filled cocktail shaker and strain into the chilled glass. Garnish with a lemon twist.

NORTHERN PINE

Rachael and I once traveled to the lake region in northern Italy and were nicely surprised that it looked a lot like Lake George in upstate New York, where Rachael grew up and where we still have a home. This cocktail reminds me of both.

The sage-infused base spirit used here is one of a few that are available for purchase. You can also make your own simply by placing a hearty bunch of fresh sage into a container and topping it with a bottle of vodka. Close the container tightly and let the vodka steep for a few days, then strain it back into the original vodka bottle.

1 sprig fresh rosemary, plus a sprig for garnish
2 ounces sage-infused vodka
1½ ounces fresh lime juice
½ ounce simple syrup
7 dashes of Bittermens Boston Bittahs or Angostura bitters

Fill a cocktail glass with ice and water and set aside to chill. Muddle the rosemary at the bottom of a cocktail shaker. Add the vodka, lime juice, simple syrup, bitters, and ice and shake well. Strain into the chilled glass. Garnish with a fresh rosemary sprig.

CREAMSICLE

My parents are both from Brooklyn, and the candy store was a neighborhood meeting place for the kids after school, where they could grab a sweet treat, an egg cream, or a phosphate soda, in which different tangy phosphate flavor bases would be mixed with sugar and seltzer at the counter to order. Phosphates are now being produced by several bitters manufacturers and can be purchased online. Orange phosphate imparts a Creamsicle flavor to this cocktail.

2 ounces vodka
1½ ounces fresh orange juice
½ ounce heavy cream
½ ounce simple syrup
2 dashes of orange phosphate
Orange twist, for garnish

Fill a cocktail glass with ice and water and set aside to chill. Shake the vodka, orange juice, cream, simple syrup, and phosphate in an ice-filled cocktail shaker and strain into the chilled glass. Garnish with an orange twist.

SUNRISE SPARKLER

Tangerines are slightly sweeter than oranges. You can also substitute fresh blood orange or clementine juice. Grand Marnier lends a sophisticated balance to this variation on a mimosa.

1½ ounces Grand Marnier
1 ounce fresh tangerine, blood orange, or clementine juice
Chilled prosecco, to top
Citrus twist, for garnish

Pour the Grand Marnier and citrus juice into a champagne flute and top with chilled prosecco. Garnish with a citrus twist (whichever citrus you use in the drink).

ACKNOWLEDGMENTS

Thank you to my coauthors and very robust eaters and drinkers: my sister, Maria Betar, who provided desserts for this book, and my sweet husband, John, who provided the cocktails to make everyone cheerier. Great job! Thank you to my mom, Elsa, and to Grandpa Emmanuel for teaching me about life and food and how to appreciate both. Thank you to Andrew Kaplan for being my wingman and working with seven hundred single-spaced pages of my book. Thanks for saying after finishing the read, "I'm gonna cook the sh*t outta this book!" It made my year. Thank you for the organizational superpowers of my colleague Michelle Boxer. Thanks to our teammates at William Morris Endeavor and Atria Books with whom I worked hard to get this book done the way I envisioned it in my head. Thank you to the food stylists and photographer who understood me when I said it had to look more rustic, messier—more gusto! The book looks more than edible. Pass the cheese and bread!

Index

Pilaf with Zafferano (Saffron), 306
pulled pork:
  with Arugula, Meyer Lemon, and Pasta, 231
  Sandwiches, Ultimate, 230
Puttanesca, 124
  Pizza, 90
  Sauce, Raw, 214

Q

quinoa, 199
  with Roasted Snap Peas and Hen-of-the-Woods Mushrooms, 198
  and Vegetable Stuffed Peppers, 199

R

The Rachael (pizza), 91
ragu:
  Bean and Porcini, Quick, 130
  Cinghiale (Wild Boar), 131
  Hot Sausage, 136
  Lamb, 133, 250
  Lamb, Spicy, 132
  Lamb, with Meyer Lemon and Olives, 134
  Meat, 177
  Mushroom, 128, 129
  Short Rib, 108, 135
  Veal and Eggplant, 138
  Veal and Sage, 136, 137
  White, 127
ramps:
  Pasta with Bacon, Ricotta and, 161
  Risotto Milanese with, 186

Spaghetti with, 144
rapini, see broccoli rabe
raspberry puree, in Rubino, 366
Ratatouille, 345
  Frittata, 5
  and Ricotta–Stuffed Peppers, 335
  Roasted Garlic Potatoes Stuffed with, 336
ravioli:
  Pear and Pecorino, 171
  with Spinach and Four Cheeses, 172
Raw Sauce, 142
red wine:
  Barolo, Beef with, over Taleggio Mashed Potatoes, 268
  Chianti Burgers, 271
  Half-and-Half Short Ribs with Polenta, 258
  Roast Chicken Thighs on Bread, 291
  syrup, in Roman Sour, 373
  see also Marsala
Regina Pizza (Tuna and Tomato), 98, 99
relishes:
  Giardiniera, 31
  Orange, 211
  Tomato, Fresh, 204
Ribollita, 72, 73
Rib Roast, Easy, with Roasted Garlic and Herbs, 252, 255
rice, 181–89
  Arancini, Classic (and variations), 55
  and Chicken Balls, 53

Drunken Risotto, 189
  Lemon Risotto, 187
  Pilaf, 182
  Primavera, 182
  Pulled Chicken Pilaf with Spinach and Garlic, 306
  Pulled Chicken Pilaf with Zafferano (Saffron), 306
  Risi e Bisi, 184
  Risotto Milanese, 180, 185
  Risotto Primavera, 185
  Risotto with Porcini and Celery, 188
  Salad with Golden Beets, 183
  Walnut Risotto with White Truffle and Gorgonzola Dolce, 187
ricotta (cheese):
  Baked Ziti, 175
  Cannoli Cream, 355
  Cheesecake, 359
  Flatbread Pizzas with Greens, Eggs and, 7
  Fresh (homemade), 40
  Fried Green Tomato, and Zucchini Flower Pizza, 96
  Fritters, 353
  Galette with Greens and, 18
  Gnudi, 114
  Mascarpone Cheese Spread, 40
  Mashed Potatoes with Honey and, 338
  Mushroom, and Sausage Calzones, 105
  Pasta with Bacon, Ramps and, 161
  with Pistachios, Baked, 41

and Ratatouille–Stuffed Peppers, 335
  and Sausage–Stuffed Mushrooms, 47
  and Spinach Calzone, 106
  Spinach Stuffed Chicken Tied in Speck, 305
  Stuffed Shells, 173
  Walnut, and Zucchini Pizza, 85, 90
ricotta salata:
  Broccoli Rabe (Rapini) with, 108, 314
  Drunken Spaghetti with Sweet Roasted Beets and, 146, 147
  Roasted Beets with Walnuts, Balsamic Dressing and, 312
  Sauce, 248, 249
riggies:
  Chicken, Ridiculously Good, 164, 165
  with Hot Sausage Ragu, 136
Risi e Bisi, 184
risotto, 185–92
  Barley, "Green," with Roasted Carrots, 191
  Barley, with Butternut Squash, 192, 193
  basics, 184
  Broken Spaghetti, with Kale and Hazeluts, 148
  Broken Spaghetti, with Mushrooms, Walnuts, and Gorgonzola, 148
  Drunken, 189
  Lemon, 187
  Milanese, 180, 185
  with Porcini and Celery, 188

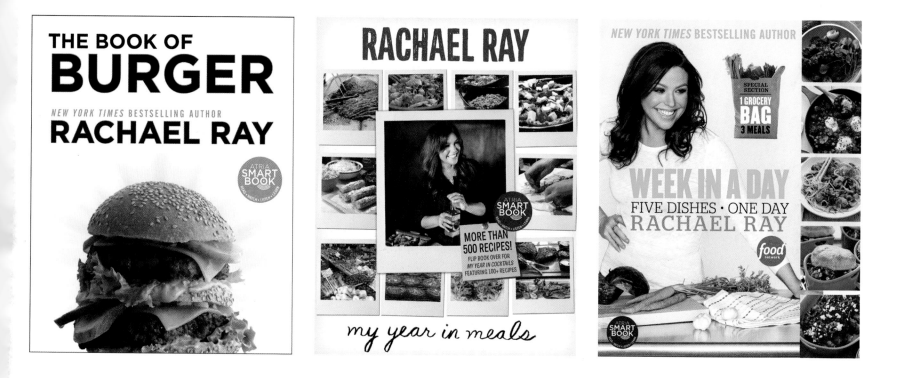